Angels in Late Ancient Christianity

Angels in Late Ancient Christianity

ELLEN MUEHLBERGER

OXFORD
UNIVERSITY PRESS

Oxford University Press is a department of the University of Oxford.
It furthers the University's objective of excellence in research, scholarship,
and education by publishing worldwide.

Oxford New York
Auckland Cape Town Dar es Salaam Hong Kong Karachi
Kuala Lumpur Madrid Melbourne Mexico City Nairobi
New Delhi Shanghai Taipei Toronto

With offices in
Argentina Austria Brazil Chile Czech Republic France Greece
Guatemala Hungary Italy Japan Poland Portugal Singapore
South Korea Switzerland Thailand Turkey Ukraine Vietnam

Oxford is a registered trademark of Oxford University Press
in the UK and certain other countries.

Published in the United States of America by
Oxford University Press
198 Madison Avenue, New York, NY 10016

Library of Congress Cataloging-in-Publication Data
Muehlberger, Ellen.
Angels in late ancient Christianity / Ellen Muehlberger.
p. cm.
Includes bibliographical references and index.
ISBN 978–0–19–993193–4 (alk. paper)—ISBN 978–0–19–993194–1 (ebook)
1. Angels—History of doctrines—Early church, ca. 30–600. I. Title.
BT966.3.M84 2013
235′.309—dc23
2012026415

ISBN 978–0–19–993193–4
ISBN 978–0–19–993194–1

1 3 5 7 9 8 6 4 2
Printed in the United States of America
on acid-free paper

For Gina

Contents

Acknowledgments

THIS BOOK IS a revision of my Indiana University doctoral dissertation, and I owe many debts to those who helped nurture it from a host of elusive thoughts toward something more tangible. First among them is my mentor David Brakke, whose expert guidance about the project and about being a scholar and teacher came with a sizable helping of humanity and wit. The conversations I had with my readers Steven Weitzman, J. Albert Harrill, and Constance M. Furey clarified and expanded the elements of my project; I am grateful for the time they spent thinking with me. My work at Indiana was supported by grants from the Department of Religious Studies and the Borns Jewish Studies Program, both nurturing environments for a new scholar.

If you were just starting out and had to pick a field of study solely by gauging the generosity and brilliance of the scholars who occupy it, you would be hard pressed to find something better than the field loosely gathered under the heading of "late antiquity." The following list does not fully address the debt I owe to these engaging and careful readers, all of whom spent time with portions of this book as it developed: Mira Balberg, Adam Becker, Jason BeDuhn, Daniel Caner, Catherine Chin, Elizabeth Clark, Charles Cosgrove, Mark DelCogliano, Elizabeth DePalma Digeser, David Frankfurter, Chris Frilingos, Diane Fruchtman, Mark Graham, Adam Gregerman, Andrew Hofer, David Hunter, Anders-Christian Jacobsen, Aaron Johnson, Dayna Kalleres, Joel Kalvesmaki, Blake Leyerle, Heidi Marx-Wolf, Candida Moss, James J. O'Donnell, Anders Klostergaard Petersen, Taylor Petrey, Andrew Radde-Gallwitz, Philip Rousseau, Samuel Rubenson, Charles Stang, Bradley Storin, and Edward Watts. I am deeply grateful for their comments and advice, as well as the guidance I have received from my colleagues at the University of Michigan, especially Kathryn Babayan, Gabriele Boccaccini, David Potter, Ray Van Dam, and Terry Wilfong.

Portions of this work first saw daylight at sessions of the American Academy of Religion, the North American Patristics Society, the Midwest Consortium on Ancient Religions, and the Society of Biblical Literature. I am grateful for the opportunity to present my ideas there and to the audiences I was invited to address at Aarhus University, the Catholic University of America, DePauw University, Indiana University, Michigan State University, the University of Michigan, and Western Michigan University. An earlier version of Chapter 5 appeared as "Ambivalence about the Angelic Life: The Promise and Perils of an Early Christian Discourse of Asceticism," *Journal of Early Christian Studies* 16 (2008): 447–78. Copyright © 2008 The Johns Hopkins University Press. Koninklijke Brill NV graciously allowed me the use of a text originally published by Dayna Kalleres in "Demons and Divine Illumination: A Consideration of Eight Prayers by Gregory of Nazianzus," *Vigiliae Christianae* 61 (2007): 157–88.

My warmest thanks to Cynthia Read at Oxford University Press; her encouragement and professionalism stand out as examples of what all authors should hope to encounter when they approach a press. Charlotte Steinhardt shepherded the manuscript—and me—through the publishing process with skill and good cheer. Perry Janes's watchful eye kept me from many a mistake.

I am also grateful for the support I received from my family. My mother, Clare Muehlberger, continues to encourage me and to help me see what is important. Phone calls, packages, recipes, and jokes from Amy Kakkuri kept me upbeat. Pat Ketelaar went far above and beyond the role of mother-in-law, offering equal doses of humor, sympathy, and fashion advice precisely when I needed them.

Finally, I simply cannot express how lucky I was to meet my beloved partner and co-conspirator, Gina Brandolino, who came attached to the finest of all cats, Sweet Pea. Over the last thirteen years, she listened to me work out the ideas in this book and she read so many different versions of them that any way I render my gratitude will not do justice to her patience, intellect, and love. The best I can do is to dedicate this book to her.

Abbreviations

ACW	Ancient Christian Writers
AP	Apophthegmata Patrum (*Sayings of the Fathers*)
CCL	Corpus Christianorum, Series Latina
CSCO	Corpus Scriptorum Christianorum Orientalium
CSEL	Corpus Scriptorum Ecclesiasticorum Latinorum
ECCA	Early Christianity in the Context of Antiquity
GCS	Die Griechischen Christlichen Schriftsteller
HTR	*Harvard Theological Review*
JECS	*Journal of Early Christian Studies*
JTS	*Journal of Theological Studies*
LCL	Loeb Classical Library
LXX	Septuagint
Mus	*Le Muséon*
OECS	Oxford Early Christian Studies
PG	Patrologia Graeca
PL	Patrologia Latina
PO	Patrologia Orientalis
ROC	*Revue de l'Orient chrétien*
SC	Sources chrétiennes
SH	Subsidia Hagiographica
TCH	The Transformation of the Classical Heritage
VC	*Vigiliae Christianae*

Angels in Late Ancient Christianity

Introduction

LIKE OTHER PRIVILEGED men in late antiquity, Gregory of Nazianzus had been raised to be bold. As a young person, he studied rhetoric and philosophy at schools in Athens and Antioch, learning from demanding teachers how to form and defend ideas, to challenge opponents, and to persuade an audience.[1] These skills were meant to advance a man's career, and they certainly had that effect for Gregory. It was his talent as an articulator of ideas, along with his allegiance to a particular theological position, that led to Gregory's being asked to join a small community of Christians in the empire's capital, Constantinople, in 379 CE. These Christians, and the emperor, were supporters of the theological position on the nature of God first advanced at the Council of Nicaea in 325 CE and contentiously debated among Christians in the fifty years since. Most Christians in the capital did not support the pro-Nicene position, and it was Gregory's task to reinforce and build the community of those who did. He accepted the invitation, and in just over a year, Gregory had so gainfully defended his minority theological viewpoint that in the late fall of 380, the emperor made him bishop of the city. Gregory displayed a polite rhetorical humility about these events in his later reflections on his career in Constantinople, composed after he had resigned the office of bishop and had returned to his home in Asia Minor, for he credited the Holy Spirit with the growth of the community of Nicene Christians in the capital. Tellingly, though, he also described Constantinople as a place "not even worthy of being called a field" before his arrival, unprepared and underdeveloped, waiting for the right plowhand to produce growth among its Christians.[2] None in his audience would have missed the hint. In his retrospective on his short time in Constantinople, Gregory subtly presented himself as the person who had taken a rough patch of land and turned it into a blooming, productive farm through his tireless and constructive work as an author and speaker contesting for the superiority of the Nicene position.

Given Gregory's reputation as a skillful defender of ideas and his self-portrayal as the person who led the Nicene community in Constantinople to prominence, it is striking to see Gregory shy away from certain subjects as though they might exceed his abilities. The *Five Theological Orations*, delivered when he was yet the embattled leader of the small Nicene group, are evidence of his highly articulated style and his fearless creativity with respect to complex subjects. In the second of these orations, Gregory argued for a particular conception of the incorporeal nature of God, a position that required him, for a moment, to consider the nature of angels. Advancing more conservatively than his reputation would suggest, Gregory offered the few tidbits of information that could be gleaned from reading the New Testament: angels are made as "spirits" and "flames of fire," as they are described in Hebrews 1, and they can be identified with the "thrones, dominions, rulers, and authorities" of Colossians 1, in addition to the "powers" mentioned in Ephesians. Then, poised atop these scriptural references, Gregory stopped, asking his listeners to sympathize with him as he was overwhelmed by the sheer number of angelic orders. He cried, "You see how I entirely lose my head about this subject, and how I do not have it in me to make any forward progress!—except to know that there are some angels and archangels, thrones, dominions, rulers, authorities, splendors, ascents, and intelligent powers."[3] The same person who had been called to Constantinople for his boldness in argument, and who would eventually be elevated to bishop of the city because of his success, in this way revealed that he thought angels and their natures were subjects beyond his ken.

Despite his complaint, Gregory did make forward progress on the topic of angels in the *Second Oration*, laying out an exposition of the nature and function of angels more intricate than his claims of having lost his head would indicate. He explained a vast system of divine communication in which angels, subjected to the divine will, relay the illumination given them from above; appear anywhere in the universe to enact their service; and "bring unity to all things, at the single nod of the demiurgical director of all things."[4] This explanation was a necessary plank in Gregory's argument about the incorporeal nature of God, in that as long as angels were available to accomplish the divine will, God himself did not need to have a body with which to act in the universe. The text of the *Second Oration* and the whole of Gregory's work show that he was, by no means, ever truly at a loss for what to say on any theological topic.[5] Instead, he did what he had been trained to do as an elite Christian in the fourth century: he articulated then forcefully defended a matrix of difficult ideas before an audience, striving to gain imperial patronage and civic power in competition with other Christians and their ideas. Thus the text of the *Second Oration* records a rather unusual situation—that of a late ancient Christian leader and intellectual known for his inventive and well-developed theological arguments portraying himself as unable to think about angels, and doing so in the very text in which he put forward a theory of angelic nature and communication.

In reality, the *Second Oration* is less unusual than it may seem, because the topic of angels evoked displays of reticence from many late ancient Christian intellectuals. At the time when Gregory was asked to lead the Nicene community in Constantinople, the writer Augustine was in his mid-thirties and was working as a teacher of grammar and rhetoric in Carthage. Though he experienced many changes in orientation in his life (turning to philosophy, to Manichaeism, to Christianity), Augustine never turned away from his rhetorical training. His skill in the articulation of ideas only grew, and eventually this talent led to his being pressed into service as the leader of a community of Christians, a minority dwarfed by the larger group of purist Christians in the same town. Like Gregory, Augustine was recognized and rewarded for his prowess in defending a contested version of Christianity, and like Gregory, he balked when it came to the topic of angels. Two instances in particular illustrate how he claimed ignorance about the angelic world.[6] In the *Enchiridion*, a "handbook" of Christian answers intended for a lay reader, Augustine apologized for his lack of understanding on a number of questions about angels. The earliest Christian texts might speak of "angels" and "archangels," "thrones, dominions, principalities, and powers," but Augustine did not think himself prepared to offer the lay Christian more information about what these beings were or how they related to one another. "Those who can answer these things should, if they indeed can prove what they say," he wrote. "As for me, I confess my ignorance."[7] On the other end of the spectrum of complexity from the *Enchiridion* lies Augustine's work *On the Trinity*, a dense and meandering theological treatise composed over the course of a decade and a half. In it, Augustine suggested that just as those neophyte Christians who did not yet understand the mysteries of the sacraments they saw acted out by priests should be aware of their limitations, he too should be mindful of the things he did not know, as should other Christians, "lest we wander into deeper waters than human weakness can safely bear." While others might speculate about the deeds of angels, their physical appearance, or how they accomplish tasks in the material world, Augustine warned that he was not prepared to do so. "I certainly lack the acuteness of vision," he wrote, "to tell by observation, or the confidence of reason to work it out by calculations, or the range of intellect to grasp it in such a way that I could answer all the questions which might be asked here."[8] The most famous Latin Christian writer of antiquity, the community leader who advised other influential writers whether Christian or not, the commanding speaker who changed the face of North African Christianity, this same Augustine suggested that he did not have the intellectual resources to think through the problems associated with imagining the angels spoken of in Christian Scripture.

It was not indifference that kept Augustine from exploring further, but rather a sense that thinking about angels was transgressive. Frequently, when he protested about his limited faculties, Augustine also spoke of the danger he felt at the very prospect of theorizing about the angelic world. His combination of reticence and concern is visible, for instance, in a treatise written in the early fifth century. Rhetorically, *To Orosius (Against the Priscillianists)* was designed to exhibit the full range of Augustine's power as an author. In it, he tackled intricate and perplexing topics for a concerned man who had approached him for an authoritative answer about a growing heresy in his own country. Playing the role of expert, Augustine grandly made reference to many of his earlier works, showing Orosius his confidence as a thinker of long practice and great productivity. Even this carefully constructed authorial persona, however, did not keep Augustine from displaying caution when asked about the names of angels listed in Scripture.

> Certainly the apostle says, "Whether thrones or dominions or principalities or powers," and thus, I firmly believe there are thrones, dominions, principalities, and powers in the celestial army and I hold that they indubitably differ from one another. But regarding the matter because of which you look down on me, whom you suppose to be a great intellectual, I really do not know. I am certain that I am not in danger because of that ignorance, at least not as much danger as I would attract by disobedience, if I forgot the commandments of the Lord.[9]

While Scripture did not fully explain the angelic orders it mentioned and while some persons may, at some point, be given a "higher revelation" about the angels, Augustine argued that this should not lead the person who receives the revelation to think himself better than the writers of Scripture. "However far anyone advances in knowledge," Augustine wrote, "he discovers himself below those writings which God has placed, like a firmament, over all human hearts."[10] The parameters set by scriptural descriptions of angels were boundaries Augustine was not willing to cross. They deterred him—and from his perspective, "all human hearts"—from speculation.[11]

To hear Augustine suggest that creative thinking might be best avoided certainly strikes us as strange in a general sense—the Augustine familiar to historians would not win a prize for reticence—but it is even stranger when we consider how Augustine's writings, in reality, did transgress previous Christian traditions about angels. In *On the Trinity*, the very text in which he lamented his lack of vision, Augustine almost entirely reworked the way that the appearances of God or the Lord in the Old Testament were read by inventing new natures and new functions for angels. Previous interpreters had seen these appearances of God or theophanies as appearances of Christ and took them as proof of Christ's co-eternity with God; Augustine, however, turned the Christian hermeneutic tradition on its head, arguing that Christ did not participate in any appearance of the Lord, the angel of the Lord, or any other divine actor portrayed in the Old Testament. Instead, the theophanies of the Old Testament were all appearances of angels, who materialized in order to be messengers of God.[12] This novel reading technique also played a part in Augustine's *City of God*, where he theorized that angels were capable to stand in for God like this because they truly had no will of their own. Though Augustine's idea of angels as divine drones differed greatly from the prevailing assumptions among Christians about angels as actors, it quickly became the foundation for later Christian, and especially Latin, conceptions of the nature of angels. In works as important for understanding late ancient Christianity as *On the Trinity* and *City of God*, it is not surprising to see a writer of Augustine's reputation lay out such intricately developed and bold ideas. However, it is confounding to see Augustine also display in such works—early and late, large and small, pedagogical or theoretical—his "constant insistence on his lack of privileged access to knowledge" about angels.[13]

It is also intriguing. If men like Gregory and Augustine were so innovative in their thinking about angels, why do they make so much noise about not being able to understand them? Of course, pointing out one's imagined intellectual shortcomings is a rhetorical device at least as old as

Moses; it is possible that such reluctances, once put on display, served as the brushstrokes of larger portraits these men created of themselves as learned and authoritative, but humble, intellectuals. Yet both Gregory and Augustine were expansively imaginative writers with respect to other divine topics, unafraid of speculation, and even unapologetic in their defense of controversial theological positions. In fact, their boldness defines them: the reason we speak of these men now as central to ancient Christian history is that they endeavored to make their intellectual work central to ancient Christian culture. The new ideas they introduced about angels stood alongside other new formulations about the divine world they and others like them worked out in the late fourth and early fifth century—the incarnation of the Word, the relationships among members of the Trinity, the nature of God—and yet the angelic is the subject that consistently drew their protests of ignorance. The intellectual and rhetorical prowess of these writers stands in tension with their claims of ignorance, and that tension hints at careful cultural construction and maneuvering under the surface. In fact, it was this tension that initially made me suspect that late ancient Christian developments in thought about angels were worth examination.

Not all historians of early Christianity have shared my suspicions. The most recent monograph on the topic of angels in Christian late antiquity appeared more than a half a century ago. What is more, it began with an apology. The tireless church historian Jean Daniélou opened the introduction to *The Angels and Their Mission according to the Fathers of the Church* by acknowledging that "to devote an entire book to the subject of angels might seem at first glance unwarranted."[14] However, Daniélou argued that his book was necessary in order to correct those who had mistaken the tradition: in the wrong hands, the angels spoken of in Christian writings could be fodder for psychoanalytic interpretation, or be mishandled by those who shared "a lively interest in the invisible world" inspired by "spiritism or theosophy," rather than accepted ecclesiastical methods of interpretation.[15] Daniélou's justifications for producing his "unwarranted" work, then, were explicitly theological. Written as a remedy, *The Angels and Their Mission* was intended to bring investigation of Christian angels back from the opposite but equally troubling provinces of secular theories of human nature and overly fervent religious investment. Daniélou's conclusions about Christian traditions were correspondingly conservative. Arguing that early Christian conceptions of angels were both founded in Scripture and internally consistent over time, Daniélou presented an intermediate, yet orthodox, account of angels in Christianity, one coherent with his understanding of Christian history. A similar motive had inspired Erik Peterson's earlier work *The Angels and the Liturgy*, which appeared in 1935. Like Daniélou, Peterson was invested in the study of angels for the sake of Christian tradition. His explicit purpose was to demonstrate that "holy Scripture provides evidence that the Church's liturgy is a participation in the liturgy celebrated in heaven by the angels and the saints."[16] As an explanation for the frequent mention of angels in modern Christian rituals, he argued that ultimately, such practices were already found in Scripture (and thus, for Peterson, the first century) and had remained constant throughout the early Christian period. Like *The Angels and Their Mission*, *The Angels and the Liturgy* provided a confessional answer to the question of the origins of Christian ideas about angels, an answer supported by a view of Scripture as a faithful and historical representation of the earliest Christian practices.

Both Daniélou and Peterson were working within Catholic intellectual circles, but Protestant scholars also avoided delving into research about angels beyond what information might be available to them in Scripture. In his work *Drudgery Divine*, Jonathan Z. Smith has explained how anti-Catholic polemic led certain Protestant scholars to long ignore or overlook early Christian history outside the earliest writers of the "apostolic" period.[17] Smith's analysis focused on scholars who studied the earliest centuries of Christianity, but trends in modern Protestant theology also bent the focus of historical investigation about angels in other eras toward Scripture and away from any other source. In his gargantuan theological treatise *Church Dogmatics*, Karl Barth directed other Christians to engage with ideas about angels only infrequently and even then, cautiously. There was no benefit in taking angels as a topic of study, because their nature offered nothing important to know. As Barth explained, "angels are not independent and autonomous subjects like God and man and Jesus Christ. They cannot, therefore, be made the theme of an independent discussion.... They are essentially marginal figures."[18] What little should be investigated about them was already available in Scripture, especially the New Testament, which for Barth as it had for Peterson represented a portrait of the earliest century of the church. "The angels have an original form in the witness of Scripture," he wrote, and any knowledge that comes from sources outside Scripture was "ballast" that "we can and must jettison."[19] Moving beyond the first century was counterproductive, for "if we try to find angels in the Bible and elsewhere [at the same time], we shall see only hazy pictures."[20] What few more recent scholarly monographs there are about angels in early Christianity have followed the boundary lines laid by these earlier scholars: whether explicitly confessional or not, recent historical investigations have concluded that late ancient Christians did not think about angels very much, nor did they advance theories about angels beyond what information could be found in Christian Scripture.[21] In a way, early Christian historians of the last hundred years, occupying diverse confessional and nonconfessional viewpoints, have taken Gregory and Augustine at their word and have avoided exploring angels in late ancient Christian tradition.

In contrast to these previous studies, which considered both early Christianity in general and early Christian thought on angels specifically to be monolithic, bound by orthodox scriptural traditions, this book offers a different perspective by arguing that Christian ideas about angels were tremendously diverse, especially in the century following the legalization of Christianity. As a cultural historian, I have assumed that religious ideas are shaped by their historical contexts; like any other cultural products, religious ideas are constantly under negotiation, fungible and in many ways inclined by circumstance and opportunity. The changing political climate for Christians in the fourth and early fifth centuries altered the character of Christianity and the practices of Christians. Historians of Christianity have long acknowledged that no single continuous orthodox thread of culture or theology naturally triumphed during that time. Instead, the late ancient evidence reveals a vigorous, at times raucous, contestation among Christians on almost every subject, along with an impassioned search among Christians for the best ways of practicing a Christian style of life. This book contends that in that environment of experimentation, Christians pioneered many new ways of thinking, both expanding and selectively narrowing the ideas, practices, and structures that constitute late ancient Christianity. Their experimentation produced a wildly diverse array of ideas about what angels were, how they came to be, how they interacted with humanity, and what they would eventually become. It would be almost impossible to represent the full extent of this diversity in this book, but in my research, I have noticed that two discourses about angels were more prevalent than the others, in the frequency of their expression and the extent of their influence on other Christians. In one, angels were one type of being among many in a shifting universe, and their primary purpose was to guard and to guide Christians who attempted to cultivate specialized bodily practices and types of prayer in order to return, like the rest of creation, to their original unity with God. In the other, angels were characters described in the emerging canon of Scripture and available to enable readers to transform the mostly narrative material in that Scripture into foundational proof for theological propositions.

I call these ideas "discourses" because they were not articulated by one writer. Rather, they were the collective and evolving efforts of groups of individuals in shared social situations. The first discourse developed in the particularly Egyptian context of a certain style of asceticism, associated with, at its earliest, Antony of Pispir and at its latest, Evagrius of Pontus. The second developed in the urban context of publicly contested authority, often but not always associated with bishops and theological conflict. Like all discourses, these two complexes of ideas did not remain exclusively in the social provinces in which they each developed. Instead, traditions about angels that were first developed in the disciplined atmosphere of Antony's small monastic circle influenced the cultural products created by the most persuasive voices in Christian late antiquity, and ideas about angels initially revealed in the orations of powerful Christians attempting to legitimize the lifestyle of their urban congregations influenced the workings of Christian ascetic circles and larger monastic communities. Conversations in late ancient Christianity were far-reaching and complex—far more so than historians often realize—and the resulting contact and influence between these two discourses created the most recognizable angelic tropes of Christian late antiquity: the guardian angel, the desert dweller who lives "the angelic life," and the priest who celebrates an angelic liturgy on earth. In short, I wrote this book because I think Gregory of Nazianzus and Augustine were protesting too much: thinking about angels did not tax the abilities of late ancient Christians any more than other ideas, and to suggest, as some scholars have, that ideas about angels were unimportant in late antiquity, or worse, unchanging, is to leave unexamined fundamental developments in Christian tradition.

The following three sections of this introduction provide background to the argument of the book. In the first, I discuss the social roles that emerged for Christians in the fourth century, after the legitimization of Christianity and the increasing cultural experimentation and construction among Christians that followed. Here I trace how the scholarly conversation has moved from opposing the categories of "bishop" and "ascetic" toward investigating the various methods of displaying power in late ancient Christianity. I offer a description of two modes of being Christian that are important to this book: cultivation and contestation. In the next section, I offer some methodological observations that ground the book as a whole. As products of the religious imagination, angels are not reliably physical, material, visible, representable—in short, they are not "real" in our modern sense of the word. Yet religious practitioners operate as if they are, and so I discuss how best to think and write the history of these mental representations of religious practitioners from late antiquity. I conclude by providing an outline of the chapters, tracing in broad strokes the argument of the book.

Contestation and Cultivation

The fourth century was a time of significant changes in the social position and cultural potency of Christians, and those changes were set in motion in part by the changing policies toward Christianity adopted by Roman emperors. In Christian memory, the start of the fourth century was marked by a disaster: the systematic and cruel oppression of Christians by the emperor Diocletian in the "great persecution." Lasting almost a decade, this period of imperial intervention in the lives of many—though not most—Christians threatened a dark future.[22] In consequence, it was predictable that when Constantine, a new emperor, embraced a policy of tolerance for monotheistic religious and philosophical traditions, Christians hailed him as their champion.[23] As emperor, Constantine certainly was an important figure, but scholars have questioned whether his reign represents a single fulcrum of intense change within Christian history. For example, Claudia Rapp has argued that Christian traditions of office and the exercise of specific types of power were relatively continuous in the time before and after Constantine.[24] While it is good for historians to recognize that no single person or act can change the whole of a culture in one moment, it is also good to recognize the thoroughgoing nature of imperial power, the kinds of resources it makes available or denies to those living in the culture it dominates, and the lasting structural changes it inspires, even in communities ostensibly separated from official expressions of power. Variance in matters theological and practical had always existed among Christians, but the culture of imperial sponsorship formed by Constantine's way of interacting with Christians established different, more trenchant consequences for that variance. The attention of emperors to theological ideas changed the nature of Christian attention to theological details, while Constantine's financial decisions—both the money he lavished on new Christian buildings and the patronage and finances he extended to individual Christian leaders—established a method of relationship and appropriation that inclined some Christians to adopt and others to retract from such power. The emperors who followed Constantine expanded their interactions with Christians, such that the approbation of one or another emperor was often a deciding factor in Christian cultural and theological disagreements in late antiquity. Many ideals and practices were continuously in use by Christians before and after the turn of the fourth century, but no cultural continuity remained unrefracted by the movement of Christians from intermittently persecuted minority to increasingly accepted and ultimately dominant majority.

Our view of the evolution of the nature of Christian authority under these conditions has advanced considerably. At the middle of the twentieth century, Hans von Campenhausen's study of ecclesiastical power relied on an influential sociological model to compare the worldly broker of church goods, the urban bishop, to the world-renouncing arbiter of charismatic authority, the desert ascetic.[25] The idea that bishops were the ultimate insiders, while ascetics were outsiders—holy fools with the untainted authority of the social critic—was extremely influential, and the categories of "bishop" and "ascetic" were the scaffolding for several subsequent historical accounts of Christian power in late antiquity. More and more scholars toward the end of the twentieth century, however, have worried the neat lines of such a model, opting instead to examine the places where the categories of "bishop" and "ascetic" seemed to bleed into one another. Both Philip Rousseau and Andrea Sterk have explored how the ideal of the practiced ascetic—pious, humble, and removed from worldly concerns—became the standard to which would-be bishops aspired.[26] Rebecca Krawiec and Caroline T. Schroeder have demonstrated the ways that Shenoute, not a bishop and ostensibly an ascetic, exercised power over the community at the White Monastery and the surrounding villages in ways that would fit neatly into what was expected of a "bishop" exercising his institutional authority.[27] Claudia Rapp explicitly called for what these studies have implied was necessary: the abolition of the categories of "bishop" and "ascetic" as units of research meaningful in their own right, to be replaced by the investigation of the valences of power gained in public discourse by demonstration of different talents—ascetic, pragmatic, and spiritual.[28] We do not see clearly when we divide ancient Christians by offices whose trappings we impose; it is better to recognize that cultural power was a fluid commodity and that there was a "*single arena* available to *all*" late ancient Christians in which to contest claims of authority.[29] Among historians of late ancient Christianity, the idea of different authorities, separated within offices and available only to the holders of those offices—ascetic on the one hand, bishop on the other—has collapsed, with scholarly perspectives converging instead on the common public contestation of cultural power among Christians.

While the move away from the bishop-ascetic dichotomy is a welcome one, the fact that in antiquity Christians *themselves* seem to have recognized some difference between bishops and ascetics should give us pause. The distinction is especially visible in texts that address the issue of ascetics taking on offices in episcopal hierarchies. Many bishops, like Athanasius of Alexandria, went to great lengths to incorporate ascetics into their own organizational structures, and their initiatives can be interpreted in two ways.[30] The impulse of bishops to ordain ascetics may have been, on the one hand, a sign that bishops considered ascetics and the authority they carried as natural extensions of episcopal hierarchies, thus supporting the interpretation that episcopal authority and ascetic authority were parts of the same whole. On the other hand, the rush of bishops to ordain ascetics may have been a sign that bishops were interested in locating, then coopting, alternate authority structures that had arisen separately from their own authority. While the actions of expansionist bishops can be read at least these two ways, the responses of ascetics to the prospect of ordination seem on their face less ambivalent. Most ascetic texts problematized the desire on the part of ascetics to be ordained, and several ancient stories imply that good ascetics should outright refuse to accept any office. Of course, these texts, too, may be read in multiple ways. Refusal to accept an office was precisely the mark of humility needed to suggest that one was worthy of office; the only person truly qualified for the job was the one who did not want it. Many Christians, ascetics and others, displayed their humility by refusing offices for a time before eventually taking them.[31] By these lights, it appears that even those works that protest about ascetics becoming bishops and insist on there being a divide between the two in reality speak to the continuity between the categories rather than their separation.

Yet there were some Christians for whom avoidance of office was a real, and not rhetorical, concern, and their discussions of the problems associated with becoming leaders in the church are quite revealing. As a young adult, Evagrius of Pontus had followed a promising track, first serving in a minor church office under Basil of Caesarea in Asia Minor during the late 370s, then as a deacon under Gregory of Nazianzus when he had gone to Constantinople to work with the Nicene community in 380 CE.[32] Evagrius abruptly left that career path, spending time in an ascetic commune in Palestine before moving on to live with other ascetics in the communities of northern Egypt. When he later wrote about the temptations that ascetics were likely to encounter, Evagrius identified the call to ordination as a tactic of the demons with whom individual Christians did battle. The demon of avarice would first cast in the mind visions of all the work an ascetic could do if he were wealthy, wielding power to do good for suffering people in a poor town. Avarice would then turn the ascetic over to the demon of vainglory to deliver the crucial blow. Bringing to mind "a crowd of people who gradually speak among themselves about the priesthood," vainglory would tempt the monk by "predicting the death of the incumbent priest" and suggesting the now bewildered ascetic might be the natural successor to the office.[33] Elsewhere, Evagrius described the demon of vainglory revealing to the ascetic in a similar scenario that, though he might resist, "he will eventually attain the priesthood." In fact, people would come to him and demand his service, and "if he should be unwilling, he will be taken away in bonds."[34] The most poignant and dangerous elements of such demonically inspired fantasies were the people: people who needed help, people who saw potential in the great ascetic, people who clamored for his accession. Ordination was no empty temptation; in these warnings about the demon of vainglory Evagrius acknowledged the tangible benefits of accepting church office, which included the glory that came with the recognition of others as well as the ability to do good by edifying a community of Christians.[35] Yet Evagrius still painted even these duties as temptations, suggesting that ascetics should reject church offices as they would any other temptation.

Why avoid something so promising? Evagrius himself never spelled out his reasons for avoiding ordination, but his erstwhile student John Cassian did.[36] Cassian spent almost ten years in the communities of northern Egypt near the end of the fourth century, and at least part of that time he spent studying with Evagrius. When he left Egypt, finally settling in southern Europe to begin a monastery, Cassian attempted to translate Evagrius's advice about demonic temptations for a Latin-speaking audience.[37] In his discussion of vainglory, which borrows from Evagrius's ideas, Cassian famously pronounced a simple rule for monks who wished to be successful: "flee women and bishops," the idea being that a bishop was as liable to ordain an ascetic as a woman was to seduce him. The context of this dictum reveals a deeper motivation for why an aspiring ascetic should avoid such creatures. Cassian wrote:

> This old saying of the fathers is relevant even now—it is a saying that I cannot quote without shame on my part, since I could not evade my sister, nor escape the hands of the bishop—namely, that a monk must, by all means, flee women and bishops. Neither one of these allows him, once he is joined in close intercourse with it, to pay any further attention to the quiet of his cell nor to cling to divine contemplation through the understanding of holy things gotten through the purest of sight.[38]

Cassian's extended account of avoiding ordination tells us that refusal was sometimes more than a rhetorical feint at humility. It was possible to recognize the honors and glory that came with church office and yet to privilege something else: the solitude of the cell and the practice of contemplation, both of which would be interrupted by contact with a woman or a bishop. For some Christians, avoiding ordination was the means to a more important end, namely preserving a unique way of life unavailable to those taking on public positions of authority.

This special way of life has come into clearer view over the last fifty years. In that time, scholarly understanding of all early Christian ascetic movements has advanced, with extensive archaeological and papyrological work, the reconstruction of Shenoute's corpus and other texts, and better theorized accounts of the geographical and cultural location of the large communities of ascetics in Egypt with respect to their Christian and non-Christian neighbors. But there has been an especially intense focus by some scholars to reconstruct the words and ideas of Evagrius, whose assumptions about human nature and cosmology caused controversy after his death, first at the turn of the fifth century and later again in the mid-sixth century. The result of those controversies—Evagrius being declared a heretic and being deleted from traditional retellings of Christian history—had the effect of removing from circulation many texts by him and related to him. Only the efforts of several scholars to restore and recontextualize Evagrius's works have clarified the importance of his system of progressive Christian development.[39] Evagrius expected Christians to be able to pass through several stages of progress by cultivating the *nous*, a mental faculty akin to the intellect or reason. Through intense practices aimed at ridding oneself of the passions, which were thought to darken the *nous* and impede its function, Christians could first contemplate divine beings and then inch ever closer to acquaintance with God. These ideas, though inventive, were not entirely new. The system that Evagrius wrote about inherited structure and content from philosophical and reading circles like those maintained by scholastic teachers of Alexandria: Origen and Didymus the Blind are two paragons of this tradition.[40] Furthermore, ascetics in Egypt long before Evagrius's arrival had built systems of ascetic training in this mold of the philosophical school: Antony of Pispir, the same Antony made famous by Athanasius's *Life of Antony*, also was influenced by Origen's cosmology and style of reading. Early Christian ascetics like Antony; Ammonas, the next leader of Antony's community; Macarius of Egypt, an ascetic influenced by the same models; and Evagrius were not primarily interested in the exercise of public power or the recognition of other Christians. Instead, the ascetics in this loosely gathered tradition of cultivation were interested in the progress of the individual Christian through reading and prayer—a return to an intellectual realm of the divine, facilitated by the ascetic lifestyle they adopted. In the expectation that the whole of the created universe would eventually return to unity with the uncreated God, these Christians made cultivation a priority, forgoing certain activities to preserve time and space to work on their development.

The focus on cultivation in this ascetic tradition is quite different from the focus that captured the attention of so many other Christians in late antiquity: contestation, or the wielding of power by means of skillful persuasion.[41] Because of the imperial sponsorship of Christianity, the stakes of public contestation were high. Not only did emperors call and ratify councils—engendering the forum in which Christians articulated in a legal way the theological propositions they considered most pressing—but emperors frequently championed some leaders while deposing and exiling others, funded some communities while ignoring others, protected some Christians while exposing others.[42] Within the field of competition established by such actions, Christians in the fourth century strived for legitimacy; their endeavors included developing certain styles of reading for holy texts and the canonization of one particular set of texts as the "New Testament." When such Christians made arguments, they made them for an audience: of other bishops, of lay Christians, of monks, of imperial officials, of non-Christians. Those embracing the mode of contestation did so because they had "a more acute awareness of the public image of the representatives of the church," an awareness born of the shift toward a Christian cultural majority.[43]

None of these actions or dispositions were necessarily tied to the office of "bishop" nor, in truth, any other office. Indeed, the writers I examine in this book who had powerful public voices were often ordained into service *as a result* of their success in contestation, rather than coming by their power because they were ordained to certain offices. Both Gregory and Augustine did not gain their skills from being made bishops, but rather were hastily asked to become bishops because of their already evident persuasive authority. Some of the best representatives of contestation were particularly bad at remaining in office. Athanasius spent almost one half of his career as bishop of Alexandria *not* being the bishop of Alexandria, in a strict sense; he was exiled multiple times by emperors supporting other factions of Christians. That is to say, Athanasius in exile in Rome or Trier was not "the bishop of Alexandria" in any meaningful way, except perhaps from hindsight and the peculiar viewpoint of those who would trace an eventual "orthodoxy" already existing in the late ancient Christian community. Yet this fact did not impede his efforts at contestation. Indeed, his most lasting legacy, the casting of the multiple opponents to the Nicene creed as one sprawling family of "Arians," was conceived during an exile, precisely when Athanasius was not technically holding any office.[44] Athanasius is one example, but there are many others. Even the usual way that we refer to Augustine, as "bishop of Hippo," obscures the fact that the congregation he led was in the minority in North Africa, its numbers dwarfed by the prevailing community, whose dominance we obscure in turn when we call them "Donatists" and not simply "Christians." All of this is to point out that those who were engaged in contestation truly were contestants, struggling against others for intellectual, religious, and social legitimacy, and failing as often as they succeeded. It is important to remember that their fates were not ever settled, from their perspective, nor the meaning of the "office" they all at one point or another held, namely that of "bishop."[45] What characterizes these men is their developing method of contestation, focused on the emergent authority of Scripture and the power of a skillful voice to capture and convince an audience.[46] Such a mode is one way of being Christian in the fourth century, one that, if we note the sources carefully, we can see was discursively different from the mode of cultivation represented in traditions associated with ascetics from Antony to Evagrius.

The two realms I have tagged here as "contestation" and "cultivation" are themselves contingent; they do not describe late ancient realities but instead help me parse the important differences between the way that someone like Augustine or Athanasius lived and the way that someone like Evagrius or Antony lived. Because Christian institutions were continually under formation during late antiquity, we cannot discern anything reliable solely by learning the name of an office or social role that an early Christian claimed. Instead, we should seek more detailed information: What and how did this person read? What and how and for whom did this person write? Did he seek to debate with others, dominating by rhetoric, or did he turn his attention and energy to practices of the body and soul as he understood them, toward cultivating a path of progress? Was he looking to create a change in society or a change in the self? When we ask such things, we see that some Christians applied religious energy and political capital toward garnering and persuading an audience, and for some, toward leading a congregation. Others put those same resources toward the transformation of their own moral or ontological state. These two choices are not mutually exclusive—Augustine certainly paid attention to his moral development, and Evagrius certainly had a community to which he felt responsible and which he attempted to teach—but they are paths, vocations, and one or the other often dominates in the career of the individual Christian in late antiquity. The ideas about angels I examine in this book were inclined to these two approaches to the new power available in the world after the start of the fourth century because they are products of the religious imagination.

The Religious Imagination

To write about angels is to write about the processes of cultural construction. The cultural phenomena labeled "angel" can be analyzed with the same apparatus used to analyze other cultural objects, such as "tree" or "city," because those, too, are objects of cultural construction. Yet angels have a special feature that requires more attention: they are not as easily referenced and known as things like trees and cities because they are not as reliably available to be investigated. Instead, they are products of the religious imagination. Underlying this book are several methodological assumptions about the religious imagination, none of which are my invention, and many of which will already be familiar—indeed, intuitive—to most readers.

First, the religious imagination produces representations, a term which I use in a technical way to mean cognitive representations. Although the word "image" is lexically related to the word "imagination," the human imagination does not deal solely in images. While we often call things to mind by visualizing them, as often as not, we imagine things without using any visualization at all. This is also true of objects of a religious nature. To ponder, "what is an angel?" is not necessarily, or even primarily, a matter of making a mental picture of an angel. Even a basic narrative statement like "a frightening angel visited her sister" does not require me to create a cinematographic scene in order to hold it in my mind, although such figuration can certainly be a part of how I represent the idea to myself. Cognitive representation is as often a matter of holding open a space for agency: What does an angel do? What might an angel think? Where might an angel come from? All of these are questions that can be considered without any recourse to visualization. I do not mean to say that visual representations—whether images made in the mind, or images made in the world—are unimportant. Late ancient Christians explored the visual world, its properties, and its possibilities, in an intense way, and the visibility of divine beings was a topic of much theorizing and debate.[47] However, images are not the only way, nor even the most important way, that late ancient Christians imagined angels. If debate about and diversity among cultural products serve as signals of human interest, then it is significant that the physical representations that Christians made of angels, when they made them, were surprisingly stable throughout late antiquity, hewing to a similar and familiar form.[48] The lack of innovations in visual patterns for depicting angels suggests that what interested fourth- and fifth-century Christians about angels was not what they looked like, but what they are and what they do.

What angels are and do matters so much because angels were real to late ancient Christians. That seems like a simple statement, but let me explain what I mean. The term "real" can mean different things, and some contemporary meanings of the term are not useful for this book. First is the common idea that "real" is a synonym for "apparent." In this frame, the "real" is that which exists right in front of our noses: material, visible things are real. Angels were not reliably material or apparent to late ancient Christians, but they were still real. Another common meaning has the word "real" as the opposite of "illusionary." One believes in the existence of what is real and disbelieves what is not real, whether these things are visible or not. Late ancient Christians were more inclined to cast "belief" as the hopeful expectation of some future event (I believe that I will win the jackpot) than to use "belief" as a simple predication of something's existence (I believe the jackpot exists). In these terms, late ancient

Christians did not use belief to describe their relationship to angels; they did not speculate about certain angels being illusory in the sense of not existing. Instead of either of these common meanings of "real," I take the term to be synonymous with "culturally operational." In late ancient Christian literature, there are signs that Christians expected angels to exist and to persist, and that they accepted that angels could interact with human beings, even if only select ones.

To illustrate what I mean, let me introduce a contemporary object that is real in the way I use the term about angels: cholesterol. I have never personally seen cholesterol, nor have I gone through the processes that would verify its existence. Yet I do not wonder whether it exists, and I have a reasonable expectation that with effort I could locate someone who has seen it and who could verify its existence. Even on this shaky epistemological foundation, cholesterol is culturally operational—is real—for me, and its reality changes the way I act and think. I evaluate the food I eat based on my estimation of how eating it will change my cholesterol; I alter my physical activity to affect my cholesterol; I visit specialists and ingest preparations, often at significant cost, to control my cholesterol. The fact that cholesterol is as real to others as it is to me certainly helps: when I forgo a second helping of bread pudding at a dinner party "because of my cholesterol," the hostess does not even blink an eye; she does not need an explanation, and she may even be managing her own cholesterol. It would be insufficient to say that she and I "believe" in cholesterol. I suppose we do, but "belief" does not adequately convey the *givenness* of cholesterol for us. Most of us would protest that cholesterol is a "real" thing, even though it does not occur to us to try personally to verify its existence—indeed, our easy acceptance of something that, practically speaking, most of us cannot know is precisely the point. Angels are real to religious practitioners in this same sense, inspiring neither belief nor disbelief, yet influencing behavior and the generation of new ideas because they are given parts of late ancient Christian culture.

Remembering that angels are real and therefore operational in the world of late ancient Christians can help avoid another pitfall, namely, assuming that angels are a symbolic system by which Christians theorize about other things. In the past, some historians and theorists of culture understood cultural systems by considering the function of their parts. This was a fruitful approach in many ways, especially because it allowed investigators to suspend judgment about the reality of cultural phenomena under study that seemed strange or unbelievable to them, especially when those phenomena were part of cultures distant from their own. While functionalism has fallen out of favor as a scholarly approach, one element from the heyday of functionalist studies persists: the idea that some cultural systems or cultural products exist because they are "good to think." The phrase originated with Claude Levi-Strauss's study of totem animals, in which he opposed some species of animals, those that were "good to eat," to others that were "good to think." Anthropologists Edmund Leach and Stanley Tambiah, responding to and expanding Levi-Strauss's work, popularized the idea that animals could be "good to think," and as ethnographic models took hold across the humanities, "good to think" flourished as an idea with strong, but implicit, explanatory power.[49] Its use naturalized foreign cultural systems by subsuming them under an intuitive banner: some part of another culture may not be indisputably real to scholarly observers, or immediately sensible to them as a choice for cultural expression, but it at least must be "good to think," a good way to work out the problems facing one's culture in elaborate, but risk-free thought experiments. At first glance, angels seem perfectly germane to this peculiar way of parsing a distant culture: as we will see angels in late ancient Christianity were thought to be very close to humanity, yet not at all like humanity, and thus would seem to be fitting subjects for late ancient thought experiments about humanity.[50] Yet I would argue that saying angels in late antiquity are "good to think" is uncritical and, worse, misleading.

The phrase suggests a utilitarian motive behind the maintenance of the cultural systems to which it is applied. Religious adherents are using angels (or animals, or women, or whatever categories the investigating scholar deems "good to think") as a theoretical practice field for something else, which is their actual concern. There are several problems with this approach. First, it allows the scholar to divide the culture under study into parts and to separate those things that are "good to think" from other concepts, as if those other concepts were not themselves also cultural constructions. Indeed, if angels appear to serve a function in the cultural work of late antiquity, that is only an effect produced by valuing them as less consequential than the other equally constructed concepts in late ancient Christian culture: the human being, the Christian, the priest, the ascetic, Scripture, the church, God. To accept the analysis implicit in stating that angels were "good to think" is to privilege one or more of these cultural constructions above others, instead of seeing all of these things as mutually constructed, interdependent identities central to grasping what we mean by "late ancient Christianity." A reader may object that late ancient Christian writers themselves say that angels are unimportant, pointing to the very protests I cited at the start of this chapter. But the explanations offered by late ancient Christians are not the only proper pathway for a scholar to follow, nor are they unquestionably the best starting point for analysis. Second, if whatever is "good to think" symbolically reproduces another set of problems, then it cannot be the origin of new thought, or new ideas, whether harmonious or discordant, constructive or destructive to the culture from which it came. In this book, however, we will examine the ways that various ideas of angels inflected and changed other developing Christian cultural forms, including things that we often assume are central to understanding the late ancient Christian world: Scripture and the rules for reading it, asceticism, and the emerging network of public leaders. For these reasons, "good to think" is a scholarly tool that is not particularly useful in understanding angels in early Christian traditions, and for one more: angels in the time of the turn to Christian majority were very often, as we shall see, quite disturbing for Christians to think, in that they altered the discourses of which they were a part, in unpredictable and creative ways.

The texts on which this study is based are drawn from many parts of the late ancient world and were written or survive in translation in many languages. I have gathered extensive references to other texts in the notes, but those references do not document every instance in which an early Christian mentions angels or similar beings. That is for a simple reason: to do so would not clarify late ancient Christian thought about angels and runs the risk of simplifying it to a catalog. Angelology—the systematic investigation and cataloging of the role and nature of angels within a wider account of all divine beings—is mostly a medieval pursuit.[51] It is actually quite foreign to much of late antiquity. We have seen how writers like Gregory of Nazianzus and Augustine seemed to content themselves with listing those beings mentioned in Scripture and in any case did not attempt explicitly to create a comprehensive account of angels and their roles. As further evidence of the lack of a concept of angelology in late antiquity, consider the absence of treatises written "On the Angels" to match the overwhelming number of late ancient Christian treatises produced, say, "On the Trinity," or "On the Holy Spirit." One late ancient author, Pseudo-Dionysius, created an angelology by listing in order nine categories of angels named in Scripture and detailing their essences and actions. But that work, as I argue at the end of the book, represented a break from other late ancient thought, in that it treated angels as a discrete subject, a "hierarchy" that stood between God and Christians. Its influence, though, has prompted scholars to excavate similarly discrete angelologies for various early Christian thinkers, literatures, or locations. Such reconstructions can be helpful, but they obscure an important fact: late ancient Christians did not consider angels separable from the rest of Christian ideas, did not think of angels as supplementary or extraneous divine beings worthy of treatment in a list, and did not resect their ideas about angels from ideas about God, humanity, the cosmos, and the form of Christian practice. As is increasingly obvious, late ancient Christians lived in an intricate world, one far stranger than what we might imagine for them; the concerns of that world, its organizing categories, are quite different from the concerns of our world. For that reason, I have worked here to reconstruct, as best I can, the complexity of late ancient Christian ideas and practices regarding angels, and so have avoided adopting the genre of angelology, which ultimately simplifies. Instead, I offer a historical argument about the two most salient ways that late ancient Christians, navigating the novel social and cultural territories that came with the turn to cultural majority, imagined angels in new, exacting, and transformative detail.

Chapter Outline

The argument of the book unfolds in the following way. Chapter 1, "Late Ancient Theories of Angels," illustrates the diversity of thought about angels in late ancient Christianity by comparing the ideas held by two writers working in roughly the same time period, the decades around the turn of the fifth century: Evagrius of Pontus and Augustine of Hippo. Evagrius had begun a career as a church official but left that career and went to study in the academic and ascetic circles of Egypt. His emphasis on the cultivation practiced by individual Christians was the frame within which he wrote about angels as one unstable class within the larger category of "rational beings," a group that included human beings and demons as well. According to Evagrius, human beings could, depending on their attention to the development of the *nous*, an intellectual faculty, become more like angels and thus begin their return to complete unity with God; angels, for their part, could help human beings in this process. Such ideas had their foundation in the cyclical and changing universe imagined by Origen, the third-century Alexandrian writer, but Evagrius further developed Origen's ideas in the context of ascetic practice to articulate a program of progressive development for Christians. In comparison, Augustine of Hippo held quite different expectations about angels. Augustine's rhetorical training prepared him to advocate and to advise other Christians, particularly with respect to the coherence of the Christian worldview. In his writing, he sought to prove Christianity's superiority and to invalidate competing religious and philosophical traditions; particular ideas about angels were central to his case. For example, his work *City of God* proposed a way of seeing world history in which angels were citizens of a holy city that Christians could hope one day to join. The reality of the city was guaranteed by the reality of its inhabitants, and the specific qualities of these heavenly citizens were forged in Augustine's mind in conversation with other traditions. It was precisely Augustine's aim of circumscribing philosophy, literature, alternate versions of Christianity, and Manichaean traditions that led him to his specific ideas about the place of angels at the very start of creation and their eternal stability and happiness with God. The chapter's comparison of Evagrius and Augustine reveals two basic facts. First and most important, late ancient Christian thought about angels was not unified. While Evagrius elaborated an entire cosmology within which angels occupied one stage in the return to the highest God and were mobile by their very nature, Augustine fashioned angels as beings that had lost mutability, indeed any agency, at the beginning of time. Second, variant Christian ideas about angels took shape in distinct, recognizable social situations born of the transformation of Christianity from a minority to a majority culture. The ideas of Evagrius and Augustine typify the ideas arising in the modes of cultivation and contestation in Christian discourse in late antiquity.

The next two chapters step backward to examine the cultural and intellectual trajectories that led to the different ideas held by Augustine and Evagrius. The first of these treats Augustine's predecessors and Augustine himself. In Chapter 2, "Locating Christ in Scripture," I consider several Christians engaged in contestation, demonstrating how Augustine's ideas of angels were the result of a late ancient tradition of reimagining angels in order to preserve the coherence between Scripture and developing theological positions. For those involved in contestation, Scripture was a powerful base of authority, but only powerful when it supported one's argument—that is to say, when it was protected from alternate interpretations and was not legible in the theological frameworks staked out by others. Over the course of the fourth century, Christians involved in theological debate tested various ways of reading Scripture, especially in pursuit of a foundation for knowledge about Christ. Two approaches were particularly popular. First, viewing Scripture through a historical lens: Christians had long read Scripture as a record of the past, often to establish the presence of Christ as the Word in historical time. In addition to the historical lens, late ancient Christians directed ever more attention to reading Scripture with a grammatical lens, breaking passages down to phrases and words that, in their singularity, reflected much more of the reality of the divine world than narrative passages did. The chapter begins with Athanasius's early articulations of a pro-Nicene position in the *Orations against the Arians,* the basis of which was formulated during his time in exile in Rome with Marcellus of Ancyra; the germ of Athanasius's reading depends on a particular understanding of the comparison of Christ to angels in the letter to the Hebrews. Thirty years later, the interactions of Basil of Caesarea and Gregory of Nyssa with Eunomius of Cyzicus, recorded in several treatises, reveal these men's ideas about the limits of language to represent divine reality and the role of the reader in producing interpretation. Angels in Scripture were put to use to mark the boundaries of appropriate interpretation and specifically used by Basil, then Gregory, to undermine Eunomius's more grammatically conservative readings. Taking part in this intellectual tradition, Augustine created a way to understand angels that encompassed both historical and grammatical readings. Considering certain words in Scripture that seemed to rule out the presence of Christ in the appearances of divine actors in the Old Testament, Augustine argued that all such theophanies were appearances of angels—a position that changed Christian historical reading practices in place since the first century. Thus, during late antiquity, changing ideas of angels were key to the development and sustainability of Christian practices of reading Scripture, particularly reading Scripture with an eye to deriving information about Christ.

At the same time that the changing imperial conditions of Christianity were shifting how Christian interpreters used angels, such conditions were also making possible a new style of Christian life aimed at individual cultivation undertaken in renunciatory practice. In Chapter 3, "Angels as Equipment for Living," I look back at the genealogy of acetic and academic Christians whose ideas influenced Evagrius and explore ideas about angels developed in the particular style of asceticism that Evagrius eventually adopted. Those Christians in the lineage Evagrius joined had enacted a program of asceticism that followed most closely the structure and curriculum of the academic Christian circles that had flourished in Alexandria, which themselves reflected the model of philosophical school circles. The first part of the chapter therefore explores how philosophical expectations of a divine guide for wise men informed the experience of a student in one of these academic Christian circles, Gregory Thaumaturgus. Gregory learned from his teacher Origen of Alexandria that all Christians have a divine guide protecting them, whose status varied according to the moral progress of its charge. A similar teaching influenced Antony of Pispir, an ascetic whose letters described the gradual development of a Christian and the emergence of a guide for his practice. Antony alternately called this guide a power, a spirit, or an angel, and for the chapter, I adopt the term "companion angel" to represent all of these. The assistance of this companion angel was not guaranteed but could be earned by enacting what he termed the "sacrifice" of ascetic practices. The remainder of the chapter traces the continuation of the companion angel tradition in the letters of Ammonas, Antony's successor at Pispir, and texts surviving from other ascetics in their lineage like Macarius the Egyptian and Evagrius of Pontus. Recognizing the tradition of companion angels can provide context for stories included in the early fifth-century collections of literature meant to capture the details and tenor of Egyptian ascetic life. In the world of Christians cultivating their own progressive development, angels were guides earned as markers of moral advancement and coaches who enabled the success of their athletes. In this way, the first three chapters of the book demonstrate the diversity of ideas about angels in late ancient Christianity and reveal the intellectual and social genealogy of those ideas as they were developed by Christians practicing cultivation and contestation.

The second part of the book, Chapters 4 through 6, shows how the discourses about angels that developed in these modes of piety did not stand apart from one another. Though they were discrete and each had a primary social environment in which it operated, ideas from both discourses influenced the cultural products and institutions of other Christians. To start, Chapter 4, "Crossing Over," demonstrates that the tradition of companion angels, first articulated in ascetic circles, influenced two popular biographies composed by writers who exemplify the mode of contestation: Athanasius of Alexandria and Gregory of Nyssa. This chapter first examines the evidence of the tradition in the *Life of Antony* written by Athanasius in the late 350s CE. Athanasius himself speaks in the *Life* of collecting the existing stories about Antony, and it is clear that he redacted some of the material in the *Life* from a written source that had described Antony receiving and using a companion angel. The second part of the chapter demonstrates that the companion angel tradition also influenced a later biography, Gregory of Nyssa's *Life of Moses*, written in the 380s or 390s CE. The presence of the companion angel tradition in these two works demonstrates that there was an extended conversation between those Christians interested in personal cultivation through ascetic practice and those interested in the persuasive value of exemplary biographies for advocating certain models of Christianity to a wide audience. The implications of this chapter are significant: though the style of asceticism associated with the cosmology of Origen and the practices of Antony and Evagrius was eventually disfavored among Christians, its idea of a companion angel lived on in works that were extremely influential both in late antiquity and in later idealizations of the Christian way of life.

Conversely, Chapter 5, "Defining Others," demonstrates that the work of those Christians focused on contesting social authority could influence the communities of cultivative Christians in Egypt. Several fourth-century orators sought to explain to their congregations the existence of other Christians who practiced a different method of Christianity, one focused on discipline and separation from the social attachments of family and community. These orators naturalized ascetic Christian practices by use of a trope borrowed from the gospels: the idea that unmarried, renunciant Christians were normal, because Jesus had praised the practice of celibacy as something that made humanity "equal to the angels." From there, the shorthand of "the angelic life" was used in increasingly broad ways, coming to refer to ascetics and their communal practices in general. It both familiarized ascetics to and distanced them from urban congregations of Christians. The preaching of John Chrysostom exemplifies the way that orators branded the alternate practices of Christian life enacted by ascetics as "angelic," but he was by no means the only one to do so. The trope was widely used by Christian leaders and deeply pervaded Christian culture, so much so that it even affected the day-to-day lives of renunciant Christians living in ascetic communities. By exploring the evidence left by Evagrius of Pontus, the collected *Sayings of the Fathers*, and the extensive works of Shenoute of Atripe, I show that ascetics knew others referred to them this way and often put the trope of "living the angelic life" to use among themselves. While the idea that those ascetics might be living in an angelic community helped reinforce certain values and helped ascetic leaders negotiate the difficult territory of communal life, it also created problematic expectations among those who joined ascetic communities. Thus, much of the surviving ascetic literature shows wariness about ascetics expecting themselves to be living as angels, or among angels, who appeared to them in their practices.

Chapter 6, "Bringing Angels into the World," treats the pedagogical works written in the fourth century by church leaders in order to train new Christians how to participate in rituals. These works stand in direct tension with the warnings issued in ascetic literature that I examined in Chapter 5. Unlike ascetic communities, where the practice of envisioning angels was most often viewed with disdain, catechetical programs in fact encouraged Christians to see angels and to imagine themselves standing among angels during the performance of rituals. What is more, the way teachers asked Christians to imagine angels changed over the course of late antiquity; these changes reflect the shifting social position of Christians in the wider Roman world. In the earliest treatises, which date to the mid-fourth century, Christian rituals were described as reproductions of an angelic service acted out in heaven. However, as Christians gained cultural power, Christian writers began to imagine angels coming down into the world to watch humans enact their rituals. Instead of being a dim reflection of a ritual taking place somewhere else, the Eucharist in particular became the central event, transformative not just for Christians on earth, but for angels from heaven, too. Ultimately, the refiguration of ritual in these texts elevated the status of the officiant of the ritual; such a change in catechetical texts also shows us both the power of the leader who headed the late ancient Christian congregation and the developing confidence of the Christian cultural majority.

In my conclusion, "The Limits of Angelology," I discuss Pseudo-Dionysius's *Celestial Hierarchy*, a sixth-century Syrian text that many scholars have taken as the definitive account of ancient Christian ideas about angels. The *Celestial Hierarchy* is an important text, but two of its features have induced the unwarranted pride of place it enjoys in reconstructions of ancient Christian culture. Its pseudonymity and its genre—the fact that it is a "hierarchy," a term this author coined—are rhetorical features that can, and have, supported the notion that early Christian thought about angels was solely drawn from Scripture and did not change during late antiquity, a stance that continues to inflect historical studies of early Christianity. Given that the purpose of this book is to overcome that tendency, I suggest in the conclusion that *Celestial Hierarchy* be taken as the witness of one small part of late ancient Christian culture and that angelology, the form of study it pioneered, be avoided in favor of more historically contextualized ways of investigating the past. My goal is to demonstrate that angels were intrinsic to late ancient Christianity, rather than separable from it.

1

Late Ancient Theories of Angels

EVAGRIUS OF PONTUS AND AUGUSTINE OF HIPPO COMPARED

IN HIS SECOND letter to the Corinthians, the apostle Paul warned the community he had founded that other teachers might follow him, bearing messages contrary to the one he preached. Given the force of Paul's language when he spoke against these latecomers, it seems clear that he was not conjuring up a hypothetical situation; other people had already visited the Corinthians and had already introduced a different gospel among them. Paul ridiculed these teachers as "false apostles, deceitful workers, those who pass themselves off as apostles of Christ." The community should be able to detect the wicked nature of such interlopers, whom Paul sarcastically branded "superapostles," and they should distrust whatever message the visitors bring. It was not easy, however, to tell the difference between a true apostle and a false one. Paul chided the Corinthians: "Do not be surprised! Even Satan can pass himself off as an angel of light, so it is no trouble for his ministers to pass themselves off as ministers of righteousness." If the highest of the fallen angels could masquerade as a good angel, so too could a "deceitful worker" appear to be an edifying teacher of the true gospel to those who were unsuspecting (2 Cor 11.13–15).

Corinth was not the only one of Paul's communities to be approached by missionary preachers with whom Paul disagreed. The churches he founded in Galatia, it seems, had also been taken in by other apostles, other messages. Paul's surviving letter to the Galatian communities defended the authority of his unique gospel with unmeasured vitriol. He threatened his readers, "even if I or an angel from heaven proclaim something to you outside that which I have already proclaimed to you, let that one be accursed!" (Gal 1.18). Paul's concern stemmed from the fact that at first, he had been welcomed among the Galatians as "an angel of God, as Christ Jesus" and his message had been granted the authority of a missive from heaven (Gal 4.14). Now others had come to disrupt it. If an angel or another missionary could persuade the Galatians to follow a new teaching, the gospel Paul had taught was, in his absence, unstable in the extreme; his words call into question the ability of the Galatians, or any Christians, to discern the intent of the missionaries and messengers that come to them. If the most evil of demons can appear to be an "angel of light," then even Paul's eternally true message—itself received by the Galatians as if it had come from an "angel of God"—may be usurped by another, later, "angel" preaching a deceitful gospel. Aside from Paul's obvious fears about the endurance of his own message, also latent within the rhetoric of the letters to the Galatians and to the Corinthians is the suggestion that it was difficult to grasp the identity of angels with any certainty, given how closely they may resemble demons or human beings.

These passages of Paul's letters record a theme that proved remarkably persistent in early Christian conversations about angels. It is rare for a late ancient Christian author to speak about angels in a systematic way without also, like Paul, wondering about human beings and demons in the same breath, because most early Christians assumed that these three groups held something in common.[1] They were all "rational" beings, categorized as such because they all possessed a thinking faculty; with that faculty came a common psychology, a basic nature shared among all. As Paul's anxiety demonstrates, Christians often worried the boundaries between the three, expecting rational beings sometimes to present themselves in the form of another one of the classes (a demon appearing like an angel of light, or an angel taking on a human form).[2] Such transformations were disconcerting because, for many early Christians, the three classes of rational beings were not just ontologically different, variant in their natures, but also morally different. Human beings were morally ambivalent, angels good, and demons evil. Shifts in appearance, or even shifts in status from class to class, raised questions about a consequent shift in morality. Because of these implications, most early Christian discussions of angels also addressed questions about the moral nature of creation as well as the God who oversaw it.

Within these general parameters, though, early Christians held a strikingly wide array of theories about the place of angels in the Christian cosmos and their role in the progress of individual Christians. The purpose of this chapter is to impress upon the reader the fact that there was no single unified Christian conception of angels in late antiquity. The best way to do that is to take a sort of snapshot: in what follows, I compare the positions of two important Christian intellectuals, both active around the turn of the fifth century, whose careers exemplify the social contexts I highlighted in the introduction. The first section of the chapter focuses on Evagrius of Pontus (ca. 345–399 CE), who departed a career in church leadership and developed an ascetic program of cultivation in Egypt during the last fifteen years of his life. His account of Christian progress and the ultimate salvation of Christians rested on an elaborate theory of the cosmos in which human beings and indeed all rational beings had been, at one point, intellects unified with God. Having fallen away, those created beings who retained some quantum of intellectual character were to return to God. Evagrius's specific program by which Christians could accomplish that return assumed the assistance of angels, who reinforced the activity of the intellectual faculty—the *nous,* in Greek—and defended practicing Christians from the attacks of demons who wished to stop their progress. Though Christians enjoyed the help of angels, Evagrius placed heavy emphasis on the responsibility of the individual Christian to find his way, through special practices, back to a state in which his intellect was again the center of his being. This responsibility and Evagrius's progressive account of Christian salvation were intertwined with his understanding of all rational beings—angels, demons, *and* human beings—as inherently impermanent, mutable in their nature. That is to say, for Evagrius, angels, like other rational beings, were defined by instability in status, inasmuch as they too were responsible for improving in order to return to unity with God.

The second section of the chapter examines the way that Augustine of Hippo (354–430 CE), who served as the leader of a Christian community in North Africa during the last three decades of his life, imagined angels in his moral account of the universe and the place of Christians in it. In direct contrast with Evagrius's position, Augustine considered angels to be defined not by instability but by stability; they were creatures of God who always enjoyed unity with God's nature and will. Their fixity was central to the project of Augustine's later career, namely, resolving the insecurity of human social institutions with the hope of future security that he found Christian salvation to promise. As he wrote the *City of God,* the stability of angels served Augustine, helping him articulate the certainty and promise of the city in the title; angels resided in that city, secure in their citizenship, and Christians could strive toward the same citizenship when earthly institutions failed them. Angelic fixity was something that Augustine had designed and understood in conversation with non-Christian authors, but it ended up being the guarantor of his own theory of political life more generally, as angels became the exemplars of the eternal life promised in the City of God.

Comparing Evagrius and Augustine in this way demonstrates both the diversity and complexity of thought about angels in late ancient Christianity. Though their estimations of what angels were and how angels interacted with humanity were quite different, for both men, angels were deeply integrated into their conceptions of Christian progress and Christian history. It was impossible to understand the aims and work of either without a clear and detailed idea about the nature and place of angels. At the same time, we will see that the social locations in which these men developed their ideas and the ends to which those locations were oriented—Evagrius to the development of the individual Christian, Augustine to the cultural construction of a narrative of Christian superiority—inexorably shaped their ideas about angels.

Angels as Rational Beings: Evagrius of Pontus and the Cultivation of the Nous

What little we know about Evagrius's life before he moved to Egypt is based on a short biography written twenty years after his death. The *Lausiac History*, a work commissioned by an imperial official, collected the details of the lives of some fifty notable Christians who had chosen to enact several kinds of ascetic practice in Egypt. Some, like Alexandra the servant, lived by themselves, in tombs or in caves, while others, like Macarius of Egypt, John of Lycopolis, and Evagrius himself, lived in loosely organized groups of ascetics close outside the city of Alexandria, in places like Nitria and Kellia.[3] These ascetics ate special, limited diets; abstained from sexual acts and, when they could, sexual thoughts; and studied Christian writings in the hope of advancement toward salvation. The biographies in the *Lausiac History* often focused on the practices of these Christians in Egypt but some, like the biography of Evagrius, also offered a wider portrait of their subjects. In Evagrius's case, it is clear that he experienced a radical reorientation during his adult life, which led to his joining the small community of Christians he entered outside Alexandria. As I mentioned in the introduction, Evagrius had served in church offices under Basil of Caesarea and Gregory of Nazianzus; he had stayed in Constantinople as a church official even after Gregory had left, until the time that a personal crisis caused him to leave. Turning away from the capital and ultimately from the public life that had been his path, Evagrius visited an ascetic community in Palestine, then went on to spend the last part of his life in Egypt. Though in some ways this series of geographical moves represented a contraction of Evagrius's horizons, transporting him away from the center of public power and the positions of leadership for which he was being groomed, it was also an expansion of his horizons: once he arrived in Egypt, Evagrius wrote prodigiously. The texts that survive from that time are intensely detailed guides for making progress as a Christian and as a human being. Their subtle and erudite, yet humane, insights establish Evagrius as "the most accomplished theorist of the monastic life" in late antiquity, a feat he realized only in the latter part of his life.[4] In the context of the narrative provided by the *Lausiac History* and the evidence of his own writings, Evagrius departed one stage of his career when he left Constantinople, but he began a second, extremely productive stage when he joined a small community of ascetics in Egypt, first studying and then developing a more detailed version of their Christian program of cultivation, which aimed at restoring Christians to their original, intellectual natures.

Understanding the role angels played in Evagrius's advanced Christian practice requires knowledge of a theory of the universe that deeply influenced Evagrius's assumptions about the origin of the created world and the natures of the beings that inhabited it. Like the author of the *Lausiac History* and a significant number of other late ancient Christians, Evagrius made sense of the world in the terms first laid out by the third-century Christian philosopher and interpreter Origen of Alexandria. In his treatise *On First Principles*, written in the early third century, Origen had explained that all beings that now exist had once existed only as intellects, rational entities encircling and adoring the one highest God, who was himself intellect. At one moment, some of these intellects grew stale and saturated in their adoration of God and fell away from him, becoming souls. God, in his compassion, created the world as a safe place for these fallen souls to reside; he provided bodies to be their vehicles, which they could use to eventually learn of their fate and try to correct it by returning to unity with God. The only intellect that did not depart from God was Christ; he remained unified with God and thus was an emblem of the way back for those who had fallen. The others have a stature in the universe that corresponds to the extent to which they departed from God: archangels, angels, gods, human beings, demons, and the devil were each increasingly distant from their original state. The classes that existed in this hierarchy above humanity had fallen less than humanity, and thus beings like angels and archangels could also serve as useful paragons of a life closer to God.[5] Of course, those beings that had fallen even further away from God than human beings might exist to offer a negative example; demons may show us the way by tempting us, and thus educating us about what things to avoid.[6] Eventually, these rational beings would return back to the adoration of the God they had abandoned and, no longer needing bodily vehicles, be simple intellects joined with him again. In this way, Origen had provided an explanation of the diversity of beings in the world and at the same time had indicated the way these beings would in the end regain their original unity with God.

Evagrius probably first heard this explanation of the created world and its diversity of beings from his early teachers in Asia Minor, Basil of Caesarea and Gregory of Nazianzus.[7] As young adults, Basil and Gregory had compiled a selection of Origen's works, an anthology designed to be a resource for Christians struggling with questions about reading Scripture and about free will.[8] The compilation continued to be an important source of ideas and answers for them; for example, Gregory in particular sent the book to a friend, Theodore, in the year 382, more than two decades after its creation.[9] The existence of the compilation and its persistence in Gregory's library suggests his continuing trust in Origen's writings as valuable and authoritative sources of Christian teaching, something he was likely to share with his own students. Evagrius was one of those students; he later spoke reverently of Gregory, his teacher, as the one who had "planted" him in knowledge.[10] While he had left the path of church service that Basil and Gregory had laid out for him, Evagrius was nevertheless influenced by those ideas that Gregory found important, including Origen's teachings about the universe. This early influence was likely reinforced when Evagrius finally arrived in the Egyptian desert and met other Christians whose assumptions about the cosmos and the beings in it closely matched those he had learned from Gregory of Nazianzus. Evagrius's works make reference to a limited circle of teachers and traditions in Egypt, among whom were Macarius the Alexandrian and Macarius the Great (or the Egyptian).[11] It is clear that they and Evagrius revered the teachings of Antony, an ascetic of the same circle, although a member of the previous generation. The texts that survive from these men—a letter from Macarius the Egyptian and letters from Antony—prove that teachers in Evagrius's ascetic tradition had a deep familiarity with Origen's cosmology and based their systems of practice on its assumptions.[12] When he moved to Egypt Evagrius joined an ascetic tradition that embraced the same general cosmology he had learned from his early teachers, in which there had been a falling away of intellects from unity with God and in which all beings would at some point return to that unity.

As Evagrius came to articulate his program of development for individual Christians, the worldview he had learned from his many teachers pervaded his understanding of the psychological mechanics of human existence. Evagrius's surviving works reveal that he shared with Gregory, Macarius, and Antony the same basic narrative about the origin of beings in the created world, in which the "judgment of God" on those intellects that had fallen away from God by neglect granted all rational beings a body "according to the proportion" by which they had fallen.[13] Human beings had a unique type of body: a person, for Evagrius, "is the *nous* that fell away from the Unity through neglect and came down to the rank of work because of its imprudence. The indication of the rank of humanity is the human body."[14] Having such a body meant also gaining a soul, a novel constitution that Evagrius sometimes divided into two faculties. The first, the concupiscible faculty or the *epithumikos,* was desirous by nature. The second, the irascible faculty or the *thumikos,* was the seat of strong emotions like anger. The original intellect, or *nous,* remained, but now was joined with the soul as a result of having acquired a human, and consequently material, body. Thus the subjectivity of a human being was most precisely described as having three faculties—*nous, epithumikos,* and *thumikos*—an arrangement that closely reflected the philosophical conceptions of humanity held in ancient culture.

These three faculties of the human being were also the basis of the subjectivity of the other two kinds of rational beings: angels and demons, who had, like humans, fallen away from the single intellect known as God and had received bodies according to their distance from God. What distinguished all these rational beings from one another was the relative strength of each of the faculties. Additionally, all the faculties were associated with a characteristic element, whose concentration also varied from one kind of rational being to another. As Evagrius explained, "angels have a predominance of *nous* and fire, humans of *epithumikos* and earth, and demons have more *thumikos* and air."[15] These faculties and elements were not exclusive to the class they characterized: all rational beings have all three elements and all three faculties, but that which is strongest determines the identity of the rational being. An angel differed from a human being precisely in that it comprises mostly fire, and its faculty of *nous* supersedes the other faculties; a human being differs from a demon in that the demon has more air and is controlled by its *thumikos*. Humans are a mixture, located midway between angels and demons.[16] In this way, Evagrius's understanding of the psychology natural to every rational being mirrored the classifications among rational beings. The three parts of the rational being correspond to the three types of rational beings: angels, in a way, simply are *nous*; human beings are *epithumikos*, while demons are *thumikos*.

Within this scheme, making progress as a human being meant managing the three faculties in order to free the *nous* from any hindrance it might receive from the other two, restoring it as much as possible to its intended function. Those dispositions that we, as moderns, might think of as residing in our whole selves, Evagrius associated with specific faculties, each of which was susceptible to different vices, had its own virtues and thus its own labors, and could be trained to accomplish different effects.[17] Evagrius's first level of Christian progress, what he called the practical level, aimed at detachment from the processes of sense impression and evaluative judgment, things that took place in the faculties of *epithumikos* and *thumikos*. By working to control these faculties, which together Evagrius sometimes collectively referred to as the "soul," a Christian could be free from the "passions," a philosophical term that encompassed many subjective states, including anger, jealousy, gluttony. While passionlessness was, for Evagrius, the "glory and brilliance of the soul," yet another level required the mastery of the remaining faculty of the self: "The glory and brilliance of the *nous* is knowledge."[18] Once a Christian had domesticated the *epithumikos* and the *thumikos*, reaching the point of passionlessness, he had a choice to continue his development by pursuing a new exercise: contemplation, or what Evagrius called "pure prayer," that activity for which the *nous* was particularly well suited.

Working through different stages of contemplation was the task for the Christian at the second level of Christian progress, the "gnostic" level. Gnostic Christian practice was a training program for the *nous*, but it was a difficult undertaking, because the *nous*, though it did not produce sense impressions, was able to be affected by them. It was possible, for example, for the lower faculties of the soul, having once been contained by the work of the practical stage, to overcome their bounds and begin sending "thoughts" or "impressions" to the *nous* again, impressions that would all but scuttle the chances that the *nous* might be able to sustain a state of contemplation. "Temptation," Evagrius explained, "is a thought that rises through the passionate part of the soul and darkens the *nous*."[19] However, if a Christian could reach a state of passionlessness and remain unaffected by whatever thoughts or impressions were being generated in the lower faculties of the soul, the *nous* could turn to its proper action, the contemplation of intellectual knowledge. This work involved two specific topics: gnostic Christians tackled first the task of contemplating the nature of the divine beings, something that Evagrius alternately described as "contemplation of beings" or "contemplation of living beings," and after that, the task of contemplating of the Trinity.[20] Success in these pursuits meant detachment from sensible things and entry into an entirely different realm of knowing:

> The *nous* that is stripped of the passions and sees the intelligible things of the living beings truly no longer receives idols by sensible means. Rather, it is as if there is another world created by its knowledge, drawing his intelligence to itself and casting aside from him the world that is sensible.[21]

A *nous* that remains susceptible to the passions "wanders," but if and when a Christian were able to manage his responses to sense impressions and leave his *nous* to its natural work, he would be able to envision that other world, one made by the intellect; he would arrive in the company of "those who are incorporeal."[22] The practical Christian, at the first stage of progress, was training to control his lower faculties in order to produce a passionless state, but the more advanced gnostic Christian focused on the *nous* and its function in order to achieve the final goal: new knowledge, contemplation of the Trinity, and eventually, acquaintance with God.[23]

According to Evagrius, when Christians attempted to master the practical stage and move to the gnostic stage, with its exercise of the *nous*, they would receive assistance from angels. These angels acted by a certain psychological sympathy, because, as we have noted, angels were distinguished from other rational beings in this system by the predominance of *nous* in their constitution. When a gnostic Christian attempted the exercise of the *nous*, namely contemplation, an angel would be present and "with a single word he puts an end to every opposing activity within us and moves the light of the mind to an unerring activity."[24] Even the very practices like prayer and contemplation were given to human beings by these divine supporters. As Evagrius explained, it is the "grace" of an angel which "instils [*sic*] knowledge of true prayer so that the mind stands thereafter free of all turmoil, acedia, and negligence."[25] When the practitioner experienced difficulties, perhaps being dragged down again by the problems of the soul, angels acted as physicians, diagnosing the soul's maladies and offering cures to set the Christian back on the path of progress.[26] Thus, as coaches, as supporters, as trainers, angels worked to assist the Christian in practices that depended on and further developed the activity of the *nous*, a faculty to which angels were sympathetic because of their own constitution.

The protection and encouragement offered by angels to the practicing Christian only represented one half of the battle. For as much as angels attempted to influence the Christian toward pure prayer and support the light of his *nous* as he practiced contemplation, demons also attempted to influence him. Evagrius taught that demons pursued human beings, enjoining humans with a "great contest" to "keep us from knowing both the contemplation of beings and acquaintance of the Trinity," those tasks specific to the gnostic stage of progress.[27] In this quest, demons employed a number of tactics, with specialized demons approaching the gnostic Christian and intent upon "darkening the *nous*."[28] For example, Evagrius warned about the actions of the demon of fornication.

> Even when you seem to be with God, keep guard against the demon of fornication, for he is very deceitful and most jealous. He pretends to be swifter than the movement and vigilance of your mind so as to distance it from God while it is standing before him with reverence and fear.[29]

Or slander could emerge as a tactic: the gnostic Christian could expect to receive accusations without cause, because by these accusations, demons could lure the *nous* toward themselves.[30] Even the presence of emotions created an ongoing demonic hindrance, as Christians who experienced anger thereby allowed demons to extinguish the brilliance of their *nous*: unbridled anger, Evagrius explained, was an opportunity for the demons to "drag us toward worldly desires and compel the irascible part, contrary to its nature, to fight with people, so that with the mind [*nous*] darkened and fallen from knowledge it may become the traitor of the virtues."[31] Indeed, even anger that is not expressed but simply remains to fester could give control to demons, who can "strike fear in our souls and [thus] render our minds more cowardly."[32] Evagrius spoke of this moment as a time when a "cloud descends" over the *nous*, tempering its light. This short tour of the problems that demons caused shows that any lapse of the concentrated effort of a Christian to maintain detachment from sensible events and attention on the contemplation natural to the *nous* could be disastrous, for the demons "are violent against the soul as the passions multiply and they make the person incapable of sensing," and will do all they can to make sure that their target cannot "bring up his *nous*, as if it were mired in a deep pit."[33]

Of course, Evagrius did not invent the idea that demons try to hinder Christians intent on making progress. Many types of ascetic practice in Egypt were structured around battle with demonic temptations, such forces attacking the monk at the same time that their attacks and the practices of defense they inspired formed the monk.[34] Some ascetic traditions and teachers placed more emphasis on defense against demons; specifically in the case of Evagrius, he likely learned to think of Christian progress as a battle against opposing demonic forces from those teachers I mentioned before: Macarius the Egyptian, Macarius the Alexandrian, and Antony. For example, the sole letter surviving from Macarius the Egyptian details the way that a Christian who progressed in practice would be attacked, his efforts matched at every step by the efforts of the enemy. Once a Christian had mortified the body, had renounced material things, and had dedicated himself to weeping and prayer, then Macarius explained "our enemies come, dispersing wily thoughts…saying, 'you are weak in the body.'"[35] Demons notice ascetic success and respond in kind, attempting to stand in the way of Christians proficient in asceticism. Evagrius knew the traditions of Antony, revered Antony's practice, and he almost certainly also knew the text of Athanasius's *Life of Antony*; this in turn means that Evagrius knew that text's long discourse on demonic attacks and the methods Christians could use to discern demons and overpower them. The ascetic tradition that Evagrius had joined had already envisioned demons at the center of the Christian struggle, long before Evagrius offered his more specific theories of how demons and angels championed and hindered the work of the Christian in the gnostic stage of practice.

Evagrius was primed to activate these ideas about both demons and angels in his own writing and to develop them further because he had also learned about the role of such beings in Christian progress before he ever moved to Egypt. His earlier teacher Gregory of Nazianzus, in addition to teaching Evagrius about a certain cosmology, may have taught Evagrius about the role of demons.[36] Gregory composed a group of poems in which he placed the developing Christian in the midst of both enemies and friends. In an especially realistic tone, Gregory's words painted the picture of a human being struggling to protect himself from the attacks of demons even as he calls on angels to defend him. The crush of the battlefield is disorienting and the Christian who speaks in the following poem is desperate.

> Go away, go away, evil one, manslayer;
> Go away, sight of terrible sufferings, raging evil;
> Go away, Christ is within, to whom I have offered
> and given my soul. Flee, giving up as quickly as possible.
> O help, angels standing by!
> O a tyrant, and a thief is approaching.
> From them take me away, yes, beloved ones, I am being stoned.[37]

The help Gregory sought was quite specific: he struggled to protect his *nous* from the attacks of demons, and he called upon angels to assist him in keeping his identity. Gregory taunted the demon in terms that divided his identity between body and intellect: "Go away, go away, for I sense the battle. Even if you might possess my body, still in my mind [*nous*] I will not suffer." These poems demonstrate that Gregory could think of the central struggle in a Christian's life as a battle between angels and demons; Gregory may have taught such scenarios to Evagrius, with the result that Evagrius had not one but two contexts from which to draw the conclusion that such struggles defined a Christian: both the Egyptian desert and the Cappadocian church.[38]

These environments certainly laid a foundation for Evagrius's ideas about rational beings, but what made Evagrius's program different was its level of demand: Evagrius placed far greater responsibility on the individual Christian than either previous ascetics or Gregory of Nazianzus had. Christians needed to cultivate a certain cast of mind in order to get the help of angels or to fend off the attacks of demons; sustained and evenhanded management of the self affected both the Christian's susceptibility to attack by demons and the likelihood that angels might step to his defense. Where Gregory had pleaded for angels to help him, offering a solicitous prayer, Evagrius shifted the focus, warning that neglect on the part of the Christian could cause an angel to refuse to help.

> Know that the holy angels encourage us in prayer and stand present with us, at the same time rejoicing and praying on our behalf. If then we grow careless and admit contrary thoughts, we vex them greatly, because they struggle so hard on our behalf but we on our part are not willing to beseech God for ourselves; rather disdaining their service and abandoning their Lord and God, we consort with impure demons.[39]

In his attempts at prayer, the Christian had help, but he also had a role to play.[40] He could choose those with whom he "consorts," and in response angels chose to be with him only "when evil diminishes."[41] Unlike Gregory in his prayers, Evagrius did not offer a picture of a human being who needed to solicit others to save him. Instead, at every stage, the Christian was as responsible as other beings for his defense. Angels can support the gnostic advancement of the Christian, can teach the Christian the practice of pure prayer, but the presence of angels alone did not sustain him in that state. Rather, his continued advancement was a mutual creation, with angels and the individual Christian both contributing to the end result.

Such responsibility entailed the willingness to avoid "careless thoughts," but it also required the development of particular skills. Christians who wished to make progress had to become proficient at discerning the difference between angels and demons, a difficult prospect because demons could appear in the form of humans, if they so chose;[42] they could even appear to be angels, as Evagrius warned in his treatise *On Prayer*.[43] The resultant pressure on a practicing Christian must have been immense: not only did he need to curate his own emotional state but he also needed to guard against the appearance of false assistants. Those who were seemingly there to help could turn out to be dangerous, and thus the Christian needed to develop his reliance on his own judgment. Even that, though, was not a simple matter. All three types of rational beings were so close in their natures and both demons and angels so powerful that they could implant ideas into the very thoughts of Christians.[44] Evagrius considered the thoughts to be both prime ground for the temptations of demons and, at the same time, to actually be the demons in a certain way. As David Brakke has explained, "Evagrius can speak of 'the demon of vainglory,' 'the thought of vainglory,' and simply 'vainglory' interchangeably—they all refer to the same thing."[45] Christians could, with practice, resist the thoughts of demons, but not of angels. Evagrius wrote,

> It is not possible to oppose all the thoughts inspired in us by the angels, but it is possible to overthrow all the thoughts inspired by the demons. A peaceful state follows upon the former thoughts, but a troubled one follows upon the latter.[46]

Elsewhere, Evagrius offered a mechanical description of how the connection between angels and human beings works. All rational beings had "seeds of virtue" in them from their original creation, traces of the good that resonated in sympathy with the thoughts planted by angels.[47] In a world where even one's thoughts were potentially the presence of demons or angels and thus required scrutiny, self-reliance took on a meaning far graver than it had in most other contexts.

The permeability of the mind of the practicing Christian was certainly disconcerting, but in it also lay the promise of the Evagrian system of progress for Christians. Human beings, demons, and angels were not guaranteed to remain within the class of rational beings that they occupied but instead were liable, and even expected, to shift from class to class. Because the differences between the three types of rational beings were indexed by the preponderance of certain elements and parts of the soul, Christians in Evagrius's program could theorize about the possibility that a single rational being might move from one class to another: demons might become humans, humans might become angels, or demons, for that matter. This was certainly the case with respect to the world to come, for Evagrius several times mentioned the possibility that "among human beings," at some later point in time, "some will feast with angels, some will be part of the troop of demons, and some will be punished with defiled humans."[48] Some humans when they die go to spend time with demons, their appropriate counterparts, while others spend time with angels.[49] Predicting who will end up in each category can be a simple matter of noticing the prevailing character of the human being. The "angry" man was one of Evagrius's favorite examples: "in the world to come, the angry man is not reckoned among the angels.... For he does not see as a result of passion, and readily he is irritated about those who conduct themselves against him, and he falls from vision, and he casts them in danger." The angry man was just like a demon because of the predominance of *thumikos*, and for that, both demons and angry men were "estranged from the order of the angels."[50] In one letter, Evagrius was even more direct, describing a demon as being simply a departed human being who was filled with anger.[51] Additionally, at times, the three classes of rational beings could collapse into two for

Evagrius: demons and impious human beings in one class, angels and righteous human beings on the other.[52]

Yet none of these possibilities were presented as faults in the system or obstructions to its eventual end. Instead, the flexibility in nature among the rational beings, dependent upon the influence they allowed to each part of the soul, guaranteed the effect of Evagrius's Christian program. For him, angels were just one kind of fallen intellect, and like the human beings they helped, they were meant eventually to return to their original position as intellects. In fact, the entire cosmos was in flux, always in progression or regression from this ultimate goal. Christian progress was cosmic progress, with its end being nothing short of unity with God, a state held out as the natural potential of all rational beings. At once hopeful about the prospects of humanity and challenging to the individual human who attempted to live up to those prospects, Evagrius's mode of Christian practice was founded on the idea that all beings, including angels, were unstable.

Augustine's Angelic Citizens: Securing the Promise of the City of God

Augustine of Hippo and Evagrius of Pontus were contemporaries, loosely speaking; their respective careers flourished at the end of the fourth century. But while Evagrius died in 399 CE, Augustine, the younger of the two men, continued to write and to lead a community of Christians until his death in 430 CE.[53] Born in central rural North Africa in 354, Augustine went to Carthage as a young adult to study rhetoric. He taught in Carthage and in his hometown, Tagaste, until he moved to the Italian peninsula in 383, first spending time in Rome, then taking a teaching position arranged for him in Milan. It was there that Augustine met Ambrose, who was leading a Christian community in the city; soon after becoming acquainted with Ambrose, Augustine underwent a "conversion" and began identifying with Christianity, being baptized in 386.[54] Within five years of his baptism, Augustine was serving as a presbyter in Hippo Regius, a coastal town back in North Africa; within ten, he was bishop of a Christian community in that town. Over the next thirty years, Augustine wrote and preached extensively, in Hippo and in Carthage; through his letters, he influenced a large network of Christians, some of whom had actively sought his help (and others who had not). In one sense, Augustine experienced a definitive change in his life path—at one moment, he was a rising young teacher in a system of schools, and at the next, he had moved home and had changed course, aligning himself with a small Christian community. Very much like Evagrius, Augustine acted against the expectations of the powerful people who had groomed him, relinquishing his career in the teaching of rhetoric as Evagrius had relinquished his as a church official. Yet to consider Augustine's writings from the last thirty years of his life is to realize that the rhetorician and teacher had not gone away: Augustine's voice was still that of the expert, the persuasive and knowledgeable guide who explained difficult matters in inventive, convincing terms.

The character of Augustine's voice is clear in the *Enchiridion*, a small book he wrote in 420 CE or shortly thereafter. Augustine had been the leader of his community for more than two decades and during that time had proven himself a sedulous and learned writer, but many of the things he had written were long, unwieldy for any but the most devoted ancient reader to put to use. Prompted by the request of a certain Lawrence for a brief manual of Christian teachings, one that could be "carried in the hand," Augustine compressed his most important ideas into the *Enchiridion*, which comprised short, digestible paragraphs.[55] When it came to the topic of angels and their origins, Augustine explained how fixity was the very essence of angelic nature.

> As some angels abandoned God through impiety and pride and were cast out from their home in the heavens to the deepest darkness, the remaining number of angels persisted in eternal blessedness and holiness with God. For it was not from a single fallen and condemned angel that the others were descended, making them bound to an original evil by a series of chains, like human beings were, and thus were all on the hook to pay the penalty. No, instead, the one who became the devil was haughty (as well as were his impious associates), and by his haughtiness was laid low with them. The others adhered to the Lord in pious obedience, thus receiving that which they had not had previously: a certain knowledge by which they would be secure of their eternal stability and their assurance of never falling.[56]

Pithier than most of Augustine's writings, this little paragraph demonstrates that Augustine shared many of the same concerns as Evagrius—the origin and eventual moral status of angels and demons, the event of some of them "falling away," and their ultimate relationship to God. And yet, the positions taken by Augustine could not have been more different from those of Evagrius: where Evagrius's estimation of the cosmos and of the place of Christians in it was founded on the instability of angels—the fact of their movement in return to God, along with all other rational beings including human beings and demons—Augustine's estimation was founded in stability. The events that defined the moral standing of angels had happened long ago: when some fell away from God, becoming demons, others remained, and thus were granted their eternal surety of place and moral orientation. How can these two men have come to such different answers to their common questions?

It is possible to construct an answer to this question because the short paragraph from the *Enchiridion* that I reproduced above is, in reality, a summary of a matrix of ideas and interpretative positions about the morality of angels and demons, their respective relationships to God, and the meaning of those relationships that Augustine had developed over the previous three decades. The issues that informed Augustine's explanation of angelic fixity in the *Enchiridion* are treated at much greater length in a text that Augustine had worked on from 412 CE to 426 CE, *The City of God against the Pagans.*[57] While not Augustine's longest work, *City of God* is a sprawling text. In it, Augustine meandered through discussions and proofs of theories about the beginning of the world, the usefulness and flaws of philosophy, contemporary politics, and the ultimate Christian track toward salvation. The length of *City of God* is a boon to us, because it allows us to visualize the conversations and paths of reasoning in which Augustine formed and tested his ideas. The view of angels that Augustine had summarized in *Enchiridion* was the result of a long thought process which I will unpack in this section by examining Augustine's arguments about angels in the *City of God.* As Augustine sought to provide an explanation of Christian salvation and world history, the moral stability of angels was a foundation on which he could build the promise of the title, the existence of the City of God. That stability was, itself, underpinned by Augustine's positioning of himself as an authority, his understanding of the nature of Christian Scripture and his proposals for how to read it, and importantly, his desire to engage other ancient authors in conversation.

That desire shaped the outward-looking perspective of *City of God,* which was quite different from the perspective of many of Augustine's other works. Instead of interpreting Scripture directly and at length, like the *Ennarrationes in Psalmos,* or polemically refuting another Christian's ideas, like the slew of works against Pelagius, or even explaining his own

Christian journey, like the *Confessions*, *City of God* speaks from a much wider platform and encompasses a broader scope of issues. Modern biographers have noted its singularity in tone; while the *City of God* certainly engages Christian learning and Christian Scripture, it is also a demonstration of cultural mastery, flaunting its knowledge of the traditions of philosophy and literature centered outside Christian discourses. Augustine worked very hard to have *City of God* be "a monument to the literary culture of the Later Empire," presenting his opinion as one point of light in a constellation of literary voices from the past—a "whole range of literary authorities" explicitly named and quoted at length.[58] These lengthy quotations were the basis of Augustine's engagement with the experts of his world, however outdated; the scope included, yes, literary giants, but also writers of political and moral theory. Their inclusion established Augustine as an authority in command of the culture of the elite Mediterranean world. The way he drew these voices into conversation, analyzing them and revising them, also shows us his continuing rhetorical orientation.[59] The author of *City of God* trusted in a certain kind of presentation of argument: the strongest case is the one made by a well-read and persuasive man, whose ideas comprehend and explain all others in their universality. The *City of God* offers a portrait of Augustine as precisely that man.

In addition to presenting Augustine, its author, as a certain kind of man, *City of God* presented the world as a certain kind of place, uncertain and unstable, where the promise of security could only be found in an alternate narration of human history.[60] Though in many ways the beginning of the fifth century was a time of stability in civic order, particularly for those in the wealthiest families, a person who sought evidence of political uncertainty did not have to look very far. The once-unified and lauded Roman Empire was creaking audibly, with eastern and western structures of authority increasingly isolated from one another. Armies outside the empire were testing its stability, with the most famous moment being the siege and attack on the city of Rome—no longer the official center of power, but still an emotionally charged symbol of a fading institution. Among Christians, and particularly in Augustine's home of North Africa, divisions of religious doctrine and practice sustained multiple communities vehemently separate from one another, contributing to the sense that the world was already fragmented and threatened to fly apart entirely.[61] The project of *City of God* was to accomplish a different sort of history, one in which Augustine offered a single, unifying narrative in response to these things, "the challenge of his own troubled times."[62]

Over this unruly reality, Augustine superimposed the existence of two invisible cities. One was a holy city, the City of God from which the title of the work took its name, the other an earthly city. Though most of humanity remained unaware of these cities, they were a part of them; specifically, most human beings were citizens of the earthly city, and as they chased wealth, advancement, and political security, they were honoring the values of their mother city—values that were hollow, based on institutions bound to crumble. Human beings, Augustine pleaded, should awaken to the vanity of their city and strive instead to become citizens of the City of God, a place of real pleasure and happiness, where Christians, and any who follow the Christian God, would reside in the future. The prospect of that future—both the reality of the invisible City of God and the promise of joining it—was guaranteed, in Augustine's figuration, by the fact the city was already populated. Its citizens were the angels in heaven, who already had the security and freedom that other citizens would enjoy, once they arrived. Christians were to think of this earthly scene with its struggles as a temporary place, a stop before arriving at their true home, the heavenly city. Joining as its citizens should be their deepest desire, because having learned there is such a place, "we have longed to become citizens of that city, with a love inspired by its founder." For Augustine, the resolution of the manifest fragmentation of the world lay in the Christian path, namely, the commitment to a Christian community and Christian life now in order to have later the delight and security of the City of God, which the angels already enjoy.

Augustine based his proof of this city and the promise it held for Christians not on any visible reality nor his own logic, neither of which was to be trusted, but instead on "Scripture," conceptualized as a well of authoritative information comprising the words of God himself. Augustine doubted that he or any person could have secure knowledge of divine realities. Though like Evagrius, he reckoned humanity was endowed with an intellect that likened us to God, he had little faith in the faculty of the human intellect, especially as it was joined with a body. "The mind of man," Augustine lamented, "is itself weakened by long-standing faults which darken it. It is too weak to cleave to that changeless light and to enjoy it; it is too weak even to endure that light."[63] According to Augustine, Christ helped humanity overcome its lack, acting as a mediator and showing the way to divine knowledge. When Christ's example was not enough, Christians also had an artifact of the path Christ had exemplified: his words.

> This Mediator spoke in former times through the prophets and later through his own mouth, and after that through the apostles, telling man all that he decided was enough for man. He also instituted the Scriptures, those which we call canonical. These are the writings of outstanding authority in which we put our trust concerning those things which we need to know for our good, and yet are incapable of discovering by ourselves.[64]

In this way, Augustine considered Scripture as much more than a collection of texts. It was the words of the Mediator, of God, and thus the assurance of those things that cannot be known or cannot be seen by the faulty faculties of human beings. Augustine's absolute certainty about there being a City of God depends on the reliability of Scripture, which he figures as the highest form of knowledge. Scripture has "supremacy over every product of human genius," as it does not "depend on the chance impulses of the minds of men, but is manifestly due to the guiding power of God's supreme providence."[65] The specific references to the City of God in Scripture, which Augustine finds in Psalm 46, 48, and 87, are less important individually than they are as indications of the weight of Scripture, a whole and unfragmented body of knowledge given directly from God.

So, the city itself was not so difficult to find—"in testimonies too long to quote them all," Christian Scriptures consistently spoke about the blessed City of God.[66] What was far more difficult to locate, however, were the citizens who inhabited the City and exemplified the life it promised to humanity—the angels. Angels were certainly mentioned in Scripture, but their specific status as the blessed citizens of the holy city, forever with God and forever unchanged, was not easily to be found in scriptural passages. And that presented quite an issue, for the City of God was not a model, or a symbol; it was not an empty place that waited for Christians to inhabit it later. Instead, Augustine insisted, it was a real, if invisible, place, with real, if invisible, inhabitants. If the inhabited City of God was to serve as the emblem of the eternal and stable society that Christians should strive for, its constituency must be eternal and stable. As Augustine explained, "I have undertaken to treat the origin of the Holy City, and I have decided that I must first deal with the subject of the holy angels."[67] To deal with angels entailed accounting for their origins, too, and Augustine took concern with the fact that the scriptural narration of the creation of the world did not include the explicit description of the creation of angels, that is, of the citizens of the City of God. If angels were indeed those entities that had never fallen away from God and were granted, at the start of time, an eternal stability with God, then it would defy logic that they not be part of the creation account of the book of Genesis.

Yet they were not. Alternatives were few; as Augustine questioned, "Will anyone now venture to suppose that the angels were created after all those things which were enumerated in the six days? However, if anyone is silly enough for this, he is refuted by another passage in Scripture, of equal authority, where God says, 'When the stars were made, all my angels praised me with a loud voice.' That shows that angels already existed when the stars were made."[68] Augustine placed trust in Scripture to offer an account of the cosmos, and the account pointed to the creation of angels in the first three days of the Genesis account. Logic had ruled out days two and three, as the products of those days were named with enough precision to discourage interpretative introduction of angels into their meaning. The third day involved land and water, the second the firmament, and neither of these were particularly open to being read as if they included an implicit creation of angels.[69] There remained one possibility, and that was what Augustine chose: he coded angels into creation as "that light which received the name of 'day.'" Their inclusion under "light" was fitting because angels, "as they are illumined by the light through which they were created, they became light and are called 'days' by participation in the unshifting light and day, the Word of God."[70] Through inventive reading and the assumption that Scripture would certainly describe the constituents of his imagined city, Augustine located the creation of angels in the work of God's first day of creation.

This interpretative stance was not a random selection for Augustine; it had the logical force of placing angels at the very start of the world, and in addition light and illumination were tropes Augustine had already utilized in other texts to speak of the presence of good and to explain the appearance of evil. In a sermon recently discovered, for example, Augustine spoke of the diversity of beings existent in the universe, accounting for their origins with a narrative of illumination.

> Every life that can be illuminated and arrive at wisdom, as long as it is of a good will, loves the God that illumines it. Turning itself toward him, it goes forward, and being a part of him it is formed to the integrity and perfection of wisdom, and the fullness of blessing according to its type: the rational and intellectual life, whether it be

> of angels or humans. And such a life, being praiseworthy, loves its illuminator, but every such life that through an evil will deserts the one illuminating it darkens and becomes full of pride. This is the life of both the iniquitous angels and iniquitous humans. They do not want to adhere to God, but they by their own arrogance want to be taken as God.[71]

In this sermon, the mechanism of illumination allowed Augustine to theorize the origins of angels and demons, as well as both good and evil human beings, without having to posit their creation by God in these moral states. God had illumined all beings, whose individual wills then determined whether they remained with God or departed from him. Augustine's presentation was similar in the *City of God*, where he argued that neither darkness nor evil were created by God. Evil angels are not motivated by some larger principle of evil, but simply "become darkness, deprived as they are of partaking in the eternal light."[72] Even more to the point, "evil is not a positive substance," but was simply the lack of light, the lack of good.

Yet this accounting of the beginning of creation introduced an element of instability into Augustine's schematic description of the universe. Though he compensated for it in many ways, there remained a moment after angels were created when they had made a choice; those who chose to change their state by departing from God fell.[73] Thus even the account of how angels came to have an unmoving attachment to God contained a subtext in which some angels did experience change, both in their status with respect to God and in their constitution. The solution to this dilemma lay in a new way of thinking about angels and their constitution, one that drew on Augustine's textual conversations with other writers in other traditions, alongside a novel way of reading Scripture.

To unpack the details of Augustine's solution to the problem, I need to explore for a moment a subject that may seem far afield: Christian techniques of historiography and Augustine's use of them. Several centuries before Augustine's time, when Christians were still a minority within a dominant non-Christian culture, Christian authors sought to explain the place of Christianity in history, to apologize for its novelty in time and its variance from Judaism, the religious tradition within which it found meaning and from which it claimed its antiquity. One of the primary charges that Christians needed to answer was that they gave their allegiance to a human being whom they mistakenly thought divine; the perception among critics was that those who followed Jesus were confused about him and had been misled. Consequently, the first Christian attempts to engage with other traditions and to defend the worth of Christianity addressed Christians' understanding of divine beings like demons, gods, and angels. In Origen of Alexandria's treatise *Against Celsus*, for example, a major argument about the truth of Christianity turned on learned Christians who already knew how to discern the divine world. They recognized that pagan sacrifices were run by demons, and that "the holy angels of God are of a different nature and will from all the demons on the earth."[74] Origen's imaginary Christians engaged in conversations about such topics on a regular basis, not only knowing by rote the difference between angels and demons, but reasoning about it for themselves. "They speak much, too," he wrote, "both regarding the angels of God and those who are opposed to the truth, but have been deceived; and who, in consequence of being deceived, call them gods or angels of God, or good demons, or heroes who have become such by the transference into them of a good human soul."[75] Instead of being mistaken about the divine world, Christians were, in reality, the only ancient people who saw its members clearly. They were wise to the ways of demons and had not been fooled by them in the way that those in other religious traditions had been.

Origen was defending Christianity during a time when Christians were a minority within the public culture of the Roman Empire, but as Christianity grew in stature and gained political capital, apologetic writers shifted tactics, going on the offensive against non-Christian traditions and decrying *them* as mistaken about the divine world. In the course of the early fourth-century treatise on the *Divine Institutes*, for example, Lactantius wrote quite polemically about Christianity's superiority to a number of other traditions, using the texts of those traditions to point out logical inconsistencies that undermine their claims of truth. He cited an oracle of the itinerant Apollo, given in response to the query, "What is God?" Apollo answers with a long poem, which starts, "He is self-natured, untaught, without a mother, unaffectable, separate from word or name, dwelling in fire—shortly put: God. We his angels are a small portion of him."[76] In the traditional Hellenic system of thinking, there was one supreme and matchless God, unable to be in contact with humanity, and around whom there are several lesser gods, but Lactantius was eager to show that Apollo's oracle dismantled such a tradition. Apollo, *in his own words*, Lactantius seemed to wink, demonstrated that those beings surrounding the one God are not "gods," but lower beings called "angels."

And, what is more, Apollo identified himself as one of these, as he says that "*we* his angels are a little fraction of him." Yet, at other oracle sites Apollo responded to questions about what he should be called, and twice he answered in terms that did not identify him as an angel, but instead as a demon.[77] "Angel" and "demon" are terms easily interchangeable in oracular literature, both meaning in general "middle divine beings," but Lactantius cited these oracles in order to marshal evidence from them, not to explore the range of names for divine entities. In Lactantius's argument, Apollo's fluid identity was key to understanding his inferior nature: not only did Apollo attempt to deceive, but by speaking in multiple terms about his identity as a divine being, he reveals himself to be morally suspect as he does so. For Lactantius, the oracle's fluidity was the clearest possible indication of its falsity.

I give this brief history of Christian apologetics because this is the thread of conversation that Augustine entered in his discussion of angels and demons in *City of God*. Much like Lactantius used the texts of the oracles to disparage the gods who spoke in oracles, Augustine chose to present the work of other traditions directly in order to reveal the inconsistencies he saw in the ideas of non-Christian versions of the divine world. For example, Augustine cited the second-century Latin writer Apuleius often in the *City of God*, focusing his attention on Apuleius's account of the shared psychological experiences of demons and human beings. In a text discussing the mechanics of having a personal demon, Apuleius had explained that demons were "capable, in the same manner as we are, of suffering all the mitigations or incitements of souls; so as to be stimulated by anger, made to incline by pity, allured by gifts, appeased by prayers, exasperated by contumely, soothed by honors, and changed by all other things, in the same way that we are."[78] The similarity between demons and human beings, their common psychology, was a benefit to humanity whom they assisted: demons could understand human motivation and needs because those motivations and needs were also their own. Augustine, however, argued that the demons' commonality with human beings was a problem, rather than a benefit. Notice how closely Augustine's citation of Apuleius followed the examples Apuleius had used, but subtly shifted them toward the negative. Paraphrasing Apuleius, he wrote,

> The Platonist also treats of the character of the demons, and says that they are liable to the same emotional disturbances as human

> beings. They resent injury, they are mollified by flattery and by gifts, they delight in receiving honours, they enjoy all kinds of rites and ceremonies and they are annoyed at any negligence of these.[79]

Even though Augustine described demonic experiences in a way that closely mirrored the examples Apuleius had given, his examples made demons out to be little more than impish dictators: they were first liable to "disturbances," then resentful, were "mollified by" and "delight" in human attention, and could be "annoyed" if not given the proper honors in ritual. Rather than the basis of common feeling for humans among demons, as Apuleius figured them, these experiences—really, changing subjective moods—made demons out to be worse than humans. Demons, Augustine argued, do not have the same internal resources as the wisest of humans; they lack the most rational part of human subjectivity, an entity that can exert rational restraint against the impulses of the passions.[80]

On this point, Augustine pivoted, finding in the demonic experience of the passions the very fault of those angels that fell to become demons. What had been a report of the character of demons contemporary to Augustine became the foundation for an account of how demons came to be in the first place. As he described the moment in which angels fell away from God, Augustine returned to language reminiscent of the effects of experiencing passions; the angels that would become demons fell because of their "own wills and desires." They have "chosen pride in their own elevation in exchange for the true exaltation of eternity; empty cleverness in exchange for the certainty of truth; the spirit of faction instead of unity in love; and so they have become arrogant, deceitful, and envious."[81] Thus the strange and disrupted emotional lives of demons were the traces of their original departure from God; they experienced a perversion of their nature when they fell, and that perversion was visible in their emotional, fickle personalities.[82] In contrast, angels, who did not ever depart from God, were entirely without these disruptions. They were eternally in bliss, having the permanent assurance of never being separate from God or God's will. Such adherence was natural to them, and their unity with the unchanging God meant that they, too, were unchanging. In Augustine's estimation of the origin of divine beings, angelic passionlessness was the foundation for understanding the emergence of both good angels and evil angels, commonly called demons.

By extending the unchanging nature of God to include, in an oblique way, the unchanging allegiance of angels, whose natures were thus aligned with God and not liable to perversion, Augustine introduced a novel understanding of angelic nature. Precisely how novel it was in the context of late ancient Christianity is clear when we compare Augustine's claims about angels and their passionlessness to the assumptions readers tended to make about angels in Scripture. When angels appeared in Scripture, they interacted with human characters in ways that signal an emotional continuity with humanity: they reassure those who appear to be frightened (Luke 1.29–30, 2.9–10); they are moved to free those who are imprisoned (Acts 12.6–9); angels are liable to punish those who do not listen to their instructions (Ex 23.20–22); angels hear thoughts and warn the faithful against bad decisions (Matt 1.19–24). In short, angels act like the characters with whom they communicate, having their own responses and motivations. Remember that Augustine considers Scripture a well-designed vehicle by which humanity could learn what it needed to know about both "visible things which we ourselves have not seen" and "invisible things which are out of reach of our own interior perception."[83] For him, the very language of Scripture was a revelatory medium by which readers could know something of the divine world, and the reports of angels in this special text suggest they are perceptive emotional beings, changing and adjusting to the human beings whom they contact. That is to say, Scripture read in the plainest of ways indicates that angels act in ways contrary to Augustine's proposal about their passionlessness. Within the text of *City of God*, the very work in which he praised Scripture as the ideal vehicle for divine knowledge, then, Augustine also questioned the language of Scripture as a real representation of the divine world.

He introduced a new way to deal with the representations of angels in Scripture, namely, by proposing the discernment of language on the part of the reader. In a passage in which he explored the possibilities of human experiences of the passions, Augustine acknowledged the issues raised by the way angels were depicted in Scripture.

> There is another question which merits examination. Are we to suppose that our experience of such emotions, even in the practice of good works, is one of the disabilities involved in this present life? Do we then assume that the holy angels feel no anger when they punish those who are consigned to them for punishment by God's

> eternal law? That they come to the help of the wretched without feeling compassion for their wretchedness, and have no fear for those whom they love when they rescue them from danger? Certainly, we follow the conventions of human language in applying to the angels the words denoting these passions, but this is perhaps because of the analogy between their actions and those of men, not because they are subject to the infirmity of our passions.[84]

In Augustine's reasoning, angels only appear as beings subject to experiences like those of demons and humans on account of a quirk of human language, not because our language reflects the real interiority of angels. Human perception makes the mistake of linking the actions undertaken by angels with a particular psychology of experiencing passions, but this is simply a hazard of narrative. Though angels may outwardly appear to act as humans act because we see them interacting with humans and acting in stories that humans can understand, they do not share in the same mechanism of intention, or passivity, that fuels human action. Like God, angels can seem to be angry, but remain philosophically undisturbed.

The distance between scriptural representations of angels and Augustine's portrait of them as impassive beings created at the very start of the world points to the work involved in creating a comprehensive explanation of the world that also cohered with Scripture. Augustine undergirded his argument in *City of God*, and even the very existence of such a city to which Christians should strive, by revising the received understanding of angels. His engagement with other authors—especially his adoption of the discourse of experiencing passions, first to disprove Apuleius and ridicule his religious tradition, but then as a way of understanding the origin of moral difference among divine beings—centered his argument. In a way, Augustine's attempt to provide a universal explanation, to persuade others of the eternal truth of the Christian world, also allowed him access to ideas that supported that truth. His interaction with literatures and writers beyond Christianity and his desire to encompass other systems within his explanation ultimately gave him the thought models he needed to explain how angels could be invulnerable to the vagaries of the material world and of human society. His argument about the City of God, which influenced political theory in Christianity and in Western Europe in particular for centuries, was founded on a newly invented way of thinking about angels.

Common Questions, Different Answers: The Importance of Social Context

Evagrius and Augustine may have disagreed about the fundamental nature of angels and their role in helping Christians attain some level of salvation, but this chapter reveals that these two Christian authors were actually concerned about many of the same questions. They both wondered about the diversity they saw among divine beings—angels and demons in addition to God—and sought explanations for that diversity. Their explanations focused on the earliest moments in time, questioning whether and how these beings could keep their alignment with God, or whether it was necessary for at least some of them to leave God. In their handling of creation, both Evagrius and Augustine cast the universe in moral terms: angels remained closest to God and thus were either naturally good, or as naturally good as a rational being could hope to be. Both thinkers saw angels as an indication of the Christian path back to God. If we look at their positions in more detail, though, we see that their explanations of just how angels filled that role were quite different. Evagrius's understanding of Christian life involved participation in a progressive return to God by the fostering of the *nous*, aided by angels who were themselves seeking a return, while Augustine told his readers about the future that Christianity offered them in the City of God, a future exemplified by the angels who were already citizens of that city and would never leave it. Though they engaged similar questions, Evagrius and Augustine had different, even contradictory, conceptions of what angels were and what role they served.

Comparing their ideas demonstrates the variety of thought in late ancient Christianity, but it also demonstrates something more: that angels were not the focus of some separate discourse, removed from Christian ideas about more important divine actors, but were fully integrated into the programs of salvation espoused by late ancient Christians. If we were to ask what these two men thought about angels and report their ideas detached from their context, we would have a sharp, clear answer about angels, but at the same time, we would have no real idea what purpose or influence angels had in their understanding of Christianity. Both Evagrius and Augustine laid out extremely detailed visions of what it meant to live as a Christian. Significantly, it was not possible for these writers to imagine creation, human subjectivity, and the eventual end of human history and the world without specifying exactly what angels were and what they signified for humanity's prospects. Angels were inherent in the way these men were Christians and how they taught others to think of Christianity.

Correspondingly, their ideas about how angels interacted with humanity were influenced by the modes of piety they had embraced. Evagrius, who had turned away from the beginnings of a career in church office in Constantinople in order to focus on intellectual development in an ascetic sphere, imagined angels as one part of a constantly changing constellation of rational beings, making progress on their return to God. As the life of the ascetic was one of constant minute adjustments, struggle, and trial in the cultivation of the *nous*, so too was the life experienced by all rational beings, including angels. Augustine, who had aimed toward an authoritative account of the world and of world history, circumscribed the entirety of human learning and politics within his theory of the City of God, imagined angels to be eternally secure, in the happy circumstance of being assured of their stability with God. As Christians would be in the future city, so too were angels, already aligned with the will of God and working only according to that will. The ways these two men were Christian—one pursuing cultivation, the other contestation—contributed to the ways they understood angels as an integral part of a divine system.

Neither Augustine nor Evagrius invented the modes of piety they inhabited. As I said at the start of the chapter, comparing their ideas has been a way to take a sounding of Christian culture at one point in time, the era around the turn of the fifth century. In the next two chapters, we will step back to see the roles angels played in the development of the two traditions of piety of which Evagrius and Augustine were exemplars—first, in the world of those wishing to garner authority by creating theological claims founded on readings of Christian Scripture, and second, in the world of those ascetics who sought a return to God through progressive practices of body and mind.

2

Locating Christ in Scripture

ANGELS IN THE DEVELOPMENT OF THEOLOGICAL READING

IN THE MIDDLE of the second century, the Christian apologist Justin Martyr constructed a philosophical dialogue between himself and a Jewish character, Trypho. This earliest of dialogue texts strove, through questions and answers carefully controlled by its author, to explain emergent Christian doctrines and to demonstrate Christianity's superiority to the tradition Justin figured as its predecessor: Judaism, represented by Trypho. Such a project necessarily focused on the person of Christ, and Justin correspondingly made sweeping claims for his identity:

> Christ is "king" and "priest" and "god" and "lord" and "angel" and "human being" and "commander in chief" and "stone" and a "begotten child" and the first to "suffer," first rising into heaven and then "returning in glory"; he is proclaimed to "have the eternal kingdom"—which I can demonstrate from all the Scriptures.[1]

Justin's unrestrained confidence in the broad identity of Christ was supported, as he said, by his knowledge of Scripture. For Justin, "Scripture" meant the Septuagint, the Greek body of literature that many Jews of Justin's time also considered authoritative. Part of Justin's project in the *Dialogue* was to demonstrate that Christ, who had lived as a human being during the first century, was the eternal entity Jews had long identified as the Logos or Word.[2] Even more specifically, he wished to demonstrate that Christ as the Word was the actor present at the moments when the

Septuagint mentioned all the things he had listed: when the text said "king" or "stone" or "commander in chief," it was an implicit reference to Christ, giving proof that Christ was active in history long before Jesus was born. The idea that the Word, as Christ, had been continually present in history would help Justin's case for Christianity, because the divine figure at the center of the religion had existed long ago and had already appeared to Jews in history. Taunting Trypho, Justin suggested, "if you had conceived of the things said by the prophets, you would not have denied him to be God, son of the only, the unbegotten, the ineffable God."[3] In the *Dialogue*, Justin did not persuade his character Trypho to read different texts, but to read the same texts differently. He reasoned that the right kind of reading would lead to the right kind of thinking about the divine world.

Justin's style of reading depended on a particular principle, which I call "continuity of character," to convert scenes played by characters in the Septuagint into statements about the identity of Christ. He expected readers to understand that characters who fill the same function in successive stories in a larger narrative are, indeed, the same entity, regardless of the names applied to them. In one chapter of a novel, a teacher may enter a classroom and begin lecturing, and generally readers are not shocked to begin another chapter that makes reference to a "Ms. Jones" who leaves the classroom at the end of the hour; we have the cognitive resources to imagine and identify characters with more than one designation. Under this principle, Justin directed Trypho to consider the three visitors to Abraham at Mamre, a scene depicted in Genesis 18. While Justin and Trypho agreed that these visitors were angels—itself already an interpretative position—one of those angels, Justin argued, was also Christ. Of the visitors, one had vowed to return, promising that Sarah would have a son (Gen 18.10). When the narrative shifted to focus on Sarah and her struggle with Hagar three chapters later, the text specifically said that "God" spoke to Abraham to reassure him that it would be Sarah's child Isaac who would give him progeny (Gen 21.12). Because the promise uttered by the angelic visitor in Genesis 18 was explained by one identified as "God" in Genesis 21, Justin was satisfied that the angel of Genesis 18 was also the God of Genesis 21, the same entity.[4] However, in Justin's theology, this angel-God could not have been the highest God; rather it was a "rational power," alongside God, which "God begat from himself before all the creatures."[5] That is to say, the angel at Mamre who promised Sarah a son was God, but not the high God; instead, it was the Word—Justin's Christ. By relying on continuity of character, Justin aimed to establish for Trypho the meaning of the text of Genesis, ultimately by converting Trypho to accepting this rule of reading.

All reading is work, but applying such finely wrought reading tools to narrative is a manifestly complex process, one open to more vulnerabilities than Justin's triumphant tone may have led his readers to believe. In Trypho, the *Dialogue* voices the concerns that a reading audience—others with an investment in the same text being interpreted by Justin—might have with his style of reading.[6] Trypho observed that if Christ, the Word and God, was indeed present at Mamre as one of the three angels, he must have eaten what Abraham had prepared for those angels as his guests. After all, as he noted, the manna the Israelites ate in the wilderness is described in Scripture as "the angels' food," so it was clear from their shared text that angels do in fact eat. Trypho adopted the reading technique Justin had proposed in order to raise questions about Justin's interpretation—how can this angel at Mamre eat and yet be God in the form of the Word? Was not Justin substituting an angel for God?[7] To answer Trypho's challenge Justin adopted the reader of narrative's most incisive tool: distance from the historicity of the text. Saying that the "eating" at Mamre must have been symbolic, Justin assured Trypho that the incident of the visitors eating food would "trouble no one" accustomed to poetic license. Even as he sought to establish the historical presence of Christ at Abraham's table in Mamre, Justin vacated some of the more literal implications of that claim. His turn to symbolism was a turn away from the logic underlying continuity of character, executed when that logic no longer served his purpose. His interpretative shift points out a significant issue for understanding reading practices: reading techniques are not stable processes, applied once for all, but are available for the use of the reader, whose concerns and ideas ultimately shape interpretation.

The dialogue between Justin and Trypho foreshadowed several themes that occupied early Christian interpreters and were the object of intense focus in the fourth and fifth centuries. Many ancient Christian readers would follow Justin's practices, locating Christ or the Son in the appearances of divine beings as characters in the Septuagint, or those books that Christians increasingly understood as the "Old Testament." Using these appearances, or theophanies, as situations from which information about Christ could be drawn, Christians expanded the ways they could know divine entities. At the same time, they developed reading practices to square their reading of Christ in the theophanies with their emerging theologies of Christ. Such conversations about Christ's identity in late antiquity had the highest of stakes; arguments had to be persuasive, not just locally, but for a wide audience of other Christian writers and for imperial spectators.[8] Alongside one's personal persuasive power stood the appeal to a common set of texts, to "Scripture."[9] Despite its forces as an authorizing mechanism, the role of scriptural interpretation in the theological conversations of late antiquity is easily overlooked. The history of late ancient Christian theology is often told as a succession of increasingly precise propositions about the God, especially Christ, offered at imperial councils and contested in turn, with certain propositions drawing public and imperial support and others losing it. That same history, though, could also be told as a succession of carefully winnowed and defended set of reading practices, negotiated and used to authorize an expanding body of texts alongside an ever more precisely determined knowledge of God.[10]

In this chapter, I explore how angels, variously imagined and deployed, sustained the changing constellation of reading practices that were adopted in late antiquity, especially among those Christians seeking to establish reliable knowledge of Christ's identity from Scripture. In the first section, I discuss how Athanasius of Alexandria learned to adopt extremely detailed scriptural interpretation to support his theological positions about Christ and to delegitimize other positions. His first extended scriptural argument against Arius, developed in the early 340s CE, was a reading of Hebrews 1.4, in which Christ, the Son, is said to have "become superior to the angels." In his discussion of the Son and angels, Athanasius offered precise arguments about individual words to support his vision of Christ's uniqueness among other divine beings, even as he employed other, more well-established modes of reading in order to locate Christ historically in stories from the Old Testament where angels appeared. In the second section, an extended conversation among three theologians from Asia Minor—Eunomius of Cyzicus, Basil of Caesarea, and Gregory of Nyssa—allows us to see how increasingly precise theories of language and knowledge inflected Christian ideas about Christ and angels in the 360s to 380s CE. While these readers still used the lens of historical location, finding Christ in Septuagint appearances of angels, the specific meaning of words applied to Christ, including "angel," came under even greater scrutiny. The later parts of their conversation were inflected by the shifting political and social situation of Eunomius on the one hand and Basil and Gregory on the other. Gregory, in particular, activated a novel discourse to criticize Eunomius, branding his reading of the Son and angels as a "heresy" and as a "Jewish" error. In the third section, I read Augustine's discussion of

Christ and angels from *On the Trinity*, a work completed in 420 CE, in the context of the methods advocated by these earlier writers. The reading practices they share—both the impulse to locate Christ in history and the impulse to more clearly define words that might yield knowledge of his nature—overlapped in precise, difficult ways for Augustine. Augustine's attention to words written about Christ, especially his having been "sent" from the Father, precipitated novel reading strategies that redefined angels even as they redefined Christ. As we will see, angels were central to the shift in reading practices among late ancient Christians. Ideas about them were also central to maintaining the coherence of the evolving conception of Scripture as a body of authoritative texts and the ever more precise discourse about knowledge of the divine that developed during late antiquity.

Discovering the Meaning of Words

In the first chapter of this book, I presented Augustine of Hippo as an example of a Christian living in the mode of "contestation," but Athanasius of Alexandria is an equally good example. As a young assistant to Alexander, leader of a community of Christians at Alexandria, Athanasius attended the first imperial council at Nicaea and experienced both the power of imperial attention and the promise of Christian unity. When he became bishop of the same community in 328, Athanasius was inspired by the ideal of unity he had seen dramatized at Nicaea, and he attempted with varying degrees of success to consolidate several different communities under his hierarchical model of episcopal Christianity.[11] During his career, however, Athanasius also experienced setbacks and losses; he was exiled from Alexandria five times, his seat as bishop occupied by others, and he continually struggled with other communities of Christians, both within Alexandria and beyond. Through these ups and downs, the constant theme of his life was a deep trust in the power of conviction. In writing and in speech, Athanasius used the tools of rhetoric, polemic, and persuasion to support and at times to regain his position as the leader of an important Christian community.

The changes in the way that Christians discussed theological matters during Athanasius's career inflected his way of reading Scripture. In the early part of his career, Scripture served Athanasius as a persuasive fount of examples and exhortatory language. For example, while serving as an assistant to Alexander and during the early years of his own time as bishop, Athanasius often wrote documents in which scriptural citations were exemplary in a general way.[12] In the letter known as "One Body," Athanasius brought scriptural phrases to bear as illustrations of points he meant, finishing his own thoughts or sentences with words quoted from Scripture.[13] In a way, his writings from the 320s and 330s ventriloquized his thoughts through Scripture, taking on the voice of Paul or the voice of the gospels to better say what his own exposition might also have expressed. In his first major polemical work, the paired texts of *Contra Gentes* and *On the Incarnation of the Word*, Scripture was deployed in this vein: the logical and philosophical arguments Athanasius presented were the framework of the treatise, while scriptural citations entered to expand and anchor the prose.[14] In his festal letter from 339, Athanasius also cited Scripture in this hortatory way, offering, for example, Paul's words as a restatement of his own exposition. Athanasius's early works are surprisingly light on interpretative work, depending as they do instead on more traditional polemic fare: logical deconstruction and positive philosophical construction of one's case. These texts are instrumental for understanding Athanasius's developing theology, especially with respect to his theory of the Incarnate Word, but none depends so completely on proof from texts that its case would be empty without reference to Scripture.[15]

Athanasius developed a remarkably different way of utilizing Scripture in persuasive argument while he was exiled from Alexandria between the years of 339 to 346 CE. His removal from the position of bishop resulted from the judgment of an imperially sponsored council in Antioch; the emperor Constantius and gathered Christian leaders deposed Athanasius, selected a different man to serve in Alexandria, and sent that man to take over the position.[16] Athanasius fled, eventually ending up in Rome, where he spent time with Marcellus of Ancyra, himself also in exile—a collaboration that would transform Athanasius's style of argumentation. Both men were bishops without chairs, looking for an audience they had lost, and skilled interpretation of authoritative texts was their tactic for preserving what little of their influence remained and for regaining their power.[17] Scholars have long recognized that Athanasius developed a far finer sense of the type of interpretative arguments needed to engage with his opponents during his time in Rome.[18] Much of his new strategy of reading focused on the specific historical and ontological implications of the individual words of Scripture, particularly for the nature of Christ.

Evidence of Athanasius's shift in strategy survives in his *Orations against the Arians*, which evince his new intensive reading style and his novel rhetorical approach to the theological conflicts that had occupied him for close to two decades. The *First Oration* in particular is well known for the way Athanasius painted his opponents, borrowing a technique from early Christian heresiologists: he posited a genealogy of heretics threatening the true Christian community, with Arius, the Alexandrian presbyter condemned at Nicaea, as the father of the entire family. Grouping a large collection of different theological positions under one inimical category—"Arians"—and presenting himself as the champion charging against it, Athanasius did much to create the reputation he still enjoys today, as a defender of an orthodoxy established at the Council of Nicaea. Though the genealogical argument of the *Oration* has influenced subsequent accounts of early Christian theological diversity, it was not even Athanasius's primary complaint. Arius and other opponents of Athanasius were one heretical family, but what defined them as heretics was the way they read Scripture. Unlike Athanasius's earlier writings, the *First Oration* was dense with arguments about the meaning of individual words of Scripture, especially those cited by the "Arians" in support of their theological position.

Evidence in the *First Oration* suggests that Athanasius found his opponents' interpretation of Hebrews 1.4 to be the reading most in need of correction. Within the larger text of the *Oration*, there is a pair of passages, focused on this verse, in which the Son is said to have "become superior to angels" (κρείττων γενόμενος τῶν ἀγγέλων). Those passages are linked by a narrative trope, one even more specific than Athanasius's genealogical system of heretics: that Arian interpreters of this passage were distributors of poison, like the devil. Athanasius warned that the positions voiced by Arius in his theological hymn, the *Thalia*, were heretical and that readers should not think otherwise even though Arius supported them with words from Scripture. After all, other "heretics"—for Athanasius, Jews and Manicheans—also read the Scriptures, but this did not make their interpretations legitimate. His case in the early part of the *First Oration* culminated in a distinctive set of themes.

> If they think they can turn blasphemies into praise by the inclusion of certain words of the holy Scriptures in the *Thalia*, then they might as well deny Christ right alongside the present-day Jews, watching them read the law and the prophets. Or, they could deny the law and the prophets with the Manichees, since they read some part of the gospels. If they are ignorant, and thus are distressed and blurt out such things, then they will learn from Scripture that even the

> devil, the conceiver of heresies, through the same bad odor of evil has used words of Scripture, holding them as a cover for dispersing his own poison, so as to fool the guileless.[19]

In Athanasius's estimation, the followers of Arius were just like the devil, who chose to "disperse his poison" (τὸν ἴδιον ἰὸν ἐπισπείρας) and "fool the guileless" (ἀπατήσῃ τοὺς ἀκεραίους) by incorporating quotations of Scripture into theological positions. Additionally, Arians were like those other misguided readers of Scripture, Jews and Manichees. These tropes are significant because they link this early part of the *Oration* to passages that come much later, toward the end of the work. For only in the last part of the *Oration* did Athanasius return to this particular tableau of images. In *Oration* 1.53, Athanasius listed the most problematic scriptural passages his opponents use—Proverbs 8.22, Hebrews 1.4, Hebrews 7.22, Acts 2.32. He argued there that heretics were "deceived about the sense" of these passages, thinking the texts represent Christ as a creature, a work of the eternal God rather than something continuous with that God. To describe the effect of their misguided readings, Athanasius adopted the same set of themes he had compiled earlier in the *Oration*: instead of the devil, it is now these Christians who "deceive the brainless [ἀπατῶσι τοὺς ἀνοήτους], putting forth words and dispersing their own poison of heresy [τὸν ἴδιον τῆς αἱρέσεως ἐπισπείροντες] against the true interpretation"; after this, Athanasius quickly repeated his complaint about Jewish and Manichaean readers.[20] Under this rubric of poisoning the foolish, Athanasius spent the remainder of the *Oration* handling the implications of the specific words of Hebrews 1.4. These themes and the time that Athanasius spent interpreting the passage from Hebrews 1 reveal a literary relationship between *Oration* 1.1–1.8 and 1.53–1.64. They are logically paired, make sense together without the intervening arguments in the middle of the *Oration*, and thus may have been the building blocks of an original, shorter composition.[21] All this is to say that Athanasius's case against his opponents seems to have originated with his attempt to correct their readings of a passage in which Christ was compared to angels.

It was perhaps natural for Athanasius to have started his case against Arius there because Hebrews 1 was, itself, an exercise in using Scripture as proof of the identity of Christ. The author of Hebrews, who chose to open his discourse with the stark thesis that the Son had replaced the prophets as God's vehicle of speech, founded his claim upon an extensive investigation of passages from the Septuagint. By placing texts he read as references to this Son next to texts that spoke of angels, the author used what was said or not said about angels as the standard against which the Son was to be judged. The majority of the passages favored by the author of Hebrews were songs of evocative praise from Psalms, mostly written in the first-person voice of God which Christians had been reading as applying to Christ. The author of Hebrews queries the reader: "To which of the angels did God ever say, 'you are my son'?" (1.5). About the Son, God had said that angels would worship him, but to angels, God had said they would be servants (1.6–7). "To which of the angels had God ever said, 'sit at my right hand, until I place your enemies as a footstool for your feet'?" (1.13). The litany of these passages demonstrated in the highest form of divine speech, God's own words available in the Septuagint, that those things said about the Son had outstripped those things said about angels.[22] And yet, the juxtaposition of these two registers of speech naturally solicited direct comparison, which the author of Hebrews readily provided: the Son had "become superior to the angels" (1.4). On the foundation of a record of divine speech, the author of Hebrews compares the Son to models of divine authority of the past and finds the Son surpasses them.

The fact that this comparison could yield information about the nature of the Son meant that establishing a proper reading of it was crucial. Athanasius's discussion of Hebrews 1 in the *First Oration* quickly narrowed focus to center on the importance of single words in the passage to establish the identity of the Son. This was, in part, a response to his opponents' use of particular words. Arius's *Thalia* had treated Christ and words about him primarily as indices of the way God should be understood, even while it suggested that no amount of comparison could reveal the nature of God.[23] Similarly, the opponents Athanasius attacked used Hebrews 1.4 to insist that the Son had been created like angels and other creatures, because the participle γενόμενος has been applied to him. This Athanasius rejected out of hand:

> Things written this way do not indicate, O Arians, that the Son is originate [γενητός], but rather that he is other than things originate, proper[24] to the father, existing in his bosom. And even the fact that [the passage] uses "became" [γενόμενος] does not mean that the Son is originate [γενητός], as you think.[25]

Athanasius relied on a grammarian's precision, insisting that the linguistic similarity between "became," actually here in Greek a participle, and "originate," an adjective, was a false indication about the Son. To support his claim, Athanasius engaged in a word study, seeking out other ways the variations of the word had been used in biblical texts. He cited examples of Scripture where human sons are spoken of as "originate" (γενητός) (Job's sons in Job 1.2, Isaac in Gen 21.5), then compared them to John 1.3, where it is the Son through whom "all things came into being" (πάντα δι' αὐτοῦ ἐγένετο). Athanasius argued that the passage from John marked the Son as a creator, while ordinary human beings were among things created. The result was direct: "Since the Son is other than things originate," Athanasius argued, "and is himself the only proper offspring of the Father's substance, this notion about the word 'became' is worthless for the Arians."[26] Instead, for Athanasius, the true meaning of the word, and thus the passage, revealed the Son's role adopted in time; "becoming superior to the angels" refers to the Son's recent office as mediator to humanity at the moment of the incarnation.[27]

Next, Athanasius investigated the other relevant words in the phrase from Hebrews 1, an exercise that brought him to consider the implications of comparison it made between the Son and angels. "Superior" (κρείττων) drew his attention, as it seemed to suggest that the Son and angels might be, or might have been, in the same class. Becoming "superior" implied at one point having been equal; the phrase as a whole implied that the Son was better than but in essence still comparable to angels. Athanasius rejected both of these options, denouncing the very idea of comparison. "There is no sameness shared between the angels and the Son. The word 'superior' is not used for comparison (συγκριτικῶς), but for differentiation (διακριτικῶς), because of the difference between his nature and theirs."[28] In Athanasius's reasoning, if the author of Hebrews had said that the Son was more than the angels "by so much," or that he "was so much greater than they," then it would have been proper to assume that the Son and angels share the same nature and can be compared. However, since the author said the Son is "superior" and that the Son differs from the angels "as a son differs from servants," it is clear that the Son has a different nature from that of the angels.[29] In this small beginning to his wider case against Arius, Athanasius read Hebrews 1 with a very fine lens, aiming to invalidate the readings that suggested the Son was a creature. Thus, by attention to the definition—and redefinition—of words fragmented from their larger context in Hebrews, Athanasius ruled out comparison between the Son and angels.[30] That this took place in a discussion of a text that, itself, had directly compared the Son to angels only throws Athanasius's interpretative ingenuity into greater relief. In the *First Oration*, we see how Athanasius learned to read Scripture to counter the arguments of those he saw as his opponents. The first exercise of that new reading style centered on deconstructing an implied relationship between the Son and angels.

This fine-grained attention to words in Scripture—their usage, their meaning, the information they might convey about Christ, if read correctly—was not Athanasius's dominant mode of reading, but he continued to explore its potential for denouncing the interpretative practices of those he saw as his opponents. In the *Second Oration against the Arians*, written slightly later, Athanasius turned back to comparison—not a comparison about Christ and angels directly, but a comparison of the frequency and semiotic range of words used about them in Scripture. Developing a theory of the correspondence of language to meaning, Athanasius used the multiplicity of certain words of Scripture to disconnect those words from any concrete correspondence to an ontological reality. According to Athanasius, words like "created" and "servant" appeared in Scripture in so many different contexts that they could not possibly have reliable referents in the real world.[31] As a result he argued that they should not be taken as indications of anything essential about the characters and entities to which they were applied. However, some words that appear in Scripture were reserved for Christ alone: "Son," "Word," and "Wisdom" are Athanasius's examples. Working against the reality that these words, too, appeared in many contexts and with many referents in Scripture, Athanasius anchored his claim about them in cosmological numbers: just as there are many angels, yet one Christ, there are many variable words, but only a few whose use in certain situations belies a unique status. Despite their frequent occurrence, the singularity of words like "Word" and "Wisdom" were for Athanasius tethered to the literal singularity of Christ, and thus they are reliable indicators of the permanent essence of Christ.[32] Here, Athanasius was also pioneering the possibilities of reading intently, searching out meaning in grammatical structure and the linguistic details of a text, rather than solely the meanings of the words. Words about angels were the comparative context, the emblem of multiplicity, against which Athanasius placed certain words about the Son, privileging those words as unique.

Though Athanasius developed new attention to the meaning of language in his *Orations*, he did not abandon other methods of interpretation. Instead, he balanced his grammatical attention to words with the other prevailing interpretative rubric of his cultural context: finding Christ in Old Testament passages that mentioned an angel and reading Christ's presence in events recorded in Scripture as an indication of his presence in historical time. This is the sort of reading that we saw Justin engage in even when it created conflicts with the theological position he was advocating; Athanasius also preserved historical interpretation, even when it brought unruly associations to the fore. In the *Third Oration,* for example, written four or five years after the first, Athanasius tackled those passages in the Old Testament that he saw as representing Christ when they spoke of an "angel" or an "angel of the Lord." Reading Genesis 38, in which Jacob prays for an angel to protect his grandsons, Athanasius saw a plea to Christ. At the same time, though, his novel understanding of the power of individual words changed how he presented the reading: he was careful to argue that the "angel" so called revealed nothing about the nature of Christ.[33] Athanasius's use of the record of Scripture as a record of history did not override his distrust of any text that associated Christ with an angel, even if by name only. Indeed, Athanasius appealed to the reader to check his experience: the one who says he has seen the Son knows that he has not seen an angel or a creature, but God.[34] In this *Oration,* therefore, we see Athanasius working to negotiate two reading systems. In one, Christ is located under the names of other characters in the Old Testament, and by this, is proved to have been ancient, or eternal, or at least known before the first century. In the other, individual words taken in or out of narrative context carry information about the nature of Christ. The passages from the Old Testament where readers had traditionally located Christ stood at the point of conflict between these two systems, because the first involved reading a character identified as an "angel" or an "angel of God" as Christ—a situation that under the second would imply that "angel" relayed important information about his nature. Athanasius recognized the problem, but his solution was ad hoc, an appeal to experience. As we will see, however, those passages in the Old Testament that mentioned angels, but which Christians identified with Christ, continued to be a source of contention among Christian readers and inspired ever more complex practices of reading.

Exploring the Limits of Reading

Athanasius's engagement with Scripture in the *Orations against the Arians* demonstrates that reading practices were developing among those who sought scriptural authority for evolving theological positions. Moving beyond judging particular interpretations as acceptable or unacceptable, Christians had begun to interrogate the processes that led to particular interpretations, developing theories of both the capacities of the reader and the mechanics of the act of reading. How such theories evolved and how they were negotiated are perhaps best seen in a series of works produced between the 360s and 380s CE which record an extended conversation among three Christian intellectuals from Asia Minor. Eunomius of Cyzicus argued for his understanding of the Son and Father and the relationship between them in an apologetic work, a version of which was likely presented at an ecclesiastical council in Constantinople in 360.[35] As we shall see, Eunomius's *Apology* detailed a conservative approach to reading: he trusted the ability of words to represent specific, unique meanings, and he drew conclusions about Christ based on words that could be said of him. Within a few years of Eunomius's work, Basil of Caesarea had written a treatise *Against Eunomius*, similarly focused on how to extract knowledge of the Son and Father from Scripture, using a far less conservative reading style.[36] Basil distrusted words to represent the real nature of things; words were, instead, the building blocks from which readers could form "concepts" about a subject—not true knowledge, but as close as a reader could get to true knowledge. Basil's treatise prompted Eunomius to write an *Apology for the Apology* some time near 380 CE. Basil of Caesarea had died by that time, but his brother Gregory of Nyssa took up the thread of conversation, writing a defense of Basil's position during the years 380 to 383 in his own work *Against Eunomius*, responding to Eunomius's second *Apology* and articulating the type of divine simplicity that would come to be a significant part of later Christian theology.[37] Though there is a much larger network of social and political contacts within which their conversation took place, I want to focus here on how the reading assumptions Eunomius, Basil, and Gregory made in turn can highlight for us the intricacies of reading Christ in those scriptural passages that mentioned angels.

Let us start with Eunomius of Cyzicus. Though his theological position and his intellectual community were deemed heretical by later Christians, we must remember that Eunomius was a prodigious writer, influential in Christian intellectual culture both during and after his lifetime.[38] His theory of reading espoused a strict correspondence between language and the objects of knowledge represented in language. With respect to Scripture, the particular names of divine beings were meaningful; names—that is to say, words—were conceptually linked to the entities they marked. As he held, "We do not think that substance [οὐσίαν] is one thing, while that which indicates it is another. But, the entity [ὑπόστασιν] itself is that which indicates the name [τοὔνομα], for the designation [προσηγορίας] speaks truthfully about the substance [οὐσίᾳ]."[39] Though Eunomius did not distinguish what some of his contemporaries would eventually deem different categories—names being different from designations, substance being different from entity—his main point was clear. Words relate reliably to what they represent; the nature of a thing determines its name, and to discover the meaning of a name or designation was to uncover the named thing's nature. In accordance with this theory of language, Eunomius argued that Christ was different and inferior to God the Father in two ways. First, Eunomius argued, if the God the Father was described in Scripture as "unbegotten" (ἀγέννητον), then the Father was, by nature, "unbegotten," a unique state that excluded others, including Christ. Second, by the fact of Christ being called a "Son" in Scripture, a name that in its very meaning indicated a hierarchical relationship to a Father, astute readers of Scripture knew that the Son was inferior to the Father. As a reader who trusted language to reveal divine realities, Eunomius was confident that the designations granted to God the Father and God the Son in Scripture reveal the substance of both entities as well as the relationship between the two.

Indeed, Eunomius so trusted the language of Scripture that his theory of reading included a second way to discover knowledge of divine beings like Christ in Scripture. For him, scriptural texts were such an accurate depiction of reality that what they implied was as reliable as what they explicitly said. Even more precise, any verb of action that appeared in Scripture designated an object of that action, whether the actual proper name of the object appeared in the text or not. Therefore, because Psalm 2 presented God speaking to a Son and God saying "today I have begotten you" (ἐγὼ σήμερον γεγέννηκά σε), Eunomius reasoned that the Son of this God must be a begotten thing. This was still, in his view, proof from Scripture: "We say that the Son is a begotten thing [γέννημα] of the Father, according to the teaching of the Scriptures."[40] Here, Eunomius relied on the fidelity of the verb γεγέννηκά to the reality of its action, reasoning that the thing so produced can be truthfully called something "begotten," even though γέννημα does not itself appear in this passage. Similarly, Eunomius extrapolated Peter's statement in Acts that "God has made [ἐποίησε] him both Lord and Christ" to indicate that the Son is a made thing (ποίημα)—again, a word itself not available in this passage, but implied as the object of the verb that is, in fact, in the passage. For Eunomius, knowledge about the Son was available through careful investigation of the names given him; some of those were directly available in Scripture, but others no less informative were made available through the process of reading him as the object of the Father's actions in Scripture.

Like Eunomius, Basil of Caesarea generally trusted scriptural language to guide readers toward knowledge of the divine in some way, but his lengthy response to Eunomius's *Apology* sought alternate methods for readers to extract knowledge from scriptural designations. Basil acknowledged that Christian readers could find many titles in Scripture for the Son; these titles, however, were not indications of his essence, but rather of something less specific. Basil explained:

> As our Lord Jesus Christ intimates in Scripture about himself both the philanthropy of divinity and the grace which comes from [divine] economy, he indicates these things by some properties [ἰδιώμασί τισι] that may be contemplated with respect to him: he calls himself "door" and "way" and "bread" and "vine" and "shepherd" and "light"... but all these names do not mean different things about his [nature or substance].... He is one in substrate, a single and simple, not composite, substance; he speaks differently about himself in different places, harmonizing the designations that lead to certain concepts with each part. According to the variance of works and the scheme of his different activities, he provides names for himself.[41]

If scriptural designations conveyed knowledge of divine substance, the sheer welter of names that Christians had found in scriptural passages about the Son—and even the tradition of reading the Son in those passages—would make no sense. The Son cannot literally be the door, as well as the way, and bread, and a vine; if Eunomius's method of reading were followed, it would lead a reader to think that all these designations represented something of the real nature of Christ. Instead, Basil argued, the equation Eunomius would have between name and nature could be loosened to allow that names inform, in a general way. A scriptural name would lead a reader to form an idea about a property, that is, a quality proper to a divine entity, which could allow some knowledge of God, though not of his nature.[42] The properties one understands by reading such names cohere through human thought into a single "concept" of the Son—a product of human intelligence and nowhere close to the knowledge of the divine substance that Eunomius claims, but useful as a handle for managing one's relationship to the divine.[43] Basil's method of interpretation was at once conservative, in that it reserved knowledge of God beyond the ability of humanity, and liberal, in that it placed great emphasis on the work of the reader to form such "concepts" about divine beings. It was also productive, in that it allowed for an almost infinite number of data from Scripture to reveal something about Christ without making those data equivalent to Christ's nature.

As potentially expansive as this reading technique may have been, Basil also recognized certain limits to reading. Worried that readers driven by a desire for knowledge of the divine world might seek to artificially enlarge the data given, he was concerned by titles applied to the Son which were derived from, but not extant in, Scripture. This was a direct response to Eunomius's reliance on the relations of subject and object to investigate the Son. Seeing ποίημα implied in the verb ἐποίησε, for example, constituted for Basil a dangerous move toward innovation. Therefore he warned, "do not let Eunomius"—or any reader, for that matter—"say that he has the authority in discourses about such great matters to conceptualize certain variations and transformations of names. For if we indeed are called to account for 'careless' words on the day of judgment (Matt 12.36), then how could the hewing of new things regarding these great matters be set aside from us without account?"[44] The point was this: only words that were predicated of the Son in Scripture were, to Basil, legitimate for deriving knowledge of any sort about Christ—whether conceptual or directly ontological. If Scripture can call the Son "glory" and "axe," "cornerstone" and "stumbling block," but scrupulously avoids calling him "creature," then "creature" must be discarded as a name that even applies to the Son in the formation of concepts, let alone one that conveys direct information about his nature.[45]

The case Basil argued against such reading methods culminated in his reading of a text that Christians had long identified as speaking of Christ, namely Isaiah 9.5: "a child has been begotten for us, a son has been given to us, the beginning rests on his shoulder, and his name is called 'angel of great counsel'" (LXX).[46] Following Eunomius's method of interpretation, the fact that Scripture says that this child "has been begotten" (ἐγεννήθη) necessitated that the Son could be identified as a begotten thing (γέννημα). But Basil found it significant that the title given to this Son is not γέννημα, but something else:

> That the Father has begotten, we have learned everywhere; that the Son is a begotten thing, we have never heard up until today. "For

> unto us a child is begotten, and unto us a Son is given, and his name was called" not "begotten thing" [γέννημα] but "angel of great counsel." If "begotten thing" did signify substance, we would not have received another name from the Holy Spirit, different than one which would clearly provide his substance.[47]

If Scripture had intended Christ to be understood as something begotten (γέννημα), it would have called him just that, instead of naming him to be the "angel of great counsel." For Basil, though, "angel of great counsel" did not inform readers of the Son's nature any more than the invented "γέννημα" would. In fact, "angel" in this passage was proof that the divine words of Scripture themselves favored Basil's reading practice, invalidating the entire process of attempting to find in names the indication of some deeper reality. In Basil's view, "angel of great counsel" may indicate something about one of the Son's properties, as other names and designations from Scripture do, but not his substance. It was entirely empty of direct meaning about Christ.

Yet it was not empty of meaning regarding the location of the Son in historical time. Just as Athanasius had preserved historical reading methods alongside newer grammatically focused ones, Basil, too, kept earlier methods in use. Shortly after his argument against the validity of deriving natures from names, Basil entertained the "angel of great counsel" as a title of the Son in order to respond to another plank in Eunomius's platform: the claim that the Son was recently created from nothing.[48] By assuming continuity of character in Scripture, as had Justin and Athanasius before him, Basil demonstrated the existence of a single divine actor who was called both "angel" and "God." In Genesis 31, for example, Jacob was approached by "the angel of God," who announced to him, "I am the God of Bethel." Later, in Exodus 3, "the angel of the Lord" appeared to Moses in the burning bush, then announced "I am the God of your father, the God of Abraham, the God of Isaac, and the God of Jacob." Finally, the entity who spoke with Moses announced, "I am who I am." Unless one is willing to read "God," "the Lord," and "the angel of the Lord" as different characters—and narrative logic strongly counters this desire—then one must assume that all these names refer to a single being. This was what Basil asked his readers to assume, and with that established, he asked "Who is he who is both angel and God? Is it not the one whose name, we learned, is called 'angel of great counsel'?" By taking all these names as titles of one being, Basil established something Eunomius had rejected:

the Son, who existed from the same time as "the Existent," the God whose title he shares, was represented in these stories as both "God" and "angel" and interacted with figures of the past. Even with an awareness of changes in narrative time—seeing, for example, that the angel of great counsel in Isaiah may have been a title given to the entity born in the incarnate Son—Basil maintained that "angel" has indicated a property of the Son since before time. As he explained, "Even if he became the angel of great counsel recently, he did not reject earlier the designation of 'angel.'"[49] If the Son had borne the titles of God and angel for all existence, his co-eternity with the Father could not be questioned. Equating the Son with an angel mentioned in a passage from the Old Testament allowed Basil to prove this particular christological claim, using a technique that had allowed others before him, like Justin and Athanasius, to establish the eternity of Christ.

While it may have been a viable response to Eunomius's idea of a recently begotten Son, one less than the Father, Basil's association of the Son with the two titles of "God" and "angel" remained open to other kinds of reading. Near the year 380 CE, Eunomius composed a response to Basil's accusations against him. In what survives of this *Apology for the Apology*, Eunomius confirmed Basil's reading of Christ in the characters represented in passages like Genesis 31 and Exodus 3.[50] Then, he applied his own theory of language to these passages. The historical location of the Son in such passages formed the basis for a more precise claim about the Son's status, a claim based on the very words of the two passages. Eunomius contended again that the Son occupies a mediate position between the angels and God the Father. Proof again lay in words: the Son is the one

> Who, by being named "angel," on the one hand, clearly showed the one [i.e., God] through whom he announces his words and [clearly showed] who is the Existent; and, on the other hand, by being addressed as "God," demonstrated his own authority over all things. For he [the Son] is the god of all things coming about through him, angel of the God above all things.[51]

Because Eunomius correlated names and substances, passages like those used by Basil are rich with information: the Son's title of "angel" reveals information about his relationship to God, while his title of "God" reveals information about his relationship to angels. In this way, even Basil's admission of the historical placement of Christ proved to be meaningful when combined with the assumptions about the reliability of language that Basil had rejected. Unfortunately, no response survived from Basil to this second statement of Eunomius's case for his particular reading practices; Basil died in 379 CE without writing another installment in his ongoing argument with Eunomius.

A few years after Basil's death, however, his brother Gregory of Nyssa wrote a rebuttal of Eunomius's *Apology for the Apology* in three books composed between 380 and 383 CE, in which he continued to explore the ramifications of Basil's and Eunomius's reading practices. Gregory's polemic put the practice of historical reading in the spotlight, relying heavily on the assumption of continuity of character. For example, the paired names of "God" and "angel," which led Eunomius to see the Son in a middle position, to Gregory was evidence that even characters in the Old Testament embraced his, and not Eunomius's, theology of the Son. He developed the following counterargument to Eunomius based on a reading of Exodus 22 and 23.

> Moses supplicated the Lord not to place an angel in charge of leading the nation, but for he himself to guide its journey. Thus we have from God himself: "Walk, go down and lead this people into the place which I tell you. And behold, my angel will travel before you on the day when I oversee" (Ex 32.34). And again, a little later on, "I will send my angel to your presence" (Ex 33.2, slightly adapted). Next, a little after the following, comes the supplication from the servant toward God, "If I have found favor in your eyes, send my Lord with us" (Ex 34.9). And again, "unless he travels with us, do not send me up" (Ex 33.15). Then, the answer of God toward Moses: "that which you have said I will do. You have found favor in my eyes and I know you past all [others]" (Ex 33.17). Thus, if Moses asks that not the angel, but the one discoursing with him, be the attendant and leader of the army, clearly [Scripture] demonstrated through this that the one who made himself known by the name of "Existent," the only-begotten, is God.[52]

And, we should understand, not simply an angel. An observant reader may come to the conclusion that the extended conversation taking place over these two chapters signified that the angel was one being, "the Lord" another, God another, and that, given that the passage makes no mention of the Son, there is no reference to the Son in the passage. Gregory, working here through an extended conversation between Moses and God, used the assumption that the actors have remained constant throughout the conversation in order to make the point that "the Lord," Christ, is *not* the angel of God, but rather God. Most damning for Eunomius's position, moreover, Gregory argued that even *Moses* understood this. Thus Christ, whom Gregory located in all these theophanies, was identical to God and not merely something sent out from God. With this interpretation, Gregory ruled out other interpretative options that see Christ in texts that speak of "angels" as a messenger or as something inferior to God.

Here I have traced at length the specific charges and responses in the debate between Eunomius, Basil, and Gregory, staying very close to their arguments, but it is important also to understand how the wider social context of their conversation was reflected in the positions they took. During the two decades since Eunomius had first written the *Apology*, the political landscape for Christians seeking public legitimacy had shifted considerably, tilting toward Gregory and Basil's favor.[53] Once a powerful and well-connected figure, Eunomius was discredited at an imperial council in 381 CE.[54] It is thus not surprising that, as the latest salvo in the debate, Gregory's warnings against Eunomius's reading styles involved social arguments alongside interpretative and epistemological ones. Though Gregory participated in arguments established by Eunomius and Basil about language and its ability to represent the divine world, the rhetoric in his treatise *Against Eunomius* included a level of emotional commitment that went beyond mere argument. Gregory was outraged by the way Eunomius had read the substance of Christ in the name "angel." He fairly exploded: "Immediately anger falls on my heart and cuts short my logic, and my reason is confused by passion, transformed into anger set in motion by the things [he says]. Maybe I will not be pardoned for such passion—but whom would anger *not* seize when he heard such things?" Gregory's indignance persisted: "What *should* I feel," he wrote, "hearing from this fighter of Christ that the Lord of the angels is an angel—when he does not let this fall by chance, but indeed struggles to maintain this totally inappropriate position?!"[55] The intensity of this anger was a departure from Basil's more nuanced, if not neutral, stance.[56] But it also signaled the changed context for reading Christ in passages that might associate him in any way with an angel. The Son simply had to be equal to the Father, God the Existent. Gregory warned, "If someone says anything against this, he is an advocate of the Jewish persuasion, not taking the Son as the savior of the people." Furthermore, he argued that anyone who says that the Son is not God himself, that being who speaks in Exodus 33.17, has turned away from Christianity, and "nothing other than the doctrines of the synagogue has he brought into the church of God."[57] Additionally, those who advocate that the Son was not also the Lord referred to in the Old Testament, in Gregory's mind, were "clearly Judaizing, taking away from doctrine the reality of the only-begotten."[58]

Gregory's charges of heresy and Judaism against Eunomius were clearly made possible by the changes in Eunomius's fortune, but those charges were also part of a much wider discourse that was developing in late ancient Christianity. Most Christians accused of heresy by early Christian writers were also at some point accused of Judaism.[59] By the time Gregory was writing his discourse *Against Eunomius*, Christians in many locations had begun to argue that theological positions associating the Son with an angel were "Jewish." Two examples will illustrate what I mean. First, in a letter to Paulinus, now recognized as a record of a Roman synod held in 377 or 378, Damasus the bishop of Rome listed the practices of groups that he anathematized. He first noted the Christian practice of reading "gods" in Scripture as angels, but cautioned against extrapolating that title to a particular practice. "The name of 'gods' is given and imposed by God to angels and all the saints," he argued, "for the father, the son, and the Holy Spirit, by one equal divinity, they are not given the name of 'gods' but of 'God.' Let us only be baptized in the name of the Father, Son, and the Holy Spirit, and not in the names of archangels, or angels, in the way the heretics, Jews, and the senseless Gentiles do."[60] Second, the Christian writer and translator Jerome composed a letter to the widow Algasia, in or near the year 406 CE. In the letter, Jerome interpreted Colossians for her, taking the text's reference to the "religion of the angels" to be an indictment against Jews. "The entire cult of the observations of the Jews is destroyed, and whatever sacrifices they offer, they do not offer them to God, but to fugitive angels and to unclean spirits."[61] Jerome's reading of Colossians explained the phrase "religion of the angels" as the temple sacrifices that took place after the arrival of Christ, but he also saw it having a wider sense, indicating any Jewish "observation." Within the space of a few decades, the equation of Judaism and "angel worship" had become a commonplace, one that Christian intellectuals shared with their correspondents. Understanding the voices in Christian literature that drew associations between Judaism and the worship of angels helps us to see the impact delivered by Gregory's accusation that Eunomius was verging on "Jewish" territory. By participating in the developing fourth-century tradition of accusing Jews of worshipping angels, Gregory marked Eunomius not just as an inaccurate reader of Scripture but as a heretic.

Thus Gregory's installment of the conversation shows us how reading practices had changed and how arguments enforcing them had shifted. While Eunomius, then Basil, sought to articulate theories of reading that would lead to the right interpretative conclusions, Gregory supported Basil but wielded a blunter instrument, simply ruling some readings heretical on their very face. He sought to preserve the practice of reading Christ historically in Old Testament passages while at the same time ruling out the specific implications that the characters representing Christ, especially angels, would have had for understanding Christ's nature.

Supporting Salvation History

Augustine of Hippo may seem a strange interloper in this discussion of language and its ability to accurately represent divine realities, but his social position, reading practices, and engagement in persuasive argument put him in the company of Athanasius, Eunomius, Basil, and Gregory. Like these men, Augustine trusted the force of persuasive words to explain ideas and to shape communities. His trust was founded in his early educational training and his career; Augustine's first vocation was as a teacher of rhetoric, and the dispositions of that teacher are evident in his writing. Almost more than any other late ancient author, Augustine left behind documents testifying to his practice of self-fashioning: the *Confessions*, his extensive body of letters, and the *Retractions* he made at the end of his life all point toward Augustine's efforts to craft his public persona. Other documents testify to Augustine's efforts to shape Christian communities, both the small community he led in Hippo and the wider, dispersed Christian community in the western Mediterranean: the audiences for his anti-Pelagian writings and pieces like *City of God* ranged far beyond those in his small North African congregation. His exposition in all these writings was deeply influenced by the assumptions and structures of rhetorical argument.[62] In his efforts to construct his own position and to be a persuasive advocate for his style of Christianity as the "universal" or "catholic" one, Augustine is at home among the writers I have treated so far in this chapter.

Scholars have not often put Augustine in conversation with them, however, because while he wrote in Latin, they wrote in Greek. In fact, Augustine himself complained about this language barrier in his work

On the Trinity. Though he was aware of an intense intellectual tradition of investigating the Son in Scripture, he felt that he remained outside the conversation, unable to participate.

> Sufficient texts on these matters either do not exist in Latin or they cannot be found—or, better, cannot easily be found by me. On the other hand, I do not doubt, based on the scarce works that *have* been translated for us, that Greek texts contain everything that we might profitably seek, though we are not in any way good enough at Greek in order to read and to understand such matters in them.[63]

Augustine's humility about Greek discourse has reinforced judgments by theologians that Augustine was too intent on preserving the unity of God to engage in and comprehend the intricacies of the Greek conversation about the three persons of God. I count his humility as a rhetorical stance more than a factual description because I have been convinced by recent scholarship, which sees more continuity than distance between Augustine on the one hand and Greek writers on the other.[64]

In terms of reading practices, Augustine was motivated by many of the same concerns as the other writers I have examined so far. First among these was the examination of Scripture as if it were a historical record, which could reveal information about Christ as an actor in the past. Augustine knew how to view stories through the historical lens, reading both for knowledge of the eternal Christ, as Justin had, and for knowledge of the incarnate Christ, as Athanasius had. As fits his early trepidation, though, Augustine conservatively described his particular historical method of reading as something itself drawn from Scripture:

> Regarding our Lord Jesus Christ, we hold that there is, both dispersed in the Scriptures and explained in the books of learned catholics, a rule to which we hold quite firmly: he is to be understood as the Son of God, equal to the Father, according to the form of God in which he exists, but also less than the Father according the form of a servant, which he took on.[65]

That is, Christ is the Son, but this Son is understood in two ways: first and in most cases, he is divine, equal to God the Father, whose "form" he represents; second, he is less than the Father at the moment when he becomes incarnate. For Augustine, taking on the flesh marked a decrease in the Son's status, but one that was undertaken willingly, a reading based on Philippians 2. Thus a reader could interpret a passage as speaking of the Son "in the form of God" or "in the form of a servant"; these two options allowed interpreters a great deal of latitude to understand scriptural statements about the Son and to relate them to the identity of the Son in particular moments. That latitude was accompanied by a certain amount of difficulty. Augustine observed that some Christians read about the Son being "from the Father" and became confused, trying to see in this the lesser of the two interpretations, instead of understanding the Son's production from the Father to be a reference to the Son's equality with the Father. Others still seemed purposefully to mistake the rule, taking words like "the Son can do nothing on his own, but only what he sees the Father doing" (John 5.19) to mean that the Son in his form of a servant must be lower than the Father. Augustine rejected interpretations like these. The purpose of the "form-of-God" rule was to make such readings impossible: it was "intended to show not that one person is less than the other, but only that one is from the other. Yet some people have extracted from it the sense that the Son is less than the Father," Augustine complained.[66]

One of the most vulnerable points in Augustine's system of historical reading occurred when its results intersected with the results of the other reading practice Augustine shared with Eunomius, Basil, and Gregory: attention to specific grammatical sequences and words. Augustine considered individual words of Scripture important; while he did not seem to be aware of the details of the argument, say, between Eunomius and Basil about the mechanisms of reading and producing knowledge and had not specifically theorized the capacity of language, he did assume that words in Scripture conveyed deep meaning. Such a rubric was, at times, difficult to maintain when used in combination with the sense that Scripture was a historical record. This is easiest to see in Augustine's discussion of the Son as one who is "sent." In John 17, Jesus prays to the Father, hoping that all people "may know you, the single true God, and Jesus Christ, the one you have sent." The grammar of this prayer could not be clearer, as Jesus, *speaking about himself*, refers to himself as an object of the Father's mission. Beyond the Gospel of John, other early literature also referred to God "sending" Jesus; most interesting for later Christians was Paul's statement that "when the fullness of time had arrived, God sent [*misit*] his son, made of a woman, made under the law" (Gal 4.4). These verses troubled Augustine. First, he was bothered by the issue of mission itself and its implications. Augustine's opponents claimed that "sending" was an action, which implied a dominion of one person over another. As the Son is one "sent," so these interpreters conclude that "the Father is greater than the Son, because the Son is constantly referring to himself as sent by the Father."[67] The specific word "sent" seemed to confirm what certain readers had found in the descriptions of the Son as a servant.

But there was a second, much larger issue that Augustine's attention to the meaning of "sent" precipitated. References in the New Testament called Christ "the Lord," so most early Christians readers saw Christ in passages like Genesis 12.7 ("the Lord appeared to Abraham") or Genesis 18.1 ("the Lord appeared to him..."). If Christ had been the entity that was sent to visit biblical ancestors, however, it would be superfluous for a writer like Paul to say of him that "God sent his Son" in the "fullness of time" (Gal 4.4), as if God had not "sent" the Son until the time of his incarnation.[68] Put another way, for the word "sent" to have meaning in Paul's letter, there must have been a time when God had not yet "sent" the Son. Thus Augustine was led to call into question the identity of the theophanies that Christian writers had traditionally identified with Christ, those moments when "God" or "angels" appeared to characters in the Old Testament. In the case of Abraham and the three angelic visitors of Genesis 18—a story where Christians had long read Christ—Augustine would question those who saw Christ as one of the visitors among them.

> How can he "be found in the condition of humanity," having his feet washed, eating human food, before he took on flesh? How could that have happened while he was yet "in the form of God, not thinking equality with God to be robbery"? Of course, he had not already "emptied himself, taking the form of a servant, made like humanity and found in the condition of humanity." Because we do know that he was found in that condition by being born of a virgin, so how could he "appear to Abraham" as a single man before that?[69]

Augustine understood the Son having been "sent" as a reference to the incarnate Son, Jesus, having appeared in flesh at one moment. As a result, it was difficult then to find that same character appearing to others in the historical context of Abraham, or Moses. How can a Son who only became enfleshed "in the fullness of time" also be in the flesh at Mamre, eating the lamb of Abraham's hospitality? The inclination to read Christ in the historical contexts of Old Testament stories, combined with the specificity assumed of all scriptural language, led to an untenable situation: Christ, who by most Christians before Augustine had been read as appearing in the theophanies of the time before Christianity, also had spoken of himself in words that could only mean that he had, in fact, *not* appeared in those same theophanies.

This was not Augustine's only headache. Reading techniques often have far greater effects than their primary application, and Augustine's insistence that the incarnation of the Son was the pivotal moment of divine mission hinted toward a second difficulty he found in reading the Son in these theophanies. Because being "sent," when applied to the Son and the Holy Spirit, means "coming forth from the hidden world of the spiritual into the public gaze of mortal men in some bodily shape," Augustine wondered whether the Father should not also be described as one "sent," "if he was made manifest in such bodily ways as appeared to the eyes of the ancients."[70] That is, traditional readings of the theophanies of the Old Testament required the manifestation of whatever divine actor one sees in them; Moses, for instance, "saw" the hind parts of God because those parts are material, manifest to human beings like Moses. However, one plank in Augustine's philosophical understanding of the divine world was that visibility was intrinsically linked to mutability, a trait that could not be applied to divine actors, who were perfect and unchanging. If an entity can be seen, it is material; if material, then it is liable to change; if liable to change, then inferior. Because Augustine assumed something visible could not be the highest of the divine, it became impossible for him to read any member of the Trinity in these theophanies. If the Father is immutable, it is out of the question for him to appear to the sight of humans; the same applies to the Son and the Holy Spirit. With these assumptions in place, Augustine was left with the question: just who appeared to Moses, to Abraham, to Jacob?

The solution itself was simple: Augustine concluded that any appearance of a divine actor in the Old Testament was materially manifested by angels. Though a particular theophany may have been instantiated by the will of any member of the Trinity, what was actually sensed by the human beings involved was a created, sent being—an angel. Surprisingly, Augustine supported this reading position by using the technique of continuity of character, precisely the same technique that had led earlier Christians like Basil and Gregory to locate Christ in the very theophanies that caused Augustine such trouble. Let us return to Exodus 3, the same passage that drew the attention of Basil, Eunomius, and Gregory. Readers first encounter "an angel of the Lord," who quickly announces, "I am the

God of Abraham and the God of Isaac and the God of Jacob." Instead of seeing this speaker as a divine being who has the title of both "God" and "angel," as previous readers had done, Augustine explained that these titles indicated an angel had acted as a mouthpiece for God, who could not himself be part of the physical reality of human beings. As he wrote,

> The person of God itself is not represented in all that which is announced to us by the Lord God. When it is represented, it sometimes manifests in an angel, and other times in another form which is not an angel but is arranged by an angel. When it is in a form which is not an angel, sometimes it takes on a body that already exists and adjusts it for the manifestation, while at other times, a body is produced just for the moment and is dissolved again once it has done its job.[71]

The entities that appeared to characters in the Old Testament were angels, or material creations arranged by angels; none were God or Christ. Previous interpretations had relied on certain titles to locate Christ in these stories—seeing "Lord," for example, was a sure sign to previous readers that Christ was the entity appearing. While it might make sense, then, under the assumption of meaningful nature of divine language for Scripture to specify that an "angel" was appearing to human beings in all theophanies, Scripture nevertheless used "Lord" in places where it did not mean a higher divine being, like God the Father or the Son. This, Augustine reasoned, was something like the workings of a courtroom: angels are the recorders of God, who speak for him as a clerk speaks for a judge. What the record will show is that the judge spoke, though physically he did no such thing.[72] Similarly, when Old Testament passages said "God," "the Lord," "the Lord God," "an angel of the Lord," or an "angel" had appeared, all of these were materially manifested by angels, leaving the members of the Trinity outside the realm of the material world and preserving Christ as an immaterial being up until the moment when he was "sent" to become incarnate.

Augustine's solution was revolutionary. Those same passages of Scripture that others had used explain that Christ, the Son, had been the entity represented in Old Testament theophanies, Augustine used to bolster his claim that all theophanies were appearances of angels. At times, Augustine directly challenged older interpretations. Previous readers, such as Basil, had seen Christ in the "angel of great counsel" named in Isaiah, yet Augustine preferred to rely on other evidence to understand the context of the passage. The New Testament bolstered his innovation, and the statement in Hebrews that the "message spoken through the angels became steadfast" was particularly significant to him. Augustine cautioned,

> There are some who wish to think of the angel as the Son of God speaking on his own behalf, because he is said to be an angel by the prophet [Isaiah], meaning that he announces both his will and the will of the Father. However, I would like to point out that in the letter [Hebrews], it does not say "through an angel" but rather "through angels."[73]

The plurality of angels in the phrase from Hebrews demonstrated for him that all appearances of the divine in the law, that is, in the Old Testament, were actually accomplished by angels. Instead of seeing the Son as nominally called an angel and expanding Christ's character to cover most of the theophanies, as had previous interpreters, Augustine divested the Son of any tie to the material appearances of the divine that took place before his incarnation, expanding the role of angels to cover the theophanies. In this way, Augustine vacated several centuries' worth of interpretative tradition and rejected the claim that this "angel of great counsel" or any other appearance of a divine actor was Christ.

Augustine's method of reading was a complex combination of several factors, but its heft was balanced by its utility. Reading the theophanies in this way eliminated several thorny textual problems created by the interaction of developing reading practices with increasingly more detailed theological positions about the Son. The benefits of Augustine's new approach to theophanies is best typified by a look at Genesis 22. Augustine interpreted the story of the binding of Isaac in a way that made it impossible for the divine actor (or actors) involved to be anything but angels. In the specific language of this passage, it is "God" who tests Abraham by ordering the sacrifice of his son, but at the crucial moment, it is "an angel of the Lord" who tells Abraham to lay off and not to harm the boy. Augustine scoffed at the possible misinterpretations:

> How will they respond to this? Would they say that God had ordered Isaac to be killed, but the angel prohibited it? That the father, against the warning of God who had ordered him to kill Isaac, submitted himself to the angel and spared him? This interpretation is laughable and should be rejected! Scripture disallows such a ridiculous

> interpretation anyway, adding as it does, "for now I know that you fear God, since, for my sake, you did not spare your beloved son." Who is this "my sake" referring to if not the one who ordered him to kill?[74]

Rather than suggest that an angel be able to override God's own command, Augustine came to see that all the divine speakers in Genesis 22 were angels, acting as mouthpieces for God. This explains why the speaker in verse 12 would pronounce, awkwardly, "I know you fear God" instead of "I know you fear *me*"; it was an angel who acknowledges Abraham's fear of God, the one who also had sent him. Additionally, a reader might interpret the second clause of the angel's announcement, "you have not spared your son for my sake," as meaning this: "you have not spared Isaac simply because I, the angel, had ordered you to do so; in reality, it was because it was an order from God that came to you through me." Here and elsewhere, Augustine solved the issue of multiple titles for the divine in biblical theophanies by eliminating the members of the Trinity as possible actors and making all divine appearances of one class: those worked by angels on behalf of God.

While this may, in one sense, be seen as a moment when angels become quite literally tools for reading, in another sense, Augustine's reading technique expanded the status of angels by making them the main actors in the dramas of the Old Testament. Those appearances that were previously thought to be manifestations of Christ—pivotal moments such as the staying of Abraham's hand during the near-sacrifice of Isaac or the giving of the law to Moses—were now seen by Augustine to have been manifestations of angels or manipulations of the material world accomplished by angels. In his new interpretation, angels were present at the most significant events in pre-Christian history, accomplishing pivotal divine interactions with humanity. This style of interpretation relinquished a long-standing Christian method of reading: proving Christ's eternity, or at least antiquity, by reading him as present in the events recorded in the historical narrative of Scripture; at the same time, it brought angels into human history, not just once, but hundreds of times.

The identification of Christ in the Septuagint had served Justin and other early Christians in an apologetic way, offering evidence that Christianity was not novel and that Christ had long been present, latent in religious traditions like Judaism. The same assumption underscored many of the interpretative debates among Christians in the fourth century: we have seen how passages from the Old Testament were sites of contestation for

Eunomius, Basil, and Gregory, and though the discussion in this chapter focused on Athanasius's use of Hebrews, he too interpreted Old Testament passages as significant for understanding Christ. For all these Christians, reading the Old Testament as if it contained thinly veiled references to Christ was a way to prove the existence of Christ in time—no mere man, the entity who was Jesus also existed long before the first century—as well as to illuminate specific details of his nature. Augustine, by contrast, was far less interested in proving to others that Christ was eternal. He was more concerned with preserving the meaning of individual words about Christ and spoken by Christ, as represented in Scripture—so concerned that he abandoned a long-established Christian reading practice.

Reading Changes

Reading is one of the most complex, variable, and difficult cultural actions accomplished by human beings. Its intricacies make for delicate management. As we have seen, late ancient Christians renegotiated what practices of reading were appropriate under social and political conditions that were quite different from those of the first three centuries of Christianity. Athanasius conceived a new style of theological argument, one based on the authoritative interpretation of the collected texts in an emerging canon of Scripture; he discovered this style while he was exiled, seeking legitimacy and an audience willing to grant him authority. His first foray into this style of argument was to reread an important text comparing Christ to angels: Hebrews. From there, Athanasius worked to keep the name "angel" from signifying any particular meaning about the Son, whom it identified in Christian readings of the Old Testament. The three Cappadocian writers whose arguments I explored wondered about the reliability of language and the human intellectual contribution to reading. Their concerns about grammar and naming were particularly intense regarding the name "angel" and its being read with or applied to Christ. Augustine stood Christian interpretative tradition on its head by removing any divine actors from the Old Testament, substituting angels instead. As messengers for God, angels literally spoke and appeared on behalf of other divine actors, moving in the material world in order to make possible contact between humanity and the divine. In this way, Augustine preserved the capacity of words like "sent" to carry a real meaning with reference to Christ; additionally, he resolved the difficult issue of materiality and visibility being, in his thought, inimical to the nature of divine beings.

It is important to recognize that all of these writers developed new ways of reading angels as they articulated theological positions in conflict with others. The redefinition of angels I have traced in this chapter took place in the context of contestation—the struggle to authoritatively define one's conception of Christianity and acceptable Christian thought.

Angels were not just tools for producing certain readings, though, and their role in the changing reading styles of late ancient Christian intellectuals was not incidental. From a certain perspective, we might look at these debates about reading in antiquity and conclude that the way angels change in them is not significant; angels were not even the central focus of the debates I have recounted here—instead, Christ was. But viewed from another perspective, these debates remade both the world readers lived in and the cosmos, changing the place of angels and making them important actors in both. That is because these Christians did not take reading Scripture as a mere exercise. Proper interpretation provided information about God and the divine world and allowed one to support with scriptural warrant one's theories about the nature of divine actors. That is to say, to know about the divine, or to try to know about the divine—in other words, to conduct theology—one needed to develop a trustworthy system of reading, one not vulnerable to the faults of the human intellect. It is not inevitable or even necessary that reading and theology be linked in this way. Revelation directly from the gods or through a mediator, divination by a skilled human being, logical derivation—these are potential ways to establish the identity of divine beings, and in fact, all these have been used by Christians, at one point in time or another. But reading as a way to establish the properties of a divine being, or the entire welter of divine beings in the cosmos, took a special place among the many Christian uses of texts during late antiquity. As it was becoming particularly significant in the public forum fostered by imperial sponsorship of church meetings and imperial attention to theological detail, reading and the changes that supported reading were anything but functional. They held the highest of stakes, both religious and political, as they were considered the only way to secure correct information about God and his nature.

The purpose of this chapter was to trace the context in which a thinker like Augustine could arrive at the views of angels he espoused: divine beings that interacted with the material world, heavenly citizens that guaranteed the reality of the City of God. In the next chapter, I will do the same for Evagrius of Pontus, tracing how ideas about angels forged by academic Christians were the context in which he developed his peculiar theory of angels.

3

Angels as Equipment for Living

THE COMPANION ANGEL TRADITION IN EVAGRIAN CHRISTIANITY

THIS CHAPTER EXAMINES the ascetic network of teachers that Evagrius joined when he came to Egypt and in which he developed his extensive theoretical knowledge of Christian progress and the divine world. Ascetic renunciation had been a theme in Christian writings as early as Paul's letters and the gospels, which offered attentive readers the twin resolutions of control of the body and development of a radically new self. During the first three centuries of the Christian movement, many put these resolutions into practice through special social arrangements, choosing to avoid traditional expectations of family and community in the search for a specifically Christian way of life.[1] In the fourth century, the changing material conditions of Christianity—its acceptance as a legitimate religious tradition and the political and financial opportunities that came with that—led to new contexts for practicing these resolutions. Christians experimented with new models of asceticism across the Mediterranean, but especially in Egypt—not in the city of Alexandria, but rather in the small ribbon of land between the farmable area near the Nile and the drier, harsher inhabitable land beyond the flood zone. Though the communities and individuals who lived there had deep economic ties to and continuing relationships with the towns and villages nearby, ascetics emphasized the differences between their culture and the culture of settled Egypt and, by extension, the world. They understood themselves to have withdrawn from the social life normal to Egypt to focus on their salvation as Christians. The distance such Christians constructed between themselves and the world, a discursive reality if not a physical one, allowed for the cultivation of intense practice, including physical labor, renunciation, prayer, and reading.[2]

Among the many different models for community that early Christian ascetics adopted, prominent in Egypt was the model of the academic or philosophical circle. Such circles were loose associations comprising mostly students, bound together by allegiance to a teacher and reverence for his lineage. If the ancient educational system as a whole was a basic introduction to a common culture, teaching a person "how one was to act, how he was to treat other men, what role he was to play in his community, and the manner in which he ought to approach the divine," then smaller academic circles were the advanced upper reaches of the system, with intense and specialized cultures of indoctrination and practical training.[3] Their work often centered around reading: interpreting the right texts, implementing the directions yielded by correct interpretation, imitating one's teacher in his reading practices—these were the core activities of academic circles, and they had the single goal of perfecting the life of the practitioners. That is to say, life as the advanced student of a particular teacher was often far more involved than our modern notion of "school" allows; it is best to think of academic circles as all-encompassing communities, which demanded time, loyalty, and dedicated practice.[4] As Christians experimented with methods of renunciation in Egypt, the academic model was a natural option. Not only was there a long history of Christian academic circles in Alexandria from which to draw inspiration and in which at least a few ascetics must have participated, but the academic model also melded easily with the intense focus on practice and progress embraced by those who had withdrawn from the urban centers of Egypt.[5]

When Evagrius of Pontus came to Egypt, he aligned himself with teachers whose established program of asceticism closely resembled a philosophical circle. Evagrius credited several men with introducing him to the ascetic life, speaking often of a lineage of fathers who shaped him; among those he mentioned most frequently was Macarius of Egypt.[6] Macarius belonged to a tradition of teaching that had a long history in Egypt; his forebears included men named Ammonas and Antony, ascetics whose letters in turn show their dependence on the ideas and practices laid out by the great Alexandrian thinker, Origen. To understand Evagrius's complex theoretical apparatus about angels, we need to understand the multigenerational intellectual tradition in which he was formed and particularly how angels were conceived in that tradition. While none of these earlier writers had quite the extensive system of angels and demons for which Evagrius is so famous—that appears to be his own creation—they did imagine angels as a part of the ascetic and intellectual program they taught. In fact, these teachers trained students to expect the direct assistance of an angelic guide and companion.[7] In this, Egyptian ascetics had created a new version of a standard feature of ancient academic culture: the expectation that demonstrated prowess as a student of philosophy would earn one a divine guide. That belief was the foundation upon which Evagrius built his more exquisitely detailed understanding of angels, demons, and human beings, which we examined in Chapter 1.

The present chapter will unfold in three stages. First, I will detail the traditions about divine guides that were operative in academic circles, which took their lead from ancient discussions of the famous philosopher Socrates and the "divine sign" said to guide him. Second, I will demonstrate how the notion of the divine guide was adapted by Antony and other teachers following him. Supported by their reading of Christian texts, they called the guide multiple names—sometimes a "spirit," a "power," or an "angel"—but employed a consistent set of expectations for how the guide was gotten and, in some cases, how it was lost. Third, I will explore the evidence of this ascetic tradition about an angelic guide surviving in the collections of stories about Egyptian ascetic life that were redacted outside of Egypt, mostly in the first half of the fifth century. Meant to represent the essence of the Egyptian ascetic tradition, some of them were edited to avoid mention of notions associated with Evagrius and those tied to him. Even so, ample evidence remains in these collections for the distinct tradition of the angelic guide earned by success and embraced in the Evagrian tradition. In the context of the cultivation of a specific ascetic program, late ancient Christians assumed an angel would be given to those who had performed particularly well. Though it was first honed in the teaching lineage of which Evagrius was a part, this assumption permeated later representations and recollections about the ideal Egyptian past.

Philosophical Guides

To understand how the tradition of the divine guide developed in Christian ascetic circles, we need to look back, improbably, to classical Athens and its most famous criminal, Socrates. Socrates was placed on trial in 399 BCE, having been charged with corrupting the young men of the city by asking irreligious questions. The charge was likely motivated by a general sense of exasperation, for while Socrates was famous and revered as a teacher, he was not known for his tact. His method was to examine students persistently, calling into question even the most basic of social assumptions and striving to prod Athenians toward more rational behavior. One might imagine that Socrates's interest in the moral health of the Athenian public would have led him to politics. That never happened, yet it was not his lack of tact that kept Socrates out of public life; instead, something else intervened. As Socrates explained,

> Perhaps it would seem odd that I go around giving advice in private and sticking my nose into other people's business but don't dare step up and give the city advice about your concerns in public. The reason for this is the one you've often heard me give in many places, namely, something divine and spiritual comes to me.... It's come to me since childhood—this voice—and whenever it comes, it always turns me away from what I'm about to do but never turns me toward anything. This is what opposes my engaging in politics, and I think it's wonderful that it's done so.[8]

Socrates was prevented from entering public life by the intervention of a voice, something divine that steered him away from harm. Socrates's follower, Plato, later described the voice as rare, available to only to a "small remnant" of people who "consort worthily with philosophy."[9] Among even the select group of those who "have tasted the sweetness and blessedness of this possession," namely philosophy, not all have such a guide. This "divine sign" had been given "to few or none before" Socrates.[10] From Plato's descriptions, it is clear that Socrates's sign was considered the mark of an advanced philosopher, something granted to the person willing to dedicate himself to the restrictions of the philosophical life in order to gain the "sweetness" that such a life holds in promise.

The divine sign has long been an object of curiosity for those who study Socrates, whether modern scholars or ancient philosophers. In antiquity, many philosophers claimed Socrates as their intellectual ancestor, seeking to emulate his teaching and his equanimity. For them, the ideal of Socrates as an intelligent, rational, independent seeker of truth did not square easily with stories about him having been guided from his youth by a voice or divine sign. We can see the centrality of this problem for thinkers who idolized Socrates in their attempts to explain the divine sign and its work. In one dialogue imagined by the first-century writer Plutarch, mention of a divine sign precipitates a wild discussion of whether it is ever appropriate for a philosopher to entertain the guidance of a sign. The subsequent conversation quickly turns to stories of Socrates's sign, and the group works in concert to preserve the image of Socrates as a rational thinker by redefining his sign as an instinct, a hunch that was the product of unseen, but not irrational, thought processes in the eminent philosopher.[11] The sign was special, but it was not something external to Socrates.

One participant in the conversation, however, embraced the idea that Socrates's sign was the voice of a special assistant that only the worthiest of human beings received. According to the character Theanor, the sign was a daemon, a type of divine being invested in the fate of humanity and able to affect the fortune humanity experiences. Socrates had been granted the sign because he had already demonstrated his virtue in his constant pursuit of philosophy; the sign respected his progress, which far outpaced that of others who struggled in philosophy. As Theanor related at length, those who succeed in their struggle for virtue eventually become daemons themselves, and thus

> do not hold what is done and said and striven after in this world in utter contempt, but are propitious to contenders for the same goal, join in their ardour, and encourage and help them to the attainment of virtue when they see them keeping up the struggle and all but reaching their heart's desire. For daemons do not assist all indifferently, but as when men swim at sea, those standing on the shore merely view in silence the swimmers who are still far out and distant from land, whereas they help with hand and voice alike such as have come near, and running along and wading in beside them bring them safely in, such too, my friends, is the way of daemons: as long as we are head over ears in the welter of worldly affairs and are changing body after body, like conveyances, they allow us to fight our way out and persevere unaided, as we endeavour by our own prowess to come through safe and reach a haven; but when in the course of countless births a soul has stoutly and resolutely sustained a long series of struggles, and as her cycle draws to a close, she approaches the upper world, bathed in sweat, in imminent peril and straining every nerve to reach the shore, God holds it no sin for her daemon to go to the rescue, but lets whoever will lend aid. One daemon is eager to deliver by his exhortations one soul, another another, and the soul on her part, having drawn close, can hear, and

> thus is saved; but if she pays no heed, she is forsaken by her daemon and comes to no happy end.[12]

In this soliloquy, Theanor described a system of progress in which human individuals making an effort in this world are watched by entities that were once like them; if such humans prove worthy by their athleticism in the struggle, these now-divine beings reach out to aid them; each person can thus garner his or her own guide. That guide is a former human being's soul, now a daemon still interested in the goings on of the world, who supports and coaches a still-living person in the athleticism of his "training" (ἄσκησις), so long as the athlete is "stripping for the same goal"—that is, preparing his body for the contest of virtue.[13] If the human beings who merit this attention ignore the daemon helping them, it is at their own peril. We understand from Theanor's speech that such guidance was never guaranteed, but given only as the result of continuing hard work. In this way, the character Theanor voiced an alternate perspective on Socrates's sign: rather than an internal product, the directions of the sign came from another entity, separate from Socrates himself, a daemon who had recognized his valor and elected to help him.

Though Theanor's perspective was not the dominant point of view in Plutarch's conversation, it had staying power. In the century after Plutarch's dialogue was published, other writers attempted to mitigate the impression that Socrates was guided by a daemon, an external entity whose care he cultivated. Apuleius, the Latin writer I mentioned in Chapter 1, dedicated an entire treatise to justifying the legitimacy of the sign with Socrates's philosophical integrity. The problem was simple: if Socrates were cultivating a daemon, he could not have been following his own rationality or sense of what was right, and thus was not worthy of acclaim as a philosopher. Furthermore, the suspicion that Socrates was controlled by a daemon easily turned to the presumption that Socrates was superstitious, in that he devoted himself to a middle divine being, whose moral nature was increasingly understood to be ambivalent by second-century thinkers.[14] Therefore, Apuleius argued that Socrates would never have submitted himself to a morally questionable "demon." Instead, there was another kind of daemon, which had deigned to witness and guard the thoughts and actions of each human being.[15] The solution was ingenious: while it might have seemed to others that Socrates worshipped a capricious divine being, cultivating it with rituals and gifts, in truth the daemon was pleased only by human beings who undertake the "sacraments of philosophy."[16] No superstition, the very acts of inquiry and reason so integral to the philosopher's career were the things that placated the daemon, whose guidance was available to all those who performed philosophy as well as Socrates. Because Socrates was the most accomplished in the aims of philosophy—detachment from the world, wisdom about affairs divine and human, a bemused attitude regarding humanity's arrogance—he had earned the most reliable and highest of guides.

If Socrates, the paragon of rationality, had a divine guide, wouldn't all engaged in philosophy strive to earn the same? The answer in antiquity was overwhelmingly "yes." In the academic circles of the second and third centuries, students were led to expect some manner of guide. The very youngest students had human guides, known as pedagogues, to protect them on their way to and from school, but more advanced students required more advanced guides. A remarkable document from the third century reveals how students thought about their teachers, their schools, and the help that might lead them on their path to greater understanding. Gregory Thaumaturgus, one of the students Origen of Alexandria had taught during his time in the city of Caesarea, composed a lengthy speech in praise of his teacher. A central character in Gregory's narrative about his time in Origen's school was the "personal pedagogue" who had first brought him to meet Origen.[17] Telling the story of how he came to travel to the city where Origen taught, Gregory relates that he had the assistance of a soldier. "It was not the soldier," however,

> but a divine escort, a good guide and guardian, who had preserved us all the way through life as if a good journey, passing over other things . . . and stopping to set me up here [in Caesarea]. He did all things and organized by all methods so that we be together with this person who was cause of so many benefits for us.[18]

Where other children had human pedagogues, Gregory already had the help of a divine guide to guard him. The guide brought Gregory to his teacher, yet once he had arrived at Origen's school, Gregory asked the divine escort to step aside so that Origen could guide him; Gregory also expected the guide to return to help him again once he left Origen's care.[19] Gregory's description reveals that he expected to have assistance in his education; when he needed help, something divine directed him, just as something divine had directed philosophers like Socrates.

The education Gregory received at Origen's hand would have changed how he understood this divine guide, because the texts Origen prepared students like Gregory to read offered a novel context for making sense of it. Akin to other philosophers, Origen considered reading the highest practice of an intellectual life. It was far more than a way to learn new information; because Origen assumed that language itself was a trace of the divine rationality that governed the cosmos, attentive interpretation of words could link the reader to the divine world in a deep way. Words about divine actors were especially rich sites for understanding the nature of the divine and the meaning of its interactions with humanity. For this reason, the intellectual training Origen offered students was entirely aimed at preparing them to participate in the exegesis of texts, and in this, he did not differ from the leaders of other academic circles.[20] What did make his school different from others was his choice of texts for exegesis. Origen placed the texts valued by Christians at the apex of his curriculum—books from the Septuagint, the gospels, and some letters of Paul. Where other philosophical teachers focused on the exegesis of Platonic dialogues, Origen's students read Scripture; "becoming a person capable of perceiving the deeper significance of the Bible" was the purpose of his curriculum.[21]

For readers prepared in the philosophical tradition, an abundance of information about the divine guide could be found in Christian texts. Many stories included characters from the past being granted divine assistance, but three were particularly resonant with the expectations of Christians in academic settings. First, in God's directions to Moses in Exodus 23, readers could find details that confirmed the reality of the divine guide. After giving Moses a long list of religious commands, God instructs him, saying,

> I am going to send an angel in front of you, to guard you on the way and to bring you to the place that I have prepared. Be attentive to him and listen to his voice; do not rebel against him, for he will not pardon your transgression; for my name is in him. But if you listen attentively to his voice and do all that I say, then I will be an enemy to your enemies and a foe to your foes.[22]

Here, readers could see that the guide would make Moses's path clear, as long as Moses heeded the voice, just as Socrates had done. If Moses did not obey the voice, he could lose the assistance of the guide; if he did obey,

God would protect Moses in all situations. Other texts similarly suggested that righteous people had the protection of a guide. Readers trained in a philosophical curriculum could see Jacob's blessing on "the god who nourished me from my youth, the angel who rescues me from all evils" in Genesis 48 as a dual description of the divine guide, both a god who nourishes and an angel who rescues.[23] Those who were trained to be attentive even to the precise lexical details of a text would not miss the same verb in Psalm 34 as in Genesis 48, "to rescue," when the Psalmist spoke of a guardian: "the poor one cried out and the Lord heard him and saved him from all his afflictions. The angel of the Lord will encircle those who fear him and rescue them."[24] For readers using Scripture as a guide to the divine world and looking for information about the interaction of human beings with divine ones, passages like these provided a linked matrix of proof that could be unlocked by proper exegesis. Divine guides like those expected in academic circles existed in literature important to Christians: there, these guides were called angels.

Gregory's education with Origen was centered on the reading of these texts, so it is natural that his ideas about his divine guide were informed by them. In his reflections on his education, he praised Origen, but he also took a moment to praise his divine guide. It was, he said

> that one, of all those invisible and divine beings that are allied to humans, who was appointed by some great judgment to keep me safe, to tend me, and to be a guardian for me—this holy angel of God, the one who has "nourished me from my youth," as the beloved man of God said, clearly referring to his own.[25]

Gregory identified his divine guide as an angel, one of the same class that had been protecting individual human beings since the time of the patriarchs. But Gregory's understanding was even more deeply formed by his reading of Christian literature. Just as a graduated hierarchy of angels was available to be read in Christian texts, so too was a graduated system of divine guides available to Christians. Working with the assumption that greater Christians merited greater protection, Gregory found in Scripture an angel superior to others in the way that Origen was superior to those students around him and even to other philosophers. He considered Origen to be so brilliant a teacher and upstanding a Christian that Gregory theorized Origen to have not just an angel as his companion, but the "angel of great counsel" itself, described in Isaiah 9, to guide him.[26]

For students like Gregory, Scripture was a source of information that coincided with the expectations typical of academic culture, but it also allowed him to expand his understanding, because the grades of angels available in Scripture confirmed the corresponding hierarchy Gregory saw among human beings.

It is possible that Gregory arrived at the correlation between the rank of the divine guide and the status of the human being it protected on his own, but it is more likely that he learned this notion from his teacher. Origen's ideas about angelic guides are best seen in his *Commentary on Matthew*. In a style reminiscent of the rhetoric of Platonic dialogues, Origen there presented an array of different claims that could be made about guiding angels. Some may think that angels are provided to Christians at birth, a position supported by several passages in Scripture.[27] Others may think Christians receive the protection of an angel only at baptism, and Origen listed a number of number of scriptural passages that could support them.[28] His own position was more complex, blending scriptural reading with the moral hierarchy of divine beings which was emerging in third-century philosophical discourse. Increasingly, Christian and non-Christian philosophers classed "demons" below angels, some going so far as to consider demons morally ambivalent or evil and angels morally good. For Origen, all people were under the influence of a divine being from their birth: those born Christian have an angel, but those not born Christian have a demon as their guide. The identity of that being could change, however, as a person became Christian, for human beings are coupled to their divine beings just as a wife is coupled to her husband. When one is saved, Origen explained, the other tends to follow.[29] This situation was reflected in the scriptural language that suggested humanity is at one time "under the spirit of fear" (a demon) and at other times "under the spirit of adoption" (an angel).[30] With these texts, Origen came to the understanding that humanity has always had a connection to the divine world, but the stature of the human being determines the kind of divine being it receives as a guide: a demon, an angel, or in the case of those most perfect ones who need something more than an angel, "the Lord himself."[31]

Latent within Origen's understanding of multiple levels of guides connected to human beings was an evaluation of humans themselves, who could be inferior or superior on the basis of their advancement in learning and virtue. As we saw, Gregory assumed that Origen had a greater angel as his guide than did more human beings; Origen, for his part, expected humanity to be aligned with the guide most proper to it, whether a lowly demon or a higher angel. Yet according to Origen, these arrangements were not automatic. Instead, they involved the evaluation of individual humans by the guides they might merit. The presence of an angelic guide depended on the actions, thoughts, and dispositions of the person guided as well as the willingness on the part of the guide to be involved with the human being. Both were necessary conditions for a relationship to develop, but the ultimate factor was the disposition of the divine being: it decided when to be visible to humanity. Presenting an example from Scripture, Origen wrote that "it was by grace that God appeared to Abraham and some others among the holy ones—Abraham's well-practiced eye of the soul was not enough to allow God to appear to him, but rather God presented himself to the sight of a righteous man, who became worthy by his sight."[32] Abraham may have had all the visionary skill in the world, but without the willingness of God to be seen, he could not have produced a vision of God. By extension, this is the case with all divine beings, including all types of angels. It is in their very nature to be able to will whether they are seen or not. As Origen argued, "whatever angel does not wish to appear to one of us may be present without being seen. Do not be surprised that if God is willing, he appears to Abraham, but is not willing to appear to others, and the angel willingly appears to Zechariah, but is unwilling to appear to another."[33] Origen suggested that the willingness of the divine being was inspired by the righteousness of the person to whom it would appear.[34] The moral evaluation implied here is radical, because these beings are intimately involved in the lives of the persons they guard. Angels are "those that will nurse us, will bear us in their bosoms."[35] They know their charges as well as they could possibly be known, and they see the moral success or failure of those they examine.

Companion Angels

During the first part of the fourth century, the nature of the Christian community in Alexandria shifted dramatically. While the academic circle, centered on a teacher and reading practices, had been central, an episcopal model increasingly dominated the culture of urban Christians in Egypt. Much of this change can be traced to the powerful writer and speaker who vied to maintain his position as bishop of Alexandria during much of the fourth century, Athanasius. In response to the controversy over the ideas of Arius, whose writing suggests he was shaped by philosophical culture, and as a way to consolidate authority in the single leader of the church, Athanasius articulated a new model of Christ as the sole legitimate teacher, thereby invalidating the place of various Christian teachers and the practices of reading and speculation they espoused.[36] While his efforts were not entirely successful in driving Christian teachers and Christian students out of the city, Athanasius did succeed in displacing the academic circle as the center of the urban Christian community.[37]

Even as this model of the philosophical tradition faded in the city of Alexandria, it thrived in the smaller ascetic communities established outside the city. Our best evidence of the earliest Christian ascetics suggests their deep reliance on the model of academic circles. Ascetic conversations were influenced by prior academic cultures; much of the vocabulary of athleticism and struggle so prominent in ascetic writings was already in use in philosophical schools before Christian ascetics adopted it.[38] What is more, the collections of letters from men like Antony, Ammonas, and Macarius of Egypt demonstrate their formal and intellectual inheritances from Alexandrian teaching traditions.[39] Yet these teachers were not passive recipients and transmitters of past academic culture; they developed and expanded the models on which they depended in order to cultivate a Christian life in their new context—not the city, but the "desert." In this section, I trace one part of that development, specifically how these ascetic teachers understood and developed the academic tradition of the divine guide to fit it to their new needs.

To start, let us consider the earliest collection of letters: those from Antony, who started his life of renunciation in the late third century and lived until 356 CE. His letters survive in various collections in multiple ancient languages—Latin, but also Georgian, and Arabic, with small parts of the collection in Syriac and Greek.[40] Though the collections vary somewhat, they are consistent in their representation of their author and his intellectual lineage. They show that as a teacher, Antony displayed a deep intellectual dependence on the ideas and practices of the academic Christian circles that preceded him.[41] Though the letters are not written as systematic theological treatises, it is clear that they share a general cosmology with Origen of Alexandria, along with the attendant ideas about the origin of divine and human beings.[42] Antony spoke of an original unity interrupted, from which all levels of rational beings—angels, humans, demons—were produced and to which all would return.[43] Like the schools in Alexandria from which he took his inspiration, Antony's program involved a commitment to the work of interpretation as a spiritual practice; to read Scripture and to find new lessons in it was the basic task of any Christian.[44] Antony considered biblical texts to reveal the divine world to the one whose mind was attuned to its message, and in this, he resembled other academic teachers. Like them, Antony promoted specific practices to support such rare levels of advanced reading. Fasting, keeping vigil, remaining celibate were all enacted as a way to purify the intellect. Overall, the program he promoted aimed to produce nothing short of a complete transformation, a way of life in a Christian venue, focused on the intense refashioning of the individual toward a higher existence and return to an original unity with the divine.

While Antony positioned himself as the wise guide for those who joined his circle, the letters also reveal that ascetics pursuing this program could expect help, even beyond the direction Antony offered. The best among them could expect that a divine guide would join them to ease their way. As he oriented students to the path they would follow, Antony emphasized the importance of their dedication to that path, difficult as it may have been, because their singleness of purpose was the main factor that elicited the help of the guide, which Antony often called a "spirit." As he wrote,

> I believe that those who have entered the struggle with all their heart, and have prepared themselves to endure all the trials of the enemy until they prevail, are first called by the spirit, who alleviates everything for them so that the work of repentance becomes sweet for them. He sets for them a rule for how to repent in their bodies and souls until he has taught them the way to return to God, their own creator. He also gives them control over their souls and bodies in order that both may be sanctified and inherit together.[45]

When a student dedicated himself to the program Antony taught, a cascade of things occurred, if all the conditions were right. As soon as an ascetic could will himself ready to enter the contest, he would find that his way was smooth; the spirit both teaches and enables the practices the ascetic needs in order to arrive at his goal—salvation of soul and body. The rest of Antony's letter offers extensive detail regarding the spirit given to the dedicated ascetic: when the ascetic begins to fast and keep vigil, taking on the "exertion and the exercises of the body," the spirit becomes the ascetic's "guide, testing him" to see whether he can manage the work.[46] It also "opens the eyes of the soul," then goes on to teach the mind "how to purify the body and soul through repentance."[47] When the mind "accepts this struggle," it can accomplish the purification of all parts of the person, in prayer and in communion with the spirit that guides the ascetic and teaches him, because that spirit "strengthens" the mind and "makes firm" the soul to support the student's progress.[48]

By Antony's description, a cycle of attachment and abandonment characterizes the relationship between the student and the spirit who guides him. While we might think of the exercises adopted by ascetics as external and visible—like fasting, or celibacy, or even a dedicated system of prayer—what the spirit evaluates, according to Antony, is the work of the mind or the soul. If the ascetic fails in that work, there are significant consequences. As Antony warned his brothers, "if the mind spurns the testimonies which the spirit has given it, then evil spirits override the [natural] constitution of the body."[49] These evil spirits take the place of the good spirit that had come to the ascetic to help him. Without the guidance of the good spirit, the ascetic's soul falls into a disordered state. Yet Antony offered reason for optimism, because once the "soul grows weary [of its deprivation] and asks from where it can receive help," it is allowed to return to the company of the good spirit and is, finally, made whole again.[50] In these ups and downs we see the demanding nature of Antony's program: when an ascetic masters the basics, he stands to receive the guidance of a spirit, yet that spirit could withdraw if the ascetic's will and internal struggle were lax; it could return when the ascetic seeks it again. The effect of this cycle was to encourage vigilance of a radical kind on the part of the ascetic, because his success was never final.

Most scholars have thought of the spirit Antony described in these letters as the Holy Spirit, that is to say, the biblical character later understood by Christians as a member of the Trinity, but doing so needlessly forecloses on the ambiguity yet present in early fourth-century Christian culture.[51] When Antony wrote these letters in the 340s, Christians had not yet reached a consensus about the Holy Spirit, its activities, or its stature among the many divine beings that were part of Christian tradition.[52] It was only in the later fourth century that the Holy Spirit became the object of concentrated attention and extensive theorizing among Christian intellectuals: in the 370s, Christian writers in Cappadocia explored a number of ways of conceiving the Holy Spirit, culminating in the position articulated at the Council of Constantinople in 381 CE. In the middle of the fourth century, during Antony's life, evidence of Christian ideas about the Holy Spirit from Egypt hints that there was more controversy than consensus. For example, Athanasius wrote several letters between 358 and 361 to a

Serapion of Thmuis, answering concerns Serapion had expressed about a group of Christians who considered the Holy Spirit to be a "created and superior angel" on the basis of their readings of 1 Timothy 5.21, which names not "Father, Son, and Holy Spirit," but "God, Christ Jesus, and the elect angels."[53] Athanasius responded with his own view of the Holy Spirit, which ruled out its identity with any angel.[54] Given that Athanasius needed to argue for his view at the end of the 350s, there is no reason to conclude that Antony's letters from at least a decade earlier would have a concept of the Holy Spirit that aligned with the later Christian consensus about it. It assumes too much to say that Antony considered *the* Holy Spirit, the member of the Trinity, as the thing that guided ascetics, even though he spoke at times of the guide as a spirit of holiness or even a "holy spirit."[55]

Furthermore, there is evidence in the letters that identifying this guide as the Holy Spirit would confine the rather expansive understanding Antony had of the help members of his circle could enjoy. As we know, Antony's program was based around meticulous attention to language, particularly scriptural language. In his fourth letter, Antony detailed the help of the guide by quoting from the Wisdom of Solomon, writing that "the spirit does not enter a soul that has an unclean heart, nor a body that sins. It is a holy power, far from any deceit."[56] Or, more precisely, Antony here created a sentence that reflected the structure of a verse from the Wisdom of Solomon, rather than quoting directly from the book. For the text of the Wisdom of Solomon 1.4–5 actually reads as follows: "Wisdom does not enter a soul aimed at doing evil nor does it dwell in a body that honors sin. A holy and well-trained spirit will flee deceit."[57] What appears in Antony's recreated quotation of this verse are the subjects "spirit," substituted for "wisdom," and "power," substituted for "spirit."[58] It is possible that Antony was using a much different version of the Wisdom of Solomon, one that is otherwise unattested from antiquity. Yet it is far more likely that Antony composed a biblically inspired piece of almost-scripture to speak of the "spirit" accompanying ascetics being a "holy power" that would leave them if they were deceitful. As he formed this new text from the substrate of the biblical text, Antony equated the primary actor with the "spirit" that guides, substituting for the name of the "holy spirit" his preferred phrase for the guide, "a holy power."[59] Indeed, these were not the only phrases Antony used to refer to the guide.[60] Most often, he simply referred to the "spirit." At times, he qualified this, using "the holy spirit," or "the guiding spirit." Elsewhere, he used language familiar to us from

Origen's description of the guide: the "spirit of adoption." There are many other ways he spoke of the guide: in Antony's letters, the "spirit of repentance," the "spirit of consolation," "spirit of wisdom," "spirit of comfort," "hidden power," and "angel" all refer to the entity that could help an ascetic in his practices, but could also leave him.

Antony may have varied the name he called the divine guide, but the letters he wrote sounded a consistent theme: ascetics must continually strive to be worthy of its attention. He urged the brothers in the sixth letter, for example, never to "fail to beseech the goodness of the Father that perchance a helper will come to you," then specified precisely what one must do in order to cultivate the presence of this helper.[61] Sacrifice is the biblical metaphor he adopted to instruct his readers:

> Lift up the body in which you are clothed and make it an altar and lay upon it all your thoughts and leave all evil counsels before God, and lift up the hands of your heart to him, that is to the creator of the mind, and pray to God that he gives you the great invisible fire, that it may descend from above and consume the altar and all upon it, as well as all the priests of Baal, who are the hostile works of the enemy, that they may fear and flee before you as before the prophet Elijah. Then you will see as it were the track of a man over the sea, who will bring you the spiritual rain, which is the comfort of the spirit of comfort.[62]

The ascetic's interaction with his own body was, in Antony's rendering, a consuming sacrifice meant to please God and burn up the "hostile works of the enemy." Elsewhere, Antony reiterated his plea, telling ascetics to offer themselves as "a sacrifice to God."[63] He directed ascetics to make this effort continually: "Do not neglect," he wrote, "to cry out day and night to God, entreating by the benevolence of the Father...help from above."[64] Their constant attention must be directed to the practice of asceticism, an ongoing "sacrifice" of the body to bring help for the mind.

Those who produced acceptable sacrifices gained a guide, whose services included but extended beyond many of the expectations traditionally voiced in philosophical circles. Guides kept philosophers safe—Socrates was prevented from entering politics, Gregory Thaumaturgus was protected as he traveled—but the primary danger for Egyptian ascetics was far more sinister. As has been recognized in recent scholarship, Egyptian ascetic culture was distinct for being permeated by the discourse of demonic attack.[65] And as we saw in Chapter 1, Evagrius had theorized the progress of the individual as including, at the first stage, a consistent battle with demons, and Antony, too, expected that demons would seek out Christians.[66] So, the "hidden powers" serving ascetics in Antony's circle did offer guidance to the ascetics, but their primary duty was to fend off the hostilities of demons, who, Antony warned, "watch out for us always." Appealing to Psalm 34, Antony pitted the hidden power, the "angel of the Lord," directly against the demons who attack the ascetic. As Antony reasoned, it was on account of these demons that "it is written, 'The angel of the Lord encamps around those who fear him and delivers them.'"[67] The opposition of the demons created a veritable battle: an ascetic, with the help of his angelic guide, was to fight off temptation and demons in an epic struggle.

In spite of (or perhaps because of) the emphasis he placed on individual effort leading to ascetics receiving a guide, Antony's letters undercut any claim ascetics might have had to crow about their performance in these struggles or their ascetic advancement. To this end, Antony sharply warns, "You should not regard your progress and entry into the service of God as your own work; rather a divine power supports you always."[68] The help they received—in the form of what Antony described alternately as a "spirit," a "helper," a "divine power," and an "angel"—existed to guide them and to protect them from the demonic interference that was an inevitable part of life in Egyptian ascetic communities. Antony encouraged them all to try to gain this power by figuratively sacrificing themselves through deeds of concentration and renunciation, acts that would purify body and thus mind to receive and maintain the presence of this power, even as he reminded them that it, and not they, brought ascetic excellence and closeness to God. It was their job to be vigilant and exert effort, but their efforts were never the direct cause of their success.

Though Antony died in 356 CE, the small group of ascetics he had shepherded continued to live and thrive. In the literature that survives from the period after Antony's death, it is clear that the community maintained and elaborated upon the tradition of the divine guide, gotten by means of ascetic sacrifice. In fact, having an angelic helper was a primary way that Antony's community defined progress in the ascetic life, so much so that even those outside the community knew its importance for Antony's followers. Serapion of Thmuis, the same man who had written to Athanasius about the Holy Spirit, wrote a letter to Antony's students, commiserating with them about the loss of their leader and offering them hope for the future of their practice.[69] He acknowledged that Antony's presence seemed to have made the whole world holy, but even without Antony among them, it was still possible for them to try to maintain the holiness. To do this, Serapion encouraged them to pursue the help of the power that had guarded Antony. "It is fitting," he said, "that we acquire the power of one in the many. Therefore we pray that as many as you are, you acquire that many powers—that every one of you might become, through his power, blessed Antony himself." The text of the letter is quite clear here, for the language in which it survives, Syriac, specifies that the power mentioned, the "power of one," was the power that belongs uniquely to Antony.[70] The brothers should utilize this personal power of Antony's in order to get powers of their own, which will in turn help them to become like Antony. Serapion continued: "As you become many Antonys, many powers will come to you and a great remedy, a perfecting cure, will pour forth upon you."[71] Though it is possible that Serapion had some abstract concept of power in mind—what we might call the magnetism of personality, or the force of the will—his description of Antony possessing a unique "power" that might lead the remaining brothers to be able to draw "many powers" to themselves suggests that these powers were discrete entities, things to be gotten and kept by each ascetic as he emulated the life that Antony had led. When moved to console Antony's students, the outsider Serapion cited Antony's teaching about a holy power to them, in terms that would motivate them to persevere in their discipline and acquire such a power for each of themselves.

Not only did others outside Antony's community like Serapion know this tradition, but the ascetics who lived on after Antony's death continued to teach it, advancing its assumptions and showing their own students how to participate. One line of transmission is visible in the letters surviving from Antony's student and likely successor as the leader of the small community at Pispir, Ammonas.[72] He wrote to many, both nearby and distant, dissecting their personal issues and directing them to better discipline; his advice follows the model that had characterized philosophical and religious teachers' writing in Egypt for at least the previous three centuries.[73] As a teacher, Ammonas painted the moral situation of his readers starkly. In one letter, he told his charges that he could see that, in the realm of "invisible things," their bodies were "entirely alive" but could become dead bodies were they to neglect their practice.[74] Creating such black-and-white alternatives served a pedagogical purpose—to make the eventual advice he would give seem the only natural choice—and

Ammonas followed his diagnosis with directions no less subtle. Ascetics should avoid vainglory—that is, the state of hoping others would think well of them—and with vainglory, pleasures in general.[75] Supporting his prescription with passages from a number of biblical books, from Isaiah and Proverbs to Hebrews and 2 Timothy, Ammonas exhorted his readers to continued vigilance and against the seeking of approval.

The injunction against vainglory was a general theme of Egyptian ascetic texts—an attempt to temper the heady achievements of the ascetic lifestyle with humility—but Ammonas's letters had even more specific advice. In these more detailed instances, they reveal Ammonas's deep and lasting connection to Antony's teaching. Ammonas offered his charges information about garnering divine assistance that echoes the metaphor of "sacrifice" Antony employed to characterize ascetic effort. Here is how Ammonas had described getting a divine guide:

> If any man love the Lord with all his heart and all his soul and with all his might, he will acquire awe, and awe will beget in him weeping, and weeping joy, and joy will beget strength, and in all this the soul will bear fruit. And when God sees its fruit so fair, he will accept it as a sweet savour, and in all things he will rejoice with that soul, with his angels, and will give it a guardian to keep it in all its ways as he prepares it for the place of life, and to prevent Satan from prevailing over it. For whenever the evil one sees this guardian, that is, the power encompassing the soul, he flees, fearing to approach the man, and afraid of the power that is about him.[76]

Though this letter did not immediately reproduce Antony's precise way of teaching about the tradition of getting help, it did outline stages corresponding to the acquisition of the divine power described in Antony's letters. First, an ascetic must devote himself to the Christian life; next, his efforts must produce a "fruit" that God accepts as a "sweet savour," a phrase that alludes to the pleasing fragrance God received with sacrifice; then, God provides a guardian, or a power, for the ascetic, who wards off any approach of Satan. An ascetic's efforts produced sweetness that could be offered to God, and God would return to the ascetic a protector, one who encompassed his soul (an allusion to the angel who "encamps around" those who fear God); this "power" would protect the ascetic from attack. Ammonas's teaching coincided with Antony's at all these points, though it was voiced in slightly different terms.

Though Ammonas's advice can be traced to the tradition Antony also taught, the differences between their positions signal development in the way divine guides were imagined. Ammonas's letters placed more responsibility on the ascetic for acquiring this divine helper than had Antony. The expectations Ammonas had for ascetics were numerous, intensive, and concrete. The active pursuit of the angelic helper was necessary, if indeed ascetics "desire to receive it." Their task, Ammonas argued, was to give themselves over "to bodily toil and toil of heart," extending their "thoughts up to heaven night and day."[77] It was not enough simply to "enter the struggle" with one's whole heart, as Antony had urged; instead, there were specific practices of cultivation, of "divine labor" to be done:

> If the righteous have the divine power with them, there is nothing that is able to hinder them. And so, this is the divine labor [to be done] until it dwells in a person: that he despise all dishonor, but also honor, among human beings; that he hate all the necessities of this world and hate all the needs of the body; that he cleanse his heart of every foul thought and all the empty wisdom of this world; and that he make supplication with fasting and tears night and day. And God, who is good, will not delay to give it to you. Once you have received it you will pass all the time of your life in ease and freedom of care, and you will find great boldness before God, which he will grant you.[78]

Such a project of cultivation required the ascetic to be vigilant in a number of different venues: emotional, social, physical. Those capable of these acts of body and mind proved worthy of the divine power, and God hastened to give it to them. Given the extent of the program and the responsibilities placed on the ascetic, it is perhaps natural that some may doubt their ability to cultivate a divine power—and even that doubt is a subject for vigilance. "Watch out," Ammonas warned, "lest thoughts of division or doubt alight in your heart, causing you to say 'who is ever able to receive such a thing?'"[79] In the place of doubt, ascetics should adopt a comprehensive effort, an effort that included the fight against vainglory Ammonas had introduced at the start of the letters. There, Ammonas had even spoken of vainglory as an entity: "My beloved, you who are loved by my soul, you whose fruit is reckoned to God, contend with all your deeds against the spirit of vainglory so that you might completely conquer it, that your whole body might be acceptable and remain as a living thing with its creator, and that you receive the divine power, which surpasses all these things."[80] The path is clear—commitment to the ascetic program Ammonas advocated, in its large and small details, would result in the acquisition of a divine power.

Just as the responsibilities of the ascetic were more extensive in Ammonas's letters than in Antony's, so too were the benefits allowed an ascetic who had merited the presence of a divine power. Those benefits accrued on many levels. First, accepting the divine power meant accepting a general feeling of joy, a fervor for one's practice, and the "sweetness of God," along with a cascade of goods that would allow ascetics to "prosper."[81] At the same time, ascetics could expect a more subtle personal change, in that the power would be "dwelling in them"; its presence strengthened them but also allowed them to heal others in turn.[82] Most distinctively, Ammonas may have promised those who earn a guide direct access to divine knowledge. From an allusion in one of the letters, we know that Ammonas read and expected his readers would recognize the *Ascension of Isaiah*, a text that included a vision of an angelically guided tour of the heavens. Perhaps this is the best hint by which to understand what Ammonas suggested when he punned on the word "power": "I have written to you so that you might be empowered in what you perform and so that you know it was in the quiet that the holy ones prospered. Because of this, the divine power dwelled in them and thus made the heavenly mysteries known to them."[83] Knowing and befriending an angelic guide allowed ascetics to succeed, to be suffused with buoying emotional states and strength, and even possibly to make contact with other angels in heaven.

These were heady promises, and Ammonas balanced them with warnings about the various ways ascetics could lose the presence of a divine power once they had acquired it. Motivations were key. If an ascetic were too proud, or driven by his own will rather than God's, "this [power] will not be a helper and it will not go out with" the ascetic during his practice.[84] When an ascetic fell to pleasing others, the power might desert him. Ammonas lamented those in the past who "acted not out of faith but for the sake of human beings." They suffered from obsequiousness and "because of this the divine power did not dwell in them but rather all their works are sorrowful. Thus they did not know the divine power, nor petition its protection, its ease, or its joy."[85] Such motivations might be hidden from other human beings, but the guide itself could know them. "When the power gazes on them," Ammonas said, "it reckons them to be comforted in this world and the passions, both of soul and of body; thus, it is prevented from overshadowing" these ascetics, who are "not worthy of the divine sweetness, so the divine power does not dwell in them."[86] As this suggests, in actuality, not all received the power.[87] Ammonas frequently mentioned how scarce were the ascetics who deserved one:

> Not many monks or virgins have known this great and divine sweetness since they have not acquired the divine power, except some few here and there. For they were not cultivating the power, and therefore God did not give it them. For to those who cultivate it God gives it; for he is no respecter of persons, but gives it to those who cultivate it in every generation.[88]

The collective impact of these warnings is to make clear that the help of a divine power was not a recipe for ease in life for those few who receive it, but only ease in the dedicated and continual labor of the ascetic program.

Another letter surviving from the early Egyptian ascetic movement resonates with the expectations and promises laid out by both Antony and Ammonas. It is a short piece, attributed in antiquity and by most contemporary scholars to Macarius the Egyptian, a revered ascetic and longtime teacher. The terms and stages of the ascetic path as he described them will be familiar to the reader: once a person commits himself to the work of fasting and praying, demons come to attack him. "In such battles," Macarius admitted, "the heart becomes utterly weak."[89] It is precisely at that moment when the heart lost strength that the ascetic could expect help. He wrote,

> When the heart becomes weakened in these things so that it is dissolved in the sufferings of these battles, then the good and merciful God sends to him a holy power and supports his heart and gives him weeping and easy speech and repose in the heart, so that he becomes strong against the enemies, who are no longer motivated, as they fear the power that is dwelling inside him. Just as Paul cried, "you will struggle" and "you will receive a power" (Acts 1.8). For this is the power of which Peter spoke, saying, "an incorruptible inheritance, undefiled, reserved in heaven" for us, "who are kept in the power of God through faith" (1 Pt 1.4–5).[90]

Just as we saw in the advice from the other two teachers, Macarius encouraged ascetics to steel themselves for the difficulties they would experience as soon as they began the program they had chosen. Demons would invariably take their dedication as license to attack, and it was precisely when things had looked the worst that God would send "a holy power," which discouraged the demons who fear the "power dwelling inside" those who have practiced well. As Antony and Ammonas taught about a power whose presence in an ascetic repelled attacking demons, Macarius taught his charges a similar lesson, using an expanded set of biblical passages as his proof.

What is more, Macarius thought the cycle of attachment and abandonment that we saw in other letters to be a necessary, if painful, part of the ascetic's progress. The contest of ascetic life was to remain always a contest, even it if meant that God had to withdraw the divine power he had given in order to let ascetics struggle further on their own. As Macarius explained, "when the good god sees that the heart has been so empowered against the enemies, then he takes away the power from time to time."[91] Without the presence of the power, the demons can tempt the monk in whatever way they wish, but eventually "the good god, thinking about his creation, sends him the holy power again and supports the heart and soul and the body and the rest of the members."[92] Ascetics must understand that vigilance over even the heart and soul were the central occupation of their work. As Macarius warned, "Whenever a thought disparages the arrangements of the spirit, then the power withdraws once again and what is more, battles come to the heart; and the troubles and passions of the body trouble him as a result of the movements which the enemies sow."[93] The wisest of Christians would come to understand that "great humiliation and the crushing of the heart" were actually instances of their primary goal, namely, as Macarius painted it, "sacrifice to God."[94] In his articulation of the vagaries of ascetic life, we see Macarius's debt to Antony and Ammonas: the attack of demons, the protecting power, and the metaphor of sacrifice all point to a shared lineage.

It was this lineage that Evagrius of Pontus elected to join when he came to Egypt in 383 CE. As I have mentioned, Evagrius boasted multiple times about his affiliation with Macarius, but even without those displays of gratitude, the two men's ideas are so compatible as to signal a relationship. As a small example, consider in the previous paragraph how Macarius paints the attacks of the demons: they create passions by sowing movements in the hearts of ascetics. This language, which alludes to a

Stoic-influenced theory of the passions, also lies at the center of Evagrius's account of the mechanics of the ascetic soul.[95] For Evagrius, both angels and demons could produce "movements" that often led to altered emotional states or visions. Dreams, too, could be produced by either kind of divine being. For instance, Evagrius explained: "there is a simple movement of the memory, coming from either ourselves or the holy powers, thanks to which we encounter holy people in our sleep and converse and eat with them."[96] What little survives of Macarius's teachings suggests his weighty influence on Evagrius with respect to how angels and demons worked in the souls and minds of human beings.

This detailed exploration of late ancient ascetic letters demonstrates that, in his guidance for ascetics trying to make progress, Evagrius imagined several scenarios that accorded with the tradition of the divine guide as it was developed by Antony, Ammonas, and Macarius. Like other ascetics in his lineage, Evagrius expected his followers to read texts in a particular way, and even to use texts as weapons against attack from the outside.[97] He gathered these texts in a collection titled *Talking Back*, which offered practical solutions in the form of scriptural passages to cite back to the eight most difficult kinds of demons liable to attack ascetics: the demons of gluttony, fornication, greed, sadness, anger, listlessness, vainglory, and pride. *Talking Back* is no theoretical book but was meant for daily use. Therefore, the particular situations for which Evagrius offered solutions were, we can assume, plausible as possible events in the daily life of ascetics in Evagrius's tradition. Some of the scenarios he discussed regard ascetics who do not have the proper respect for the angel that could guide them. In one case, Evagrius offers advice to the monk who is so prideful that he "rejects the angel who assists" him: he urged that monk to remember Genesis 48, the blessing of Joseph calling specifically on the "angel who rescues me from all evils."[98] Other monks become prideful and think they need no angelic assistance; to them, Evagrius compelled the use of the first part of Exodus 23: "Look, I am sending my angel before you.... Pay attention to him and listen to him, and do not disobey him."[99] Both of these exchanges are meant to reinforce the proper attitude of humility in the monk who thought angelic guides were unnecessary for success.

Humility was the right salve to apply to pride but did not help those ascetics who lacked confidence in these angelic companions, fearing that because they were not visible, they were not real. To these, Evagrius assigned the use of the same passage from Exodus 23, insisting: "Look, I am sending my angel before you!" If that were not sufficient to assuage "the thoughts of terror that come upon us because the angel who assists us is not visible," an ascetic could counter his doubts with this: "With a secret hand the Lord wages war against Amalek from generations to generations."[100] Evagrius's biblical interpretation is clear—angels who assist monks are not the Lord, but his "secret hand," who persist in all ages. More biblical passages support these monks—if one were sad or frightened by the number of demons who are visible as they attack monks, he should remember the words, "do not be afraid, for those that are with us outnumber those that are with them."[101] These angels could be seen by some, but even for those who do not see them, it was important to offer thanks to "the angel of the Lord" who inhabits the intellect and drives out thoughts of evil.[102] Thus multiple situations show us that Evagrius, like his teachers, knew that ascetics could gain the help of a divine guide. Following his teachers, at times he called this a "holy power," while at other times, he simply used the term "angel."[103]

In concert with his predecessors, Evagrius also instructed ascetics that the guide they had worked so hard to gain could be lost from time to time. Abandonment by one's angelic helper was always a possibility, because its presence hinged on the continuing efforts and success of the monk. In his *Commentary on Proverbs,* Evagrius warned ascetics that "wealth of knowledge and wisdom provide for us many angels, but the impure person is separated even from the angel given to him as a child. Spiritual friendship is virtue and knowledge of God, through which we are bound to the friendship of the holy powers."[104] The glue that held this relationship together was the virtue of the ascetic, his ongoing purity of heart. Without it, the angel was liable to leave. The prospect of abandonment inspired trepidation among ascetics: in *Talking Back,* Evagrius offered retorts to be used by the ascetic who feared being "briefly abandoned" by the angels who guard him.[105] Ascetics must have known their internal states were under surveillance because Evagrius offered strategies to the monk afraid angels would see his "unclean thoughts" and leave him because of their disgust.[106] Such pieces of strategy suggest the existence of monks who might need to use them, meaning that the threat of abandonment by one's angel was a real part of the ascetic experience.

My purpose in tracing the tradition of the angelic guide—from the early accounts of Socrates's sign, to Christian academic circles in Alexandria, through the academic circles of Egyptian ascetics—was to show how the idea, which is present in Evagrius's writings, took its shape in a particular environment. But how is this tradition related to Evagrius's more extensive theoretical ideas about the human self, like those we explored in Chapter 1? Evagrius had learned a great deal before he came to Egypt, but it was in Egypt that he incorporated the practical aspects of an all-encompassing ascetic program. There he learned that angels protected human beings, and this idea was the foundation for his explanation that angels were sympathetic to humanity because they shared a particular nature—precisely that nature that ascetics were attempting to strengthen in their practice of prayer, reading, and renunciation. Evagrius's theory of angels as rational beings, ever improving toward a reunification with God, traces its source to the teachings Evagrius encountered when he entered the realm of cultivation. Those teachings continued to influence the representation of Egyptian ascetic life, even after Evagrius's death.

Looking Back at Egypt

I must confess to the reader: All of the sources I have just used to reconstruct the tradition of an angelic guide common among a certain strain of ascetics in Egypt have not typically been used as the starting point for historical research on Christian asceticism in Egypt. There is an easy explanation: most of the sources I cited in the previous section survive in ancient languages other than Greek, which takes pride of place among historians of ancient Christianity. As I mentioned, Antony's letters are best preserved in Arabic and Georgian; Ammonas's letters have a Greek form, but it is clear that the extant Syriac version is closest to the original; and Evagrius's works are notoriously scattered, with *Talking Back*, my main source for the daily expectations of monks, surviving in Syriac, Armenian, with some fragments in Sogdian. These are not simply accidents of time. Instead, a controversy that engaged much of the Egyptian ascetic world in the late fourth and early fifth centuries pruned the sources that survive to this day. The Origenist controversy, as this conflagration is known, led to the destruction of many authors' writings, including works of Alexandrian writers like Origen and Didymus, as well as those who lived outside Alexandria, like Antony, Ammonas, and Evagrius.[107] In the case of some of these figures, like Antony, alternate narratives of their lives became popular, dominating later historical reconstructions, while in the case of others, like Didymus or Evagrius, the shunning had a chilling effect—their works survived in fragments, in translation, in highly edited versions, under the name of other authors, or sometimes not at all. The practical effect of the Origenist conflict was to severely restrict the literature available from those who were the object of controversy, including many of the earliest Christian ascetics active in Egypt.

Ironically, the same controversy that fragmented these texts also consolidated one ideal representation of Egypt because it seems to have inspired the collection of reports and sayings meant to typify a particular interpretation of Egyptian ascetic life.[108] These texts, produced outside of Egypt, fall into two categories. First are the tourist accounts: several writers claim to have traveled to Egypt, presenting themselves as apprentices in order to gain access to ascetics and credibility with their readers. The resulting works, like the *History of the Monks in Egypt* or the *Lausiac History*, read like notes from a visit to the Egyptian desert.[109] Second are the multiple collections of the *Sayings of the Fathers*: editors, likely from Palestine, attempted to package and export the essence of Egyptian asceticism by collecting vignettes about individual monks. Over the course of the fifth and sixth centuries, different versions of the *Sayings* were created, organized according to various rubrics, and translated into many ancient languages. Much of what has traditionally been known about asceticism in Egypt has followed the narrative of these kinds of sources, which historians have often trusted as accurate and uninflected. Their pared-down, reportage style makes the ascetics they feature seem directly accessible to readers, but that is a rhetorical effect. We now know and can at times trace some of the ways these collections have been edited, their stories carefully chosen or changed to fit a particular conception of the structure and goals of ascetic life. We need always remember that these, like any other sources, speak to us through a veil.

In some collections, that veil is tinted positively toward ascetics like Antony, Ammonas, and Evagrius, so we should not be surprised to see reflected in them the traditions developed by these men. The *Lausiac History* written by Palladius, for example, had a positive view of Evagrius and others like him, and not surprisingly contains the most extensive ancient description of Evagrius's career. Palladius included stories and details about Evagrius along with Macarius the Egyptian, Macarius of Alexandria, and Paul the Simple that other, later epitomators of Egyptian asceticism found troubling. His accounts of these teachers' lives also give us a glimpse into their teachings. As he created his *History*, Palladius assumed that gaining a divine guide was a natural, if rare, part of ascetic life. For example, he related that one woman who had been successful in her program was abandoned by her assistant as the result of a specific disposition and an even more specific sin:

> Finally, she fell completely abandoned because of her overweening pride. She opened her door and received the man who had ministered to her, and she committed sin with him, because she had practiced asceticism for the sake of human applause rather than for religious purposes and out of the love of God. Vainglory and evil intentions are the cause of that. For as her thoughts were occupied in running down others, the guardian of her chastity [prudence] was absent.[110]

From the cause—vainglory and pleasure—to the result—abandonment—this vignette was an object lesson in how to keep a companion and, more important, how to lose one. In its components, the lesson echoes the tradition of the angelic companion as it was taught by Evagrian ascetics. Elsewhere in the *Lausiac History*, an ascetic named Paphnutius delivers a sermon explaining all those who have been abandoned in this way. If a person has been "swollen with pride" and speaks highly of himself, attributing his wisdom to his own great talent and not, as he should, to God, then "God takes away the angel of providence from him." As the angel goes away, the devil approaches, knowing that the "witness of his prudence has gone."[111] Though some of the words used in the *Lausiac History* to refer to the guide are different from what remains from the letters of Antony, Ammonas, and Macarius, readers will see the pattern of their teaching in Palladius's work: pride and vainglory lead to abandonment, which exposes the ascetic to demonic attack.

Interestingly enough, the *Sayings of the Fathers*, which were edited to obscure certain parts of the Evagrian ascetic lineage, nevertheless contain many reports conforming to that same pattern. For instance, one unnamed ascetic who was being "disturbed by fornication" went to a more experienced monk to share his troubles. The elder saw the problem at once.

> God showed him about the brother, and he saw him sitting, with the spirit of fornication nearby, chatting him up; there was also an angel present, who had been sent to him as help, and he was irritated at the brother, since he no longer cast himself upon God, but took pleasure in thoughts, giving over his mind to impulse.[112]

The ascetic had had a guide, but when he lost vigilance over his thoughts, he irritated the angel sent to help him and it departed. As a result, the spirit of fornication troubled him—something impossible without the tacit negligence of his companion angel. Other companion angels in the sayings collections follow a more traditional model, simply and directly warning their charges what to avoid. One angel sent "to help" another monk warns him not to go and live in the city.[113] Angels intervene when a monk is about to judge another brother or when a monk is anxious about another brother's sin of hoarding gold.[114] I call this "more traditional" because these angels acted for ascetics in ways that echo Socrates's guide. They were coaches who directed their athletes away from what might be harmful to their progress. What is more, they evaluated the worth of their athletes through constant surveillance, judging whether they were performing to their potential. Here is the advice of one ascetic to another who was concerned about the thoughts that come to him in his bed.

> In bed, in effect, impressions of women accompany the monk, but the angels persevere near him. And, it is precisely to keep guard over him that they are assigned. Also when your heart tells you during the night or during the day "Stand and pray!" know that this is the angel that keeps himself near to you, that it is he himself who speaks to you. And when you get up, he stays near you and prays with you and chases away from you the demons who grind their teeth against you. If, on the other hand, you turn a deaf ear and get up late, at that point it is his time to go away from you and you will then fall into the hands of your enemies.[115]

The call to vigilance could not be more clear: monks must pay close attention to the perils of the night. They had assistance in the form of the angels assigned to protect them, but those angels could depart if the monk were not sufficiently dedicated to his own advancement.

Among the many stories in the *Sayings of the Fathers* that correspond to the tradition of the angelic helper, several are specifically about Antony himself. Antony had the help of an angel who made his way easy. At times, the angel literally showed Antony what he must do: he appeared as a mirror image of Antony, teaching him how to practice as an ascetic.[116] At other times, it was simply a voice that directed Antony, aiding him at moments of frustration. In one story, when Antony realized the full extent of the trials and tricks that demons lay out for ascetics, he despaired, asking "What is able to overcome such things?" A voice came to him to give the answer: "humility."[117] Antony's helper was familiar to other ascetics, who understood that he had a special relationship with something divine, which came to him in even in the reading of Scripture.

> The brothers came to Antony and said a passage from Leviticus. Antony went into the desert, and Ammonas secretly followed him, knowing his usual way of doing things. At a distance, Antony stood praying and cried in a great voice, "God, send Moses and teach me this passage." Then a voice came to him, speaking with him. Ammonas said that he heard the voice speaking with Antony, but he could not grasp the power of the conversation.[118]

Thus we have come full circle: Antony claims a voice that no others can hear or follow, just as Socrates had done with his guide so long ago. In the *Sayings* and their portrait of ascetic life in Egypt, a faint trace of the traditions of the philosophical circles of Alexandria and the earliest Christian monastic documents is open to view.

The tradition of the angelic guide, gotten by the demonstration of moral prowess and kept by success at ascetic struggle, may sound to readers like a distant cousin to the more famous late ancient Christian doctrine of the guardian angel, given to all Christians, and indeed, it is. Writers like Eusebius of Caesarea and Basil of Caesarea spoke of all Christians receiving an angel, assigned to protect them: in their estimation, however, the angel was a permanent companion; it did not judge or leave them.[119] While discussions of this style of guardian angel dominated the conversations among those outside the ascetic world, the tradition of the divine guide, understood as an angel, also exerted its influence. As we will see in the next chapter, two extremely influential pieces of literature produced by those enacting cultural contestation were inflected by the more hierarchical, merit-based, tradition of the angelic guide.

4

Crossing Over

THE COMPANION ANGEL TRADITION IN EXEMPLARY LIVES

THE CHRISTIANS WHO attempted to cultivate a particular life of study and bodily discipline in Egypt created a distinct culture, with traditions and expectations different from those held by urban Christians. In the last chapter, we saw how the line of Christian teachers that included Antony, Ammonas, Macarius, and eventually Evagrius developed a unique understanding of the position of the Christian who sought perfection by joining an ascetic circle. Much like the philosophical circles on which they were modeled, ascetic circles emphasized the total dedication they required of members. In Antony's and Ammonas's letters, such dedication was described as the equivalent of a biblical sacrifice—a valuable offering that pleased God and inspired him to work on behalf of the person who made the sacrifice. According to these teachers, the assistance God gave came in the form of a companion angel, whose nature was similar to the intellectual nature residing in all humanity. Its similarity to the human intellect inspired sympathy for those who were cultivating the strength of their intellect, so the angel protected the successful ascetic from distraction and even from attack by demons. As this chain of causality reveals, the idea of the companion angel was an intimate part of an entire system of Christian ascetic progress; it was linked to assumptions about the nature and origin of humanity, humanity's ultimate purpose, and the specific path to salvation and unity with God that the ascetic Christian life offered.

Knowledge of the companion angel tradition and the complex of teachings that undergirded it should inform our interpretation of late ancient

Christian literature. This is certainly the case with other letters and treatises produced by ascetics themselves. In the last chapter, I argued that we should use this tradition to understand those collections of materials meant to represent Egyptian ascetic life to others—the tourist catalogues like the *History of the Monks in Egypt* and the *Lausiac History*, and the redacted collections known as the *Sayings of the Fathers*. We should also seek out the contours of the companion angel tradition, as well as the ascetic program of development and cultivation of which it was a central part, in other late ancient Christian literature, not just those texts immediately associated with the lineage of Antony, Ammonas, and Evagrius. Early Christian networks of communication were extensive, allowing the propagation of ideas at speeds and over distances we, as people reliant on electronic communication, might not imagine possible in a pre-modern setting. The companion angel tradition is both complicated (it has multiple stages) and eccentric (its assumptions are quite different from the mainstream of Christian thought). These two qualities make its influence easy to discern when it appears, even in literature where we least expect to encounter it.

Perhaps a natural place to begin looking is the other main source of information about Antony that survives from late antiquity, beyond his letters: the *Life of Antony*, written by Athanasius. Completed in the late 350s CE just a few years after Antony's death, the *Life* became the most popular text in Christian late antiquity. With its popularity, it carried Athanasius's particular message about the ideal Christian, the beliefs about the divine that Christians should espouse, and the ideal structure of a Christian community.[1] To create the *Life of Antony*, Athanasius depended both on reports from ascetics who had contact with Antony and on written sources. Though Athanasius's efforts at editing these sources to support his proposals for Christian culture have made it difficult to see, at least one of the sources he used conformed to the version of Christian practice presented in Antony's letters. The first part of this chapter will show that the tradition of the companion angel underlies several important passages in the *Life of Antony*, beginning with the climactic scene in which Antony has a vision that protects him from demonic attack and promises to make him famous, and including many other events and lessons from Antony's career.

The second part of the chapter will examine another piece of late ancient literature that resonates with the companion angel tradition, one that, to this point, has been assumed to be unrelated to Egyptian ascetic traditions: Gregory of Nyssa's *Life of Moses*. Written in the 390s

CE, this text presents the events in the life of the biblical character of Moses—his birth in Egypt, his experiences as a slave there, his leading the Hebrews out of Egypt, the destruction of the pursuing Egyptian army and Pharaoh—all as an extended metaphor for the progress of the Christian. Its most lasting contribution has been its argument that a Christian's desire to know God is never entirely fulfilled; as perfect as humanity may wish to become, the goal of virtue, and with it knowledge of God, is ever receding, staying just out of the Christian's reach. As a whole, it has been understood as the product of Gregory's late-career engagement with a general Christian quest for knowledge of God. Yet there is a far more specific late ancient context in which to understand this work: the *Life of Moses*, like the *Life of Antony*, coheres to the expectations of the companion angel tradition as voiced by Antony and the line of Christian teachers who followed him.

The authors of the *Life of Antony* and the *Life of Moses* were not, themselves, a part of the teaching lineage that developed from Antony's small community. Instead, they operated on a much larger stage. Both were at one point in their careers named bishop, but more important, both were prolific writers whose articulation of Christian ideas and cultural forms dominated conversations among Christians, during their lifetimes and beyond. Athanasius's specific version of the meaning of the Incarnation determined subsequent Christian conversations about Christ; Gregory's understanding of the Holy Spirit and the human capacity to know the divine similarly inflected later conversations on the Trinity. Their extensive influence on others was no accident. Men like Gregory and Athanasius sought to persuade, and their writings were designed to argue and to convince. Presenting models like Antony and Moses was a different way of arguing for one style of Christian practice and disparaging others, their biographies rendering an ideal Christian life in line with the thoughts of their authors. The *Life of Antony* and the *Life of Moses* were products of the argumentative and dominant public culture of the Christian fourth century, that which I have called "contestation," and yet they also reflect the influence of traditions, often overlooked, which were developed in the esoteric study circles populated by ascetic Christians in Egypt. More specifically, the ideas about companion angels taught by Antony, Ammonas, and Evagrius are present in these *Lives*. Thus, the most enduring products of Christian writers engaged in contestation actually represent the traces of a long conversation between these men and those ascetic Christians who focused on cultivation.

The Helper in the Life of Antony

The *Life of Antony* was the most successful piece of Christian literature in late antiquity. Written shortly after Antony's demise in 356 CE, it was read by so many so quickly after its publication that it determined the way most Christians imagined the ascetic movement in Egypt. Two important urban interpreters of asceticism, Gregory of Nazianzus and John Chrysostom, cited it as an authoritative source about Egypt before the year 400 CE. It was swiftly translated from Greek into several different languages; of those translations the Syriac and Coptic versions were particularly influential.[2] For example, the sixth-century Coptic writer John of Shmun argued that Coptic literature was the best Christian literature by contending that all other Christian writers eventually depended upon Antony as a model.[3] His claim was a stretch, but the fact that John found it plausible, and expected his readers to find it plausible, speaks volumes about the reach of Antony's shadow over Coptic Christian culture. In Latin, not one but two translations were made and were in wide circulation within about fifteen years of Antony's death. One of those Latin versions found its way north to Trier, where it inspired the piety of two adolescent Christians who, in turn, enflamed the zeal of a young North African visitor to Milan—namely, Augustine, the man later famous for his account of the conversion Antony's example had incited.[4] Ambrose, the bishop of Milan who guided Augustine during this transition, cited Antony's life as the model of practice for Christians to adopt.[5] Last, Jerome, not a person particularly known for his accession to the ideas of others, went so far as to try his hand at making a Christian celebrity like Antony by writing his *Life of Paul* in loose imitation of Athanasius's text, finding "it necessary to co-opt and modify the vision set forth in the *Life of Antony*, rather than supplant it."[6] All of this demonstrates the *Life of Antony*'s popularity within Christian literary culture and its power as a portrait of Egyptian monasticism.[7]

The events in Antony's life make a compelling story all on their own, but much of the dominance of the *Life of Antony* as a piece of literature can be traced to the skill of its author, Athanasius, the man who was bishop of Alexandria during parts of the fourth century. The *Life* he created had a particular literary quality, for it presented the details of Antony's career in a form that was relatively new to Christian literature—the documentary biography. Adopting tropes and structure from traditional biographies of philosophers like Pythagoras, Athanasius wove Antony's actions into a narrative that advocated a certain exemplary style of life for other Christians, even as it showcased Antony's unique effort.[8] By balancing Antony's surpassing excellence against the seductive suggestion that all Christians could imitate him, Athanasius harnessed the force of Antony's example to present his own political vision of Christianity. The *Life of Antony* promoted allegiance to bishops and to Athanasius specifically, disparaged Arius and the academic system of Christianity that produced him, and promulgated the idea that Antony was a solitary ascetic, dissociated from others—all by the skillful deployment of Antony's speeches and life events within the wider form of an extraordinary biography.[9] Put more shortly, Athanasius's *Life of Antony* signifies as much about Athanasius as it does about Antony. There is a certain irony in the fact that Athanasius, adopting a philosophical genre, turned the Antony we saw in his own letters—a highly literate philosopher and teacher of Scripture, one who cultivated a dedicated community of students—into an illiterate monk who ventriloquized the needs of his bishop between sessions of advice to unknown crowds of visitors.

We know that Athanasius did not compose the *Life of Antony* from scratch but rather shaped previous traditions to meet those needs. The preface to the work makes clear that Athanasius collected evidence about Antony that was already in circulation. There, Athanasius apologized to the person who solicited him to write the *Life of Antony* because the text was not as complete as it could have been. Though Athanasius had tried to document as much as possible about Antony, he admitted he was unable to collect reports from all those he wished to interview. His apology is a boon to us, because it demonstrates that Athanasius was working with existing stories about Antony. It was his hope, he said, that by "learning more" from those other sources that presented Antony's life in various lights, he might be able to send "something fuller," but the sailing season, and with it, the season for sending letters, was ending, so Athanasius asked the solicitor to be content with the fact that he was forced to complete the *Life of Antony* only with what he had to hand.[10]

Some of the things he had to hand must have been written sources. As several scholars have observed, the *Life of Antony* is stitched together in a way that shows the seams of documents that were used in its creation. One example comes from an early part of the *Life*. In its depiction of Antony's youth, the text at times refers to Antony going to "church" (ἡ ἐκκλησία), Athanasius's usual way of speaking of an assembly of Christians, while at others it speaks of him going to "the Lord's house" (τὸ κυριακόν), a locution Athanasius himself never used in any other writing.[11] Scholars argue, therefore, that Athanasius had adopted a written narrative that happened to call a Christian assembly "the Lord's house," then amended it by interspersing his own phrases to fill out the story—phrases that included his more customary way of speaking about an assembly, namely, as a "church." A second example of Athanasius's editorial intervention is visible in *Life of Antony* 7, where the text summarizes the lessons to be learned from Antony's first encounters with multiple forms of demons.

> This was the first contest Antony had against the devil—or, rather, this was in Antony the success of the Savior, who *condemned sin in the flesh, so that the justice of the law would be fulfilled in us, the ones who do not walk according to the flesh but according to the spirit*—but Antony was not then careless or presumptive, even though the devil lay at his feet. . . .[12]

The section bounded by dashes reads like an interjection, one that directly contradicts its surroundings by suggesting that "the Savior" and not Antony was responsible for Antony's victories. After all, if Antony were not the triumphant architect of his victory over the devil, why would the story reassure us that he had not become "careless or presumptive" as a result of that victory?[13] Still other examples pointing to Athanasius's work as an editor can be drawn from Antony's extended speeches in the *Life* on the topic of demonology, in which slightly different trains of thought are spliced together with rather clumsy transitions—signs of those speeches having been compiled.[14] Additions and adjustments like these abound in the *Life of Antony*, providing ample indication that Athanasius consulted and edited written sources as he created his version of the career of Antony.

The *Life of Antony* presents the mechanics of asceticism—what constitutes the human being and how ascetic practices change him—in a way that hints at still other, previously unidentified sources Athanasius may have adopted. Early in the *Life of Antony*, when a group of monks asks Antony for instruction about progress in virtue, he gives a speech explaining how human beings came to be and detailing their eventual return to their original state. "The beginning of virtue," he says, "takes place when the intellectual part of the soul [τῆς . . . ψυχῆς τὸ νοερόν] remains according to its nature," the state "in which it was created."[15] This intellectual part was made beautiful and straight, but often it "bends and falls away from how it was made," a situation that Antony identifies with "wickedness of the soul," a state directly opposite the state of virtue.[16] Such ideas accord with earlier Christian academic accounts of human existence. For example, the "intellectual part of the soul" was theorized by Clement of Alexandria, a third-century teacher and philosopher whose presuppositions about human existence influenced later teachers like Origen and, with him, early ascetics outside Alexandria.[17] Even the letters of Antony, for instance, assume a similar origin of the human race, and indeed, a similar origin of all beings possessing an intellect—angels and demons among them. All these intellectual beings at one point diverted away from God and will eventually return to God.[18]

In addition to these general assumptions, the practical advice Antony gives in the *Life of Antony* about how monks can return to that original unity with God also accords with what appears in Antony's letters. In the *Life,* Antony suggests that bodily practices, like restricting food or sleep, can support the original nature of the intellectual part of the soul, something Antony's character considers in shame whenever he entertains the idea of relieving hunger, fatigue, or his "other bodily needs."[19] Attention to one's thoughts was also necessary. In another speech made just before his death, Antony summarized the secrets of the ascetic life, telling the gathered monks to "guard the soul from filthy thoughts and have zeal toward the holy ones," Antony's way, in some parts of the *Life*, of referring to angels.[20] It was the same message he had delivered "habitually" to all who visited him—to "have faith in the Lord and his love and to guard themselves from filthy thoughts and fleshly pleasures."[21] Doing so preserved the intellectual part of the soul as it was created by God and given to humanity, "entrusted to us like a deposit," worth all the attention one could muster.[22]

Maintaining such attention required an effort out of proportion to normal life, and for that reason, *Life of Antony* sounds the same unyielding tone again and again: the core of asceticism is dedication of purpose. First, the preface of the *Life of Antony* draws attention to Antony's expression of purpose (πρόθεσιν) in his asceticism and hoped that the reader would imitate Antony in order to develop and to strengthen his own purpose.[23] The character Antony himself emphasized the need for singleness of purpose, encouraging monks with a distinctive refrain: "do not lose heart in the practice of asceticism."[24] Antony spoke of the requisite dedication in quite specific terms: its fruit is simply "labor" (πόνος). The entire point of practice was to accustom the body to "labors" and to keep one's strength despite ongoing labor.[25] These elements coincide so neatly with the emphasis on struggle and dedication in the letters of the ascetic teachers that we should wonder whether any part of the *Life of Antony* reflects the program these teachers developed.

The answer is yes. Though it has been subordinated to the narrative Athanasius wished to establish about Antony, the companion angel tradition we examined in the previous chapter persists in the text of the *Life of Antony*. Portions of Antony's career, his actions, and his words trace the stages that Antony's letters set out for ascetics to go through in their acquisition and retention of a companion angel. As I just explained, Antony's character in the *Life* encourages monks to demonstrate unfearing commitment to their program. In their letters, Antony and Ammonas his successor encouraged full commitment to the program of asceticism they taught. In addition, they also warned that the moment when an ascetic first began to show real resolve in practice was a moment of danger, because the display of his resolution would draw the demons to attack. In the narrative of the *Life of Antony*, Antony himself experiences precisely this kind of attack. Just when he dedicated himself to excelling in virtue,

> The devil, the jealous hater of good, could not stand to see such purpose [πρόθεσιν] in one so young, and started to do to him those things which he had the habit of doing. First he tried to lead him away from asceticism, casting [ὑποβάλλων] the memory of his property, his care for his sister, the relationships of family, love of silver, love of glory, the diverse pleasure of food and the other recreations of life, and, finally, the harsh nature of virtue—how great its labor! He pointed out both the weakness of the body and the length of time it would take. In sum, he raised in Antony's awareness a dustcloud of thoughts, wishing to sever him from his upright resolution.[26]

While Antony was attempting to make progress in his asceticism, the devil was at the same time attempting to dissuade him from it; his technique consisted of "casting" thoughts of other pleasures and the difficulties of ascetic life in his mind. Later, when he spoke to other monks, Antony gave lessons based on this experience to explain this tendency of the devil. He warned that when demons "see Christians, but especially monks, loving labor and making progress, first they set upon them and tempt them, putting stumbling blocks in their way—these stumbling blocks are filthy thoughts [οἱ ῥυπαροὶ λογισμοί]."[27] The wise monk will know the correct response to such attacks, which is to ignore them. Antony told ascetics they should pay no attention to the thoughts demons cast, treating demons "as if they were strangers to us" [ὡς ἀλλοτρίων ὄντων ἡμῶν].[28] According to the *Life of Antony*, having demons attack new and zealous ascetics was a predictable part of ascetic life; those attacks could easily be deflected if ascetics are properly prepared.

As we know, ascetics who preserved their resolve under attack could expect help. This was a central teaching of the ascetics in Antony's lineage—those who showed great struggle would likely have an angel to join them and help them—and it is, in fact, a central part of Antony's story in Athanasius's *Life of Antony*. As Athanasius told it, when Antony showed purpose, the devil attacked him, and continued to attack him, in various forms. First casting thoughts, then appearing as various sexual partners, then as menacing animals, demons pulled out every stop to thwart Antony's plan for ascesis. At a dramatic moment in the *Life of Antony*, when a zooful of terrifying demons in the form of animals appeared to "break down the four walls" of his house, seeking to harm Antony, and he was "being flogged and tortured by them, feeling the most terrible bodily labor," and "groaning on account of that bodily labor," Antony still managed to mock the devil while he was lying breathless on the floor. The demons "gnash their teeth" against him, then, all at once, his pains ceased.

> Looking up, he saw the roof as if it were being opened and a certain ray of light coming down upon him. And the demons immediately disappeared, the bodily pain immediately ceased, and his house was again set right. Antony, sensing the support, and breathing again now that his pains were lessened, questioned the vision that had manifested, saying "Where were you? Why didn't you appear at the beginning, to put a stop to my grief?" And a voice came to him: "Antony, I was here, but I waited to watch your struggle. Since you held out and were not bested, I will be to you always a helper, and I will make your name known everywhere." Having heard this, he got up to pray. And he felt so much better that he felt even stronger in his body than he had before.[29]

Though Antony was at the point of death, scarcely able to breathe or even rise off the floor, the appearance of this "ray of light" chased away the demonic attackers, relieved Antony's pain, and even fixed the seemingly broken walls of his house. A voice came to him (φωνὴ γέγονε πρὸς αὐτόν) to announce its intention to be a "helper" to Antony for the rest of his life.

Many readers of the *Life of Antony* have attempted to pin down the identity of this "ray of light" that comes and has such a bold effect on the demons who had been terrorizing Antony, as well as the identity of the speaker who promises to make Antony famous. Most of them have discovered in this scene a vision of the Lord, or of God. David Brakke hints at the agent of Antony's vision, for as he explains, the point of the scene is to show that Antony "receives an extraordinary promise from God: 'Antony, I was here....'"[30] Another interpreter of the scene, Brian Brennan, leaves the identity of the vision and the voice unresolved, but does venture a hypothesis: "When, after repeated demonic attacks, Antony remains firm in his faith, God rewards him with a vision."[31] Still a third interpreter, Tim Vivian, the most recent English translator of the *Life*, suggests that the help Antony received in this scene should be attributed to the Word, that is, to Christ.[32] In part, readers are likely to attribute the cause of Antony's vision to God or to "the Lord" because that is what the text itself encourages. The *Life of Antony* interrupts the scene of Antony's torture by the demons in his little house to preface the appearance of this ray of light, saying that "The Lord did not forget Antony's struggle during that time, but brought him help."[33] From there on, it is plausible for a reader to assume that the Lord does the speaking and is going to be Antony's helper. Close examination of the passage, however, reveals the ambiguity of the line: rather than say in particular that the Lord became a helper for Antony, or that the vision Antony saw was, indeed, the Lord, the Greek is more roundabout: εἰς ἀντίληψιν αὐτῷ γέγονεν, perhaps colloquially best translated as "the Lord came to his aid." In Athanasius's telling of this scene in *Life of Antony*, there is exegetical direction embedded within the text itself, and modern readers have followed that direction, however gently it is stated.

Like modern readers, ancient readers followed Athanasius's exegetical direction; the ancient translations that survive of the *Life of Antony* tend to identify the vision as God or the Lord as well. While most scholars agree that the Greek life written by Athanasius is the earliest version of the text, the relationships between it and the later versions that survive in other ancient languages are complex and disputed.[34] There are multiple places where the ancient translations of the *Life of Antony* do not match, but in the majority of the scene that recounts Antony's vision, the two most important ancient translations, those in Coptic and Syriac, agree with the Greek version. In particular, they, like the Greek version, consider the Lord to be the agent in Antony's vision. That is to say, the most significant ancient versions of *Life of Antony* all bear witness to a strong interpretative impulse to consider both the ray of light Antony sees and the voice he hears as synonymous with the Lord. And yet, the Coptic and Syriac versions accomplish this exegetical direction in ways that are distinct from the Greek version. As for the Coptic, the relevant portion of the story in that version proceeds directly from the demons gnashing their teeth at Antony to the moment when Antony sees the roof opening.[35] An equivalent line in Athanasius's version that identifies this help as coming from the Lord—εἰς ἀντίληψιν αὐτῷ γέγονεν—is entirely missing from this Coptic version. This does not mean the Coptic version did not attribute the vision to the Lord, just that it does so at a different place in the narrative: when the attacks of the demons upon Antony come to an end, this text tells us that Antony "sensed that the Lord saved him." As for the Syriac, it follows the Greek version in its opening, its first sentence being an approximation of the Greek "the Lord came to his aid"; the passage specifies the source of Antony's assistance, twice naming "our Lord" as the help and then having Antony pray to "God who had visited him."[36] The Syriac version accomplishes the same identification of the Lord with Antony's vision but in a way that supplements what the Greek version does.

It is clear that all three of the versions aim at identifying the Lord as the source of the vision—and indeed, there is a fourth extant version, in Greek, as reported by Symeon the New Theologian (b. 949 CE), in which Antony asks the vision directly, "Lord, where were you?"[37] Though all these translations share an exegetical impulse, the variety of ways by which they direct the reading of the scene suggests that the least redacted version of the tradition stood without the identification of the "help" that Antony had gotten as the Lord or God. That is to say, while these texts agree in substance, in their details they disagree. In that disagreement we can see that there is something unstable and perhaps problematic in the text of these scenes. Consequently, it is possible and even probable that this portion of Athanasius's version of the *Life of Antony* included at least one editorial gloss. It was an important one, for it directed readers to consider Antony visited by the Lord, to the exclusion of other possibilities, thus shifting the meaning of the scene for readers both ancient and modern.

We have another context in which to parse the scene, namely, the tradition of the companion angel. It is clear that expectations like those detailed in the letters from Antony underlie the way he, as a character, battles demons and receives a vision in the *Life of Antony*.[38] To summarize the train of Athanasius's narrative: Antony had demonstrated purpose and immediately demons set upon him. When he fought back and managed to withstand the demonic attacks, the vision appeared, the demons were quickly chased away, and Antony regained his strength. When he asks the vision what took so long, the voice tells him that it needed to see the athlete's efforts before revealing itself. It promises that, because of the virtue Antony showed, it will become Antony's "helper," making him famous. All of these stages evoke the assistance given by the angelic guide or "holy power" detailed in the letters of the ascetic teachers who followed Antony: granted in return for demonstrated skill, the power chases away demons and allows the easy practice of an ascetic life. What is more, Antony's own letters twice identify the angel that protects a monk as a "helper," the same word that the *Life of Antony* has the vision speak: "I was here, but now... I will be a helper for always." For these reasons, the scene that *Life of Antony* has presented as the appearance of the Lord to Antony should be recognized as a redacted version of a much earlier tradition of the companion angel: Antony showed his virtue, and God noticed and sent him a helper, one that waited to see Antony's prowess in his contest with the demons before revealing itself.

Additional passages in the *Life of Antony* resonate with the expectations of teachers in Antony's lineage, confirming the influence of the companion angel tradition on the materials Athanasius used to create the text. During the course of the *Life of Antony*, the helper garnered at Antony's triumph against the demons remains with him, aiding and protecting him throughout his career. As examples, consider the situations in which Antony fended off temptations. Shortly after the vision in which his helper arrived, Antony was tested by the devil, who put an unattended piece of silver in the road where Antony was traveling. The idea was to see whether Antony could be affected by greed. When Antony refused to take the silver, it vanished, revealing itself to have been a trick. Next, a piece of gold appeared, and the text of the *Life of Antony* comments, "Whether this was the enemy showing the gold to him, or whether it was some more excellent power, training the athlete and instead showing the devil that Antony truly gave no thought to money—he did not say and we do not know."[39] The narrator does not say which of these options was true, but his raising the prospect of an intervening "power" that trains Antony like a coach is a detail that tells. After Antony had passed the first test by refusing the silver, his companion angel may have conjured up the second test in order to show off the prowess of his athlete, just as it had promised to do when it first joined Antony.

This was not the only appearance the companion angel made in Antony's career. In the *Life of Antony*, the ascetic enjoyed the assistance of a guide at multiple points during his extraordinary life, even until his last days. In one passage, as Antony tired of being around people, he made plans to travel farther away from inhabited places, toward an area known for its communities of monks. Yet a "voice from above" like that from his vision interrupted his travel and asked, "Antony, where are you traveling, and why?" Antony, we learn from the text, was not surprised by the voice because "it was customary for him frequently to be hailed in this way."[40] The voice redirected him elsewhere, to the famous "inner mountain," where Antony could enjoy peace and quiet. When Antony complained that he did not know how to get there, a group of passing travelers accepted him into their party "as if they had been ordered by providence."[41] Two other passages from the *Life* show "providence" revealing things to Antony in the way of a divine guide—in one case, providence gave Antony a vision that was then explained by a "voice from above," while in another case, Antony learned the time of his death from providence.[42] Though such vignettes do not dominate the narrative of the *Life of Antony*, their presence is significant, for they reveal the connections between the *Life* and traditions preserved by other ancient literature in which outstanding ascetics are guided by voices, helpers, and providence, namely, the letters of ascetic teachers like Antony and Evagrius, as well as those collections of stories that represent their traditions.

Knowing the ascetic traditions contained in the materials used to compile the *Life of Antony* renders other previously indistinct scenes from the *Life* quite clear. The importance of discernment, that is, of being able to tell a vision of an angel from a vision of a demon, was consistently at the top of the list of ascetic teachings; it was the most useful of skills, because when all other tactics failed, demons could attack ascetics by appearing to be the very angels that were come to help them. As much is clear from the advice Evagrius later shared about a trick demons used: "at times the demons split their ranks, and if you appear to be seeking assistance (against some), the others will gain entrance in the form of angels, driving out the first ones, in order to have you deceived by them into thinking that they are really angels."[43] Evagrius's advice stands in continuity with the traditions about Antony and his experiences. For example, at one point in the *Life of Antony*, Antony tells the story of a demon who had approached him using the very trick. "Once," Antony said, "a very elevated demon appeared in an illusion and dared to say, 'I am the power of God' and 'I am providence—how do you wish me to indulge you?'"[44] This demon was not presenting itself as just any angel, but as Antony's own companion angel—a "power," a "providence" that could provide whatever he needed. It is possible that Evagrius himself was aware of this specific story about Antony. He had certainly read the *Life of Antony* and had taken it to heart.[45] Significantly, his playbook against the demons offers Isaiah 10.16 as the best response to a very similar scenario, namely, "against the demon that advised us, saying 'I will make you illustrious everywhere before all people,' and pretended that it would help us."[46] Here, an educated and well-practiced reader of the *Life of Antony* and a student of Antony's students describes the way a demon can infiltrate an ascetic's world and thoughts by pretending to be an angel. This particular demon Evagrius countered was not just any angel, but an angel that promised to make the ascetic famous among all people—an echo of the promise Antony's vision made him when it appeared to him and stopped the demonic attacks against him.

These small snippets of traditions about Antony and the companion angel made it through the editing process that created the *Life of Antony*, but there were most certainly traditions or parts of sources that did not. Still other traditions are visible in the *Life*, even if they lie under significant editorial work. We know from Athanasius's intervention in the scene of Antony's vision and other parts of the *Life* that Athanasius tended to attribute actions and events in the stories he used to the Lord rather than to Antony, to other ascetics, or to angels. His tendency could shift the lesson of a particular passage. For instance, comments distributed throughout the *Life of Antony* attest the importance of a monk's subjective feeling in the process of discernment. When a monk wishes to discern what sort of being visits him, if he finds himself reassured and any initial fear changes into joy, then he can be certain he is experiencing a visit of the "holy ones," namely, angels.[47] Fear, dread, and anxiety mark the visits of demons, who are, after all, not kin to humanity in the way angels are; these feelings, when they persist, are clear indicators of demonic presence.[48] In *Life of Antony* 35, however, the role of the monk's subjective feeling in discernment was sublimated beneath Athanasius's wider impulse to associate any divine action with the Lord. Notice how he adjusted the source of the joy in the following advice.

> A vision of the holy ones is not troubling. For "he does not argue, nor cry out, and no one hears their voice" (Mt 12.19). Quietly and gently it appears, so that joy, happiness, and courage occur for the soul. *For with them is the Lord, who is our joy, the power of God the father.* The thoughts of the soul remain untroubled and unagitated,

such that, as it is illuminated, the soul can contemplate those appearing through it.[49]

Elsewhere in the tradition, we know that joy and calm accompany the presence of an angel; here, the tradition is still evident, despite the intervention of a sentence about the Lord, which I have marked with italics.[50] Before and after that intervention, Antony offers advice about how to tell whether visions are angels. And, indeed, his advice assumes a peculiar technical process of the soul: its composure allows it to be illuminated, and in turn, to contemplate the beings that appear in the vision; that contemplation occurs "through the soul."[51] Over this complex ascetic lesson, Athanasius had layered the presence of the Lord—both explaining the subjective feelings Antony was describing and inserting the Lord into the process Antony was attempting to explain.

Passages like these remind us that the *Life of Antony* is a redacted text. At times, the needs of its compiler Athanasius have overridden the source material he used, such that its traditions have been obscured. At other times, the *Life* resonates distinctly with extant ascetic traditions that represent Antony's community and practice more directly. Reading the *Life* in conjunction with other material about and from Antony—that is to say, not treating the *Life* as the first source of information about Antony but rather as a secondary text that contains traces of other, earlier sources—allows us to see the ways it was influenced by previous material. Specifically, Athanasius's redaction contains the traces of a tradition of expecting the help of a companion angel, something first developed and handed down in the lineage of ascetics associated with Antony.

The Divine Power in the Life of Moses

Gregory of Nyssa lived during the second half of the fourth century, and to students of Christian history, he is most well known for his theological writing. In cooperation with his elder brother Basil of Casarea, he articulated striking positions regarding the Trinity, positions that became the foundation of Christian thinking about the relationships between Father, Son, and Holy Spirit. At the same time, though, Gregory wrote several works that addressed issues of practice: from his early treatise *On Virginity* to his much later *Homilies on the Song of Songs*, Gregory spent much of his career theorizing and explicating the worth of certain paths of Christian practice. Near the end of his career, Gregory created a text centered on a biblical character, Moses; his journey from being a slave in Egypt to being the leader of the Israelite exodus from Egypt Gregory presented as a meaningful pattern that a Christian might imitate in his practice. During the past century, scholars of Gregory's work estimated the *Life of Moses* to be central to Gregory's account of how one acquired knowledge of God. Jean Daniélou's 1944 epitome of Gregory's mysticism, *Platonisme et théologie mystique,* followed a three-part scheme laid out in the *Life of Moses* as the key for understanding how Gregory expected Christians to make progress in mysticism.[52] Christians who approached God first passed through light, then clouds, then darkness, just as Moses had on his approach to meeting God on Sinai. With Daniélou's presentation, the *Life of Moses* assumed importance as a text representing Christian mysticism, and its subsequent popularity and influence on later interpreters of Gregory is difficult to overstate.[53]

Discussions of Gregory's theories of mystical progress have very recently shifted away from taking the *Life of Moses* as the centerpiece of study, directing attention instead to the *Homilies on the Song of Songs*, which are loosely related to the *Life* and, some say, were written at the same time as the *Life*.[54] The causes behind this shift are diverse, but one of them prevails over the others: beyond its mystical three-part pattern of the approach to God and one section that at length specifies the qualities of darkness surrounding God, the *Life of Moses* does not entirely fit Daniélou's characterization of it. Indeed, it is an unwieldy text. If it is meant as a guide for how to advance in knowledge of God, the average Christian would likely find it bewildering. There is no step-by-step process for a Christian to enact, and any user would need a great deal of contextual information to do successfully what the *Life* asks him to do, which is to somehow imitate Moses. Because the explanations of events in Moses's life are vague, yet suggestive, they are attractive to those who seek mystery in seeking mysticism, but they are also obscure. Several portions of the *Life of Moses*, however, are entirely clear, at least when they are read in the context of the teachings of ascetics in Antony's lineage, especially the teachings of Evagrius. This section of the chapter demonstrates that the *Life of Moses*, like the *Life of Antony*, was informed by the tradition of the companion angel, as it was developed in the cultivative ascetic culture of Egypt.

Gregory's *Life of Moses* recounts the career of Moses not once, but twice. The text is divided into two sections, what it calls the "history" (ἱστορία) and the "contemplation" (θεωρία), which both narrate the events of Moses's life. The first telling, or "history," appears to be a straightforward paraphrase of the biblical account from Exodus, Leviticus, and Numbers. But no paraphrase is entirely straightforward; the exercise of retelling a story allows for interpretation and subtle renegotiation of the elements in the story. For this reason, paraphrases are especially revealing, in that the concerns of the paraphraser are visible in the changes, additions, or omissions he or she makes. In the case of the *Life of Moses*, its preface reveals that it was written for a particular purpose. Someone had approached Gregory to ask how to succeed in the "perfect life" (ὁ τέλειος βίος).[55] Gregory responded first by correcting the requester's expectations. He rejected the idea that he, or anyone, could define "perfection" or explain how one might live a life leading toward perfection. Instead, he suggested that the life "of virtue" was the thing to seek.[56] A Christian seeking virtue would understand that whatever "perfection" was, it would always recede away from the one who pursued it; thus constant effort and progress, rather than a final accomplishment, characterized the life of virtue. Such a life was "sweeter" and "more refreshing" than any "sweetness that tickles the sense of pleasure."[57] These words—virtue, sweetness—are generic words, applicable to the pursuit of righteousness, philosophy, or any other beneficial way of life, but as we have seen, they are also words that have a particular valence in Christian ascetic circles, especially those associated with Antony and the teachers who came after him.

That link, between the *Life of Moses*' retelling of the biblical story of Moses and the traditions nursed in Antony's lineage, is even easier to see when we consider that the first part of the *Life* is dominated by the intervention of a new character not represented in the biblical account: a "divine power" (ἡ θεία δύναμις). This power appears at key moments in Moses's journey. As Moses the infant floats on the Nile in his basket, that basket is "guided by a certain divine power" to come to rest at exactly the right spot on the riverbank to be discovered.[58] The cloud that manifests to lead Moses and the people through the wilderness does so "by a divine power."[59] When the Israelites arrive at the Red Sea, Moses "accomplished the most unbelievable thing, having been urged on by the divine power": he split the sea.[60] The same divine power allowed the manna collected before the Sabbath to remain fresh enough to be eaten two days later, saving the Israelites from having to collect food on the Sabbath itself.[61] When they arrive at Sinai, the divine power initiates both Moses and the people, then leads Moses through a higher initiation during which he envisions a tabernacle.[62] The divine power allows the laws Moses receives to be articulated, and it makes Aaron's rod bloom into flowers.[63] In all of these cases, the divine power works for the betterment and protection of Moses and the Israelites. Such hints render the climax of Moses's history quite interesting, for as he approaches the burning bush, the point at which he encounters the divine in the biblical account, he experiences a great illumination and is literally filled with a power, or "empowered" by the vision he sees (δυναμωθεὶς τῇ ὀφθείσῃ θεοφανείᾳ).[64] It is quickly afterward when Moses encounters Aaron, who has been himself divinely urged toward Moses, and later, Moses twice receives a "symbol" from above, which directs him, telling him what to do.[65] In all of these instances, Gregory depicts Moses as being led by a divine power, guided through his trials and difficulties, his way made smooth by the power's intervention.

Some scholars have explained this strange feature of the first part of the *Life of Moses* as a convention of the genre of biblical paraphrase. Often, when writers adapt biblical stories, they adjust the characterization of God in the story to square with their theological expectations of God. For example, the letter of Paul to the Galatians suggests that when Moses received the law on Sinai, it was "given by angels" and not by God, a typical way among early Christians to mitigate the material implications of God appearing to a human being like Moses. Michel Barnes has argued that Gregory was engaging in a similar kind of adaptation in his *Life of Moses*. His study on the use of the single term "power" (δύναμις) in Gregory's theology of the Trinity suggests that it was one of a range of options Gregory had for referring to God. Barnes's book focused on Gregory's explicitly theological writings, but in the short paragraph in which he discusses the *Life of Moses*, he contends that it is "Gregory's interest in God as cause" that led him to use the phrase "divine power" so frequently in that particular text. Gregory chose "divine power" when he wanted to indicate the agentive character of God, argues Barnes.[66] This explanation would be stronger if Gregory had avoided all use of the term "God" in causative or material situations in the *Life of Moses*. However, Gregory did not shy away from speaking of God in such terms, asking, for instance, that God guide his hand as he completed the text, or suggesting that God listen to the silent cries of Moses.[67] All of this is to say that Gregory did not elsewhere in the treatise avoid mentioning God as a causative entity who could interact with humanity, could guide the efforts of humanity, and could reveal his truth to humanity. Thus, we should not solely explain the phrase "divine power" as a traditional adaptation technique for rendering biblical paraphrase theologically correct.

A stronger explanation takes its form from the text of the *Life of Moses* itself. The second part of the text, the "contemplation" of Moses's career, offers a hint about how best to understand the divine power mentioned in the history: it is involved in the lives of those who undergo training in a system of practice that includes certain kinds of contemplation. There is, Gregory told his readers, a loud trumpet that Christians hear when they come near to the knowledge of God, much like the supernatural sights and sounds Moses experienced on his path to the top of Mount Sinai. Moses's experiences all signify something in the life of the Christian. As Gregory explained,

> When the person who has been purified and is keen of hearing in the heart hears this sound—I mean that which comes about regarding knowledge of the divine power (πρὸς τὴν τῆς θείας δυνάμεως γνῶσιν), accomplished through the contemplation of beings (ἐκ τῆς θεωρίας τῶν ὄντων)—that person is guided by it to the place where he can pass through, by understanding, to God.[68]

To Gregory, the process of making contact with God depended on "knowledge of the divine power." The method for gaining this knowledge is unique—it involves the "contemplation of beings," a phrase that calls to mind the primary task of the second stage of Evagrian progress in Christianity, the "gnostic" stage, in which knowledge (γνῶσις) of God and of the Trinity are the goal, while "contemplation of beings" is the practice that allows one to prepare to reach that goal.[69] Translators of the *Life of Moses* have left this phrase vague, rendering it relatively unspecific: the most popular English version has "contemplation of reality."[70] The wider context of the *Life of Moses*, however, makes the case that Gregory was indeed referring to the practices Evagrius espoused. Elsewhere Gregory explained that if a person wishes to attempt such contemplation, which he there terms the "contemplation of the rational beings"—namely, τῇ τῶν νοητῶν θεωρίᾳ, an alternate phrase Evagrius had used for that practice that characterized the second stage of Christian progress—that person must be purified in soul and body, because in such contemplation he would "surpass the knowledge that arises from the senses."[71] After the soul and body, the mind in particular was of utmost importance for Gregory, as it was the part of the soul that advanced "through greater and more perfect purpose in the consideration arising from observing the beings."[72] These pieces of the *Life of Moses* directly correspond to the progress in Christian practice that Evagrius urged his students to make. The rather technical vocabulary of contemplation, the emphasis on knowledge, and the presence of the divine power as something that facilitates contemplation all direct us to consider Evagrian texts as potential contexts for these passages and perhaps for the entirety of the *Life*.

Evagrius never hid the fact that progress in his system required dedication and a long period of applied training; in Gregory's biblical interpretation, Moses is the character who models just such a long training for the reader. As he describes the stages of Moses's career—slave, leader, lawgiver—Gregory frequently mentions Moses's "purpose" and "careful attention," through which he prepares himself for the spiritual meeting with God that he has on the mountain; this is the same quality we have seen praised in ascetic writings.[73] That meeting changed Moses's life, instituting him as the spiritual head of the Israelite community, and as Gregory saw it, a similar meeting with God could change the lives of his readers. "We have learned," he wrote, "that Moses, and whoever ascends through virtue according to Moses's example, empowering the soul through the enduring purpose toward the elevated and lofty life and through the guidance of the light which comes from above," have success in "leading those born kin to them to the life of freedom."[74] Furthermore, Gregory linked Moses's purpose and subsequent success to the fact that he received help: he first dedicated himself to a righteous life, then he received assistance. Gesturing toward Moses and his experiences, Gregory promised his readers that their own careful purpose would not go unrewarded. "To those who succeed in virtue, even the ally (συμμαχία) given to our nature by God is provided, this ally who came into being first, according to the first creation. Now it appears and is recognized only when we sufficiently claim the higher life for ourselves, through purpose and careful attention, and when we strip for the more difficult contests."[75] Work and dedication focused on to the life of virtue would result, Gregory assured them, in the revelation of assistance from another being, one created before humanity. On the whole, the *Life* encouraged readers to undertake the life of virtue by imitating Moses and promised them an ally who marked their incipient success and would facilitate their further progress.

In the biblical story, Gregory saw confirmation of this ally in the character of Aaron, Moses's brother. In Exodus 6 and 7, Moses is ordered by God to confront the Egyptian leader, Pharaoh, and to bring the Israelites out of Egypt, but he falters; his conviction in speaking is not strong. To help him, God designates Moses's brother, Aaron, as a spokesperson for him. When Moses loses confidence, Aaron does the talking. In words that echo other passages in the *Life of Moses*, Gregory equates the relationship of Moses and Aaron with the relationship between the virtuous practitioner and the ally that comes to his aid. In both cases, "to the one who has ascended to the greatest successes of the soul through long careful attention and the guiding light that comes on high, it is a loving and peaceful meeting when his brother is goaded by God to meet him."[76] The meeting between Aaron and Moses is part of the "historical" timeline of Moses's career, but Gregory saw that it could also have meaning for his readers if it were converted to be part of the "contemplation" of Moses's career. In that case, the message was simple and applicable to a range of people and situations: those who experience doubt and frustration can expect help, if they persevere.

Gregory was even more explicit, though, identifying Aaron not just as a general symbol of help, but as a type of the angel that accompanies successful Christians in their practices. Gregory believed that each human being was courted by one angel and one demon, both of which sought to influence the human being under their sway and to guide his decisions. The angel, like Aaron, is an "ally in the life of each person," and opposes the demon that tries to dominate the human being.[77] Gregory assured his readers that this belief was "confirmed by the tradition of the fathers." That tradition resides in the lineage of Alexandrian academic Christians and the later ascetics who emulated them. Origen of Alexandria, for instance, often referred to a passage of the early Christian text called *The Shepherd of Hermas* as he explained the influence of two spirits over humanity: one good, one evil.[78] The ascetic teachers I discussed in the last chapter followed Origen and held this belief as well. In the opening lines to his guide to spiritual warfare against demons, Evagrius set out his understanding of the divisions in the "rational nature"—that is, the division among beings endowed with intellect: "From the rational nature that is 'beneath heaven' [Qo 1:13], part of it fights; part assists the one who fights; and part contends with the one who fights, strenuously rising up and making war against him. The fighters are human beings; those assisting them are God's angels; and their opponents are the foul demons."[79] As he sought to interpret the details of Moses's career, Gregory of Nyssa offered interpretations shaped by these teachings. In the *Life of Moses*, he argued that Aaron was best seen as a symbol pointing to the "angel who fights with and stands near" Moses. The angel matches Aaron on two levels: "he is thought of as created before us, because his angelic and incorporeal nature was established before our nature, but he is clearly a brother, because of the kinship (συγγένειαν) between his intellectual part and our own."[80] The purpose of the angel, like Aaron, was to fight off any enemy that might try to attack; the motivation of the angel called upon to do this stemmed from the intellectual nature it shared with the human being it protected. Both these rather distinct notions are represented in Evagrius's writings.

Moreover, according to Gregory, the human being at the center of this struggle was not helpless. As he explained, "the person in the midst of these two who follow him closely has it within himself to make the goal of the one against his opponent prevail over the other." Moses's dedication was what brought God to send Aaron to him, and the same was true of Christians: dedication could reveal the angel sent by God to assist in the struggle. For Gregory, the kind of dedication required was quite specific and obvious, because those who contended for the human being used two opposing methods: while the angel worked by means of thoughts, the demon works by means of pleasures.[81] Thus, drawing the angel to oneself was a matter of exercising the intellectual part of the soul, the very part which made the angel "brother" to the human being who sought its help. In Gregory's estimation, if a person who is dedicated to the life of virtue manages to "estrange himself from those doing evil, turning instead toward the best of thoughts," then "the ally, his brother, is provided to him and helps him. For the angel is a brother in a certain sense to the logical and intellectual part of the human soul."[82] In this, too, Gregory followed the teaching of the ascetic Christians in Egypt. Evagrius also placed the responsibility on the Christian, making the outcome of the war between angel and demon entirely up to the person. "It is not because of the severity of the enemies' power, nor because of negligence on the part of the assistants," Evagrius warned, "but because of slackening on the part of the fighters that knowledge of God disappears and perishes from them."[83] The details of how Gregory interpreted Moses's brother Aaron are deeply resonant with the way that ascetic teachers spoke of the angel who vied with the demon for the attention of the human being.

In the context of the *Life of Moses*, such details also give new meaning to the "training" that Moses went through: it is couched in the terms of ascetic discourse, especially the discourse created by teachers in the lineage of Antony. Specifically, there is a striking resemblance between certain parts of Moses' characterization in the *Life* and the way that Antony is characterized by the *Life of Antony*. Compare for example, Moses's "longstanding purpose" and "exceedingly careful attention" to the "purpose" and dedication that Antony had shown; both characters are exemplary models of singleness of intent. Pure intent, however, is a rather generic quality to praise, something that readers could expect just about any laudatory biographer to claim for his subject. The similarity does not end there. While Gregory of Nyssa was one of the few late ancient Christian authors who did not mention the *Life of Antony* nor quote phrases from it, passages like the following show that Gregory probably had in mind an experience like Antony's when he wrote about the way that Moses's training created an excellent and virtuous person: "If such a person is empowered by the shining light and receives both strength and authority against his opponents, then just like an athlete sufficiently trained in athletic courage by a wrestling coach, he would go boldly and with conviction toward the contests with the enemies."[84] These lines are meant to describe Moses, of course, but they could easily apply to an ascetic like Antony: whatever source or sources Athanasius had used had depicted Antony going toward his enemies, seeking ways to avoid humanity and to engage demons on their own turf. He did so, we know, because he had acquired a divine helper, a "power," in the words of the *Life of Antony*. It is not difficult to see the influence of this characterization of Antony in the presentation of Moses, who again, Gregory said, was "empowered by the light appearing to him," and who went forth "boldly" because he "had acquired a brother as an ally and a supporter."[85] The discipline Moses exhibited and the process that Moses completed are examples of that which was predicated of Antony and predicted for ascetics like him.

Just as Moses's training alluded to the purpose and dedication valued in ascetic contexts, so too the struggles with his enemies also resonated with ascetic contexts. In Gregory's narrative of the "history" of Moses's career, Moses's enemies were always Egyptians. Three conflicts from the biblical story drew Gregory's attention: the moment when Moses interrupted a fight between a Hebrew and an Egyptian and killed the Egyptian; the moment when Moses confronted Pharaoh and demanded the release of the Hebrews; and finally, the pursuit of Moses and the escaping Hebrews by the Egyptian army, which ended in the deaths of the Egyptians in the Red Sea. Egypt and Egyptians can signify many things for Gregory in the *Life of Moses*, but in his discussions of these three conflicts, he interpreted Egyptians as representing demons. First, when Moses entered into the fight between the Egyptian and the Hebrew, Gregory wrote that this indicated a fight between "the enemy of the soul and its friend," the demon and the angel that Gregory had described as fighting for sway over each human being.[86] Their fight also pointed to the larger moral territory on which practice in virtue took place, and Gregory urged the Christian seeking virtue to be aware of all possible pitches of the struggle. "The human being," he explained, "lies in the middle as the prize in the struggle between those working against one another. With whichever he takes as a friend, he makes that one the victor over his opponent—idolatry over piety, intemperance and wisdom, righteousness and injustice, arrogance and humility, and whatever else can be thought up by which the opposing Egyptian brings the fight to the Hebrew."[87] Second, the same analogy lay under Gregory's interpretation of Moses's meeting with the Egyptians and Pharaoh: the "brotherly ally" is brought whenever "we come near the Egyptians" or when we "draw near to Pharaoh."[88] If the reader was already made to understand the "ally" as an angel, then Egyptians and Pharaoh slot easily here into the category of "demon."

Last, of course, is the climax of Moses's story: the pursuit of the Egyptians and their drowning in the Red Sea. This, too, Gregory interpreted as a pattern for the conflict taking place between those who practice the life of virtue and the demons that wish to interrupt them. The pursuit of the Egyptian army represents, in his retelling, the intensified attacks by demons that happen when one has dedicated himself to the virtuous life, or, metaphorically, has left Egypt: "Whenever they leave the bounds of the realm of the Egyptians, the ones who cast temptations follow them, with difficulties and fears and dangers of the end."[89] Gregory warned that Christians who accept Moses's message of freedom—namely, those who try to adopt the life of virtue—can expect to be "threatened all the more by the attacks of the temptations, which are launched by the Enemy."[90] But Moses, or a good leader like Moses, was to remind the ones leaving Egypt that they would have a "divine ally" on their journey—reassuring them using the same word Gregory used to describe Aaron and the angel he represents.[91] Interestingly enough, in other descriptions, the ally corresponded to the cloud that led the Israelites through the desert, and which Gregory in the first part of the *Life of* Moses called a "divine power." As Gregory explained,

> Whenever a person flees Egypt and, once outside its borders, finds himself terrified by the attacks of the temptations, the guide from above shows him an unexpected salvation, so whenever the enemy and his army encircles the one being pursued, the guide provides him in his time of need a path in the sea, into which the guide, the cloud, directs him.[92]

In multiple layers of interpretation, then, Gregory reiterated the doctrine of the guiding angel: it was indicated by Aaron, Moses's brother, and by the cloud-pillar guiding the Israelites. During these reiterations, the referent for the opponents of the angel was always the same: they were the Egyptians. If inference by analogy is not enough proof that Egyptians represent demons for Gregory in these cases, then consider his direct explanation, from another part of the *Life:* "Who doesn't know that the Egyptian army—that is, the horses, the chariots and those who ride them, archers, slingers, hoplites and the rest—are the same as the battle-lines of the enemies?" Standing in the ranks of the enemy are "angry thoughts" and the movements that bring us to "pleasure, sorrow and greed"—precisely those techniques and temptations that demons were known by ascetics to cast.[93] In sum, Gregory saw in Moses's interactions with Egyptians scriptural confirmation of the doctrine of an angel and a demon who fought over the human being, the expectation that demonic attack would intensify when a Christian showed dedication, and the assumption that those who were worthy would receive a guide to protect them from the temptation demons cast at them. These teachings are clearly important to Gregory, worthy enough to be the lesson of the *Life of Moses*; they were equally important to the ascetic teachers in the line from Antony to Evagrius.

If we follow these analogies and, in consequence, assume an ascetic context for at least parts of the *Life of Moses*, then certain passages of the text come into sharper focus. In a series of comments near the end of the "contemplation" of Moses's life, Gregory lectured his readers about the way the Adversary was likely to seek new and different ways of attacking a Christian as he made progress in virtue. The imagined Christian's situation and the Adversary's novel tactics are general enough to apply to the average ancient Christian, if a bit loosely. But if we place the situation and the tactics in the frame of asceticism, they become manifestly specific and sensible. Gregory first explains that the demons find it hard to get someone without possessions to be greedy, hard to get someone who is withdrawn to care about the luxuries of the world, and thus they turn to the one thing that is still available as a weapon to use against men living alone, namely, pleasure. In denouncing greed, or luxury, Gregory's advice could be directed at any Christian, but it makes the best sense if it is directed at Christians who have given up possessions and have withdrawn. What follows is Gregory's warning about the tactics that affect men who have nothing and who care for nothing.

> Those who were stronger than the enemy's weapons, who demonstrated that every attack made with iron was weaker than their own power, who turned back the flank of the enemies by force, it is they who were wounded by female darts of pleasure. The ones who were better than men became less than women. As soon as the women became visible to them, brandishing their forms instead of weapons, they neglected the firmness of their courage and dissolved their mettle in pleasure. And there were some who, of course, were filled with lust for inappropriate intercourse with foreigners. The one joining himself to the evil becomes a foreigner to the good ally.[94]

This is, of course, a reinterpretation of a scene from Moses's life, the rebellion of some Israelites against Moses. However, it is also a description of the kinds of stages of temptation a demon would attempt to use against a Christian who had given up normal social connections and property to live the virtuous life. A vice like greed is hard to instill in those who have given up what they have voluntarily. Pleasure, though, can still come calling, and can attack the Christian in the form of women, then sexually appealing foreigners. If the Christian takes the bait, the "good ally" that has previously been joined with him, Gregory tells us, removes itself and even it becomes a "foreigner" to the Christian. This sequence of images—possessionless and withdrawn men who are tempted by women who have "become visible" and then by foreigners who offer them inappropriate intercourse, while their allies estrange themselves—is suggestive in many ways. One of the primary suggestions it calls to mind is the progress of the ascetic outlined in the teachings of Antony, Ammonas, and Evagrius, and even the *Life of Antony,* as it was redacted by Athanasius: a person who is tempted in many forms, including by demons who appear as potential sexual partners, and who can lose the help of his companion angel should he act sinfully in response.

Adopting an ascetic frame through which to read the *Life of Moses* clarifies what Moses's career is meant to signify in the text. In his telling of the *Life of Moses,* Gregory recounted the process that Moses went through as a leader. Though he was not very effective at first, he subjected himself to a long training with much discipline, experienced an illumination, and received the ally of Aaron, his brother, to fend off the Egyptians and to lead the people to freedom. In his "contemplation" about these narrative events, Gregory was quite clear: Christians who undergo a long training and have experienced illumination can expect the help of an ally, an angel, that stands with them, fighting against the attacks of the enemy and his demons, which manifest themselves as passions, temptations, and ultimately the bodies of women and foreigners. Now perhaps it is clear why I suggest that the *Life of Moses* needs to be read with the literature we have from Antony and his followers close at hand. To be fair, there are parts of the *Life of Moses* that do not surrender to my reading. As a text, it has long served as an inspiration to those who wish to think more generally about mysticism within Christianity—that is, the pursuit of the knowledge of God, whatever its location, whether within an ascetic community or not. And, texts can certainly comprise multiple messages; the *Life of Moses* would not have been such an enduring text in Christian reading were it not for its ability to speak to multiple audiences. Even so, no context fits the passages I have discussed nearly as well as does the context of ascetic teaching from the academic circles of Egypt. Portions of the *Life of Moses* reflect the specific expectations, terminology, and advice of these teachers, especially Evagrius of Pontus. Gregory of Nyssa, though he did not have direct contact with Egyptian asceticism, represents in his *Life* important traces of the tradition of the divine power, an angel that was awarded to the most skilled and most righteous practitioners of Christian "training." What remains a mystery is just how these traces came to exist in Gregory's work; there are several options, all of which require us to consider the possibility that Evagrian practices and assumptions circulated outside of Egypt as early as the 390s CE. The events in Moses's life can be signposts for a Christian who takes up the practice of virtue, but Gregory's text about Moses can be a set of signposts for us, pointing out the ways that Gregory's conversation partners and prospects were often more diverse, more far-flung, than what we imagine them to be.

Is All Christian Literature Ascetic Literature?

Both the *Life of Antony* and the *Life of Moses* were written with knowledge of the traditions of the companion angel as they were cultivated by the lineage of teachers and students loyal to Antony. The *Life of Antony* by Athanasius was clearly a document made to represent stories and events in Antony's career, but it contained traditions obscured by Athanasius's editing choices, but which stand out once the text is compared to other extant literature from and about Antony. The letters of Antony and his successors described a series of stages that ascetics could pass through in their ascetic progress and in their relationship with a companion angel: dedication, acquisition of the angel and success in ascetic struggles, relinquishment of the angel in the face of vice, and return of the angel upon repentance. Those stages were present, if sublimated, in the story of Antony as Athanasius told it. Their presence should remind us that the *Life of Antony* was first and foremost an edited piece of literature. As several scholars have argued, it was shaped for specific purposes, but it was also shaped from specific sources. While none of those written sources survive, it is clear from the consistency and the editorial glossing in the *Life of Antony* that at least some of them contained teachings aligned with Antony's own advice to ascetics.

Gregory of Nyssa's *Life of Moses* also suggests an author who understood and expected the companion angel in the way outlined by teachers in Antony's tradition, but it contains ideas that relate most closely to a more developed stage in the lineage. The text praises some of the same themes that were prevalent in the *Life of Antony* and Antony's letters, but its most distinctive references were Evagrian. In its discussion of the creation of angels in the first creation, its placement of human beings between an angel and a demon both warring for the human's attention, and its oblique references to the stages of contemplation a practitioner must pass through during the life of virtue, the *Life of Moses* was intelligible only by those already familiar with Evagrius's expectations for Christians attempting to follow his ascetic program. Other scholars have compared the systems of thought created by Gregory of Nyssa to those created by Evagrius, claiming that they mutually illuminate each other as examples of late fourth-century Christian thinkers, but here I am making a more forceful claim: the *Life of Moses* is a text in the Evagrian tradition, written to showcase how Moses can serve as an ideal for those seeking to lead ascetic communities in Evagrian practice.[95]

Though the *Life of Antony* and the *Life of Moses* show connections to the lineage of ascetic teachers, they are independent from one another. As I mentioned before, Gregory of Nyssa is one of just a handful of late ancient writers who do not make reference to the *Life of Antony*, whether in the *Life of Moses* or in his other works. The *Life of Moses* was influenced by the same tradition that also shaped portions of the *Life of Antony*, but Gregory did not adopt that tradition directly from Athanasius's text. Instead, these two exemplary lives, one written in the late 350s CE, the other in the late 390s CE, are separate snapshots that capture how the teachings that were developing in the ascetic circles outside Alexandria were taken by outsiders. We have long known how ascetic programs were represented by others—in the tourism catalogs, in John Cassian's epitome of Evagrian ideas, or later in the works of Maximus the Confessor. These lives, now identified to have been influenced by ascetic discourse and separated by forty years' time, demonstrate that the ideas about angels, demons, and humanity that were forged in the laboratory of cultivation shaped the literary products of those engaged in contestation—not just at one moment but over the course of a half-century. The *Life of Antony* and the *Life of Moses* are evidence of the extended conversation that took place in Christianity, across barriers created by social standing, the influence of different material environments, and the differing aims of these Christian writers. In reality, that conversation went in both directions. More evidence of the conversation is detailed in the next chapter, where we will see how ideas about angels and specifically "the angelic life" proclaimed by urban orators, those in the thick of contestation, ended up forcefully shaping ascetic discourse in turn.

5

Defining Others

ASCETICISM AND THE DISCOURSE OF THE ANGELIC LIFE

NEAR THE END of the fourth century, a small group of monks from Palestine traveled to Egypt to observe the way of life of the ascetics living in the desert. One of the travelers gave an account of the journey and the wonders he beheld, which begins:

> There I saw many fathers living the angelic life, making progress in their imitation of our divine savior, as well as other new prophets who, by their inspired and wondrous and virtuous way of life, possess a divine state. As true servants of God, they are not concerned by anything earthly, nor think upon anything temporal. Instead, they have their citizenship in heaven while existing on earth.[1]

Although the travelers were also ascetics, monks in their own communities, they saw something different in the way that Egyptian ascetics lived. The Christians they encountered there were almost ethereal, living a life unlike other human lives, and were inspired by their relationship to, even identity with, heavenly beings. This opening to the *History of the Monks in Egypt* is only one example of a large number of texts in ancient Christian literature that utilize the special lens of "the angelic life" for viewing the feats of Egyptian ascetics. The equation of the ascetic life with the angelic one permeated ancient writing about the renunciatory efforts of Christians.

It also permeates modern scholarly treatments of asceticism in late ancient Christianity. In the mid-twentieth century, texts like the introduction to the *History of the Monks in Egypt* were read as if they revealed the intimate motivations of the ascetics who chose to go to the desert. Between the 1930s and the 1960s, at least four monographs and twice as many articles on the topic of the angelic life appeared, the majority of which accounted for the popularity of ascetic withdrawal in Egypt in the fourth century by asserting that ascetic Christians thought themselves to be enacting the imitation of angels.[2] Since the 1960s, the explanatory force of the idea that Christians were imitating angels and thus started the ascetic movement has fallen out of favor, but the trope of asceticism being "the angelic life" has not. Robin Lane Fox's popular book, *Pagans and Christians*, dedicates an entire chapter to asceticism with the title "Living like Angels."[3] A scholar no less impressive than Peter Brown discusses Syriac ascetics under the rubric "These Are Our Angels" in his book about late antique asceticism, *The Body and Society*.[4] Robin Darling Young uses "the angelic life" as a lens through which to interpret a letter from Evagrius that promised that the family of a monk can gain "the inheritance with those being made holy in light," a reference to angels from Colossians 1.12.[5] In his study of the way monastic society influenced the scriptural culture at the heart of early Christianity, Guy Stroumsa writes that the practice of writing one's thoughts was an integral part of the "*bios angelikos* which the monks are supposed to lead."[6] The concept of the *vita angelica* served as a heuristic tool for medievalist Dyan Elliott to study Tertullian's configuration of female virgins as equal to angels in stature, but separate from them in their flesh.[7] There are many more instances than these, but the point is clear: in contemporary academic writing, "the angelic life" serves as a handle by which to refer to and sometimes to interpret early Christian asceticism.

The idea that late ancient Christian ascetics lived "the angelic life" is a product of the culture of oratory and social explanation that developed in the fourth century as Christians trained in rhetoric exercised ever greater influence over urban congregations. This chapter examines the development of the discourse of the angelic life in late antiquity in three sections. The first section shows how the analogy between the angelic life and renunciation in general began as an inventive exegetical extension of a gospel parable about resurrection. In the mid-fourth century, skillful preachers adopted the trope to explain to their urban congregations how the communities of ascetics who existed separate from cities were, in fact, still part of the same Christian tradition as those who remained in cities and fulfilled normal social expectations. As for the ascetics, late ancient evidence discussed in the second section of the chapter reveals that most knew that some of their fellow Christians cast them as human beings who lived like angels. Ascetics in Egypt in particular even put the trope of "living the angelic life" to use among themselves, by envisioning angels as a constant audience for their practices and thus creating and maintaining the boundary between their communities and the rest of the world. Imagining ascetic communities to be places where angels could appear at any moment also allowed ascetics to develop constructive solutions for the sometimes difficult navigation between the strict behavioral ideal of perfection in virtue and the ready flexibility demanded by life in close quarters. At the same time, angelic appearances generated their own difficulties on occasion—both conflicts of authority and crises of identity. The third section highlights the problems that the discourse of the angelic life engendered for those living in ascetic communities. Through an examination of traditions preserved in the collections known as the *Sayings of the Fathers* and the work surviving from Shenoute, the influential leader of the White Monastery, I demonstrate that though "the angelic life" was a positive way for non-ascetics to glorify and explain ascetic practices, it was a prospect received in ascetic literature with ambivalence and at times disdain. As we watch the development of this discourse and its adoption and rejection in different contexts, we will see how in late antiquity, the product of largely urban Christian oratory influenced both the imaginative world and the day-to-day management of ascetic communities.

Equating Angels and Humanity

The first widespread use of the angelic trope to describe a particular practice lies in the late third and early fourth centuries corresponding to the increase in practices of sexual renunciation within Christianity.[8] Even though chastity was a common component of the culture of later monastic communities that constructed themselves as an alternative to an urban lifestyle, it was first a practice adopted by men and women who otherwise maintained normal social relationships and remained in their towns and villages. Many dedicated themselves to being "virgins," a special status that could signify several different models of sexual renunciation: two of the most significant were men and women who lived together, but remained chaste, and women who declined to marry and instead lived chaste lives with their families.[9] The adoption of a life of sexual renunciation by so many Christians inspired a profusion of texts that reflected on virginity and the young people who decided to dedicate themselves as virgins.[10] Some sermons gave practical advice to the fathers whose daughters lived as virgins in the family home, as forms the anonymous text *Peri Parthenias*, while other sermons, such as Gregory of Nyssa's *Treatise on Virginity*, reflected on the philosophical character of virginal purity.[11] Approaches to the topic could be abstract or concrete, but almost all treatises on virginity commented on the superiority of the lifestyle and the unsurpassed purity of the virgins themselves. These sermons used different methods to translate the admirable and transcendent nature of sexual renunciants, but one particularly compelling way was to adopt the language, inspired by the gospels, that compared virgins to angels.

Authors writing about virginity most often turned to the Synoptic story of the Sadducees's challenge to Jesus regarding the resurrection to make this comparison (Mark 12.18–27; Matt 22.23–33; Luke 20.27–40). As characters in the New Testament, the Sadducees were known to reject both the idea that the soul endures after the death of the body as well as the possibility of resurrection.[12] In this passage, they pose a question to Jesus: if a woman is married seven times in this life, who is her husband in the resurrection? For early interpreters of the story, the reality of the resurrection was the most salient lesson to be drawn from Jesus's response to the Sadducees's question. When sexual renunciation became more popular among ancient Christians, a new lesson emerged.[13] In Luke's version of the story in particular, Christians saw an affirmation that the life of the resurrection was available *before death* to those on Earth who declined to marry. In Luke, Jesus responds to the Sadducees in this way:

> The sons of this world marry and are given in marriage, but those who happen to be judged worthy of that world and of the resurrection from the dead neither marry nor are given in marriage. Indeed, they cannot die anymore, since they are equal to the angels and are sons of God, being sons of the resurrection. (Luke 20.34–36)

Two features of this version place special emphasis on the unmarried state. First is the way Luke distinguishes between those who marry and those who do not. Jesus's words make a distinction between "the sons of this world" (οἱ υἱοὶ τοῦ αἰῶνος τούτου) who participate in marriage and those, on the other hand, "who happen to be judged worthy of that world and of the resurrection from the dead" (οἱ δὲ καταξιωθέντες τοῦ αἰῶνος ἐκείνου τυχεῖν καὶ τῆς ἀναστάσεως τῆς ἐκ νεκρῶν), who do not participate in marriage rituals. According to the wording of Luke, the hypothetical group of people who do not marry are still alive: these people are simply "considered worthy" of the next world and have not yet passed on to it. These people "cannot die anymore," another detail that suggests that Luke is addressing two groups of people among the living, those who have married and those who have not. Luke's version of the answer is special for the way Jesus expresses the similarity between these unmarried people and angels. In the Gospel of Mark, the source for Luke's story, those who are resurrected are "like angels" (ὡς ἄγγελοι) and thus do not marry. In Luke, these unmarried people, the ones who are "considered worthy of... the resurrection," are "equal to angels" (ἰσάγγελοι γὰρ εἰσιν) while they are yet alive and yet in this world. The difference between ὡς ἄγγελοι and ἰσάγγελοι may seem insignificant, but it is quite provocative: constructive readers understood Luke's version of this story to mean that those who decline to marry now achieve a status equal to angels, not in the resurrection but while they are yet very much alive—and yet very much human.

The idea that renunciation of sexuality might, in some way, make human beings "equal to angels" was a powerfully attractive metaphor for the writers who sought to articulate the place of virginity in early Christian practice. Written in 371 CE, Gregory of Nyssa's *Treatise on Virginity* alluded to Luke's story, explaining that a virgin claims the resurrected life as a result of his renunciation of sexuality:

> For if the life after the resurrection promised to the righteous by the Lord is equal to the angels, and if being set free from marriage is indeed part of the angelic nature, he has already received the benefits of the promise, mingling "with the brilliance of the holy ones" (Ps 110.3) and imitating the purity of the incorporeal ones by the undefiled nature of his life.[14]

Here, what remained implicit in Luke 20 was made explicit. Humans may refrain from marriage in the resurrection, but those who remain unmarried now are *already* considered righteous and have "already received the benefits" of the resurrection. For Gregory, there were limits to how well virgins might imitate angels, just as there were limits to how well angels could imitate the model provided to them, the "beauty of the archetype" belonging to the "father of incorruptibility."[15] Other Christians were more optimistic about the capabilities of virgins, such as the author of a treatise on virginity once attributed to Athanasius but now recognized as pseudepigraphical.[16] Addressing female virgins who, instead of living in their homes with their families, had adopted separate communities, this author encouraged each individually:

> Toward the heavenly light you too have been summoned, illustrious bride, and to the lifestyle of the angels, as also their companion on account of the brilliance of the lofty beauty of virginity and the perpetuity of the unending glory. Therefore, even the angels honor the excellence of her (virginity's) splendor as their equal.[17]

The passage from the Gospel of Luke certainly informs this author's concept of virginity, but he advised much more than the simple avoidance of marriage. Rather, these women should adopt a broader program of positive dedication to the role of "virgin," an entire "lifestyle of the angels," both beautiful and glorious. In his advice, this author suggested that angels would approve the virgins' new and separate community of chastity.

More and more late ancient Christian writers legitimized the development of separate ascetic groups by comparing such communities to life among the angels. For example, the famous orator John Chrysostom utilized the trope of the angelic life in multiple ways and on multiple occasions in the late fourth century. Trained in rhetoric, John could craft his messages flexibly, adapting different concepts of angels to illustrate different lessons. When he was lecturing new Christians about the history of the church, he reminded Christians that the martyrs of the past overcame their physical pain by thinking on heavenly things.

> Because of this, that blessed apostle, who knew the strength of such a model, said "think on the things that are above, where Christ is seated at the right hand of God." Look at the forethought of our teacher, how he leads upward those who obey him—slicing through all the angels, archangels, thrones, dominations, principalities, authorities, all those invisible powers, the cherubim and the seraphim, to fix the thoughts of the faithful right before the throne of the king itself.[18]

In order to reassure Christians that they would have direct access to the power of God through Christ's intervention, John pieced together the different orders of angels mentioned in Scripture and then depicted Christ passing all of them by as he delivered prayers to God. Cognizant of multiple orders of angels, John used the idea of hierarchy of angels to make his point about the force of Christ's mediation even more vivid.

When his purpose shifted to explaining the practices of ascetics, however, John defined angels precisely by the *lack* of hierarchy among them. In his treatise *Against the Opponents of the Monastic Life*, John attempted to reassure the frightened parents of young Christians who were thinking of entering a monastery. These worried parents assumed that if their child were to disengage from marriage and family as the ascetic lifestyle requires, it would reflect negatively on the care and direction that they, as parents, had provided. John agreed with them about the gravity of their situation: neglecting the welfare of one's children, he acknowledged, is among the highest of sins and will be punished by God.[19] However, he argued, parents who consider entry into the monastery the equivalent of neglect are mistaken. Their children are actually better protected in the monastery than in society, because it was a place that allows them to avoid confusion and injustice. Only those in monasteries, John wrote,

> live in tranquility, in the harbor, in great security, observing the shipwrecks of others, as if from heaven. For they have chosen a way of life which befits heaven, and they have attained a state inferior in no way to that of angels. Just as among the angels there is no inequality, nor do some enjoy prosperity while others experience misery, but all of them share one peace, one joy, one glory, so it is likewise in the monasteries. No one reproaches poverty, no one exults over wealth. That "yours" and "mine" which overturns and upsets everything is utterly banished. All things are held in common—food, housing, clothing.[20]

If marriage and family were primary guarantors of social standing and financial security, were parents who allowed their children to opt out of marriage and its benefits irresponsibly endangering their children's future security? John's answer was no. Instead, entering the monastery actually ensured that security: all monks are of equal status, and that status happens to be "in no way inferior to that of the angels." It may not be remarkable to say that angels are not distinguished by wealth or poverty; even the earliest gospel telling of the story of Jesus being questioned by the Sadducees acknowledged that angels live free from the mundane and the material. But to say that among angels there is "no inequality," that they "share one glory," was indeed remarkable, particularly for a writer who had in other contexts made much of the hierarchical nature of the heavenly orders.

John used almost this same set of guarantees about equality and security in sermons preached not just to the parents of prospective monks, but to an entire urban congregation. In his *Homilies on Matthew*, John frequently praised ascetics to the public as those who enjoy the life of the angels. Equality among persons, poverty, and sexual renunciation were all angelic qualities in his persuasive and powerful descriptions of the benefits of ascetic communities.[21] What is more, he directed those in his congregations to go and visit such communities in order to observe the angelic life directly. When he was preaching to audiences in Antioch, for instance, he described the ascetics living outside the city, those who have abandoned society and even the bounds of the monastery, as "angels in human form" waiting to be seen. His description alone probably motivated some Christians to go see these communities, but in case his implication were missed, John also explicitly told Christians to go and visit these "angels," even if it required that they travel long distances.[22] To visit a monastery was to visit heaven, since those who live in monasteries, "being holy, are truly angels in the form of human beings."[23] In the instance when some ascetics happened to visit his congregation, John told the members of his church not to miss the opportunity to see such holiness up close: "Lest we neglect their virtue as we consider their simple appearance and the language they speak, let us observe well and accurately their angelic life, the philosophy they enact."[24] In different venues and in homilies on different topics, John told his urban audiences that the ascetics living in communities nearby were angels, who were enacting a life worthy of praise and whose example would be beneficial.

As the angelic and otherworldly character of Christian ascetic communities was presented to congregations of urban Christians by orators like John Chrysostom, it is no surprise that "some men and women became so deeply attracted to this world that they set out to see the living saints for themselves."[25] The numbers of pilgrims were so great, Georgia Frank points out, that even those writers who recorded the journeys of a single group to see ascetics could not help but notice that their protagonists were hardly alone. Theodoret, in his compilation of stories collected by pilgrims like himself, says that there were so many visitors to the ascetic practitioners of Syria that every road looked like a river, with pilgrims streaming along.[26] Accounts from pilgrims suggest that their expectations were influenced by the constant preaching that equated ascetics with angels. The narrator of the *History of the Monks in Egypt*, cited at the start of this chapter, describes the ascetics his group visited as "angels." He promises to have seen something otherworldly—humans who are "new prophets" and living in a "divine state." Having prepared his readers in this way, the author does not disappoint expectations that ascetics will resemble angels, for the *History* takes the angelic metaphor as a physical reality, its preferred way of depicting the appearance of monks being to attribute to them angelic qualities such as lustrous and shining faces.[27] For example, the author visits Abba Or and reports that he "had an angelic form, being roughly ninety years old, with a shining beard down to his chest. His face was so radiant that seeing him could stun a man."[28] For others it is their carriage that earns them the epithet "angelic." Abba Bes, who "surpassed the brothers living around him in meekness," led a life "completely silent—his manner was composed, because he possessed the angelic disposition."[29] Theon's ability to heal prompts the author of *Historia Monachorum* to label his appearance that of an angel: "A crowd of sick people went out to see him daily, and placing his hand on them through the window, he would send them away healthy. He had the face of angel, granting joy with his eyes and entirely full of grace."[30] In some cases, the epithet extends to an entire community, as was the case with those who were living with the ascetic Apollo: they looked like "a true army of angels."[31] The travel literature produced by pilgrims to ascetic communities created for expectant visitors the idea that they would see a community of angels, rather than human beings, when they arrived in the desert.[32]

By the time the *History of the Monks in Egypt* was written, its author could use the metaphor of "ascetic as angel" to convey many different impressive features he perceived among the desert dwellers. While those who had focused on virginity alone, such as Gregory of Nyssa, drew a link between the rejection of marriage and a status equal to angels in their reading of Luke 20, other Christians applied the angelic discourse to more complex systems of renunciation. For public speakers and church officials looking to normalize and to sanctify the growing movement embracing ascetic practice, the designation of ascetic lifestyles as "angelic" was a powerful rhetorical tool—it placed ascetics in a different category from that of urban Christians, distancing and valorizing their practice, even as it naturalized ascetics and their communities as a part of the Christian world predicted by Jesus. Even though the discourse of the angelic life was mostly used by those living in urban areas and the pilgrims who traveled to visit ascetics, ascetics themselves seemed to understand that others conceived of them this way.

In the Presence of Angels

Because most ascetic communities in Egypt were never that far removed, physically or economically, from the regular life of towns and villages, the idea that ascetics lived a life withdrawn, separate from the everyday lives of other Christians, depended heavily on the cultural construction of distance between themselves and "the world" they had renounced.[33] Construction of that distance was often managed by practical means. Monastic communities used elaborate mechanisms of indoctrination and reinforcement to train new members in the values of their new communities and to break new members' allegiance to normal expectations of family loyalty and social benefits.[34] In addition to structural tools of community maintenance, such as controlling sleep, access to food, and contact with other human beings, there were yet other, more imaginative resources available by which to engineer the cultural separation between ascetics and the world. One of the most effective was the idea that ascetics were living in a community of angels. A story preserved in one of the collections of the *Sayings of the Fathers* demonstrates the power of the idea:

> Two brothers who were attacked by fornication went away and took wives. Afterwards, they said to one another, "How have we benefitted by renouncing the angelic order and entering into this impurity? After these things, will we not be led into the fire and into torment? Let us go back again to the desert and repent about what we have done."[35]

The brothers frame their dilemma as a choice between two starkly different options: either life with the women, an impurity, or the "angelic order" of life in the desert. They decide to return to their community, are given a year's worth of time in their individual cells to meditate on their actions, and when they exit, they report two different experiences. The one, who emerges "pallid and gloomy," has spent his time thinking about the torment that awaits him after death, but the other, "flourishing and beaming," reports that he meditated on the God "who rescued me from the impurity of the world and from torment and who led me to this community of angels."[36] In the context of Egypt, the actual distance between an ascetic community and a town center was often only a few miles, if that. However, continually telling stories that show ascetics choosing between the impure world and their own "angelic order" created a gulf of supernatural proportions between ascetic communities and those of lay Christians—an imaginative gulf that superseded any real proximity.

Conceiving the ascetic community as an angelic order also implied that those living in such communities had definite roles to fill. Shenoute of Atripe, the leader of the White Monastery during the end of the fourth century and for much of the fifth, modeled the ways he wanted the members of his community to act by asking them to consider how angels acted. Instead of contending with one another, he wrote, "let each one of us, as a companion of God, tolerate his neighbor, whether large or small, and let us be happy to dwell with one another peacefully without sin or deceit, like God and his angels who dwell in heaven."[37] Shenoute meant this as a corrective warning for the behavior of the monks of his community, but the standard of angelic behavior could also be brought to bear on leaders like Shenoute himself. In his interpretation of the parable of the pounds from the Gospel of Luke, Evagrius wrote of those Christians who had heard about the "heavenly Jerusalem" and attempt to recreate versions of it on earth, cities of Christians anticipating the life of heaven. "Those accepting power to lead the aforementioned cities," he wrote, "will have led them in a manner closely resembling the archangels who lead the angels, as these holy cities are filled at once with inhabitants, that is, holy souls and spiritual powers."[38] Like the members of such "holy cities," ascetic leaders had a great deal to live up to. In fact, the identification of ascetic communities with angelic ones affected both sides of relationships of power, making certain behaviors imperative for members as well as leaders. Angels were more than just a model for behavior, however. Casting the organizational structure of monasteries in this way invested relations among members with cosmological weight. Their example sanctified specific hierarchies of power. Showing excellent leadership skills and obedience in turn was as much a part of the natural order as were the relations between God and his angels, or between angels and archangels.

One of the most unnatural features of the life in an ascetic community was the sheer amount of time that ascetics spent alone. That, too, was mitigated by the idea that ascetics lived in angelic communities. In the imaginative universe created by the discourse of the angelic life, the solitude of being an ascetic was broken by the presence of angels who visited ascetics and took note of their actions. According to the literature that represents the ascetic Christians of Egypt, angels were a constant audience for the practices and failings of those attempting such a lifestyle. When an inexperienced monk asked his mentor about the temptations that he was having, the elder reassured him that he was not alone in the fight: "it is impossible," he said, "that God and his angels are not present during these trials."[39] Another troubled monk is told by his elder that, though he feels beaten by the temptations, he has actually won the contest already: "Courage, my child: I have seen crowns upon your head!" The fight with temptation is a "great contest," which "God and his angels watch." Any victory that the monk may win is not his alone, for "when the athlete wins, all the angels give glory to God in a great voice, saying, 'the athlete has won an extraordinary victory!'"[40] According to one story in the *Sayings of the Fathers,* even those ascetics who tried to live entirely separate lives, seeking solitary existence far away from others, appreciated having angels present to note their efforts. In an exceedingly literal narrative demonstration of such angelic observance, a hermit is reassured that an angel has counted every one of his steps in order to be sure to give him his due reward for all his work.[41] Of course, angels were also an audience to the ascetic's foibles, there to be grieved when the ascetic falls to temptation.[42] Even in the larger monastic centers like the White Monastery, where it seems there would have been enough surveillance to obviate the utility of imagined audiences of angels, leaders still reminded those in their charge that they could receive "conviction by God, his angels, and his saints" for their false deeds.[43] The notion that angels watched over ascetics, noting their successes and failures, pervaded Egyptian ascetic culture, from the most densely populated monastic communities to the imaginative world of solitary hermits.

Just as these stories suggest that the presence of angels lent weight to the actions of individual ascetics, so too the presence of angels could help reinforce good standards of behavior for groups of ascetics. Angels could, by their very appearance, influence the behaviors—and even the speech—of community members. Consider the story included among the *Sayings of the Fathers* about the discerning monk who has visions of angels:

> One of the fathers said that when the elders used to sit around and speak about beneficial matters, there was one among them who could discern things, and he saw angels fanning them with palm branches and praising them. When another matter came up [one that was not beneficial], the angels went away and pigs full of foul odors would wallow in their midst and obliterate them. As soon as

> they spoke about beneficial matters again, the angels would come and praise them.[44]

This monk's visions both created and reinforced the community's expectations about good discourse, working on two levels. First, as angels appeared and disappeared, they provided immediate feedback on the conversation of the group. A second, more subtle effect of the presence and absence of the angels was to allow the discerning brother to avoid direct judgment of the group. Instead, he simply reported what he saw; the angels "spoke" for him. This is an important distinction, because according to the virtues idealized in collections like the *Sayings of the Fathers*, a monk should at all costs avoid judging another monk. In his work detailing the values that governed the relationships represented among desert monks, Graham Gould observes that the sheer "number of stories illustrating the necessity of not judging others, and the urgency with which abstaining from judgment was commended, confirms the importance of the problem of judgment" in ascetic literature.[45] The act of judging was perceived negatively because it represented a lack of humility or the ignorance of one's own sins, and the "possibility of being subject to demonic deceit," not to mention the undue shame it could inflict on the one being judged.[46]

The mechanism by which the manifesting angels save the brother from erring in the vice of judgment was rather simple—either he saw angels or he saw pigs—but the assumption that angels could manifest themselves in ascetic communities allowed for elegant solutions to more complex problems, particularly those that arose when the demands of multiple ascetic virtues seemed to clash. Specifically, the imagined presence of angels helped monks and their superiors negotiate the difficult path between avoiding one behavior—slander—and allowing another—heresy. The stories of two leaders of the Pachomian federation of monasteries, Pachomius himself and Theodore, illustrate the deft arbitration made possible by the presence of angels. These stories require some contextualization regarding the gravity of both slander and heresy as vices condemned by ascetic communities. First, let us consider the fact that while judgment was indeed considered an act of vice, worse still than judgment was slander—perhaps logically so, because slander involved a third person, a listener, in the act of judging.[47] As one ascetic describes it, slander comprises both "failure to recognize the glory of God and jealousy toward one's neighbor."[48] In a community that depended on humility and camaraderie, the all-too-human urge to talk about one's neighbors could be an insidious force.

It was also a necessary one. In her study of the desert ascetics and their style of communication, Maud Gleason notes that as "we examine the social behavior of these indomitable individuals, the corpus of their sayings and stories yields evidence of two processes characteristic of social groups: status negotiation and behavioral regulation. Gossip played a critical role in both."[49] If ascetics rejected the usual demonstrations of status as a part of their renunciatory project—eschewing wealth and family connections—social prestige as defined by their own community was the last marker of status remaining to them. The stories repeated about a particular ascetic and his deeds of renunciation were the building blocks of his reputation among his peers and even his spiritual progeny. In Gleason's words, "status recognition *required* gossip."[50] This view of the necessity of gossip, however, assumes that "gossip" is always positive. Negative reports could, of course, be as damaging to an ascetic's reputation as positive reports were beneficial.

Perhaps this is why the literature representing ascetic communities treats the avoidance of slander as if it were an ascetic practice itself, one at times more important than the more familiar rejections of food, drink, sleep, and sex. A saying of Hyperchios asserts that "it is better to eat meat and drink wine than to eat the flesh of brothers in slander."[51] This pronouncement was immediately followed by another that explains the special nature of slander as more than just a sin of the self: "The serpent drove Eve out of paradise through whispering. He who slanders his neighbor is like the serpent, for he both loses the soul of the one who listens and does not preserve his own."[52] Slander, unlike culinary indulgence, involved more than one member of a community and could be damaging to the whole. While we may think of sexual renunciation as the most salient of the ascetic practices treasured by early Christian monks, in sayings attributed to Poemen and Matoes, slander was unfavorably compared with fornication; in other sayings, lying, even about a potential murder, was better than committing slander.[53] Avoiding slander was, in these stories, considered equal to the basic ascetic practices that renounce physical pleasures.

Was slander, then, the worst imaginable transgression? No. According to the collected stories of the *Sayings of the Fathers*, one sin topped all others, including slander—heresy. Consider how Agathon, described as a "monk of great discernment," reacted when some brothers come to test him: he admitted to a litany of sins, including fornication, pride, and slander, but bristled at the idea that he is a heretic. He explained: "The first things I ascribe to myself, for it is good for my soul, but heresy is separation from God, and I do not wish to be separated from God."[54] Agathon may have been a fornicator, he may even have been a slanderer, but he claims that these activities and their consequences ultimately were beneficial for him and his spiritual development. Heresy alone threatened to remove him from community with God. Heresy was a problem for one's relationship with the divine, but it could also dissolve an ascetic's bond with the human community. Among the *Sayings of the Fathers* in the alphabetic collection, Theodore of Pherme offered the following advice:

> If you are friendly with someone, and it comes about that he falls into the temptation of fornication, give him your hand and draw him out. But if he falls into heresy, and you cannot persuade him to return, then quickly cut yourself off from him, lest by delaying you are dragged down with him into the pit.[55]

Fornication, while perilous to the person involved, did not threaten to endanger others around him. Heresy was entirely another story.

If slander was to be avoided at all costs, but heresy was such a danger to the community, what should happen if one brother hears that another is entertaining heretical ideas? As Maud Gleason points out, inevitably "word gets out" about deviance in ascetic communities, but how?[56] How could information about possible heresy pass among the community, or perhaps more important, from the community to its leader, without violating the injunction against offering negative reports of others—that is, against slander? No late ancient source phrases the problem in quite this way, but stories in the literature about ascetic communities demonstrate awareness of the dilemma, and these stories suggest that angelic appearances could resolve it.

In two texts from the Pachomian community superiors learn about the heretical dispositions of others through having visions of angels or receiving messages from angels, thus avoiding the more mundane transfer of information from one human being to another and, with it, the prospect of slander. The first text describes how Pachomius himself—here called "the Great Man" or "the Old Man"—relied on angelic informants to help him control the theological deviance in his community and to sniff out heresy among a group of visitors:

> As [the visitors] sat in a secluded cell, the Old Man perceived a strong stench from them. He did not know the cause of such a stench, because he was conversing with them face to face and could not learn the cause by a supplication to God. Seeing their eloquence and their familiarity with the Scriptures, he could not understand their sickening stench. After the Great Man had conversed long with them about the holy Scriptures, and the ninth hour was come, they rose up to go away to their own place. . . . The Great Man, in order to know the cause of their stench, went into his cell and prayed God to make it known to him. An angel of the Lord came and told him, "It was some doctrines of impiety from Origen that, in their souls, produced such a stench."[57]

In the remainder of the passage, Pachomius called the visitors back and counseled the brothers not to be acquainted with Origen's books, indeed to "cast them in the river, and never want to read them again, and especially the blasphemous ones."[58]

The benefit of angelic visions also applied to Theodore, a disciple of Pachomius and later leader of the Pachomian federation.[59] According to two passages in the *Letter of Ammon*, Theodore became aware of the heretical deeds of monks hidden away in private cells because angels acted as his informants.[60] In the first instance, a monk accused of improper deeds tried to avoid talking with Theodore about his actions, but Theodore had been given specific information about these hidden deeds and used that information to goad the monk into admitting his wrongdoing:

> Theodore appeared at the monastery and called the brothers together. . . . And seizing a certain young monk who was coming out of the house, he hauled him into a vaulted room and compelled him to relate what he had done. He explained that he was the one who had been pointed out by the angel and ordered expelled from the monastery. As he did not want to speak, Theodore began to relate his first act and asked whether he had another monk as a sympathizer. Falling at Theodore's feet, he requested him to remain silent with respect to his other acts and to expel [him] from the monastery.[61]

While the passage does not tell us the exact nature of the deed, the act was embarrassing enough for the young monk to decide to leave the monastery once he heard the particulars of his supposedly private actions recounted to him. As the *Letter of Ammon* would have it, Theodore apparently received regular, detailed, and frank reports on the activities of monks from an angel, and he did not hesitate to reveal such reports, if it helped his cause.

Theodore used this subtle form of blackmail more than once. In a second story, he again learned of covert deviance from an angel and used this information to his advantage. While the deeds of the monks in the first story were implied to be sexual, Theodore intimated that he received reports about heretical teachings promulgated in secret as well:

> Once, when Theodore had all the brothers together, he said to Psarphius... "Send to Patchelphius' cell and have him come here together with the youth that is with him in his cell. And summon also his elder son."
>
> And when they arrived, Theodore said to Patchelphius: "Tell [me] what you were teaching this youth during the night." And he said: "What was I teaching him? The fear of God." Theodore said: "God himself, through an angel, has informed against you. Therefore, tell the truth whether indeed your teaching is a light."
>
> But since he refused, Theodore said to all: "He was teaching him that there is no resurrection of the flesh, reproaching the nature of his flesh." Then, as he said to Patchelphius, "Say whether it is so or not," Patchelphius' son cried out and said: "He also persuaded me to think about these things last evening."[62]

The pattern in this story is much like that in the story of the young monk with the embarrassing relationship: even though Patchelphius refused to confess when confronted, Theodore leveraged the information he had, playing one witness against another. The son finally confessed that the father, indeed, had been teaching him to "reproach the flesh."

The prospect that stories like these can telegraph a model for dealing with heresy is further bolstered by the fact that two of them are marked by their involvement with *the* archetypical heresy that occupied Egyptian ascetic communities in the late fourth and early fifth century: the Origenist heresy.[63] The story of Pachomius and the foul-smelling visitors is explicit about the cause of their odor: it was because these monks "read the works of Origen" that they reek. The second story of Theodore's angelic visions has him correct a brother who taught "there is no resurrection of the flesh," one of the doctrines that characterized the position of those branded as "Origenists." It is also interesting that these stories deal with exposing "Origenists," because the main tenet of the position characterized in that way was that the divine cannot have a human form; there was no "likeness" of the divine that can be seen. Evagrius, most likely at the center of the movement to avoid picturing the divine, warned his readers against more than just imagining God. Rather, he urged them, "Hold no desire to see angels or powers or Christ with the senses, lest you go completely insane, taking a wolf to be the shepherd and worshipping your enemies, the demons."[64] In what must be seen as an ironic twist, angels appeared to Pachomius and Theodore in order to accuse exactly those people who would have suggested that angels should have no appearance, namely, probable "Origenists." These stories are doubly anti-heretical, their protagonists seeking out heretics by means of the very thing the heresy denies.

To extend the irony, we should consider that the Origenist controversy appears to have *started* with the vision of an angel, according to one of the two ancient sources describing its beginnings. The Coptic *Life of Aphou* details the reception of a festal letter distributed by Theophilus, bishop of Alexandria, in which he denies that the divine has an image.[65] Aphou, a monk who had been living alone in the desert, gathered with the other members of his community for the reading of Theophilus's festal letter. The *Life of Aphou* relates that

> while [Aphou] was still living with the wild beasts he left for the proclamation of holy Easter. He heard a statement that did not accord with his understanding of the Holy Spirit. As a result, he was very upset at what he heard. Indeed, everyone who heard it was saddened and upset over it. But the angel of the Lord commanded blessed Aphou not to be indifferent to what was read, saying to him, "You have been appointed by the Lord to go to Alexandria to take issue with what was said." The wording of that proclamation went like this: in exalting the glory of God in the proclamation, it emphasized human weakness, and the person who had dictated it said that "this weakness is not the image of God," understanding "this weakness" to be we who bear the image, that is, we human beings.[66]

As Aphou and his fellow ascetics listened to the letter of Theophilus, they had a disturbing experience: Theophilus asserted that humanity does not share in the image of God, a view that discomfits those who hear it.

Though the entire group was "saddened and upset," only Aphou took action, being emboldened by an angel. After his encounter with the angel, Aphou stood ready to challenge the text of the letter and prepared with the exact words to do so.

The initiative the angel gave Aphou to challenge the bishop must have been strong, for the gap the *Life of Aphou* depicts between a monk from the wilds and the bishop of the largest city in Egypt was quite large. Once Aphou had an audience with Theophilus, however, none of his weaknesses, be they social or spiritual, hindered the conversation.[67] Instead, because of Aphou's confident speech, Theophilus agreed to change the wording of his letter and issued a correction at once, saying "I see that your appearance is that of a peasant, but on the other hand I can hear that your words are more elevated than the words of those who are wise."[68] When Theophilus asked why he alone, of all those bothered by the phrase, was the only one to speak up, Aphou answered, "[for my part], I am confident that you will agree with me and will no longer oppose me."[69] This is a puzzling answer, for at the start of this narrative, Aphou is upset by the phrase in Theophilus's festal letter, but he appeared unprepared to do anything about it. Indeed, the text emphasizes Aphou's lowly status, a fact that militates against his challenging the bishop of the most important city in Egypt. Thus, the angel of the Lord has to instruct him specifically "not to be indifferent to what was read." However, in his response to Theophilus, Aphou did not tell the bishop about the visit from the angel. If we are to avoid charging Aphou with pride in his meeting with Theophilus, why would the text omit the reason for his challenge?

It is possible to contextualize the omission by looking at Theophilus's own role in the Origenist controversy. This episode between Aphou and Theophilus was only the beginning of the controversy, and Theophilus changed his allegiance several times, his support wavering between monks who held the idea that the divine may be partially represented in human form and other monks who did not.[70] Even though the *Life of Aphou* champions a monk who led Theophilus to allow that the divine may have a likeness among human beings, it still exhibits caution about having Aphou be inspired by the vision of an angel. Aphou's reluctance to report the source of his boldness suggests that even this text, extremely sympathetic to one who had such a vision, manifests a wariness about monks seeing angels. Such ambivalence about angelic appearances among ascetics is not limited to the *Life of Aphou*. The idea that ascetics were "living the angelic life" led many to imagine that angels might be present in ascetic communities. We have seen that appearances of angels in these communities could accomplish constructive things: angels inspire good behavior and, when good behavior is lacking, repentance; angels by their presence steer ascetics to edifying topics of conversation; angelic appearances even resolve situations that seem to demand that monks engage in one vice—slander—to prevent another—heresy. However, the concern about having visions of angels that registered in the *Life of Aphou* also informed other works of ascetic literature. In the next section, we will see how many collections of ascetic traditions still reflected the concern, even after being edited, as they explore in narrative terms the less-than-helpful effects of the equation of the ascetic life with the angelic one.

Trouble in the City in the Desert

In the alphabetic collection of the *Sayings of the Fathers*, Megethios lamented the golden days of his community: "In the beginning, when we came together, we spoke of beneficial things, encouraging one another, and we became choirs upon choirs [of angels]; we ascended up to the heavens. But now when we come together, we gossip, one against the other, and thus go down [to hell]."[71] The complaint was not a new one.[72] However, the specificity of Megethios's complaint can illumine: he contrasted the heady early moments in his community, a time when he was one of many angels, with the more recent, and all too human, behavior of his group. Other elder ascetics went further, suggesting that members of their communities have fallen even below human behavior, becoming outright animals. When an older monk named Longinus was told by several others about the deeds of one of his disciples, he complained, "Woe is me! We came here to become angels and ended up becoming irrational, impure beasts."[73] The difference between the ideal of the ascetic life and its realities was likely harsh enough, but it may have been exacerbated by the portrayal of ascetic communities as "choirs upon choirs" of angels. There is evidence that, particularly for those who had heard of ascetic endeavors and were led to join these "angels" in the desert, the expectations created by lofty descriptions of the ascetic life needed to be tempered by the wisdom of more experienced community members.

As I explained in the last section, the analogy of the ascetic project with "the angelic life" allowed those in ascetic communities to imagine that angels might appear to them. The stories collected in the *Sayings of the Fathers* treat most of these appearances as problematic and some as wholly dangerous. In the anonymous collection, one saying tells the story of a young monk who was apparently piqued that other ascetics have seen angels while he himself had not: "An old man was asked, 'How do some say, "We see visions of angels"?'—and he replied, 'Happy is he who always sees his sins.'"[74] This more experienced monk reassured the one who asked by noting that the visions of angels claimed by others are unreal, or, at the very least, inconsequential. The "old man's" response emphasized humility. Angelic visions (not to mention talk about them) distracted from the primary purpose, the struggle with one's own sin.

The disruptive character of angelic appearances in ascetic communities is entirely clear from the way these appearances were most often identified in the literature, namely, as the work of demons. In a scenario that recurs several times, striking angelic visions happen to younger monks, who then seek interpretation of their visions from more experienced monks. The advice they get is both practical and pithy:

> A brother lived in silence. Wishing to deceive him, the demons appeared to him looking like angels and roused him for the *synaxis* and showed him a light. So he went an old man and said to him, "Abba, angels come with a light and rouse me for the *synaxis*." The old man said to him, "Do not listen to them, my child, for they are demons, but when they come to wake you say, 'I wake myself when I wish but I do not listen to you.'"[75]

For as many stories as there are representing new monks as anxious and unsure about their visionary experiences, a similar number portray monks like this "old man" as entirely nonchalant in the presence of disguised demons. Even when demons made spectacular entrances and claimed great authority, well-practiced monks shrugged them off. Consider this example from the *Sayings of the Fathers*. "The devil appeared to a brother disguised as an angel of light and said to him, 'I am Gabriel and I have been sent to you.' The brother said to him, 'See if it is not someone else to whom you have been sent; as for me, I am not worthy of it'—and immediately the devil vanished."[76] The monk defended himself by means of his humility; because he did not believe an archangel had been sent directly to him, he was able to see the ruse for what it was.

The stories about visitations by demons disguised as angels make clear that the vice of pride was the intractable problem at the center of angelic appearances. As one monk explained, "All terrible things arrive on account of our pride. If the angel Satan was given to the apostle in order that he not be proud but rather be beaten, how much more then is Satan himself given to us, to trample us until we are humble?"[77] Even the advice given to less experienced monks signaled that pride was a significant factor in angelic appearances, because it made accommodation for monks' misguided belief in their worthiness to see such visions. The Greek anonymous collection of the *Sayings of the Fathers* recounts that the "old men used to say, 'Even if an angel should indeed appear to you, do not receive him but humiliate yourself, saying, "I am not worthy to see an angel, living in sin."'"[78] Psychologically astute, this piece of advice did not on the surface deny that an ascetic might see an angel but simply instructed the ascetic to humble himself regardless. The counsel, however, suggested by its wording that the elders should recognize that a misguided ascetic affected by the grandiosity that inspires—or is inspired by—a vision of an angel might not be capable in the moment of realizing that the vision is false. Thus it grants "*even if* an angel should *indeed* appear to you. . . ." Consequently, an ascetic convinced of his special status because of his experience of a seemingly angelic vision need not confront his pride until after the vision ends and the demon has been revealed.

Admonitory stories like these highlight the ascetic emphasis on practicing humility for the development of virtue, but they also show more is at stake when monks have angelic visions than just the registers of virtue and vice. While some of the emphasis on rejecting angelic visions as possible demonic appearances resonates with the general emphasis on discernment of and battle with demons that was so central to the development of Christian asceticism, especially Evagrian asceticism, there were also practical and social reasons to reject angelic visions as tainted, or abnormal, in light of the larger goals of community life. We have seen many cases where the presence of angels lent an otherwise unavailable authority to an ascetic: the old man who discerned appropriate behavior from the presence of angels or pigs, Pachomius and Theodore finding heretics through angelic reconnaissance, and Aphou speaking up to his bishop once prompted by an angel. Because angels supervised the activities of monks and helped determine community standards, it could be destabilizing to the community order for an inappropriate monk to receive angelic visions. It is perhaps for this reason that the ascetic literature collected as the *Sayings of the Fathers* went to such lengths to contain, to rebut, and eventually to reject visions of angels as detrimental to individual ascetics and to the community as a whole.

This is all the more true when, rather than being convinced they were seeing angels, ascetics were convinced of *being* angels. Even though the trope that the ascetic life is a life "equal to the angels" pervades the texts I have examined in this book, the idea that an ascetic may actually live as an angel found little purchase in them. Indeed, the literature raised the prospect only to reject it. One example, the story of John the Dwarf and his unruly expectations about the ascetic life, has drawn comment from many interpreters.[79] Perhaps it is a favorite because it strikes the sardonic tone that so satisfies readers of the *Sayings of the Fathers*. One day, John realized that he was like an angel.

> He said to his older brother: "I want to be free from care, as the angels are free from care, since they do not work, but are ceaselessly serving God." And, taking off his garment, he went out into the desert. Having spent a week thus, he returned to his brother. He knocked at the door, and [the brother] recognized him before he opened the door, saying "Who are you?" He responded "It is I, John, your brother." And he answered, saying to him "John became an angel, and he is no longer among humans." And he called for his help, saying, "It's me!" And he did not open the door to him, but left him to afflict himself until the next morning. Later, having opened the door to him, he said "You are human, it is necessary to work again so you can eat." And he was repentant, saying "Forgive me."[80]

John has overestimated his abilities, and his thoughts of living "like an angel" have, literally, left him shut out of the community. Even after he returned from his "angelic" retreat, John the Dwarf is no less proud, considering that he wished to be immediately recognized as a brother by the monk who remained in his cell. It took time—not to mention some physical affliction—to instill in John the proper understanding of his status as an ascetic.

To sympathize with John the Dwarf for a moment, were these ideas about seeing angels and being angels so extraordinary, given how ascetics were represented by their admirers? If the ascetic project was experienced by lay Christians through literature and oration, media that often described the ascetic life as an angelic one, it cannot be beyond plausibility that lay

Christians formed their expectations of ascetic practice and its rewards accordingly. Thus, when a Christian decided to join an ascetic community, part of the challenge may have been rooting out the unrealistic and even detrimental images created by his being a spectator to ascetic lifestyles.[81] In the stories examined here, those who see angels or think themselves angels are often, but not always, less experienced; those who correct them are frequently more experienced. It was in a new monk's negotiations of status and identity that conflict appeared between the expectations of an observer and the realities of ascetic practice.

Adjusting a new monk's expectations was doubly difficult because of the continuing adulation of those who came to visit the monasteries and communities of Egypt. The formidable leader of the White Monastery, Shenoute of Atripe, provides evidence that those within ascetic communities were well aware of their reputation as people who lived an angelic life.[82] The fame of ascetics under his charge frequently caused him to reflect on the distance between the world he was trying to create inside the monastery and the way that world appeared from a vantage point outside the monastery. Most often, his reflections sounded a rueful tone. He exhorted those under his leadership to remember that "there are crowds glorifying us out there while we, ourselves, do things worthy of contempt and innumerable evils."[83] Indeed, he felt it necessary to remind his monks that even though they are called "angels" by their admirers, this did not mean that they actually were angels. Shenoute took advantage of the various kinds of angels to make a point to his charges:

> Are you not called, [my] congregation, by those who glorify you "heavenly Jerusalem" and the ones who dwell among you "angel"? You are always the same—"heavenly Jerusalem"—and the angels are those among you who fear God and observe his words. . . . If those holy ones among you resemble angels or are similar to them in their righteous deeds, then they also will be with the angels in the kingdom of God, in the way that the Scripture tells us. If, however, those who are defiled or who will defile themselves at some point among you resemble or are similar to the ancient sinning angels in their unclean deeds, then they will be with them in hell.[84]

Shenoute recalled for his monks those Christians, presumably outsiders, who thought of them as a community surpassing the world; they were a "heavenly Jerusalem," glorified as "angels." But the ascetic life did not make one an angel; moral action did. In a discussion of a controversy surrounding the behavior of some in his care, Shenoute let his feelings be known: "I and others are saddened on account of you who are doing diabolic deeds, at the same time that I am greatly satisfied, and others with me, on account of those who do angelic deeds."[85] Ultimately, Shenoute linked behavior to identity, saying that those who did "diabolic deeds" were in some way devils themselves, while "those who do angelic deeds all their lives are angels."[86] Shenoute rather cleverly turned the expectation of the angelic life to his advantage: angels came in two species—heavenly and sinning—and his monks could align themselves with either group by their behavior.

Even the vigor behind such threats, though, did not blunt the disappointments created by the identification of the ascetic life with the angelic one. Consider the situation described in Shenoute's work *Why, O Lord*, a part of *Canon* 4.[87] Some monks had recently left the monastery at Shenoute's request, and Shenoute wondered who, exactly, was responsible for the fact that the monks have broken their vows by leaving. Was it he, who enforced his will and forced the monks out of the community, or was it they, whose behavior was unacceptable and led to their expulsion? As he reviewed the details of his decision to eject the offending monks, Shenoute shifted his focus to repine against the distance between the perceptions of outsiders and the reality of the constant work he had to do to keep the monastery going:

> Many times... we spend the entire day speaking and convicting, petitioning, comforting, blessing, cursing, struggling, saying words of enmity, reciting words of peace, being holy and being civilized, being gentle in patience, loving anger, being small of heart in disturbance and more anger, weeping with tears, laughing with the comfort and fear of the Lord, knowing that we are condemned by [our] laughing because the thing that allows us to laugh "turns to grief," as it is written [alluding to James 4.9], because our sins grow "we are restless," as it is written [2 Cor 6.10?], and yet "we rejoice in the Lord," according to the Scriptures. We endure and we dwell and we gather together, saying words like, "Where are our friends on the outside who come to us and call us 'angel'?" They see all of our bad deeds with our falsehood and our evil thoughts and they see us acting indecently in enmity with one another on account of our pride and our ignorance.[88]

Given the machinations that Shenoute found necessary to lead his monastery—the constant management of emotions and reactions by cajoling, pleading, comforting, scolding—the fact that those outside the monastery could refer to him and his monks as "angels" must have seemed ironic to him, even bitterly so.[89] For all his efforts, the "bad deeds" and "evil thoughts" of the community were exhibited publicly; "pride" and "ignorance" were in evidence among his monks. While being called an angel may have been meant in admiration, to Shenoute, such a term could only point out his failings as a leader.

Under no circumstances, however, would Shenoute allow the perceptions of outsiders to influence his treatment, even discipline, of those under his leadership. That was the lesson to be taken from a text that follows the previous text (and may be part of the same work). In it, Shenoute had threatened to physically visit and perhaps intimidate the people whose behavior he would like to change, and it would seem that his monks in response had mentioned to him their status as celebrities among those who observe the community. Shenoute's response was unequivocal.

> We do not see any other teaching or word except this alone—which signals in my heart that if God wishes, I will come to you, indeed, even in the body, so that I can do things that are not fitting to you in the presence of people who will hear and those who glorify you on the outside, calling you "Children of God" and saying that your congregation is "the heavenly Jerusalem." They speak to us exactly this way in our domain, and we are not worthy. Look, we the disobedient are disgraced all the more by the glory that they give us! Does the child of God or an angel or even a just man usually practice deceit, with every kind of wicked deed? Is "the heavenly Jerusalem" usually the place for any kind of sin?[90]

Surely, the answer was "no." Although he was disheartened by the distance between what outsiders thought of his monks and the reality he saw, Shenoute was also willing to use that distance to shame those he wished to punish. The standard of living the angelic life was a sharp tool by which to goad misbehaving, unruly, or haughty ascetics.

What these passages from ascetic literature make clear is that Egyptian ascetics and their leaders knew others praised them by making a connection between their practices and "the angelic life." This connection entered into the ways that ascetics thought both of themselves and of their project. Such a discourse worked constructively—establishing boundaries between the community and the world, affirming certain behaviors while allowing for others to be avoided—but it also created problems of authority and arrogance among ascetics. When we read texts, be they ancient or modern, that compare ascetics to angels, we must remember Shenoute's warning. The idea that Christian ascetics were living "the angelic life" carried varied and even contrasting effects, some worthy and helpful, like the righteous angels in the kingdom of God, and others difficult and troubling, like the defiled angels who reside in hell.

Explaining Ascetic Christianity

The equation of the angelic life with the ascetic life almost certainly originated outside ascetic communities, in the orations of urban Christians who sought to explain just what the ascetic project was. The actions of ascetic Christians may have been inspiring to others, but they could also be seen as calling into question part of urban life. If some Christians found sexual renunciation a necessary part of their devotion, did that mean that Christians in sexual relationships were less Christian? If some Christians lived as simply as they possibly could, did that imply that those Christians who enjoyed wealth and security were misguided? Explaining that ascetics were living the life of the angels both justified and normalized the existence of these alternate ways of being Christian; doing so also removed the implicit challenge of the ascetic life to the urban one, by placing the feats of the ascetics in the realm of the supernatural, something to be admired from afar, rather than adopted by all. In this sense, one effect of describing ascetics as angels was most deeply felt in the city: it preserved urban Christian life as a viable mode of piety for "normal" humanity, even as it valued those extraordinary Christians who did not choose it.

An even more salient effect of this discourse was the way it changed ascetic communities, particularly in Egypt. Ascetics, and those who would be ascetics, were aware of the way others thought of them living "the angelic life"; that knowledge influenced both the imaginative and practical life of ascetic Christian communities. At times, thinking of oneself as living "the angelic life" was beneficial as it eased the difficulties of maintaining a separate community and blunted the problems of solitude. Even so, stories collected about ascetic Christians and the works that survive from monastic leaders like Shenoute and Pachomius suggest there was a comprehensive effort to mitigate the idea that being an ascetic meant living among angels or even as an angel. Monastic leaders tried to disabuse individual ascetics of this notion, and their campaign seems to have worked. As one short exchange from the *Sayings of the Fathers* illustrates, expectations about life in an ascetic community often changed during the length of an ascetic's career.

> In the beginning, Abba Amoes said to Abba Isaiah, "how do you see me at this moment?" He said to him, "As an angel, father." And again, later, he said to him, "Now how do you see me?" and he said "As Satan. Whatever you say to me I take as a sword."[91]

When the monk first arrived, he thought of his elder as an angel and likely thought of all the members of the community this way. Over time, though, the ascetic realized that his relationship with his elder would be one that required discipline, harsh honesty at times, yet would benefit him in his pursuit of a Christian life. While their admirers may have continued to see them as angels or their communities as the "heavenly Jerusalem," late ancient Christian ascetics quickly learned to be wary of thinking of their communities or themselves as angels. Intriguingly, at the same time that ascetic texts were attempting to tamp down the expectations that Christians could enact their practices among angels, that very expectation was being cultivated and fashioned in another genre: the texts that taught new Christians how to participate in ritual, particularly in large urban congregations.

6

Bringing Angels into the World

CATECHESIS AND THE CHRISTIAN IMAGINATION

BECOMING A LEADER in the hierarchy of officials who guided communities of Christians was not a step to be taken lightly. That was the message of a work written by John Chrysostom during the 380s CE, a treatise titled *On the Priesthood.* It was such a forceful piece of rhetoric that within a decade, the Latin writer Jerome had included John on his list of "famous men," solely on the basis of having read that one text.[1] *On the Priesthood* was, at its simplest, an apology. John had avoided ordination as a presbyter for as long as he could, and in this work he attempted to explain his reluctance to serve. His strategy was to paint the duties of a presbyter in the gravest of terms; such work was holy and solemn, and John was not to be faulted for considering the option cautiously. He presented a number of arguments to establish the serious nature of the priesthood, but the part of the text that had the greatest influence on later Christian culture and its estimation of Christian leaders was not an argument, but a story. John recounted the experiences of a certain "old man, who was used to seeing visions." At one point, the old man was granted a particular vision during the ritual of the Eucharist: he saw "a crowd of angels, clothed in shining garments, circling around the altar bowing down, just as you might see soldiers bowing in the presence of a king."[2]

The prospect that a Christian might have a vision like this was not entirely out of the ordinary in late antiquity—John seems to be alluding to the vision of the third heaven that Paul reported "someone" he knew having, so anonymous visionaries have a long history in Christian literature. But John's report stood in direct contrast with the growing disquiet manifest in and about ascetic communities regarding visions that I examined in the last chapter. At a moment when those engaged in cultivation began to question the wisdom of entertaining visions of angels, either because of the authority such visions lent to seers or because of the controversy simmering near the end of the fourth century over the theological implications of seeing divine beings, John Chrysostom was blithely reporting that invisible angels were indeed present at his church and apparent to some fortunate Christians. What is more, though John's treatise was the earliest surviving description of such a vision, the perspective it records became commonplace in late ancient Christianity. Almost universally, by the end of the sixth century, Christians imagined scenes just like that seen by John's old man: angels encircling altars, present at Christian rituals in postures of submission and obedience.

Proof of this change would seem difficult to come by. Bluntly put, how can we possibly know what late ancient Christians imagined? We cannot, of course, but a development in Christian culture during the fourth century does allow us to come very close. After the political changes that supported the legitimization of Christianity in the first half of the fourth century, many groups of Christians "saw a massive influx of new members into the church, people of varied backgrounds and motives," most of them adults.[3] Correspondingly, leaders of these groups began to devise training programs for those about to be given full ritual status in their communities. Records of these instructions, classed as the genre of "catechetical treatises," survive from diverse late ancient Christian writers from almost every corner of the ancient Christian world: Cyril of Jerusalem, in the mid-fourth century, then Gregory of Nyssa, John Chrysostom, Theodore of Mopsuestia, Ambrose of Milan, near the end of the fourth century, and Augustine of Hippo, Nicetas of Remesiana, and Narsai, the Syrian writer, at the start of the fifth century all penned catechetical materials. Their works are the foundation of our understanding of Christian ritual life in late antiquity, because modern reconstructions of early Christian liturgy depend in large part on the detailed descriptions of rituals that they provide.[4]

But catechetical treatises were more than just stage directions. In addition to providing a practical education—where Christians should expect to stand during a given ritual, what they should expect to do, what they should be prepared to say—catechetical writers also gave their charges a cultural education, one with far wider horizons than the occasional ritual gathering. Christian leaders took the opportunity to advise neophyte

Christians to accept certain points of doctrine, to hold specific attitudes toward their own community and toward outsiders, and to practice certain methods of physical comportment not just during the ritual they were being trained for, but throughout the day as a general habit.[5] Moreover, because Christian catechists advocated the representation of certain images for those taking part in the ritual life of their churches—and in some cases, warned against the representation of other images—catechetical texts from late antiquity can allow us to trace changes in the religious imagination of early Christians, or, at least, how Christian leaders hoped to shape and prune that imagination in an ongoing process of education. Late ancient instructions to new Christians often asked them to imagine angels present, invisibly, at rituals, and most frequently at the Eucharist, the commemoration of Jesus's death. Yet over the course of late antiquity, the character of these instructions shifted: the angels catechetical writers taught Christians to imagine increasingly emphasized—in their attendance, attitude, and number—the importance of Christian rituals. Almost all surviving evidence suggests that, by the end of late antiquity, Christians assumed churches were full of angels that watched rituals unfold.

This chapter traces the change in how ancient Christians were asked to view rituals by the leaders of their communities. The first section briefly surveys the way angels informed the first three centuries of Christian ideas about ritual and the communities that performed it. Adopting an orientation also used by other minority religious traditions, very early Christians held angels to conduct a liturgy in heaven and cast their own ritual lives in imitation of this angelic service. This way, despite their political inferiority, Christians could imagine themselves part of a universal, heavenly majority. The second section shows how this perspective informed the catechetical teachings of two fourth-century leaders of congregations: Cyril, appointed bishop of a community in Jerusalem in 348 CE and Theodore, who became bishop of Mopsuestia in 392 or 393 CE. Both asked audiences to use discrete techniques of visualization to enhance their experiences of ritual, and both encouraged Christians specifically to see angels as they watched ritual. Such training gave Christian liturgical performances cosmic importance, but mostly because the rituals were linked thereby to activities happening elsewhere, primarily in heaven. The third section demonstrates that later Christians reversed this perspective. Beginning with John Chrysostom, Christian writers turned the traditional understanding of ritual on its head. Rather than consider Christian rituals to be reflections of some celestial angelic service, John encouraged Christians, in catechetical materials and throughout his preaching career, to imagine angels leaving heaven to become spectators to Christian rituals as they took place on earth. Writers who followed him, like Narsai, took John's innovation one step further, claiming that angels not only watched what the priest did, but that they needed the actions of the priest in the same way that participating Christians did: they relied on the priest to conduct the operations leading to their sanctity. Thus, during late antiquity, Christian practitioners were trained to imagine angels present at rituals in such a way as to place themselves, their communities, and their leaders at the center of the cosmos.

Joining the Community in Heaven

The earliest followers of Jesus were members of a loosely organized, Greek-speaking community of Jews, and as such, they inhabited a religious world that held established traditions about angels and their activities. In the literature of the first few centuries before the common era, there were hints that a multitude of angels resided in heaven with the primary job of celebrating a ritual service honoring and glorifying God. Inventive pseudepigraphical texts, like *2 Enoch*, contained narratives of supernatural travel, in which protagonists visited various heavens and verified the existence of the angels living there and singing continuously the praise of God.[6] Other revelatory visions likewise offered a glimpse of the angels who "dwell in the temples of salvation and hymn the ineffable highest God."[7] Such reflections took their cues from descriptions, mostly contained in books of prophecy in Scripture, of the angels who offered praise to God. Among these descriptions, the most influential was a scene in which Isaiah, the reluctant prophet, was granted a vision of God's holy throne in heaven. Here is how the book of Isaiah recounts that experience:

> And it happened in the year that Ozias the king died, that I saw the Lord, seated on a high and exalted throne, and the house was full of his glory. And seraphim stood, encircling him, six wings for the one and six wings for the other, with two concealing the face, two concealing the feet, and with two they flew. One cried out to the other and said, "Holy, holy, holy, Lord Sabaoth. The entire earth is filled with his glory."[8]

From this, readers of Isaiah learned that God was surrounded by angels who worship him; they also learned the specific words with which the seraphim praised God. Practitioners in the religious traditions that claimed Isaiah as their own saw these words as a way to join with the angels in the worship of the Lord: a prayer beginning with "Holy, Holy, Holy" became a regular part of the liturgy in both ancient Jewish and ancient Christian groups.[9] Thus, even as the earliest Christians and the Jewish groups of which they were a part imagined angels praising God in heaven, they also imagined themselves adding to the chorus, replicating in their own ritual pronouncements the speech of angels. Their reproduction of the angels' praise was an aspirational act, as these religious practitioners imitated the community they imagined residing in heaven.

The imaginative work ancient practitioners did to consider themselves one small part of a wider, corporate body of angelic ritual worshippers of God was quite like the imaginative work that animates a contemporary political phenomenon. In his book *Imagined Communities*, Benedict Anderson explores the improbable triumphalist tenor of modern nationalist movements; he notes that the early confidence of nationalist leaders is difficult to explain, given the originally sparse and loose character of the relationships among the people they seek to motivate.[10] That is to say, those who eventually form a "nation" often start with no wider visible entity to which they owe fervent allegiance. But this does not deter them. "The members of even the smallest nation," Anderson explains, "will never know most of their fellow-members, meet them, or even hear of them, yet in the minds of each lives the image of their communion."[11] The "image" of that communion is something that must be described and disseminated before those who will eventually emerge as a nation actually recognize themselves as such, but it does not depend on any physical or social reality. Instead, it is an imaginative construct. By evoking, then nurturing that image, a very small minority can, despite appearances, imagine itself to be powerful and populous. By means of the image of, as Anderson calls it, an "imagined community," members articulate a vision of the group for themselves, not as an unorganized, disparate minority, but rather as a "nation."

Or, as a religious tradition. In antiquity, the presence of an imagined community of religious practitioners—thin on the ground, but thick in heaven—sustained countercultural movements of the most improbable variety. For instance, some of the texts found in the caves at the Dead Sea, dating from the first century BCE, reflect the expressions of a group that considered itself the only existing ritually correct Jewish community. The polemic they offer against other Jews, whom they cast as ritual specialists gone wrong, appears to have been directed at the priesthood based in Jerusalem. Among other differences, the community at the Dead Sea drew its liturgical structure from the solar calendar, which was in conflict with the adjusted lunar calendar of the priests celebrating at the Jerusalem temple. In the face of such authority—the Jerusalem priesthood was, after all, the establishment—the small community justified its ritual difference by claiming it was following the same calendar as the angels. Their liturgy was an angelic liturgy, one that was, and always had been, executed in heaven. Instead of being ritual deviants, those Jews who left behind texts like the *Songs of the Sabbath Sacrifice* considered themselves part of a cosmic majority, only part of which was visible on earth.[12] Indeed, in a very basic way, such mental maneuverings worked for all Jews in antiquity, not just those in smaller minority factions. Ancient Jews cast the synagogue as a central institution and, at the same time, as a "reflection of [the] heavenly temple," thus "an inherently sacred space" that dominated the unseen world and outweighed the temples and gods of non-Jews.[13] Of course, most religious traditions imagine themselves aligned with the heavens or some wider reality that escapes their less-enlightened neighbors, but this notion served as an important encouragement to those in minority traditions, or in the case of the texts deposited at the Dead Sea, a minority tradition within a minority tradition.

This same strategy was easily adapted by another minority within the Jewish minority in antiquity, namely, the early followers of Jesus, who were eager to imagine themselves part of the community of angels. At the start of the second century, the author of Hebrews urged his readers to make doubly sure none "fail to obtain the grace of God" (Heb 12.15). Such grace was difficult to come by because the community in which it was to be gained was not obvious or visible to all. The author thought that his readers stood to arrive in an otherworldly commonwealth where they would exist as counterparts to "the heavenly Jerusalem and to the innumerable angels in the festal gathering, and to the assembly of the firstborn who are enrolled in heaven, and to God the judge of all, and to the spirits of the righteous made perfect, and to Jesus, the mediator of a new covenant" (Heb 12.22–24). As the author populated his imagined community with a heavenly city, an infinity of angels, and even God himself, he also loaded the message to those reading the text: though they might lose heart, they should be reassured by the gathered number of those who are part of their community—on high, and of high number. The assumption that there was an angelic cohort, available in heaven, allowed writers like the author of Hebrews to manifest a latent majority, existing invisibly behind the apparent paucity of believers. At times, the idea of an angelic community also carried a requirement of moral purity for members of the religious community on earth. The author of Revelation, for example, made clear that he was of one mind with the angels who praised God by adopting the vision of Isaiah 6 as his own revelatory experience (Rev 4.8). Other Christians, he warned, may learn the hymns that the angels gathered around the throne sing only if they remained pure (Rev 14.2–4). Like this, an imagined angelic community could be adopted to inspire Christians, giving them a larger group in which to experience the solidarity of the righteous, but it could also be adopted to discriminate among them, with texts like Revelation spelling out the cosmic consequences of deviance from the expectations of that larger, unseen group. Establishing an imagined heavenly community—the majority of which are powerful, yet silent, partners—in reality lends a great deal of weight to those visible leaders who police the community on earth, as they are the only ones who can articulate the standards of the imagined whole.

Evidence about ritual in the early centuries of Christianity can be difficult to come by, but what evidence there is suggests that imagined angels played a continuing role in guaranteeing the legitimacy of ritual traditions, especially those under scrutiny.[14] Tertullian's treatise *On Baptism*, written at the turn of the third century, defended the ritual he knew as baptism from detractors, likely Christians, who thought it to be too close to non-Christian water rituals. For Tertullian, proof of baptism's necessity lay in the gospel story of Bethesda. Available only in some versions of the Gospel of John, the story recounts a pool of water at Bethesda agitated by an angel once per year; the first person to enter the water after the angel's visit would be cured of whatever ailment he had.[15] In Tertullian's progressive view of history, Christian baptism was the better-developed version of this pool. "Moving forward in everything, the grace of God was added to the waters and to the angel," he explained. "What used to heal the injuries of the body now heals the spirit; those that used to create temporal health now make eternal health; those that used to liberate only one person, once per year, now save the people every day, taking away death by the washing away of sins."[16] The angel that prepares the water is the "mediator" or "facilitator" of baptism—in Tertullian's phrase, the *arbiter baptismi*—without which the ritual cannot proceed, but it was also the legitimator of the ritual, marking Christian baptism of Tertullian's time the product of events described in Scripture.

Other third-century Christians authorized their rituals by using the strategy of the community at the Dead Sea: arguing for the authenticity of rituals by linking them to heavenly rituals accomplished by angels. In one example from the early third century, Clement of Alexandria reported about a group that imagined human beings having angelic doubles: when the human being was baptized on earth, her corresponding angel underwent a celestial baptism in heaven.[17] Another example can be drawn from the contentious politics of martyrdom and communal identity in North Africa in the middle of the third century. Cyprian, the contested leader of one of the communities at Carthage, was in a lengthy struggle over the nature of Christian authority. That struggle centered on the authenticity of the salvation of martyrs, those executed as witnesses of the faith. Cyprian held that an angel presided over the deaths of the martyrs, making their deaths into a type of "baptism"; the presence of the angel surpassed the authority of earthly baptism, rendering the powers of the martyrs in a heavenly vein and beyond earthly reproach.[18] In situations when the legitimacy of ritual and ritual celebrants were challenged, the suggestion that an angel might somehow be involved, lending its power to the baptism, whether actual or figurative, allowed Christian leaders to invoke both authority for themselves and authenticity for their ritual communities, whether large or small. As we will see in the next section, Christians continued to evoke an imagined community of angels, even after Christianity was legitimated and gained status in the culture of the Mediterranean. In the fourth century and beyond, Christian catechesis placed this angelic community in a different relationship to the community of Christians on earth.

Harnessing the Imagination

The earliest formal catechetical instruction from late antiquity was written by Cyril of Jerusalem in 348 CE. Though Cyril had just become bishop of Jerusalem when he wrote his instructions, his social and political position was more precarious than being "bishop of Jerusalem" might make it seem. First, Jerusalem at the mid-fourth century was only beginning to emerge as a significant Christian destination city. The financial contributions and attention of the emperor Constantine and his mother Helena had begun to draw tourists and their social capital to the city; theirs was only one of many optimistic visions of what Jerusalem was meant to be.[19] These visions, however, were not reality; Jerusalem was not yet the powerful city its supporters hoped it would become. In fact, when Cyril was appointed its bishop, it was at the authority of the bishop of Caesarea—a city that in the fourth century was the most powerful in the Roman province of Palestine and which, in the Christian hierarchy, had charge of the surrounding area, including Jerusalem. So, when Cyril took the leadership of a Christian community in Jerusalem, he was working in a small, second-tier venue. At the same time, Cyril's position as the leader of the Christian community at Jerusalem was far from stable. His appointment and his theological commitments were viewed with a vague suspicion, and he was exiled from Jerusalem no less than three times during his career, as theological allegiances and the preferences of emperors for certain parties among Christians shifted.[20] During Cyril's bumpy career, Jerusalem was a growing, changing city, emergent in Christian configurations of power; its emergence, however, took place in fits and starts, such that during the fourth century, the theological and political preeminence of Jerusalem among Christians was never a foregone conclusion.

Perhaps this explains why Cyril adopted the model of an imagined angelic community as he introduced new Christians to life in his congregation at Jerusalem. Citing Ezekiel 36, Cyril told those training to partake in ritual that this was a moment to take on a "new heart" and a "new spirit," not for their own sake, or not even for the sake of the rising Jerusalem, but so that they "may become a subject of joy for the heavens."[21] New Christians should know "the angels want to delight with" them, and Cyril hoped that people joining his community would understand that the "heavenly powers" would be overjoyed at the prospect of their baptism and would welcome them as fellows.[22] When Christians joined Cyril's church at Jerusalem, they were joining the community in heaven, and the "tens of thousands in the angelic army" in heaven stood to watch them enter.[23] At a time when many different new expressions of Christian power were coming into view—the emergent episcopacy, linked across the Mediterranean; the imperially sponsored conciliar movement; the developing trade in pilgrimage and holy tourism, centered on Jerusalem—the fact that Cyril chose to have new Christians use a centuries-old technique of imagining an invisible polity of angels speaks to both the potential of that technique and to the precarious nature of both Cyril's position and those "institutions" that were emerging in the fourth century.

The prospect of an angelic community also turned out to be a powerful tool by which Cyril could advocate certain attitudes and behaviors. As he described the power of the Holy Spirit, for instance, Cyril could simply declare that it was "great, all-powerful, and wondrous."[24] He could also, though, ask his listeners to consider their wider community as the context for the Holy Spirit's work and eventually its power. "Think how many of you are now sitting here," Cyril said, then "broaden your mind's eye from this province to the whole Roman Empire; then from this, look at the whole world." In all of these places they had just conjured, Cyril reassured them, the Holy Spirit was provident; its power covered anything they could imagine.[25] The number of people that a listener could easily see, with his eyes, was already large, but the number he could easily consider, in his mind, was greater still, and the notion that the Holy Spirit had power over all of these inspired reverence in a way that a simple statement of the magnitude of the Holy Spirit could not. How much more so then, when Christians were asked to think beyond the earth? Once Cyril ran out of human beings by which to identify the authority of the Holy Spirit, he shifted and urged his listeners, "Do not remain on earth, but go up to the things above. Go up now in intelligence, even into the first heaven, and look at the innumerable myriads of angels there. Go up higher in thoughts, if you are able; look at the archangels, too, look at the spirits, also, the powers, the principalities, the authorities, the thrones, the dominions."[26] Cyril assumed audiences could envision things not present to them, which we can divide into two classes: first, things existing in the world but not readily visible to an individual human being (like a Roman province), but second, things invisible, never readily apparent to an individual human being (like orders of angels). They were to practice calling both kinds of things to mind. By leading his audience through this exercise, Cyril taught Christians to value the importance of the Holy Spirit in ways that were directly dependent on their ability to imagine the unseen.

The technique of calling such things to mind, then, could enhance a theological claim, but in Cyril's hands, it also reinforced his own authority as a leader and moral teacher. Cyril used the same technique again in a later discourse to multiply the size of the audience observing a newly baptized Christian's sins. "Look, human," he cried, "before how many you are coming to be judged"—not just those human beings in the audience but the "entire human race" will stand there, including all past generations. While all human beings who have ever lived themselves constitute a large number, Cyril warned that "it is still a small number, for the number of angels is greater. They are the ninety-nine sheep and the one sheep is humanity. The number of places that exist—that is how the number [of angels] should be reckoned. The inhabited earth is a point in the middle of one heaven; the heaven that encircles this first heaven has a number that must be quite expansive, and the heavens of the heavens are beyond conjecture."[27] The ultimate goal of Cyril's flight of fancy was change, specifically to change behavior. He gently proffered a piece of advice to those imagining the multitudes of angels in heaven watching them: "Wouldn't it be good for us to be a bit anxious? Do not think it a small thing, human, even discounting the punishment, to be condemned in front of so many! Wouldn't we rather die a thousand deaths than be condemned by friends?"[28] This bishop of Jerusalem harnessed the imagination of his listeners to create heavenly populations, powerful motivating forces that subtly aligned new Christians with one, seemingly majority, point of view. That point of view inspired specific behaviors, like guarding one's actions, but also theological attitudes, like revering the Holy Spirit.

While Cyril used the prospect of a wider angelic community in order to explore theological positions or to inspire certain behaviors, he and other fourth-century catechists also asked students to adopt techniques of visualization to bring angels into their presence as they participated in rituals. Such visualization, practiced in a ritual context, was an extremely potent pedagogical tool. Since each visible part of a ritual could serve as a template upon which images produced by participants could be projected, and since rituals were, by definition, predictable and regular, visualization during ritual had a regular, repeatable structure that supported its pedagogical impact. In an article examining the genre of catechesis, Georgia Frank argues that writers like Cyril of Jerusalem, Theodore of Mopsuestia, and John Chrysostom suggested the visualization of images in the hope that they could teach catechumens to see the rituals they watched, the agents involved, and the actions accomplished with "the eyes of faith." No simple metaphor, this phrase represents an attitude comprising several "visual strategies" that "generated a host of mental images that would reframe the physical perception" of the rituals in question.[29] When catechumens participated in the Eucharist for the first time, for example, they were taught to have a more complex experience than simply watching the events in front of them unfold. Instead, by a "steady layering of imaginal bodies over physical perceptions," imagined bodies they themselves had conjured, new Christians could understand the Eucharist and its place in Christian theology, actively recreating the links between the Eucharist and an event like the Passion or the Eucharist and the birth of Christ by the use of their imaginations.[30] Catechists of the fourth and fifth centuries took seriously the idea that faith was precisely that entity described in Hebrews 11—"the inner conviction of deeds unseen"—and instructed new Christians in a way that trained them to generate mental images of those unseen deeds as they participated in ritual. It is crucial to understand that catechetical teachers urged catechumens to generate images of the unseen, not just the first time they participated in a ritual, but reliably, each time they participated. As a training program, catechesis inaugurated a perpetual series of lessons; its effects were lasting, with learned imagery generated each time a Christian participated in a ritual, thus reinscribing lessons about divine actors, human beings, and the relationships between them at each performance.

Cyril is an excellent example of a teacher using this pedagogical method because he taught Christians to generate mental images, not just in order to encourage certain behaviors or to reinforce points of doctrine, but also to remake rituals into multilayered, complex events. In a second set of catechetical sermons, Cyril taught Christians to call an impressive array of characters to mind as they watched the Eucharist.[31]

> Let us bring to mind heaven and earth and sea, sun and moon, stars, every rational and irrational creature, seen and unseen, angels, archangels, powers, dominions, principalities, authorities, thrones, the many-faced cherubim, saying forcefully the words of David, "Extol the Lord with me." Let us bring to mind also the seraphim, who Isaiah contemplated in the Holy Spirit standing encircling the throne of God, with two wings covering their faces, two their feet, and two for flying, saying "Holy, holy, holy Lord Sabaoth." It is for this reason that we say this doxology, transmitted to us by the seraphim, and through this hymning we become fellows in the army above the world.[32]

Linking this exercise of the imagination to a specific ritual changed the experience of the ritual. First, as Christians brought the heavens and their inhabitants to mind, they created evidence, within their own minds, of the ritual having been established in heaven. By generating an image of seraphim praising God with the words "Holy, holy, holy," participants also generated an etiology for the ritual they watched. Then as Christians sang, "Holy, holy, holy," they were repeating words given them by the seraphim, the highest order of angels, who praise God in Isaiah 6. To sing these words is to perform the ritual one has been taught to follow, but it also holds more promise: as Cyril explained, by repeating the words of the angels, Christians celebrating the ritual became "participants" (κοινωνοί) in the heavenly retinue. The mental work that participants did at Cyril's behest helped them imagine the real significance of the ritual they saw taking place. More than simple imitation, full participation in a Christian ritual, with the proper additional images called to mind, allowed Christians to join the heavenly ritual, their identities to shift to participate with the angels whose singing they imitate. Cyril's instructions about ritual were based in the notion that understanding how to engage the imagination was key to experiencing all the transformational potential of ritual.

A later writer, Theodore of Mopsuestia, used similar imaginative techniques to make Christian rituals into multilayered, multitemporal events. While he was serving as a presbyter in Antioch near the very end of the fourth century, Theodore offered a series of sixteen lectures for new Christians explaining the various acts of worship in his community, including the creed worshippers said together, the prayer "Our Father," the ritual of baptism, and the ritual of the Eucharist. Given the sheer length of these lectures—each would have taken at least ninety minutes to deliver—is it not surprising that Theodore stopped often to inform his audience of the worth of the knowledge he was giving them, reassuring them that the detailed descriptions of the rituals are useful. The following passage characterizes Theodore's frequent explanations:

> It is right and necessary that we should explain before you the power of the sacrament and of the things which are accomplished in it, and the reason for which each of them is accomplished, in order that when you have learned what is the reason for all of them you may receive the things that take place with great love. Every sacrament consists in the narration of unseen and unspeakable things through signs and emblems. Such things require explanation and interpretation, for the sake of the person who draws nigh unto the sacrament, so that he might know its power. If it only consisted of the (visible) elements themselves, words would have been useless, or sight itself would have been able to show us one by one all the happenings that take place, but since a sacrament contains the signs of things that are taking place or have already taken place, words are needed to explain the power of signs and mysteries.[33]

Rituals, for Theodore, did not accomplish a simple performative function, shifting the status of participants from unbaptized to baptized, or not-yet-communicant to communicant. Instead, rituals told a story, consisting primarily of the "narration of unseen and unspeakable things." As Theodore saw it, there were always layers of meaning to be found in a sacrament, referents for which the sacrament stands, and it was his purpose and responsibility to equip his new flock with those layers of meaning. Christians must know the various levels of significance associated with ritual acts because it was necessary for Christians both to understand the narrative associated with a particular ritual and to recreate that narrative in all its details each time they experienced the ritual. Without the ability to generate those layers of meaning, Theodore implied, it would not be possible for a Christian to "receive the things that take place with great love" or "to know the power" of the sacrament. In a certain sense, Theodore considered Christian rituals ineffective unless the participants could recreate fully the meaning of the acts they saw each time they watched.

The specific teaching that Theodore offered directed Christians to see the rituals they watched as traces of another, more important reality: the ongoing heavenly service that they would join at their resurrection. In his eyes, Christians lived out their time on earth as a part of an earthly community but always were to be looking forward to their eventual entrance into the heavenly community, where waiting for them were the "innumerable companies of angels and men who are immortal and immutable."[34] As Theodore told those about to watch rituals: "We must picture in our mind that we are dimly in heaven, and, through faith, draw in our imagination the image of heavenly things."[35] To participate in a ritual with the proper training, then, was to see a preview of the heavenly service, however "dimly" represented. The central pieces from which Christians so trained would form their images of the heavenly service were, in fact, the earthly celebrants of the ritual. At the center of the performance stood the priest.

> We must think that the priest who comes to the altar is representing his image, not that he [the priest] offers himself in sacrifice, any more than he is truly a high priest, but because he performs the figure of the service of the ineffable sacrifice, and through this figure he dimly represents the image of the unspeakable heavenly things and of the supernatural and incorporeal hosts.[36]

Participants at the Eucharist did not need to imagine heaven from scratch, but instead had bare hints of it before them, located in the people they watched. The priest himself was "a likeness of the service of heaven"; he was in turn served by the deacons, who also represented a likeness "of the service of the spiritual messengers and ministers."[37] As Christians watched the Eucharist, they had access to a tableau of the heavenly community they would eventually join, but it could be fully unveiled only in their imaginations and only if they equated the actors they saw in front of them with heavenly actors. That basic requirement put Christians in the position of continually associating their ritual leaders with members of heaven, even as they hoped one day to join the community in heaven—a powerful yet subtle argument for the authority of those who enacted the rituals. As symbols, the priest and the deacons in the procession pointed to the heavenly high priest and his servants, the angels, but as people, the priest and the deacons were forever tied, by Theodore's teaching, to the well-trained Christian's imaginative representation of those heavenly beings.

Ultimately, the association Theodore sought to establish between the Eucharist and the service of the angels in heaven was itself referential, pointing to a third time and place: the moment of Jesus's execution, enacted in history. When Christians saw the Eucharist and considered its evocation of the heavenly service, Theodore wanted them also to see that both these rituals, on earth and in heaven, were enactments of the Passion. As Georgia Frank has explained, elements of the Eucharist were assigned symbolic siblings, things and people present when Jesus died: the coverings of the altar in the church bring to mind the burial shroud that covered Jesus, the bread on the altar referred to Jesus's body laid out for burial, and the participants in the offering processional should bring to mind the funeral procession, those who took Jesus to the grave.[38] Using these associations, Theodore claimed Christians should mentally behold a "complete representation" of the Passion in the details of the Eucharist. Doing so, however, created an impasse, because the ritual was missing a piece: there was nothing in its elements to correspond to Jesus's executioners.[39] For Theodore, the omission had a purpose, because to mentally represent Jews—whom he assumed were those bringing Jesus to his death—during the Eucharist would be, in his words, "incongruous and impermissible."[40] Instead, Christians were to replace the Jews with the "invisible hosts of the ministry," imagining such angels to be present when the eucharistic offerings are brought to the altar and to be those who led Jesus to his death. It was their capacity for imagination that allowed the multitemporal, multidimensional representation of the ritual to occur as Theodore wished it to happen. If the Eucharist also tells the story of the Passion, then by inserting angels in the role of those who brought Jesus to his execution, participants are both cleaning up and filling out the narrative details of the Passion and the Eucharist as they are combined. The Eucharist, in Theodore's conception, represented both of these modes, being "an imitation or memorial of the saving acts of Christ's life *and* the anticipation of the heavenly liturgy."[41] Yet it only did so when Christians engaged in the visualization in which they were trained.

That visualization placed angels in the middle of Christian ritual and, at the same time, it made skill in visualizing angels a key part of participating in ritual. Christians could understand the fullness of the Eucharist, could, in Theodore's words, "know the power" of the ritual, only when they successfully introduced angels to their view of its unfolding. They could see the past and the future at once, by receiving the image of the priest and his assistants as angels, either those angels who worshipped in heaven, or those who attended Jesus as he prepared for his death. Furthermore, Christians could access these extra events frequently over time, as frequently as they watched the Eucharist. Their imaginative work at rituals activated a sphere unseen in normal human events, transporting them back and forth, between past, present, and apocalyptic future. A ritual executed without these trained spectators was still an effective ritual, but it lacked the extra associations produced by well-prepared spectators. There was an absence at the center of the ritual when it was taken only as a set of actions performed, an absence that waited to be filled by the work of the Christian imagination.[42]

Christians filled this absence in a particular place, in their minds, but also in a particular location, as spectators in the gallery of a church. The visualization in which they engaged remade not only the rituals but also the place of rituals and those who conducted them. Taken as a whole, catechetical materials like the treatises from Cyril and Theodore that I have been discussing had the primary function of transferring information. Ostensibly, those who knew about ritual taught those who did not know, training them for participation. Their pedagogical leadership created continuity of practice and uniformity of thought among members of their communities, the end being a group of Christians united in service, fully aware of the hidden mysteries that a celebration of ritual meant. Catechesis created "churches," groups of Christians who attended ritual together and who, if trained, understood those rituals in ways that, if they were not entirely identical, were at least compatible. But catechetical programs also shaped something else, namely, the relationship between the person offering lessons and those receiving lessons. Religious leaders inhabit many different roles with respect to those they lead—exemplar, parent, servant, judge—and the roles leaders adopt can in part influence the way followers approach them and reckon their authority. The role of teacher, of ritual expert, which men like Cyril and Theodore adopted as their own, formed those who attend the lessons in a particular way: they learned, but they did not surpass the teacher in learning. If catechesis was a method of training the imagination to understand the unseen realities lying underneath the apparent actions of ritual, then catechetical teachers possessed a deep store of secret information that they could distribute at their pleasure. Followers, or students in this model, were in permanent disparity with those they followed. The fact that such training occurred as a prerequisite to joining the community and participating fully in its rituals should point to its role in shaping a particular relationship between members who join and the leaders who admit them. Catechetical programs did teach new Christians to attend rituals and trained them in strategies to see what was beneath the surface, but these programs also shaped new Christians into an audience, gathered and waiting for the revelations of their leader and their celebrant.

Translating Christian Ritual

Even at an early point in his career of service in urban churches, John Chrysostom already understood the assumption that there was an angelic service in heaven from which Christian ritual took its form. As much is evident in his discussion of the role of the ritual celebrant in *On the Priesthood,* the treatise I mentioned at the start of this chapter. It emphasized the authority and responsibility incumbent upon the priest by associating his work with an angelic service. As John explained, "the priesthood is completed on earth, but it has its order in the deeds of the heavens." He voiced a common understanding, arguing that the Holy Spirit itself had instituted the priesthood, thus persuading "those yet remaining in the flesh to manifest the service of the angels."[43] Yet the particular way John understood the work of the priest was quite different from the way Theodore of Mopsuestia or Cyril of Jerusalem had understood it. Calling on an interpretation of Matthew 18—a chapter that figures largely in conceptions of the priesthood from late antiquity onward—John applied to the priest instructions Jesus had given the disciples.

> For those who are dwelling on earth and passing their time here, they are given trust to administer the things of the heavens and they have an authority which God did not grant to angels or archangels. For it is not to them that he said, "whatever you bind on earth will be bound also in heaven, and whatever you might loose upon the earth will be loosed in heaven."[44]

As is obvious from this line of argument, John did subscribe to the notion of a "service of the angels"—there was, for him, a heavenly liturgy—but that service had been usurped, as God had overturned the established order to give the responsibility for the service to human beings instead. In John's understanding of Scripture, priests had been granted powers that surpassed and encompassed the powers previously given to angels.

While this portion of *On the Priesthood* drew its authority from scriptural interpretation, we saw at the beginning of the chapter how John had another source of authority for his claims, namely, experience. By citing the vision of the old man who had seen angels gathered and bowing at the altar during a ritual, John introduced the presence of unseen angels as a marker of the solemnity of priestly work. In the same section of *On the Priesthood*, John appealed directly to readers to imagine the position of the priest celebrating the ritual of the Eucharist.

> Whenever he calls to the Holy Spirit and completes the awe-inspiring sacrifice and reaches continually to the common master of all, tell me where should we order ourselves? What purity do we ask of him and what piety? Imagine of what kind the hands doing such sacrifice have to be, of what kind the tongue that professes such words; the soul that receives the spirit who doesn't it have to be purer than, holier than? At that moment, the angels stand around the priest, and the bema and the place around the altar are all filled with heavenly powers in honor of the one laying there.[45]

This description reveals something of the way Christians thought about the Eucharist; John referred to the priest calling the Holy Spirit and honoring the presence on the altar, likely an indication that he assumed Christ was that presence. But we should note that the trajectory of John's comments followed the status of the priest. It is his purity and his piety readers were asked to consider. Though John explicitly said that angels were present because of what was on the altar, it cannot have escaped his notice, or that of his readers, that these numerous angels were also gathered to watch a particular human being effect the sacrifice. The angels who fill the air dramatized the actions of the priest, even if they are only present in the imaginations of the readers of John's treatise.

When John turned to develop a series of lessons to train new Christians to participate in ritual, he used the same technique. Or, rather, he encouraged Christians to use the same technique for understanding the rituals they observed. Several catechetical homilies survive from John's time serving in Antioch, and in them, he insisted that angels were present at rituals. To those about to be baptized and about to join the ritual life of their congregations, John pointed out the angels who stood by to watch them, cheer them, and carry their words to heaven.[46] Even after baptism, angels continued to watch Christians, much as spectators watch athletes. "From this day onward," John explained to catechumens, "the stadium is open, the contest is at hand, and the gallery is seated. Not only are humans watching the exercises but the host of angels as well."[47] Later, in an effort to convince his catechumens to avoid swearing oaths, John recreated an imaginary Eucharist, reminding them of its power and pointing out the implements of ritual one by one. This included the box that contains the bread, later transformed into the "Lamb of God, a mystical sacrifice, at whom even the angels themselves gaze and tremble."[48] John's students heard about the angels who watched them at regular intervals during their training: as they were baptized, when they participated in the Eucharist, and in their daily lives. Catechetical training under John was in fact a retraining of one's perception, aimed at adding (or revealing) unseen spectators, not just to ritual events but also to almost every part of a Christian's activity.

Articulated in his *On the Priesthood* and voiced during his catechetical lessons, John's assumptions about angelic spectators also frequently informed his everyday preaching. Though the composition and size of the audiences who heard John preach can be difficult to reconstruct, we know by the sermons themselves that John was intending to be heard by established Christians, long removed from any initiation to their communities.[49] Yet John reached out for the touchstone of angelic presence on multiple occasions, as if he expected that his audiences would know this cultural trope and that he need only activate it. Most frequently, he brought Christians to recall the angels that were standing with them in the church. Consider how he treated the exact moment of the offering in his homilies on Ephesians: "As the sacrifice is being brought forth and Christ, the Lord's sheep, is being sacrificed, whenever you hear, 'Let us all pray as one,' whenever you see the curtain being drawn up, then imagine that heaven is opened on high and the angels are descending."[50] The Eucharist, taken by Theodore of Mopsuestia to be a reflection of a heavenly service, was here portrayed as a replacement of heavenly service; rather than wait for humans to come join them, angels choose to descend and join humans. Furthermore, these were not just any angels. John further enjoined his listeners: "Imagine with whom you are standing at the time of the mysteries: with the cherubim, with the seraphim!"[51] John's rhetoric during a feast of the ascension gave their presence in the church the feel of a foregone conclusion. "If you want to see the martyrs and the angels, open the eyes of faith and you will see the spectacle: For if the air is full of angels, how much more so the church? And if the church, how much more so on this day, when their master ascended?"[52] In a number of different sermons, written on different subjects and preached under different circumstances throughout his career, John reminded Christians about the angels they had been taught to visualize, angels who joined them as spectators in the church.

Seen from a certain point of view, John's exhortations to the use of the imagination are no different from the exhortations of other Christian teachers. Like John, Cyril of Jerusalem and Theodore of Mopsuestia asked Christians to see angels as they watched Christian ritual. And yet, the character of John's descriptions was markedly different from what previous teachers had asked Christians to see. While Cyril and Theodore had figured the works of the imagination would transport Christians elsewhere, allowing Christian participants to see a heavenly service or a historical sacrifice behind the ritual, John had figured that the angels Christians imagined would be seen arriving at the ritual from elsewhere. In John's writing, angels stood in the audience with Christians; angels "take their seats" at the opening of the ritual, as if in a stadium; at the moment of the Eucharistic sacrifice, "heaven is opened on high" and "angels are descending." No longer executing a ritual in heaven that humanity is supposed to imitate, angels instead leave heaven to watch Christians and Christian ritual. What is more, John imagined angels, and urged his listeners to imagine angels, going through motions of subservience and obedience as they gathered to see rituals. Inculcating such objects of the imagination through Christian ritual and compelling Christians to generate them each time they observe a ritual is a type of argument that is at least as strong a statement of priestly authority as was John's appeal to the scriptural warrant of Matthew 18 as it applied to priests. In reality it was likely stronger, because it was experiential, repeated in particular places, and because it was active, with participants each creating the presence of angels in their own mental landscape.

This method of imagining angels fit with a larger pattern in John's career, namely, using rhetoric and the imagination to remake the landscape of the world around him. Christine Shepardson has focused on the way John used "spatial rhetoric" during the "significant religious and political struggles to define and control civic space" in Antioch.[53] Using anti-Jewish polemic, John created a city whose spaces were defined by greater and lesser degrees of orthodoxy; when John had completed his work, an imaginary, yet very real, map lay over the features of the Antiochene landscape. What John's anti-Jewish rhetoric did for the city and for individual buildings in the city, his exhortations to imagine angels did inside church buildings. Seeing angels surround the altar recast the position of the audience and priest with respect to a third body: angels who lent their attention to the work of the priest, making him the center of their world as he enacted rituals. If the angels found the priest so important, shouldn't the congregation as well? The complex conception of ritual evinced in John's preaching and writing was just one of many possible ways in late ancient Christianity of figuring the importance of ritual and its actors, any one of which offered rich resources for theological insights and experiential fervor. Yet, of all the possible ways of teaching about ritual—some represented in the catechetical treatises that happen to survive until the modern day, with others assuredly extant in antiquity but lost to us now—John's idea, that angels inhabited churches, standing there to watch rituals unfold, dominated liturgical conversations and the imaginative landscape in the centuries after John's death.

Gauging the success of John's particular teaching about angels at ritual is as simple as considering the catechetical materials produced by Christians in the century after John's career. Like other late ancient catechists, the Syrian writer Narsai, active in the fifth century, asked Christians to adopt specific strategies of the imagination. Telling his trainees that they should use the visual cues they saw before them as the stuff from which they could form more elaborate visualizations, Narsai argued that Christians needed to seek out new sensory references in order to convert them into images as they practiced "gazing steadfastly in the mind."[54] Their purpose was to "see those things that are manifest with the manifest senses of your body, and depict hidden things with the hidden faculties of your intellects."[55] Narsai himself actively sought out new resources for writing; his catechetical homilies contain allusions, even direct borrowings, from other authors, including all three writers I have discussed so far in this chapter: Cyril of Jerusalem, Theodore of Mopsuestia, and John Chrysostom. Narsai echoed Cyril's teaching about angels watching the baptism of Christians; like Theodore, he presented the members of the procession to the altar as figures of a heavenly procession.[56]

From John, though, Narsai appears to have learned that angels stand around the altar at rituals. Even more, he learned that this celestial audience was linked to the power of the person who celebrated the rituals. Notice in this extended passage how Narsai called all kinds of angels to mind, only to find them lacking with respect to the priest.

> It is you, priest, serving spiritually on earth, whom the spirits do not have the authority to imitate. It is you, priest—the rank that you administer is so great that the ministers of fire and spirit tremble before it. Who is sufficient to evoke the magnitude of your rank, by which you passed by those in heaven, in the name of your authority? The nature of a spirit is more subtle and glorious than yours, but it is not permitted to represent the mysteries in imitation of you. An angel is great, but how should we say he is greater than you, since when he is compared with your service, he is lacking? A seraph is holy, a cherub beautiful, and watcher swift, but they are not able to run with the fluidity of the word of your mouth. Glorious is Gabriel and great is Michael—as their names demonstrate—but they are always yoked under the mystery that is revealed by your hands. By you they are examined when you draw near to minister and for you they wait, until you open the door to their holies.[57]

The faculty of the mind that Narsai had theorized worked to depict the higher realm of angels and archangels, but this was ultimately only to subvert the superiority of such entities. Even those angels at the highest part of the hierarchy must be present for the priest's service, because they were dependent on it. Michael and Gabriel, the most powerful of angels, were bowed before the priest's celebration of the Eucharist; indeed, they waited for it, because they were barred from access to "their holies" without the priest's help. Elsewhere, Narsai could hint that all beings, angels and humans, were dependent upon the work of the priest. Speaking of those in the priesthood, he wrote, "for them is reserved the authority to try human beings and watchers. They judge both the spiritual and the corporeal."[58] Despite being superior in nature, beauty, and holiness, angels could not compare to the power of the priest *as a priest*.

Narsai had used John Chrysostom's version of ritual to emphasize the status of the priest, but a later writer, whose works were preserved under the name of Narsai, went so far as to indicate John by name as the guarantor of the unseen angelic presence at Christian rituals. Recreating the celebration of the Eucharist for his audience, pseudo-Narsai marveled at "the orders of the watchers encircling the altar at that moment, exactly according to the witness of Chrysostom, who had seen them."[59] According to this writer, these angels were far more numerous than the Christians any standing church could contain. As the sacrament proceeded, he explained, "thousands of watchers and ministers of fire and spirit process before the body of our Lord."[60] Though the creation of these images may have been the exercise of a mental faculty, they were real, in that pseudo-Narsai did not consider them figments of the imagination. "Who is it," he asked, "that would separate himself from that feast, to which both watchers and human beings have been invited?"[61] In his descriptions of the liturgy, the teacher adopted the tradition of John Chrysostom's old man, originally simply a gesture of authenticity, and used it as a guiding trope for the visual imagery of the rituals Christians experienced. He hoped that, in their representation of the Eucharist as they viewed it in their minds, Christians would see and in turn be influenced by the sheer number of angels present there, encircling the ritual as it unfolded.

Whether the students of this particular Syrian writer grasped the message, we do not know. We do know, however, that Christian culture in later antiquity shifted in precisely the way that John, Narsai, and pseudo-Narsai had encouraged. Numerous cultural products in multiple locations attest to the complete acceptance among Christians of the fifth and sixth centuries of the presence of angels at Christian rituals. Exactly contrary to the way that Christians in the first three centuries had thought of them, angels were not imagined to reside in heaven but instead were presumed to be present in the church. The *Regula Magistri*, a sixth-century monastic document likely composed in southern Italy and a precursor of the more famous *Benedictine Rule*, contains an entire section dedicated to the proper execution of the liturgy. In it, the following warning appears: "Be careful during prayers: if the person who is praying wants to blow out or cast filth from his nostrils, he should aim behind himself rather than in front, on account of the angels standing before him."[62] The warning confirms an assumption about angels present at Christian rituals manifest in a number of other texts from late antiquity. A fifth-century inscription dedicating a church in Gerasa on the site of a former pagan temple boasts that where there was once idolatry, there are now "choirs of angels" inhabiting the church.[63] The sixth-century life of Jacob Baradaeus reports that a newly Christian spectator saw Jacob celebrating the Eucharist; he realized the importance of the ritual when he saw that "fire came down from heaven, and he saw tongues of flames hovering over the oblation, and hosts of angels with bowed heads before the divine sacrifice."[64] A Coptic homily on the archangel Gabriel, likely composed in the seventh century but attributed in the manuscript tradition to Celestinus of Rome, boldly states that "the church is the place of consolation and of gathering of the angels."[65] In a medieval codex from the monastery of Patmos, an illuminated initial depicts a priest incensing a structure with an angel watching over him.[66] At the end of late antiquity, a great deal of occasional evidence existed showing that Christians in locations across the Mediterranean assumed that angels would attend rituals alongside them, physically present and requiring their dignified attention.

The idea that angels attended Christian rituals was so widely accepted after the fourth century, in fact, that late ancient Christians who did not agree with that belief were universally mocked. For an example from one end of the ancient Christian world, take John Mandakuni, who was the leader of the Armenian church in the late fifth century. Displeased by those who downplayed the importance of the Eucharist, he asked, "Do you not know that, at the exact moment that the blessed sacrament arrives at the altar, the sky above has opened itself and Christ descends and arrives, that angelic armies float from heaven to earth and encircle the altar where the blessed sacrament of the Lord resides?"[67] The sentiment was the same on the other side of the Christian world. Gregory the Great, the sixth-century leader of the Roman church, railed away at those who would deride the Eucharist: "Who among the faithful could have a doubt that at the very moment of the immolation, the heavens are opened by the voice of the priest, that the choir of angels is present at this mystery of Jesus Christ—where the highest and lowest are united, the earthly and heavenly joined, and the invisible and visible made one?"[68] Christian Rome and Christian Armenia could not have been farther apart geographically, or more different theologically, in late antiquity, and yet their most influential writers agreed: the gravity of Christian ritual was best made clear to detractors by appealing to the presence of angels gathered at the altar. By the end of late antiquity, Christians in disparate contexts and language communities expected angels to be present in sanctuaries and to attend Christian rituals alongside human participants. Those angels were there at the behest of the priest and waited for his voice to open heaven, waited for him to conduct rituals for them, on their behalf.

This was a significant diversion from the way that the earliest Christians imagined angels, as residents of heaven whose rituals were imperfectly copied on earth. The information that survives from antiquity to help us interpret the mechanics of that diversion is wanting, in one particular way: almost all the evidence we can consult was written from the perspective of aspiring church leaders, bishops, and teachers active in contestation, who sought to influence the way those they led experienced ritual and more broadly, life in the communities they inhabited. We do not have, but would eagerly accept, viable reports from those who underwent ritual training, delineating how they received such advice about techniques of the imagination. But even the material we do have does suggest something about how the shift in catechetical materials affected catechetical audiences. If John Chrysostom's presentation of angels at the altar was characterized by a persuasive fervor—he told listeners to accept the testimony of the old man, and he constantly enjoined them to see angels—then the voices of the fifth and sixth centuries I have surveyed here were assured, the proclamations of writers confident that all people knew angels gather at the altar. Confident assurance can be a projection that is as persuasive in its intentions as direct argument, of course, but the change in tone from John's writing to the texts from the end of late antiquity hints at a change in the way audiences understood, and how deeply they appropriated, the Christian imaginative work of visualizing angels. The result of that work was to relocate Christian ritual and its celebrants, placing both at the center of the universe.

A New Majority

Though I have been narrating a significant change in the history of how early Christians were taught to imagine and to participate in ritual, from a practical perspective, nothing had changed in the course of the catechetical developments I have written about. Angels were, in the second century as well as in the sixth, imagined to be entities who praised and sang hymns to their divine creator. Though the location of that creator may have moved as Christians began to value the Eucharist as a moment when Christ was present on earth, angels held the same role in ritual practice.[69] With few exceptions, they remained passive in ancient Christian rituals; the activity accomplished in a performance of a baptism or the Eucharist was accomplished by other divine actors and, in most estimations, the Holy Spirit. None of the catechetical writers I have discussed suggested that angels were participating in rituals as agents, or that they were somehow necessary to enable the ritual actions of the priest. Put another way, Christian writers who multiplied angelic spectators to ritual or shifted their location at ritual were not tinkering with the mechanisms by which rituals were assumed to function—mechanisms that worked whether participants imagined the angels their teachers wished them to see or not.

However, these writers were training those who participated in Christian ritual to produce new meanings for the rituals. Perhaps most important, they taught them to value differently those who performed rituals. This was not a simple matter of proclaiming the power and importance of the priest, or persuasively arguing that priests were to be held as authorities. Instead, Christians were taught to visualize scenarios in which powerful, important, heavenly creatures gathered and ceded authority to the earthly conductor of Christian rituals. All of that work involved conjuring invisible beings only in one's mind, but what Christians imagined did influence the dignity and gravity they attributed to the real live person in front of them. As we follow the development in Christian ideas about ritual from the earliest Christians to Cyril and John toward Narsai, we can trace a change in the religious imagination: while earlier Christian communities imagined their ritual lives as reproductions of a heavenly service, later Christians expected the rituals celebrated by a human priest to be primary, and even so important that they drew angelic spectators from heaven.

In a more oblique way, we can trace in these same writings the efforts of Christians to exert cultural influence during later antiquity, in the few hundred years after the legalization of Christianity. Because an imagined angelic community had served to mark rituals conducted by minority groups as authentic and legitimate, it should not be surprising to see the model of identifying with a distant invisible majority fall to the side as Christians themselves became the majority and claimed more positions of influence in late ancient culture. Christian dominance of this sort was not supported by positing a distant community that Christians should have imitated. Instead, it was supported by the notion that Christian life was so natural and so inevitable that even heavenly beings participated in it, seeking to be partners in its primary expression on earth. We should also notice that the shift we have seen in this chapter reinforced not only

Christian power in general, but also the centrality of one particular structure of Christian life. New practitioners were not encouraged to visualize angels appearing regularly and repeatedly in their homes, in public squares, in monasteries, or even in chapels on private estates. Instead, angels visited church buildings where priests or bishops led rituals, places that were themselves significant sites of the struggle for authority in late antiquity. From these facts, we can gauge the relative power of Christian communities in late ancient culture, organized centrally and trained to attend rituals conducted by certain people, in certain places. By the end of late antiquity, Christian ritual life was universally changed, becoming so important as to be central to the welfare of those residing in heaven.

Conclusion

THE LIMITS OF ANGELOLOGY

AN ADDITIONAL TEXT could have been included in the last chapter as another example of the ways late ancient community leaders attempted to teach Christians to see ritual with more than just their eyes. The *Ecclesiastical Hierarchy*, written in Syria near the year 500 CE, was a type of training manual for the ritual life of a community, offering directions for participating in a full range of different practices: baptism, the Eucharist, a sacrament of ointment, then others that were not included in traditional catechetical materials, like rites to ordain church leaders and new initiates to a community, along with a ritual for the dead. But the text was not simply a reproduction of the stages of these rituals. As a consistent pattern, the *Ecclesiastical Hierarchy* first details the performance of the ritual, then gives a much longer exposition of what the ritual symbolizes.[1] In this, the *Ecclesiastical Hierarchy* resembles those catechetical materials we considered in the previous chapter, as it encouraged readers to create for themselves elaborate contemplative scenarios to accompany each stage of the rituals they joined, making participation in any one of them an exercise of the imagination. It also resembles catechetical materials in another respect, namely, that it placed the celebrant of the ritual at center stage. He was the one who sees everything taking place "with a clear eye," as he "looks up on the basic unity of those realities underlying the sacred rites."[2]

Though the *Ecclesiastical Hierarchy* fits the pedagogical pattern of the catechetical materials we considered in Chapter 6, it is not usually included in the literature representing religious training in late ancient Christianity. Instead, scholars normally understand the *Ecclesiastical Hierarchy* in the context of the other documents with which it appeared in late antiquity: the *Divine Names*, the *Mystical Theology*, the *Celestial Hierarchy*, and ten letters or short treatises addressed to individuals. Some of these pieces were first mentioned in Christian literature just after the start of the sixth century, and they were quickly edited to combine them into a single corpus, then translated into multiple ancient languages.[3] Their language, as we will see, is highly idiosyncratic and inventive; the ideas they express comprise an original, provocative statement about the nature of God and Christian mystical progress toward God, making their author one of the most fascinating voices from late antiquity.

Part of what fascinates readers of this corpus of texts is the intrigue regarding its author. Scattered biographical references in the corpus suggest that the author claimed the identity of Dionysius, a first-century Greek man who, according to Acts 17, was moved to convert to Christianity when he heard the apostle Paul deliver a convincing speech on the Areopagus. The edition of the works, done by John of Scythopolis, shaped the texts to put the identity of the author as Dionysius to the fore; John's work solidified for many, but not all, later readers the authenticity of the texts as products of a first-century Greek philosopher who had become Christian and adopted Christian texts as sources of divine knowledge.[4] At the same time, the texts in the corpus were clearly the product of late antiquity and so deeply intertwined with late ancient conversations about the nature of God that they reproduced very closely ideas voiced by Proclus, a philosopher active at the end of the fifth century.[5] These and other clues have convinced scholars to place the works in the early sixth century and to locate their author in Syria.[6] With that contextualization of the corpus came a perhaps inevitable complaint—that the author was a fraud, a "Pseudo-Dionysius" who tried to pass his efforts under the authority of a first-century writer, and, worse, had not done a very good job of it.[7]

There are other ways of understanding the author's complex presentation of his identity as narrator, ones that do not see his authorial persona as an elaborate fraud but rather as an intellectual and religious practice. Instead of indicting the author's carelessness by pointing to the allusions to the first-century character Dionysius alongside more contemporary concerns, several scholars have seen such allusions as proof that the sixth-century author Pseudo-Dionysius was attempting to unify two seemingly disparate realms: the tradition of rational inquiry in Greek philosophy and the revolutionary acquaintance with the divine enabled by Christian revelation. Charles M. Stang recently pursued this idea further, arguing that in addition to effecting "a new order," in which "the incipient faith and pagan wisdom of the Athenians is absorbed into and subordinated to the new dispensation, Christ, the revelation of the unknown God," the author was enacting a ritual of personal effacement, in which taking on the identity of a known character, whose actions represented wisdom and humility, was itself a religious act.[8] By adopting subject positions from the first and the fifth centuries, this author engaged in a mystical act, accessing a unified, unwavering body of information, one that did not change from century to century. Whatever it might have done as a religious practice for the author, the effect of the author's employment of pseudonymity for many later readers was to establish a totalizing character across cultural and temporal lines for the knowledge preserved under his name—it was as true for Christians as it was for philosophers, as real in the fifth century as it was in the first.

Of the texts in the Dionysian corpus, the most interesting for our purposes is the *Celestial Hierarchy*, an account of nine ordered categories of angels whose purpose was to channel illumination from the divine world to humanity. Pseudo-Dionysius drew the names of the categories from Christian Scripture: angels, archangels, and principalities made up the first group; dominions, powers, and authorities the second; then seraphim, cherubim, and thrones the third. These angels existed to transfer light and knowledge from the highest God to humanity; the existence of their order is an explanation of how a God so unique as to admit no change could possibly communicate with the changing material world. In this way, *Celestial Hierarchy* was an answer to questions that occupied philosophers in late antiquity, especially questions about the accessibility of God or even simply the divine world. If the *Celestial Hierarchy* were understood as the work of the first-century Dionysius, then he had prefigured the issues that vexed late ancient thinkers. Such a conceit demonstrated the precocious interest of Dionysius at the same time that it implied that the Scripture from which the names of angels were drawn had existed as a fixed canon in the middle of the first century; thus the canon anticipated problems that would arise hundred of years later. These appearances are, of course, anachronistic, but the scheme of pseudonymity was a powerful form: by its logic, the *Celestial Hierarchy* represents a timelessly true account of angels, one based in Christian Scripture, which is itself timelessly relevant and coherent with the most advanced intellectual problems of late ancient thought.

This is quite a heavy claim, and it required more than just the employment of pseudonymity to sustain it. In the *Celestial Hierarchy*, Pseudo-Dionysius utilized a pair of novel rhetorical techniques in order to buffer the inevitable inconsistencies and nonconformities that obtained in the five centuries of Christian and philosophical thought and the multitude of texts both Christian and non-Christian that his claim attempted to encompass. Those rhetorical techniques in turn shaped the reception of the *Celestial Hierarchy*. The first technique was a tool for reading. While some language in Scripture cohered straightforwardly with the nature or character of divine beings as Pseudo-Dionysius understood them, much of its language, especially about angels, cannot be a direct description of angels and also be coherent with Pseudo-Dionysius's understanding of the nature of the celestial hierarchy at the same time. Too many parts of Scripture speak of angels in physical terms, a fact incongruous with the nature Pseudo-Dionysius attributes to them as heavenly, divine, illuminated beings. It was not, he argued, as if angels have the faces or feet that Scripture posits of them; they do not appear as oxen, lions, horses, or eagles, as avid readers of Scripture could conclude; they are not wheels and they do not have wings, despite what scriptural passages about them suggest. Pseudo-Dionysius explained that, instead of directly describing angels in language that was fitting to their nature, the words in Scripture were meant to set the reader's mind in motion, to cause him to wonder why heavenly beings might be depicted in clearly "ridiculous" images like these. Ultimately, the astute reader would conclude that Scripture had used "dissimilar similarities," words that depict the divine in base terms precisely so that readers will reflect on how the divine world cannot be adequately represented in base terms. The resulting paradox would encourage other ways of thinking. The physicality, even animality, of portraits of angels in Scripture thus was meant to spur the intellect of the reader "to get beyond the material show, to get accustomed to the idea of going beyond appearances to those upliftings which are not of this world."[9] It also allowed readers to buffer incongruities that might suggest that the words of Scripture did not align with the sophisticated understanding of the divine world that Pseudo-Dionysius presented.

A second, equally powerful rhetorical tool for sustaining Pseudo-Dionysius's claim of universal knowledge of angels was the hierarchy itself. The term "hierarchy," which this author coined, has come to mean in modern use a group of people or things arranged according to rank. Though that conveys part of the meaning of the word in the Dionysian corpus, it was also much more. In *Celestial Hierarchy*, a hierarchy is defined as "a sacred order, a state of understanding and an activity approximating as closely as possible to the divine."[10] Thus, a hierarchy is more than an organizational chart; it is a graded network of actors, working in concert to bring its members to the knowledge of God they are capable of receiving. "Hierarchy" is an all-encompassing concept, a "certain perfect arrangement," composed exactly as it should be to be effective and lacking nothing necessary.[11] Its comprehensive nature is essential, as Pseudo-Dionysius wrote, speaking of both the celestial and ecclesiastical hierarchies:

> We have a venerable sacred tradition which asserts that every hierarchy is the complete expression of the sacred elements comprised within it. It is the perfect total of all its sacred constituents.... Indeed, if you talk of "hierarchy" you are referring in effect to the arrangement of all sacred realities.[12]

The concept of hierarchy—whether celestial, of angels, or ecclesiastical, of human beings—is a way to comprehend all of a particular realm, to speak of its members, their activity, and their purpose in a single phrase. Thus "hierarchy" is not a rhetorically neutral concept, like a simple list. The use of hierarchy, as Pseudo-Dionysius defined it, conveyed the inclusion of all entities and possibilities, without omission. It structured knowledge about the divine world, in particular, in an authoritative, comprehensive way, claiming explicitly that its account was perfect and needed no addition or revision.

The creation of an ordered, comprehensive catalog of divine beings and their activities is, itself, a kind of religious practice, which acts to draw universal knowledge from local and specific instances of interaction between humanity and the divine world. Such is the conclusion that David Frankfurter drew in *Evil Incarnate*, his study of several religious contexts in which extensive catalogs of demons and their activities were created. Frankfurter explained how demon lists worked to obscure the local and individual contexts in which demons exist. To what was often an "unsystematic spectrum of dangers," demonology as a genre and demon lists in particular "contributed the pretense of certainty, control, and ritual tradition," all toward the interest of "grasping totality, simplifying and abstracting immediate experience for the sake of cosmic structures."[13] Such accounts of the demonic world take unruly, uncategorized, deeply locally situated information and render it, creating a template through which to view past experiences and by which to collate future experiences: this is the power of demonology. As rhetorical devices, all such comprehensive schemata act to explain what has happened and to selectively direct the possible explanations for what will happen. Frankfurter's examples were drawn from exorcistic rituals, in antiquity and in the modern world, but they illustrate how cataloging actors in the divine world can act to encompass, coopt, and even obliterate other modes of knowledge. There is more than a small resemblance between the demonologies that Frankfurter analyzed and Pseudo-Dionysius's arrangement of angels in the *Celestial Hierarchy*. As Pseudo-Dionysius claimed, the very comprehensiveness of a hierarchy of angels was its strength because it already accounted for all possible arrangements and all potential actors. As a result, once one accepts the validity of the hierarchy as presented, truly new information cannot be added; rather, it must be accommodated into the perfect hierarchy. Just so, the hierarchy was a powerful rhetorical tool for directing the way that readers accept existing information and how they organize new information.

Within the boundaries of the hierarchy, however, there was room for certain kinds of intellectual discovery. The way that Pseudo-Dionysius narrated the actions of angels in the hierarchy appears to direct readers to speculate far beyond the simple fact of there being nine orders of angels or knowing their names. As he described the purpose of each order in the *Celestial Hierarchy*, Pseudo-Dionysius provided an inventive, lavish profusion of words to mark the order's activities. Consider the order of seraphim, those nearest to God in the celestial hierarchy. He noted immediately that their name is taken from the Hebrew word for fire, making them "warmers." This identification led him to an entire cascade of designations for the seraphim:

> For the designation "seraphim" really teaches this—a perennial circling around the divine things, penetrating warmth, the overflowing heat of a movement which never falters and never fails, a capacity to stamp their own image on subordinates by arousing and uplifting in them too a like flame, the same warmth. It means also the power to purify by means of the lightning flash and the flame. It means the ability to hold unveiled and undiminished both the light they have and the illumination they give out. It means the capacity to push aside and to do away with every obscuring shadow.[14]

The imagery of fire, warmth, and light is expanded from a single name to an exhaustive and rapid-fire sequence of images and capacities. A similar calculus was at work in Pseudo-Dionysius's description of the other ranks of angels. His description of the principalities, a relatively low rank of angels at the very bottom of the third order, tended toward the improvisational.

> The term "heavenly principalities" refers to those who possess a godlike and princely hegemony, with a sacred order most suited to princely powers, the ability to be returned completely toward that principle which is above all principles and to lead others to him like a prince, the power to receive to the full the mark of the Principle of principles and, by their harmonious exercise of princely powers, to make manifest this transcendent principle of all.[15]

The appearance of the overflowing cascade of qualities of the principalities—they are princely, principled, their actions directed to the Principle of principles—masks a deceptive simplicity. These extended descriptions mine the name of the level for any information that might be extrapolated from it, but a reader receives barely any license to adopt new information from these exuberant displays, as they are reformulated restatements of the name of the category of angels they describe—a name already available in Scripture. The expositions that accompany each level of the *Celestial Hierarchy* are rich and signal a wealth of knowledge available to the reader through contemplation; in a certain sense, they are the expression of the impulse we saw in the conversation that took place between Eunomius of Cyzicus and Basil of Caesarea, in that they trust in language, even individual words themselves, to reveal knowledge of the divine world. Yet they circumscribe that knowledge in a very real way. Pseudo-Dionysius's wordplay was just that—play, a practice that appears to produce knowledge without allowing for any kind of new intimacy or acquaintance with the beings it describes, outside that available through the names of the orders drawn from Scripture.

If part of the effect of Pseudo-Dionysius's description of the activities of angels was to model a set of boundaries within which speculation could occur, for whom were such boundaries established? As much as we can reconstruct from the Dionysian corpus confirms that its author imagined himself at the center of a large and complex ritual community. First, as I noted, there are directions for a wide range of rituals in the *Ecclesiastical Hierarchy*, the presence of which suggests an extensive and diverse ritual community. That community is led by the "hierarch," a human leader at the apex of the ecclesiastical hierarchy, which incorporates the diverse members of the ritual community into one group. The members of this community considered Scripture to be divine words, spoken by God to reveal the cosmic structures of the universe; their rich well of knowledge of God could be obtained by those who read Scripture and explicated its words, but also by those who participated in the hierarchy, especially when they participated in rituals.

Though it is not possible to make a historical connection between Pseudo-Dionysius, whoever he was, and other known Christian community leaders, the concerns of the Dionysian corpus I have just outlined—a desire to establish Scripture as all-encompassing; the presence of an extensive ritual community trained by a leader to experience rituals as opportunities for the imaginative production of new knowledge—are quite similar to the concerns that occupied many of the late ancient Christians I have considered in this book. Those I have presented as engaged in contestation also sought to establish Scripture as a coherent source of divine knowledge, and they did so for audiences that included their congregations, who depended on them for maintenance of the ritual lives of their communities. What is more, there are several examples of late ancient Christians who, like Dionysius, attempted to provide a full account of what angels were by listing the names of angels drawn from Scripture. At the very start of this book, I introduced two examples: both Gregory of Nazianzus and Augustine of Hippo provided lists of angel names, using those lists as stopgaps against possible wider or deeper questions about angels. Others did so as well—Cyril of Jerusalem, Gregory of Nyssa, and John Chrysostom among Greek-speaking authors, Ambrose of Milan and Jerome among Latin ones.[16] Historians have often taken these men and their lists as possible precursors to the work of Pseudo-Dionysius, arguing for their more or less direct influence on the *Celestial Hierarchy*. Such arguments present the lists produced by these fourth- and fifth-century Christians as less well-advanced versions of the ranks enumerated in Pseudo-Dionysius's text, a position that assumes *Celestial Hierarchy* was the eventual perfected form of an earlier, abortive attempt at listing angels.[17] Of course, none of these earlier writers were aiming at, and failing at, being Pseudo-Dionysius.

What if, instead, the various occurrences of the lists of angel-names drawn from Scripture—short or long, nominal or expanded to paragraphs, mid-fourth century or early sixth century—were independent instances of the same impulse, exercised by people in similar social situations: to catalog, to classify, to order what is not ordered? All of the Christian writers I have just mentioned exercised religious authority in ways that cohere with the mode of piety I have called "contestation"; often the leaders or aspiring leaders of an urban community, these men sought to unify Christians under one particular vision of Christian life.[18] A significant portion of the power they sought resulted from the precise reading practices they enjoined. In the fourth and fifth century, their actions created one version of "Scripture." By this, I do not simply mean those books that make up the contemporary New Testament, or those books alongside the books in the Septuagint. Instead, I mean Scripture conceived as a fixed authoritative canon of texts available for interpretation and persuasive deployment under closely contested community standards.[19] Notice that these authors do not compile lists of angels' names to encourage speculation or the reading of more books that might shed light on angels beyond those included in what they deemed Scripture, of which there were many available in late antiquity. Quite the opposite. The lists are delivered with finality, as if they were all one could ever know or hope to know about angels. In this they reinforce the authority of Scripture, so conceived, as a comprehensive source of knowledge. In the case of the *Celestial Hierarchy*, the added force of the practice of pseudonymity as Pseudo-Dionysius enacted it—its power to unify, under one understanding, centuries of both Christian and non-Christian knowledge of the divine—works to lead readers easily to the idea that the hierarchy it provided represents the totality of ancient Christian thought about angels.

The power of the hierarchy as a form is evident: even when the authorship of the *Celestial Hierarchy* was determined and the effects created by its pseudonymity dissipated, the use of the hierarchy as a genre persisted among scholars as a method for knowing what ancient Christians thought of the divine world. At the end of the nineteenth century, two scholars produced evidence that Pseudo-Dionysius's *Divine Names* must have been written after 485 CE, because it cited directly from the treatise *On the Existence of Evils*, by Proclus, who died in that year. Scholars reacted to the identification of Pseudo-Dionysius as a late ancient, likely Syrian, writer in two ways. Some worked to add detail to the local context of the Dionysian corpus, trying to secure the author's identity and religious alliances. Other scholars, however, undertook to produce information proceeding from other Christian contexts vacated by the identification of Pseudo-Dionysius as a sixth-century author from Syria, to fill the gaps that his new, limited place in early Christian history had opened up. Interestingly enough, those who sought to understand ideas about angels in other contexts and time periods retained the model established by the *Celestial Hierarchy*. They reconstructed ordered catalogs of angels—hierarchies, or ultimately, angelologies—for individual writers, like Clement of Alexandria, Origen of Alexandria, Ephrem the Syrian, Gregory of Nazianzus, or Augustine of Hippo;[20] for authors representing entire genres of Christian literature, like apologetic writing;[21] and, in the case of literatures other than Greek and Latin, in which individual works often remained orphaned from identified authors, entire linguistic areas, such as Coptic literature.[22] The industry of reproducing angelologies was predicated on the idea that the structure of *Celestial Hierarchy* embodied a method of knowing so comprehensive in its scope and rich in its results that if we were only to replicate it for discrete time periods in Christian history and for authors who did not see fit to write angelologies of their own, earlier centuries of Christian ideas about angels would become clear. In this way, a diminished version of Pseudo-Dionysius's practice of authorship, his rhetorical invention of the hierarchy, lives on in scholarship about angels, ordering and to some extent determining how scholars investigate the subject under view, leading them to classify late ancient Christian thought about angels in ways that reproduced the structure of the hierarchy.

But classifying and contextualizing are opposite methods. Reconstructed angelologies fall prey, as historical products, to the very quality that served *Celestial Hierarchy* so well: they present their information in an abstract way, extracted from the networks of knowledge and social action in which it was produced. The work of this book has been to reveal what the structure of angelologies like that in *Celestial Hierarchy* and in modern scholarship can obscure: that angels were central to the articulation of Christian religious traditions in late antiquity and furthermore, ideas about angels were in no way universal, but instead were shaped by specific local social contexts, fields of practice emergent in the culture that took form after the legitimization of Christianity at the start of the fourth century.[23] The two social contexts I have traced in this book, that of the Christian practitioner seeking cultivation in the academic and ascetic lineages of Egypt, and that of the Christian trained in rhetorical persuasion and seeking to assemble a congregation of Christians under his ritual and theological authority, were both experiments. When viewed from the vantage point of later Christianity, the people involved in them look very much like they are fulfilling roles we might call "ascetic" and "bishop." Yet I have avoided these labels as heuristic categories, in part to avoid reading fixed social roles as motivating factors for the actions of the very people whose cultural work brought these roles into being as later Christians understood them. All the evidence we have from the fourth century suggests that practice and progress, in both contexts, were the fruit of a constant struggle.

One result of my investigation into these social contexts has been to demonstrate diversity in the ideas Christians held about angels in the fourth and fifth centuries. That diversity existed on a very deep level. That is to say, it is not as if Christian thought about angels was simply variegated in a more-or-less repeating pattern, with different authors proclaiming the existence of more or fewer angels, or disagreeing about simple details like the different names and ranks of angels. Instead, there was dissent about what angels were, what agency they exercised, what place they took in the figuration of the divine world, and what relationship they had to humanity, whether one of kinship, friendship, or medium. Underlying these differences were the social contexts in which they took shape. Though both Evagrius and Augustine are part of late ancient Christian history defined on a broad scale, they exemplify the different motivations and responsibilities of the modes of piety they chose to pursue. It is hard to overstate the distance between their respective assumptions about what constituted being a Christian: their ideal visions of Christian progress, their estimations of God and the knowability of the divine world, their assumptions about the capacities of human beings, down to the very structure of the communities they shaped and the way they read and thought about what each of them called "Scripture"—all were distinct. Within these wide-ranging matrices of cultural training, expectation, and opportunity, Christians developed ideas about angels that took different forms. In one, which I have labeled "contestation," angels were part of a totalizing discourse, and their clarification supported theological positions and reading practices, helped those who sought to lead communities to encompass, justify, and negotiate the existence of alternate structures of Christian community while, at the same time, placing the public religious life they championed at the very center of the universe. In the other, which I have tagged "cultivation," angels were kin to humanity. In that relationship, they helped define human nature and exhibited the possibility of human advancement in intellectual terms even as they encouraged it. It is impossible to explain the extensive ramification and evolution of such ideas about angels without reference to these two emerging ways of being Christian in late antiquity.

Second, and more surprising, this study has revealed that there was a significant amount of exchange between writers working mostly in one context or another—that is to say, there was conversation where previously we assumed silence or cooptation. That conversation went both ways. Close and careful delineation about the expectations that ascetics held for companion angels throws into relief the way that tradition influenced the literature produced by urban leaders, especially in the cases of the *Life of Antony* and the *Life of Moses*. In turn, the explanations that urban orators derived to normalize the ascetic communities forming outside their cities ended up shifting the processes of community maintenance and advancement inside those communities. While visions of angels were ultimately rejected in one context, visualizing angels at ritual turned out to be a powerful pedagogical tool when wielded in another context. So though ideas of angels were nurtured and developed in response to specific social demands, those ideas were portable, and they traveled in the interconnected network of Christian intellectuals, such that notions from both contexts influenced the development of the other.

The result is this: angels reward the scholar's attention, not as a sideline to the main story of Christian cultural development, nor as a series of symbols representing something else more pertinent or essential to the development of late ancient Christian culture, but as inherent and constitutive parts of the traditions and institutions we identify with Christianity in late antiquity. Yet as should be clear from my discussions of the effects and limitations of angelology as a genre, I do not intend this book to be the last word, a definitive template through which others must now view the late ancient past. Instead, I hope to have demonstrated the intricacies of one working model for presenting late ancient Christian history as a history integrated with angels. There certainly are others.

Notes

INTRODUCTION

1. Gregory's educational background is described by the Christian historians Socrates (*Church History* 4.26) and Sozomen (*Church History* 6.17); their accounts differ from Gregory's own account of his education in *Oration* 7.6 and *Poems* 2.1.11.100–236.
2. *Oration* 42.4. Susanna Elm has interpreted this oration as Gregory's attack on the man who succeeded him as bishop, the senator Nectarius from Tarsus, as well as a presentation of his own rectitude. See "A Programmatic Life: Gregory of Nazianzus' *Orations* 42 and 43 and the Constantinopolitan Elites," *Arethusa* 33 (2000): 411–27.
3. *Oration* 28.31 (Paul Gallay, ed., *Grégoire de Nazianze: Discours 27–31 (Discours théologiques)*, SC 250 [Paris: Éditions du Cerf, 1978], 172–74).
4. *Oration* 28.31 (SC 250:174).
5. Even his silences had rhetorical purpose; see the discussion of Gregory's forty-day silence during Easter 382 by Bradley Storin in his essay, "In a Silent Way: Asceticism and Literature in the Rehabilitation of Gregory of Nazianzus," *JECS* 19 (2011): 225–57.
6. While the texts I examine here are specific to angels, see also Catherine Conybeare's observations about Augustine's overarching embrace of "uncertainty and indeterminacy" and how this stance flies in the face of Augustine's later reputation, both in her preface and her introduction to *The Irrational Augustine*, OECS (Oxford: Oxford University Press, 2006), vii–xi, 1–8.
7. Augustine, *Enchiridion* 58 (E. Evans, ed., *Sancti Aurelii Augustini Opera*, CCL 46 [Turnhout: Brepols, 1969], 80–81). As Chapter 1 demonstrates, Augustine actually did have a great deal to say about angels in the *Enchiridion* and his other works.
8. Augustine, *On the Trinity* 3.3.21 (W. J. Mountain, ed., *Sancti Aurelii Augustini de trinitate libri XV*, CCL 50 [Turnhout: Brepols, 1968]; Edmund Hill, trans., *The Trinity*, The Works of Saint Augustine: A Translation for the 21st Century [Brooklyn: New City Press, 1990], 140).

9. Augustine, *To Orosius* 14 (K. D. Daur, ed., *Contra adversarium legis et prophetarum: Commonitorium Orosii et sancti Aurelii Augustini contra Priscillianistas et Origenistas*, CCL 49 [Turnhout: Brepols, 1985], 177–78).
10. Augustine, *To Orosius* 14 (CCL 49:178).
11. See also Augustine, *Enchiridion* 59 (CCL 46:81), in which Augustine told his readers to avoid asking the questions in the first place: "For what is the purpose of affirming, or denying, or defining these subjects in detail when it is possible to be ignorant of them without blame?"
12. For Augustine's logic about how an angel might appear as the Lord, see Chapter 2.
13. Conybeare, *Irrational Augustine*, vii, where she notes its presence in his Cassiciacum dialogues, written at the start of Augustine's Christian period, even before the *Confessions*.
14. Jean Daniélou, *Les anges et leur mission d'après les Pères de l'Église* (Chevetogne: Éditions de Chevetogne, 1953); David Heimann, trans., *The Angels and Their Mission* (Westminster, MD: Christian Classics, 1976), vii.
15. Daniélou, *Les anges et leur mission*; trans. Heimann, *Angels and Their Mission*, vii–viii.
16. Erik Peterson, *Das Buch von den Engeln: Stellung und Bedeutung der heiligen Engel im Kultus* (Leipzig: Hegner, 1935); Ronald Walls, trans., *The Angels and the Liturgy* (New York: Herder and Herder, 1964), 13. See the chapter on Peterson's theology in Dieter Heidtmann's *Die Engel: Grenzgestalten Gottes: über Notwendigkeit und Möglichkeit der christlichen Rede von den Engeln* (Neukirchen-Vluyn: Neukirchener Verlag, 1999).
17. Jonathan Z. Smith, *Drudgery Divine: On the Comparison of Early Christianities and the Religions of Late Antiquity* (Chicago: University of Chicago Press, 1990).
18. Karl Barth, *Church Dogmatics, Volume 3.3: The Doctrine of Creation* (London: T & T Clark, 1960), 371.
19. Barth, *Church Dogmatics: The Doctrine of Creation*, 380.
20. Barth, *Church Dogmatics: The Doctrine of Creation*, 404. This remark is in the context of a direct repudiation of Thomas Aquinas, but all extra-scriptural material, including late ancient and medieval thought and traditions, was suspect for Barth.
21. Note the emphasis on biblical foundations for ideas about angels in Susan R. Garrett's *No Ordinary Angel: Celestial Spirits and Christian Claims about Jesus* (New Haven, CT: Yale University Press, 2008). Even a less explicitly confessional approach, such as that of David Keck (*Angels and Angelology in the Middle Ages* [New York: Oxford University Press, 1998]), can suggest that Scripture is "the foundation of angelology." That may be the case for medieval Christians, but as we will see, it is only complexly and partially true for late ancient Christians.

22. Michael Gaddis explores the reality and the rhetoric in Christian portrayals of the first decade of the fourth century in *There is No Crime for Those Who Have Christ: Religious Violence in the Christian Roman Empire*, TCH 39 (Berkeley: University of California Press, 2005), especially in "'What Has the Emperor to Do with the Church?' Persecution and Martyrdom from Diocletian to Constantine," 29–67.
23. Elizabeth DePalma Digeser describes how Constantine's action was expansive, aimed at more than just Christianity, but was also tied to Christian visions of tolerance, especially that of Lactantius, in *The Making of a Christian Empire: Lactantius and Rome* (Ithaca, NY: Cornell University Press, 1999).
24. Claudia Rapp, *Holy Bishops in Late Antiquity: The Nature of Christian Leadership in an Age of Transition*, TCH 37 (Berkeley: University of California Press, 2005), 6–16, esp. 13: "What has been lacking is a study that deemphasizes the reign of Constantine and that, instead of treating it as a watershed in the history of the institutional development of the church, follows the continuous flow of developments, both in Christian culture and in the Roman Empire, in the centuries before and after Constantine's reign."
25. Hans von Campenhausen, *Kirchliches Amt und geistliche Vollmacht in den ersten drei Jahrhunderten*, Beiträge zur historischen Theologie 14 (Tübingen: Mohr Siebeck, 1953). His estimation of Christian authority was influenced by the models proposed by sociologist Max Weber.
26. Philip Rousseau, *Ascetics, Authority, and the Church in the Age of Jerome and Cassian*, 2nd ed. (Notre Dame, IN: University of Notre Dame Press, 2010); Andrea Sterk, *Renouncing the World Yet Leading the Church: The Monk-Bishop in Late Antiquity* (Cambridge, MA: Harvard University Press, 2004).
27. Rebecca Krawiec, *Shenoute and the Women of the White Monastery: Egyptian Monasticism in Late Antiquity* (New York: Oxford University Press, 2002); Caroline T. Schroeder, *Monastic Bodies: Discipline and Salvation in Shenoute of Atripe*, Divinations (Philadelphia: University of Pennsylvania Press, 2007).
28. Rapp, *Holy Bishops in Late Antiquity*.
29. Rousseau, *Ascetics, Authority, and the Church*, introduction to the second edition, xi, emphasis in original.
30. See Athanasius, *Life of Antony* 91 and *Ad Dracontius*, discussed in David Brakke, *Athanasius and the Politics of Asceticism*, OECS (Oxford: Oxford University Press, 1995), 99–110, and Sterk, *Renouncing the World Yet Leading the Church*, 17–19.
31. Rapp, *Holy Bishops in Late Antiquity*, esp. 137–52. See also *First Greek Life of Pachomius* 27, which seems to suggest that monks should forgive other monks who are ordained, not thinking them to have wanted power, but rather imagining that they were ordained unwillingly.
32. For the longer version of Evagrius's life, see David Brakke, *Demons and the Making of the Monk: Spiritual Combat in Early Christianity* (Cambridge, MA: Harvard University Press, 2006), 48–52.

33. Evagrius, *Thoughts* 21 (Paul Géhin, Claire Guillaumont, and Antoine Guillaumont, ed., *Évagre le Pontique: Sur les pensées*, SC 438 [Paris: Éditions du Cerf, 1998], 226–28; Robert E. Sinkewicz, trans., *Evagrius of Pontus: The Greek Ascetic Corpus*, OECS [Oxford: Oxford University Press, 2003], 167).
34. *Praktikos* 13 (Antoine Guillaumont and Claire Guillaumont, eds., *Évagre le Pontique: Traité pratique ou Le moine*, SC 171 [Paris: Éditions du Cerf, 1971], 528; Sinkewicz, *Evagrius of Pontus*, 100). See also Brakke's discussion of the work of specific demons according to Evagrius (*Demons and the Making of the Monk*, 58–70).
35. Ewa Wipszycka argues that many monks in later antiquity were ordained solely for the honor of it, since they did not participate in any liturgical activities ("Les clercs dans les communautés monastiques d'Égypte," *Journal of Juristic Papyrology* 26 [1996]: 135–66, esp. 158).
36. Palladius's *Lausiac History* 38 suggests that Evagrius left Constantinople because of an affair, but no explicit report from Evagrius himself confirms this.
37. Steven D. Driver, *John Cassian and the Reading of Egyptian Monastic Culture* (New York: Routledge, 2002).
38. Cassian, *Institutes* 11.18 (Jean-Claude Guy, ed., *Jean Cassien: Institutions cénobitiques*, SC 109 [Paris: Éditions du Cerf, 1965], 444); cf. *Institutes* 4.30.
39. The exhaustive work of scholars Irénée Hausherr and Antoine Guillaumont, often with Claire Guillaumont, is the foundation on which contemporary studies of Evagrius lie.
40. Blossom Stefaniw, *Mind, Text, and Commentary: Noetic Exegesis in Origen of Alexandria, Didymus the Blind, and Evagrius Ponticus*, ECCA 6 (Frankfurt am Main: Lang, 2010).
41. The "persuasion" described by Peter Brown in *Power and Persuasion in Late Antiquity: Towards a Christian Empire* (Madison: University of Wisconsin Press, 1992) suggests something of what I mean here. Richard Lim has argued that public debate fell out of favor as a cultural practice during late antiquity, and I agree, but the contestation for positions of authority within a certain public—a reading public, a legal public, but not necessarily a physical audience—never went out of style (*Public Disputation, Power, and Social Order in Late Antiquity*, TCH 23 [Berkeley: University of California Press, 1995]).
42. Two excellent (and very different) studies of this dynamic are H. A. Drake, *Constantine and the Bishops: The Politics of Intolerance* (Baltimore, MD: Johns Hopkins University Press, 2000) and T. D. Barnes, *Athanasius and Constantius: Theology and Politics in the Constantinian Empire* (Cambridge, MA: Harvard University Press, 2001).
43. Rapp, *Holy Bishops in Late Antiquity*, 36, cf. 41.
44. For more on the construction of the Arians, see Chapter 2.
45. Conversely, not all who held the office of bishop were "power players" of the sort of Athanasius, Gregory, and Augustine. See Drake, *Constantine and the Bishops*, esp. the final chapter.

46. That audience often in turn authorized a leader. Drake, *Constantine and the Bishops*, 398–400, where he discusses the "patronage resources" available to bishops and Christians and argues that the power of acting like a patron derives from the ability to garner many clients, namely, a congregation.
47. See, for example, Patricia Cox Miller, *The Corporeal Imagination: Signifying the Holy in Late Ancient Christianity*, Divinations (Philadelphia: University of Pennsylvania Press, 2009); for angels specifically, see Glenn Peers, *Subtle Bodies: Representing Angels in Byzantium*, TCH 32 (Berkeley: University of California Press, 2001).
48. Peers, *Subtle Bodies*, esp. 21–60, with the primary question being whether angels were portrayed with wings or without them.
49. For example, Elizabeth A. Clark, most recently, has suggested that the female figure of Macrina was good for Gregory of Nyssa to think (*History, Theory, Text: Historians and the Linguistic Turn* [Cambridge, MA: Harvard University Press, 2004], 179).
50. Another entity that would also be "good to think" in these terms is Christ, yet I have not ever heard a scholar claim that Christ was "good to think" for late ancient Christians.
51. Keck, *Angels and Angelology in the Middle Ages*.

CHAPTER 1

1. For a discussion of how angels and demons were eventually understood as being members of one class of beings, see Dale Basil Martin, "When Did Angels Become Demons?" *Journal of Biblical Literature* 129 (2010): 657–77.
2. For the trouble this can cause, see Annette Yoshiko Reed, "The Trickery of the Fallen Angels and the Demonic Mimesis of the Divine: Aetiology, Demonology, and Polemics in the Writings of Justin Martyr," *JECS* 12 (2004): 141–71. For the corresponding development emphasizing the importance of discernment, see Joseph T. Lienhard, "On 'Discernment of Spirits' in the Early Church," *JTS* 41 (1980): 505–29.
3. *Lausiac History* 38, for Evagrius. The scholarly bibliography on the life and works of Evagrius is large and growing. Joel Kalvesmaki maintains an online resource that is as broad in its catchment as it is meticulous in its details (Joel Kalvesmaki, ed., "Guide to Evagrius Ponticus," spring 2012 edition [Washington, DC, 2011], evagriusponticus.net).
4. Brakke, *Demons and the Making of the Monk*, 48.
5. See Origen, *On First Principles* 1.5.1–2 and 1.8.2–4; *Against Celsus* 5.5.
6. Origen, *Against Celsus* 6.70 (in which he argues that demons can tempt humanity).
7. Still an excellent resource on Evagrius's life and early education is Antoine and Claire Guillaumont, "Evagrius Ponticus: Persönlichkeit, Leben, Wirkung,"

Reallexicon für Antike und Christentum 6 (1966): 1088–107. See also Sinkewicz, *Evagrius of Pontus*, xvii–xxi, along with Julia S. Konstantinovsky, *Evagrius Ponticus: The Making of a Gnostic* (Burlington, VT: Ashgate, 2009), 12–15.

8. *Philokalia* (*Sur les Écritures: Philocalie, 1–20,* ed. Marguerite Harl, SC 302 [Paris: Éditions du Cerf, 1983]; *Philocalie 21–27: Sur le libre arbitre,* ed. Éric Junod, SC 226 [Paris: Éditions du Cerf, 1976]). There is some question about whether Gregory and Basil actually were the compilers or simply knew the text; Junod supports their authorship of the anthology, while Harl has doubts.
9. Gregory of Nazianzus, *Letter* 115.
10. Evagrius, *Praktikos* epilogue (SC 171:712). Evagrius's *Gnostikos* 44 and 45 attribute extensive theories of contemplation and virtue to Gregory and to Basil; if these are authentic, they are even more evidence of the influence of these teachers on Evagrius.
11. Gabriel Bunge, "Évagre le Pontique et les deux Macaire," *Irénikon* 56 (1983): 215–27, 323–60.
12. For the influence of Origen's cosmology on Antony and Macarius, see Samuel Rubenson, "Evagrios Pontikos und die Theologie der Wüste," in *Logos: Festschrift für Luise Abramowski zum 8. Juli 1993,* Zeitschrift für die neutestamentliche Wissenschaft und die Kunde der älteren Kirche 67 (Berlin: de Gruyter, 1993), 384–401, and his further discussion in *Letters of St. Antony: Monasticism and the Making of a Saint* (Minneapolis, MN: Fortress Press, 1990), 185–91.
13. Evagrius, *Kephalaia Gnostica* 3.38 (Antoine Guillaumont, ed., *Les six centuries des "Kephalaia Gnostica" d'Évagre le Pontique,* PO 28 [Paris, 1958; repr. Turnhout: Brepols, 2003], 113).
14. *Kephalaia Gnostica* 3.28–29 (PO 28:109).
15. *Kephalaia Gnostica* 1.68 (PO 28:49); in Syriac the three faculties are ܗܘܢܐ (*nous*), ܪܓܬܐ (*epithumikos*), and ܚܡܬܐ (*thumikos*). Notice the expurgated version leaves out the elements (S1 in Guillaumont's edition, the facing page 48): "Among the holy angels, there is more of *nous*; among humans there is more of *epithumikos*, and among demons there is more *thumikos*."
16. "Those who say humans are midway between angels and demons are right" (*Kephalaia Gnostica* 4.13 [PO 28:141]); notice the variance of the expurgated version, "It is right that humans say they are between angels and demons," a change in syntax that emphasizes that humans claim this status without agreeing that it is correct to do so (PO 28:140).
17. Evagrius, *Praktikos* 89 (SC 171:681–89).
18. Evagrius, *Kephalaia Gnostica* 1.81 (PO 28:55).
19. Evagrius, *Praktikos* 74 (SC 171:663; trans. Sinkewicz, *Evagrius of Pontus*, 110, slightly altered).
20. Evagrius, *Kephalaia Gnostica* 2.45 (PO 28:79); on the knowledge of the Trinity, see *Kephalaia Gnostica* 3.41 (PO 28:115).
21. *Kephalaia Gnostica* 5.12 (PO 28:181).

22. *Kephalaia Gnostica* 1.85 (PO 28:57).
23. For an even more detailed account of Evagrius's progressive system, see Sinkewicz, *Evagrius of Pontus*, xxxii–xxxvii.
24. Evagrius, *On Prayer* 74 (PG 79:1184; trans. Sinkewicz, *Evagrius of Pontus*, 201).
25. *On Prayer* 75 (PG 79:1184; trans. Sinkewicz, *Evagrius of Pontus*, 201).
26. Evagrius, *Kephalaia Gnostica* 3.46 (PO 28:117).
27. *Kephalaia Gnostica* 3.41 (PO 28:115).
28. Evagrius, *Praktikos* 74 (SC 171:662); cf. *On Prayer* 46 and 47 (PG 79:1176–77) for even more specfic tactics.
29. Evagrius, *On Prayer* 90 (PG 79:1188; trans. Sinkewicz, *Evagrius of Pontus*, 202).
30. Evagrius, *Kephalaia Gnostica* 3.90 (PO 28:135).
31. Evagrius, *Praktikos* 24 (SC 171:556; trans. Sinkewicz, *Evagrius of Pontus*, 102). Cf. the description of demons distracting the *nous* in *On Prayer* 10 (PG 79:1169).
32. Evagrius, *Praktikos* 21 (SC 171:550; trans. Sinkewicz, *Evagrius of Pontus*, 101).
33. Evagrius, *Kephalaia Gnostica* 4.85 (PO 28:173).
34. Brakke, *Demons and the Making of the Monk.*
35. Macarius of Egypt, *Letter* 1.4 (Werner Strothmann, ed., *Die syrische Überlieferung der Schriften des Makarios, Teil 2: Übersetzung*, Göttinger Orientforschungen, Reihe Syriaca 21 [Wiesbaden: Harrassowitz, 1981], xvi–xxii, at xviii). For a detailed discussion of this letter, see Chapter 3.
36. David Brakke, trans., *Evagrius of Pontus Talking Back: A Monastic Handbook for Combating Demons*, Cistercian Studies 229 (Collegeville, MN: Liturgical Press, 2009), 17–19.
37. Gregory of Nazianzus, *Prayer Text* 3 (PG 37:1403; text and trans. Dayna Kalleres, "Demons and Divine Illumination: A Consideration of Eight Prayers by Gregory of Nazianzus," *VC* 61 [2007]:157–88, at 166).
38. Kalleres, "Demons and Divine Illumination," 188.
39. Evagrius, *On Prayer* 81 (PG 79:1185; trans. Sinkewicz, *Evagrius of Pontus*, 201–2); cf. *Talking Back* Listlessness 17, where Evagrius offers advice to "the soul that wants to learn whether the soul truly is handed over to temptations from demons whenever it is briefly abandoned by the holy angels" (W. Frankenberg, ed., *Euagrius Ponticus*, Abhandlungen der königlichen Gesellschaft der Wissenschaften zu Göttingen, Philologisch-historische Klasse, Neue Folge 13.2 [Berlin: Weidmannsche Buchhandlung, 1912], 524; Brakke, *Talking Back*, 137).
40. Part of that role is ensuring that he is using the *nous* for contemplation and not trying to use it inappropriately for eradication of the passions, which is supposed to be accomplished during the practical stage. Cf. *Kephalaia Gnostica* 2.48 (PO 28:81).
41. Evagrius, *Praktikos* 76 (SC 171:664); cf. *Kephalaia Gnostica* 1.85, *Letter* 43, and *Thoughts* 26, which repeat the same idea, namely that the *nous* which is able to sustain apatheia "encounters the incorporeal beings who fulfill its spiritual desires" (SC 438:246; trans. Sinkewicz, *Evagrius of Pontus*, 172).

42. Evagrius, *Kephalaia Gnostica* 1.22 (PO 28:25–27).
43. Evagrius, *On Prayer* 95 (PG 79:1188; trans. Sinkewicz, *Evagrius of Pontus*, 203).
44. See Dragoş-Andrei Giulea's argument that Athenagoras had voiced an early version of this assumption ("The Watchers' Whispers: Athenagoras's *Legatio* 25,1–3 and the *Book of the Watchers*," *VC* 61 [2007]: 258–81).
45. Brakke, *Demons and the Making of the Monk*, 54.
46. Evagrius, *Praktikos* 80 (SC 171:668; trans. Sinkewicz, *Evagrius of Pontus*, 110).
47. Evagrius, *Kephalaia Gnostica* 1.39 (PO 28:35–37).
48. Evagrius, *Kephalaia Gnostica* 5.9 (PO 28:181). Cf. *Kephalaia Gnostica* 5.11.
49. Evagrius, *Letter* 54.6 (ed. Frankenberg, *Euagrius Ponticus*, 606).
50. Evagrius, *Kephalaia Gnostica* 4.38 (PO 28:153). The expurgated verion tellingly has the angry man be "estranged from the conduct of the angels."
51. Evagrius, *Letter* 54.6 (ed. Frankenberg, *Euagrius Ponticus*, 606).
52. Evagrius, *Kephalaia Gnostica* 6.2 (PO 28:213).
53. Augustine has sustained the interest of historians and theologians for centuries, and the resulting scholarly literature about his life, ideas, and influence is immense. In what follows, I will cite a few relevant works as portkeys, which the reader can use to investigate further; alternate entry points are *The Cambridge Companion to Augustine*, ed. Eleonore Stump and Norman Kretzmann (New York: Cambridge University Press, 2001) and "Patristics Bibliography #7: Augustine & the Latin West," compiled by William Harmless, last modified August 20, 2012, http://moses.creighton.edu/harmless/bibliographies_for_theology/Patristics_6.htm.
54. Jason David BeDuhn explores the concept of "conversion" and what it meant in the context of Augustine's career in *Augustine's Manichaean Dilemma, 1: Conversion and Apostasy, 373–388 C.E.*, Divinations (Philadelphia: University of Pennsylvania Press, 2010). Still an important resource, Peter Brown's *Augustine of Hippo: A Biography* (Berkeley: University of California Press, 1967) has now been joined in English by two other modern biographies: Garry Wills, *Saint Augustine: A Life* (New York: Viking, 1999) and James J. O'Donnell, *Augustine: A New Biography* (New York: Ecco/HarperCollins, 2005).
55. Augustine, *Enchiridion* 1 (CCL 46:49).
56. Augustine, *Enchiridion* 9 (CCL 46:64–65).
57. Again, the literature on *City of God* is immense. To start, readers might consider Gerard J. P. O'Daly, *Augustine's* City of God*: A Reader's Guide* (Oxford: Clarendon, 1999).
58. Brown, *Augustine of Hippo: A Biography*, 304; cf. the comments of O'Donnell, *Augustine: A New Biography*, 122–25.
59. Caroline Humfress argues that Augustine's rhetorical training inflected his efforts at leadership. See *Orthodoxy and the Courts in Late Antiquity* (Oxford: Oxford University Press, 2007), especially "Ecclesiastics as Forensic Practitioners," 153–95.

60. A detailed and careful examination of Augustine's changing views of human society and how best to approach and to narrate its issues remains R. A. Markus's *Saeculum: History and Society in the Theology of St. Augustine* (New York: Cambridge University Press, 1970; reissued with a new introduction, 2007); the new introduction includes an overview of Augustine's interests in order and his lack of trust in human social arrangements (see esp. ix–xvi).
61. To understand the fractured Christian communities in which Augustine took part, see Robin M. Jensen and J. Patout Burns, Jr., *The Practice of Christianity in Roman Africa* (Grand Rapids, MI: Eerdmans, 2013).
62. Markus, *Saeculum*, 4.
63. Augustine, *City of God* 11.2 (Bernhard Dombart and Alphons Kalb, ed., *Sancti Aurelii Augustini De civitate Dei*, CCL 47–48 [Turnhout: Brepols, 1955], here 48:322; Henry Bettenson, trans., *St Augustine: Concerning the City of God against the Pagans* [London: Penguin Classics, 2003], 430).
64. Augustine, *City of God* 11.3 (CCL 48:322–23; trans. Bettenson, *City of God*, 431).
65. *City of God* 11.1 (CCL 48:321; trans. Bettenson, *City of God*, 429).
66. Augustine, *City of God* 11.1; cf. Psalms 46, 48, and 87.
67. Augustine, *City of God* 11.9 (CCL 48:328; trans. Bettenson, *City of God*, 438).
68. Augustine, *City of God* 11.9 (CCL 48:329; trans. Bettenson, *City of God*, 439).
69. Augustine, *City of God* 11.9 (CCL 48:329; trans. Bettenson, *City of God*, 439). Cf. 11.34, where Augustine rules out any interpretation that places the angels in the "waters."
70. Augustine, *City of God* 11.9 (CCL 48:330; trans. Bettenson, *City of God*, 440).
71. Augustine, *New Sermon* 26.26 (François Dolbeau, ed., *Discorsi Nuovi XXXV/2: Supplemento II (Dolbeau 21–31); Étaix 4–5* [Rome: Città Nuova Editrice, 2002], 654–56).
72. *City of God* 11.9 (CCL 48:330; trans. Bettenson, *City of God*, 440). See also the extended discussion on evil in Augustine, *City of God* 12.6–9.
73. *City of God* 11.9: "If an angel turns away from God he becomes impure: and such are all those who are called 'impure spirits.'"
74. Origen, *Against Celsus* 3.37 (Marcel Borret, ed., *Origène: Contre Celse, Tome I*, SC 132 [Paris: Éditions du Cerf, 1967], 86).
75. Origen, *Against Celsus* 3.37 (SC 132:88).
76. Lactantius, *Divine Institutes* 1.7.1 (Pierre Monat, ed., *Lactance: Institutions divines livre I*, SC 326 [Paris: Éditions du Cerf, 1984], 84); cf. *Orac. Apoll.* frag. 51 in J. Fontenrose, *Didyma: Apollo's Oracle, Cult, and Companions* (Berkeley: University of California Press, 1988), 223–25.
77. *Divine Institutes* 1.7.9 (SC 326:88).
78. Apuleius, *de deo Socrati* 147 (Jean Beaujeu, ed., *Apulée: Opuscules philosophiques et fragments* [Paris: Belles lettres, 2002], 32–33; Thomas Taylor, ed., *Apuleius'*

Golden Ass, or, The Metamorphoses, and Other Philosophical Writings [Somerset: Prometheus Trust, 1997], 243).

79. Augustine, *City of God* 8.16 (CCL 47:233; trans. Bettenson, *City of God*, 321).
80. Augustine, *City of God* 9.3.
81. *City of God* 12.1 (CCL 48:355; trans. Bettenson, *City of God*, 471).
82. Augustine's purpose was to have no independent cause of evil or the emergence of evil demons: see his repetitive insistence in 12.6, 7, and 9.
83. Augustine, *City of God* 11.3 (CCL 48:323; trans. Bettenson, *City of God*, 431).
84. Augustine, *City of God*. 9.5 (CCL 47:254; trans. Bettenson, *City of God*, 350).

CHAPTER 2

1. Justin, *Dialogue* 34 (Miroslav Marcovich, ed., *Iustini Martyris Dialogus cum Tryphone*, Patristische Texte und Studien 47 [Berlin: de Gruyter, 1997], 125); cf. *Dialogue* 61 (ed. Marcovich, *Dialogus cum Tryphone*, 174–75). Also see *Dialogue* 86 (ed. Marcovich, *Dialogus cum Tryphone*, 219) and *Apology* 1.6, where Christ is identified as "like angels." Silke-Petra Bergjan argues that Justin only referred to Christ as an angel in order to mark the modalist tendencies *of others* ("Qualifying 'Angel' in Justin's Logos Christology," *Studia Patristica* 50 [2003]: 353–57); it appears, however, that all these titles, "angel" included, had meaning for Justin's own idea of Christ.
2. On the Logos in early Judaism, see Daniel Boyarin, *Border Lines: The Partition of Judaeo-Christianity*, Divinations (Philadelphia: University of Pennsylvania Press, 2004).
3. *Dialogue* 126 (ed. Marcovich, *Dialogus cum Tryphone*, 287–89); cf. *Dialogue* 75, 127–28 (ed. Marcovich, *Dialogus cum Tryphone*, 200, 290–93).
4. *Dialogue* 56 (ed. Marcovich, *Dialogus cum Tryphone*, 161–67); a few other appearances of God to Abraham take place between Gen 18 and Gen 21, but for Justin, the important detail is the promise made in Gen 18 implying a visit near the time of Sarah's giving birth to a son.
5. *Dialogue* 61 (ed. Marcovich, *Dialogus cum Tryphone*, 174). In addition to continuity of character, other reading tools helped Justin argue that this rational power was Christ. At times, the same title can refer to two different entities, which made certain passages in the Septuagint intelligible, like Genesis 19.24, which uses "Lord" both as the subject of the sentence and an object of a preposition: "Then the Lord rained on Sodom and Gomorrah sulfur and fire from the Lord out of heaven." Justin assumed two characters here, and that "the one who is said and is written to have appeared to Abraham and Jacob and Moses is a different god than the god who made all things, by number but not by will"; *Dialogue* 56 (ed. Marcovich, *Dialogus cum Tryphone*, 163). See also *Dialogue* 127.
6. For a discussion of the role of the Jewish Other in Christian dialogues, beginning with *Dialogue* and ranging to fifth-century eratopokriseis texts, see Andrew

S. Jacobs, "Dialogical Differences: (De-)Judaizing Jesus' Circumcision," *JECS* 15 (2007): 291–335.

7. *Dialogue* 57 (ed. Marcovich, *Dialogus cum Tryphone*, 167–68).
8. As an example of how vital persuasion was to a Christian's public career, see Barnes, *Athanasius and Constantius.*
9. Canonization and the attendant use of Scripture as authoritative proof in theological argument is but one type of "scriptural practice" among many in late ancient Christianity. See David Brakke, "Scriptural Practices in Early Christianity: Towards a New History of the New Testament Canon," in *Invention, Rewriting, Usurpation: Discursive Fights over Religious Traditions in Antiquity*, ed. Jörg Ulrich, Anders-Christian Jacobsen, and David Brakke, ECCA 11 (Frankfurt am Main: Lang, 2012), 263–50.
10. This is not to say that I think reading practices were simply utilitarian; often, as we will see, reading informed theology as much as theology shaped reading.
11. See Brakke, *Athanasius and the Politics of Asceticism.*
12. Scholars have proposed several different dating schemes for the texts I cite here (Rowan Williams, *Arius: Heresy and Tradition* [London: Darton, Longman, and Todd, 1987] and Sara Parvis, *Marcellus of Ancyra and the Lost Years of the Arian Controversy 325–345*, OECS [Oxford: Oxford University Press, 2006] offer differing options); the point is that they are all written before the *First Oration against the Arians* and thus register as examples of Athanasius's scriptural practice before that text.
13. This letter has survived as a letter from Alexander, the bishop Athanasius served as secretary, but scholars now recognize it as Athanasius's own writing. See G. C. Stead, "Athanasius' Earliest Written Work," *JTS* 39 (1988): 76–91.
14. Robert W. Thompson, ed., *Contra Gentes and De Incarnatione*, Oxford Early Christian Texts (Oxford: Oxford University Press, 1971).
15. See Parvis, *Marcellus of Ancyra and the Lost Years of the Arian Controversy*, and James D. Ernest, *The Bible in Athanasius of Alexandria* (Leiden: Brill, 2004).
16. Barnes, *Athanasius and Constantius*, 34–46.
17. Proper reading of authoritative texts remained central to Athanasius's conception of orthodoxy and power. Cf. David Brakke, "A New Fragment of Athanasius's Thirty-Ninth *Festal Letter*: Heresy, Apocrypha, and the Canon," *HTR* 103 (2010): 47–66.
18. Lewis Ayres, *Nicaea and Its Legacy: An Approach to Fourth-Century Trinitarian Theology* (Oxford: Oxford University Press, 2006), 106.
19. Athanasius, *Oration* 1.8 (William Bright, ed., *The Orations of St. Athanasius against the Arians according to the Benedictine Text* [Oxford: Clarendon, 1873], 8); cf. 1.1, in which heretics are described as those who disperse poison.
20. Athanasius, *Oration* 1.53 (ed. Bright, *Orations*, 55, references to Jews and Manicheans on 56).
21. Note also that in *Oration* 1.54, after a very long set of arguments, Athanasius says that he wants to treat Heb 1.4 "first," as if there had not been the entirety of the treatise before that.

22. The author is citing from Psalms. Of course, all of the passages the author applies to the Son are only understood that way through a process of interpretation. Such christological readings, particularly of royal psalms, were a very early feature of the Christian movement (cf. Col 1.16, Eph 1.21, and 1 Pet 3.22).
23. Arius, *Thalia* stanza 2 and 3 (trans. Stuart Hall, ed. J. Stevenson, *A New Eusebius: Documents Illustrating the History of the Church to AD 337*, rev. ed., W. H. C. Frend [London: SPCK, 1987]; repr. in Ehrman and Jacobs, *Christianity in Late Antiquity*, 158–59); the fragments of the *Thalia* survive only in Athanasius's *de syn.* 15 (Opitz, ed., *Athanasius Werke* II/1 [Berlin: de Gruyter, 1939]).
24. ἴδιον; for this term in Athanasius's writing, cf. Ayres, *Nicaea and Its Legacy*, 114–15, and Andrew Louth, "The Use of the Term ἴδιος in Alexandrian Theology from Alexander to Cyril," *Studia Patristica* 19 (1987): 198–202, cited by Ayres.
25. Athanasius, *Oration* 1.56 (ed. Bright, *Orations*, 58).
26. *Oration* 1.56 (ed. Bright, *Orations*, 59).
27. *Oration* 1.55–56 (ed. Bright, *Orations*, 57–59).
28. *Oration* 1.55 (ed. Bright, *Orations*, 58).
29. *Oration* 1.57 (ed. Bright, *Orations*, 60). This is a slightly specious argument, in that μᾶλλον and μείζων are comparative in much the same way that κρείττων is.
30. For the wider use of fragmentation as a reading practice, see Catherine M. Chin, *Grammar and Christianity in the Late Roman World*, Divinations (Philadelphia: University of Pennsylvania Press, 2008), especially "Displacement and Excess," 72–109.
31. Athanasius, *Oration* 2.3, 2.46 (ed. Bright, *Orations*, 71, 115–16); cf. *Fest. Ep.* 39, in which Athanasius makes a similar argument about "teacher" as a title for Christ (Brakke, "A New Fragment of Athanasius's Thirty-Ninth Festal Letter").
32. As J. Z. Smith has observed, "It is when the notion of superlative value is conjoined to the unique . . . that one begins to verge on problematic modes of speech" (*Drudgery Divine*, 37).
33. *Oration* 3.12 (ed. Bright, *Orations*, 166).
34. *Oration* 3.14 (ed. Bright, *Orations*, 169).
35. Mark DelCogliano, *Basil of Caesarea's Anti-Eunomian Theory of Names: Christian Theology and Late-Antique Philosophy in the Fourth Century Trinitarian Controversy*, Supplements to *VC* 103 (Leiden: Brill, 2010), 13. For the context of the composition of the *Apology*, see Richard Paul Vaggione, *Eunomius: The Extant Works*, Oxford Early Christian Texts (Oxford: Clarendon, 1987), 5–9.
36. For an extended account of Basil's life, see Philip Rousseau, *Basil of Caesarea*, TCH 20 (Berkeley: University of California Press, 1994); Raymond Van Dam's Cappadocian triology (*Kingdom of Snow: Roman Rule and Greek Culture in Cappadocia*; *Families and Friends in Late Roman Cappadocia*; *Becoming Christian: The Conversion of Roman Cappadocia* [Philadelphia: University of Pennsylvania Press, 2002, 2002, 2003]) also provides important contextual evidence for the social networks of the writers whose ideas I discuss here.

37. Andrew Radde-Gallwitz, *Basil of Caesarea, Gregory of Nyssa, and the Transformation of Divine Simplicity*, OECS (Oxford: Oxford University Press, 2009).
38. One scholar has tried to make the case for Eunomius's importance using what might be called the "Celsus principle"; Vaggione based his estimation of Eunomius on the number of other Christians who penned responses to him: *Extant Works*, xiii. Note also the evidence of the Eunomian community, particularly at the later moments of the fourth century and the first parts of the fifth (Peter van Nuffelen, "Episcopal Succession in Constantinople [381–450 C.E.]: The Local Dynamics of Power," *JECS* 18 [2010]: 425–51).
39. Eunomius, *Apology* 12 (ed. Vaggione, *Extant Works*, 48). When he cited this, Basil omitted the portion of the passage that indicates this "begotten essence" of the Son "was begotten before all things by the will of God and Father," which would mitigate some of his concerns about the Son being thought of as part of the regular creation.
40. Eunomius, *Apology* 12 (ed. Vaggione, *Extant Works*, 48).
41. Basil, *Against Eunomius* 1.7 (Bernard Sesboüé, ed., *Basile de Césarée Contra Eunome, suivi de Eunome Apologie*, SC 299 [Paris: Éditions du Cerf, 1982], 188–90).
42. DelCogliano explains in far more detail Basil's innovation; see especially Chapter Five, "Basil's Notionalist Theory of Names," in *Basil of Caesarea's Anti-Eunomian Theory of Names*, and particularly 163–75.
43. Though see John A. Demetracopoulos, "Glossogony or Epistemology? The Stoic Character of Basil of Caesarea's and Eunomius' Epistemological Notion of *epinoia* and Its Misinterpretation by Gregory of Nyssa," in *Gregory of Nyssa: Contra Eunomium II*, ed. Lenka Karfíková, Scot Douglass, and Johannes Zachhuber (Leiden: Brill, 2007), 387–98.
44. Basil, *Against Eunomius* 2.2 (Bernard Sesboüé, ed., *Basile de Césarée Contra Eunome, suivi de Eunome Apologie*, SC 305 [Paris: Éditions du Cerf, 1983], 14).
45. *Against Eunomius* 2.2 (SC 305:14–16). As for the word ποίημα specifically, Basil noted that there are moments when the divine speaker recorded in Scripture first employed a verb to describe an action, then used its corresponding adjective to describe the product of that action. However, these passages are not in contexts that allow for them to be read as references to the Son; here Basil uses a kind of historical investigation, treating dialogue in Scripture as past speech and seeking out information in the context of narrative in order to invalidate Eunomius's methods.
46. Is 9.5 (LXX): ὅτι παιδίον ἐγεννήθη ἡμῖν, υἱὸς καὶ ἐδόθη ἡμῖν, οὗ ἡ ἀρχὴ ἐγενήθη ἐπὶ τοῦ ὤμου αὐτοῦ, καὶ καλεῖται τὸ ὄνομα αὐτοῦ Μεγάλης βουλῆς ἄγγελος.
47. *Against Eunomius* 2.7 (SC 305:28). I am grateful to Andrew Radde-Gallwitz and Mark DelCogliano for discussing this passage with me and offering their advice about its translation and its implications.
48. By "recently" I mean not from eternity. Either Basil did not understand all of Eunomius's position, did not see a text that included it, or purposefully omitted

the fact that Eunomius specifies that while the Son is indeed created, "not existing before his own constitution," he is nevertheless existent before all (*Apology* 12 [ed. Vaggione, *Extant Works*, 48]).

49. *Against Eunomius* 2.18 (SC 305:72).

50. For the context of the composition of the *Apology for the Apology*, see Vaggione, *Extant Works*, 82–89.

51. Gregory of Nyssa, *Against Eunomius* 3.9.27 (W. Jaeger, ed., *Gregorii Nysseni Contra Eunomium libri, pars altera: Liber III (vulgo III–XII). Refutatio confessionis Eunomii (vulgo Lib. II)* [Leiden: Brill, 1960], 273–74). This is a case where the Greek may be easier to understand than the English, and Eunomius's styling of the God/angel binary represented in the Son is rhetorically savvy: ὅς τῷ μὲν ἄγγελος ὠνομάσθαι σαφῶς ἐδίδαξε δι' ὅτου διήγγειλε τοὺς λόγους καὶ τίς ὁ ὤν, τῷ δὲ καὶ θεὸς προσειρῆσθαι τὴν ἰδίαν ἔδειξε κατὰ πάντων ὑπεροχήν. ὁ γὰρ τῶν δι' αὐτοῦ γενομένων θεὸς ἄγγελος τοῦ ἐπὶ πάντων θεοῦ. Cf. Origen, *Commentary on John* 1.34.

52. *Against Eunomius* 3.9.34–35 (ed. Jaeger, *Gregorii Nysseni Contra Eunomium: Liber III*, 276–77).

53. Richard Paul Vaggione, *Eunomius of Cyzicus and the Nicene Revolution*, OECS (Oxford: Oxford University Press, 2001), especially Chapter Seven, "Exile," 267–311.

54. See Vaggione, *Extant Works*, 131–34, for a discussion of 381 and the likelihood that Eunomius's *Statement of Faith* was written to justify his orthodoxy after the judgment at Constantinople.

55. Gregory of Nyssa, *Against Eunomius* 3.9.27–28 (ed. Jaeger, *Gregorii Nysseni Contra Eunomium: Liber III*, 274).

56. Even Gregory felt there might have been a difference between his and Basil's approaches; Gregory of Nyssa, *Letter* 29.1–5 (P. Maraval, ed., *Grégoire de Nysse: Lettres*, SC 363 [Paris: Éditions du Cerf, 1990], 308–12). Gregory called upon later readers of his text against Eunomius to use it to "do battle with our enemies," signifying the deeply different tone of his writing against Eunomius from that of Basil's more reasoned and persuasive text and the different situation: instead of fighting one person, Gregory had widened the field to include "heretics" more generally (*Letter* 15, to John and Maximian, two students).

57. *Against Eunomius* 3.9.34–35 (ed. Jaeger, *Gregorii Nysseni Contra Eunomium: Liber III*, 276–77).

58. *Against Eunomius* 3.9.31 (ed. Jaeger, *Gregorii Nysseni Contra Eunomium: Liber III*, 275).

59. Daniel Boyarin (*Border Lines*,14) discusses "the orthodox topos that Christian heretics are Jews or Judaizers," noting that the "'Jews' (for this context, heretics so named), the Judaizers, and the Jewish Christians—whether they existed or to what extent is irrelevant in this context—thus mark a space of threatening hybridity, which it is the task of religion police to do away with."

60. *Letter to Paulinus* (PL 13:364).

61. *Letter to Algasia* 121.10.10–11 (Isidor Hilberg, ed., *Sancti Eusebii Hieronymi epistulae*, CSEL 56 [Vienna: Verlag der Österreichischen Akademie der Wissenschaften, 1996], 44–45).
62. Lewis Ayres details Augustine's use of traditional argumentative forms in *Augustine and the Trinity* (New York: Cambridge University Press, 2010), 105–16.
63. Augustine, *On the Trinity* 3.1 (CCL 50:127).
64. Ayres, *Augustine and the Trinity*, 3.
65. *On the Trinity* 2.2, cf. 2.4.
66. *On the Trinity* 2.2 (CCL 50:81). See the more detailed discussion at Ayres, *Augustine and the Trinity*, 181–87.
67. *On the Trinity* 2.7 (CCL 50:87).
68. *On the Trinity* 2.12 (CCL 50:96–97).
69. *On the Trinity* 2.20 (CCL 50:107; prooftexts from Phil 2.6–7).
70. *On the Trinity* 3 preface (CCL 50:129).
71. *On the Trinity* 3.19 (CCL 50:146).
72. *On the Trinity* 3.23 (CCL 50:152).
73. *On the Trinity* 3.23 (CCL 50:152); while Augustine does not point this out, his argument is parallel to Paul's argument regarding offspring in Gal 3.
74. *On the Trinity* 3.25 (CCL 50:154–55).

CHAPTER 3

1. For examples, see Susanna Elm, *"Virgins of God": The Making of Asceticism in Late Antiquity* (Oxford: Clarendon Press, 1994), esp. 25–59. Readers will recognize in the title of this chapter the influence of Kenneth Burke's famous essay, "Literature as Equipment for Living."
2. James E. Goehring, "The World Engaged: The Social and Economic World of Early Egyptian Monasticism," in *Ascetics, Society, and the Desert: Studies in Early Egyptian Monasticism* (Harrisburg, PA: Trinity Press International, 1999), 39–52
3. Edward J. Watts, *City and School in Late Antique Athens and Alexandria*, TCH 41 (Berkeley: University of California Press, 2006), 6.
4. Pierre Hadot (*Philosophy as a Way of Life*, trans. Michael Chase [Oxford: Blackwell, 1995]) gives a sense of the comprehensive nature of ancient philosophical programs.
5. For the centrality of academic circles in Alexandrian Christian life before the mid-fourth century, see Brakke, *Athanasius and the Politics of Asceticism*, 59–75.
6. Bunge, "Évagre le Pontique et les deux Macaire"; see also Sinkewicz, *Evagrius of Pontus*, xviii–xix.
7. David Brakke has explored how the Greek magical papyri, also from Egypt, have several spells to garner the magician an angelic companion (*Demons and the Making of the Monk*, 229).

8. Plato, *Apology* 31c-d (Thomas C. Brickhouse and Nicholas D. Smith, ed., *The Trial and Execution of Socrates: Sources and Controversies* [New York: Oxford University Press, 2002], 56).
9. Plato, *Republic* 496a-b (*The Republic: Books VI–X*, trans. Paul Shorey, LCL [Cambridge: Harvard University Press, 1935]), 50–51.
10. Plato, *Republic* 6.496c (Shorey, *The Republic*, 52–53).
11. For a wider discussion of the reception of the sign in antiquity, see A. A. Long, "How Does Socrates' Divine Sign Communicate with Him?" in *A Companion to Socrates*, ed. Sara Ahbel-Rappe and Rachana Kamtekar (West Sussex: Wiley-Blackwell, 2009), 68–73.
12. Plutarach, *Moralia: de genio socratis* 593D-594A (Phillip H. DeLacy and Benedict Einarson, ed. and trans., *Plutarch's Moralia in Fifteen Volumes: Volume 7*, LCL [Cambridge, MA: Harvard University Press, 1927], 480–82).
13. Quite literally, those who strip for the same goal (τοῖς ἐπὶ ταὐτὸ γυμναζομένοις) and the soul that goes through great struggles (ἥτις δ' ἂν ἤδη διὰ μυρίων γενέσεων ἠγωνισμένη μακροὺς ἀγῶνας εὖ καὶ προθύμως ψυχή).
14. Dale B. Martin, *Inventing Superstition: From the Hippocratics to the Christians* (Cambridge, MA: Harvard University Press, 2004).
15. Apuleius, *On the God of Socrates* 16 (ed. Beaujeu, *Apulée*, 36).
16. Apuleius, *On the God of Socrates* 22 (ed. Beaujeu, *Apulée*, 42).
17. Gregory Thaumaturgus, *Panegyric on Origen* 43–44 (Henri Crouzel, ed., *Grégoire le Thaumaturge: Remerciement à Origène*, SC 148 [Paris: Éditions du Cerf, 1969], 112–14).
18. Gregory Thaumaturgus, *Panegyric on Origen* 71 (SC 148:122–24).
19. Gregory Thaumaturgus, *Panegyric on Origen* 206 (SC 148:182).
20. Elizabeth DePalma Digeser, "Origen on the *Limes*: Rhetoric and the Polarization of Identity in the Late Third Century," in *The Rhetoric of Power in Late Antiquity: Religion and Politics in Byzantium, Europe and the Early Islamic World*, ed. Robert M. Frakes, Elizabeth DePalma Digeser, and Justin Stephens (London: I. B. Tauris, 2010), 197–218, at 203.
21. Stefaniw, *Mind, Text, and Commentary*, 283.
22. Ex 23.20–22. The LXX differs only slightly: "Look, I send my angel before you to guard you on the way, to bring you into the land that I prepared for you. Watch yourself, listen to him, and do not disobey him. For he will not fear you, because my name is upon him. If by paying attention you listen to my voice and do everything I command you to do and guard my covenant, you will be a nation surpassing all others to me. All of the earth is mine, and you will be a kingly priesthood and a holy nation. You will say these words to the children of Israel: If by paying attention you hear my voice and do all that I say to you, I will be an enemy to your enemies and I will oppose those opposing you."
23. Gen 48.15–16 (LXX).
24. Ps 34.6–7. "Rescue" here is ῥύομαι, as it is in Gen 48.

25. Gregory Thaumaturgus, *Panegyric on Origen* 40 (SC 148:112).
26. Gregory Thaumaturgus, *Panegyric on Origen* 42 (SC 148:112). This may reflect Gregory's belief in Origen's theory of return: more advanced human beings need the example of rational beings closer to God; Gregory had enough to learn from an angel, but Origen was so far advanced that he could only learn from Christ.
27. Origen, *Commentary on Matthew* 13.27 (Erich Klostermann, ed., *Origenes Werke: Origenes Matthäuserklärung*, GCS 40.1 [Leipzig: Hinrichs, 1935], 254–55).
28. Origen, *Commentary on Matthew* 13.28 (GCS 40.1:256).
29. Origen, *Commentary on Matthew* 13.28 (GCS 40.1:257).
30. Origen, *Commentary on Matthew* 13.26 (GCS 40.1:253).
31. Origen, *Commentary on Matthew* 13.26 (GCS 40.1:254).
32. Origen, *Homily on Luke* 3.1 (Max Rauer, ed., *Origenes Werke: Die Homilien zu Lukas in der Übersetzung des Hieronymus und die griechischen Reste der Homilien und des Lukas-Kommentars*, GCS 49 [Berlin: Akademie-Verlag, 1959], 19).
33. Origen, *Homily on Luke* 3.1 (GCS 49:20).
34. For the utility of such a guide for textual interpretation, see Catherine M. Chin, "Who Is the Ascetic Exegete? Angels, Enchantments, and Transformative Food in Origen's *Homilies on Joshua*," in *Asceticism and Exegesis in Early Christianity*, ed. Hans-Ulrich Weidemann (Göttingen: Vandenhoeck and Ruprecht, forthcoming 2013). I thank Catherine for sharing a copy of the essay with me before publication.
35. Origen, *Homily on Jeremiah* 10.8 (Pierre Nautin and Pierre Husson, ed., *Origène: Homélies sur Jérémie*, vol. 1, SC 232 [Paris: Éditions du Cerf, 1976], 414).
36. See David Brakke, "A New Fragment of Athanasius's Thirty-Ninth *Festal Letter*," esp. 51–56, and his earlier article, "Canon Formation and Social Conflict in Fourth-Century Egypt: Athanasius of Alexandria's Thirty-Ninth *Festal Letter*," *HTR* 87 (1994): 395–419; cf. *Athanasius*, 58–65 and Watts, *City and School*, 170–74.
37. As evidence of continuing academic Christianity in the city, see Didymus the Blind (Richard A. Layton, *Didymus the Blind and His Circle in Late-Antique Alexandria: Virtue and Narrative in Biblical Scholarship* [Urbana: University of Illinois Press, 2004], esp. Chapter One, "The Making of a Teacher," 13–35); cf. Watts, *City and School*, 182–86.
38. See the example of Theanor's speech from Plutarch's *Moralia: de genio socratis*, mentioned earlier in this chapter, and D. A. Dombrowski, "Asceticism as Athletic Training in Plotinus," *Aufstieg und Niedergang der römischen Welt* 2.36.1 (1987): 701–12.
39. Samuel Rubenson, "Wisdom, Paraenesis and the Roots of Monasticism," in *Early Christian Paraenesis in Context*, ed. James Starr and Troels Engberg-Pedersen (Berlin: De Gruyter, 2004), 521–78, esp. 521–34.
40. Samuel Rubenson's work has made these letters, which survive in a number of ancient versions, available as primary evidence of Antony's life and ideas in

Letters of St. Antony. I use Rubenson's translation throughout, with some adjustments I note when they appear.

41. David Brakke, *Demons and the Making of the Monk*, 16–22, making the case to include Valentinian and Gnostic teachers in the academic rubric; cf. Rubenson, *Letters*, 73–74, who also mentions Clement of Alexandria.
42. Rubenson, *Letters*, 59–68, 86–88.
43. Antony, *Letter* 2.2–6, 3.10–21, and 5.15–28 (Rubenson, *Letters*, 203, 206–207, 213–14).
44. Stefaniw, *Mind, Text, and Commentary*, expands the suggestive work of Rubenson, "Wisdom, Paraenesis, and the Roots of Monasticism."
45. Antony, *Letter* 1.18–22 (Rubenson, *Letters*, 198; "the struggle" appears in the Latin version only). I have not capitalized "spirit," as Rubenson has, for reasons that will become clear later.
46. Antony, *Letter* 1.24–25 (Rubenson, *Letters*, 198).
47. Antony, *Letter* 1. 6–27, cf. 1.28–32 (Rubenson, *Letters*, 198–99).
48. Antony, *Letter* 1.47, 56, 59 (Rubenson, *Letters*, 200–201).
49. Antony, *Letter* 1.43 (Rubenson, *Letters*, 200). Rubenson in his notes provides the multiple variations available in the other ancient versions in this sentence, which is from the Latin. Georgian has "then evil spirits sow in the constitution of the body"; Syriac has "the evil spirits take dominon [*sic*] over it and sow in the mass of the body all passions"; while Arabic has "the evil spirits prevail over him and defiles [*sic*] his body."
50. Antony, *Letter* 1.44 (Rubenson, *Letters*, 200).
51. Scholars often make this assumption: see William Harmless, *Desert Christians: An Introduction to the Literature of Early Monasticism* (New York: Oxford University Press, 2004), 80, 191; as well as Lance Jenott and Elaine Pagels, "Antony's Letters and Nag Hammadi Codex I: Sources of Religious Conflict in Fourth-Century Egypt," *JECS* 18 (2010): 557–89, at 575–77.
52. Rubenson dates the letters no earlier than the late 330s, but they can obviously be no later than 356, the date of Antony's death (*Letters*, 42–46).
53. Ayres, *Nicaea and Its Legacy*, 211.
54. Ayres, *Nicaea and Its Legacy*, 212.
55. Indeed, to my knowledge, no intellectual historian has adopted Antony's letters as evidence of belief about the Holy Spirit among ancient Christians in Egypt—a detail that illustrates the strange lopsidedness of some theological arguments: the tendency is to reduce the ambiguity present in ancient texts by overidentifying all divine beings as members of the Trinity, without a corresponding tendency then to refigure one's understanding of early Christian theology to match newly claimed evidence.
56. Antony, *Letter* 4.14 (Rubenson, *Letters*, 211).
57. This is the LXX version, but as Rubenson notes, the subjects "wisdom," in the first sentence, and "spirit," in the second, are consistently represented in the Coptic, Georgian, and Latin texts of Wisdom (see *Letters*, 28 and n1).

58. This is the case in all three versions that exist for *Letter* 4—Coptic, Georgian, and Latin; see Rubenson's discussion (*Letters*, 28).
59. To be clear: when he could have cited a piece of Scripture to unambiguously identify this thing as the Holy Spirit, he did not, instead using the phrase "holy power." Given this creative shift of subject, it is difficult and probably inaccurate to maintain that Antony had *the* Holy Spirit, that is to say, the member of the Trinity, in mind as the guide he promises to his brothers.
60. This effect may be created partially by the number of languages in which the letters survive and the vagaries of ancient translation, but the range is so wide that there is no doubt Antony used multiple terms to refer to the guide.
61. Antony, *Letter* 6.44, cf. 5.5: "Now, my children, do not neglect to cry out day and night to God, entreating by the benevolence of the Father, to grant you help from above..." (Rubenson, *Letters*, 219, cf. 212).
62. Antony, *Letter* 6.93, 73–77 (Rubenson, *Letters*, 223, 221). See *Letter* 7.58n–o, in which the spirit of comfort arrives as the result of the sacrifice of the body (230).
63. Antony, *Letter* 6.83 (Rubenson, *Letters*, 222).
64. Antony, *Letter* 5.5 (Rubenson, *Letters*, 212).
65. Brakke, *Demons and the Making of the Monk*.
66. Brakke, *Demons and the Making of the Monk*, esp. 16–22.
67. Antony, *Letter* 6.101 (Rubenson, *Letters*, 223).
68. Antony, *Letter* 6.82 (Rubenson, *Letters*, 221–22).
69. Martin Tetz, "Athanasius und die Vita Antonii: Literarische und theologische Relationen," *Zeitschrift für die Neutestamentliche Wissenschaft und die Kunde der älteren Kirche* 73 (1982): 1–30, at 14–15.
70. That is to say, the Syriac is clear in its referent for the pronoun "his" (René Draguet, "Une lettre de Sérapion de Thmuis aux disciples d'Antoine [A.D. 356] en version syriaque et arménienne," *Mus* 64 [1951]: 1–25, at 5). Draguet argues that neither the Syriac nor the Armenian depend on one another, but that both are translations from an original Greek text. Here, I translate and use the Syriac, which is the older of the two.
71. Serapion, *Letter* 16–17 (ed. Draguet, "Une lettre de Sérapion," 5–6).
72. F. Nau, *Ammonas, successeur de Saint Antoine: Textes grecs et syriaques*, PO 11.4 (Paris: Firmin-Didot, 1915), 393–95; M. Kmoskó, *Ammonii eremitae epistolae*, PO 10.6 (Paris: Firmin-Didot, 1915), 563–66; and Franz Klejna, "Antonius und Ammonas: Eine Untersuchung über Herkunft und Eigenart der ältesten Mönchsbriefe," *Zeitschrift für katholische Theologie* 62 (1938): 309–48.
73. David Brakke, "The Making of Monastic Demonology: Three Ascetic Teachers on Withdrawal and Resistance," *CH* 70 (2001): 19–48, esp. 21; cf. Rubenson "Wisdom, Paraenesis and the Roots of Monasticism."
74. Ammonas, *Letter* 1.1 (PO 10.6:567).
75. Ammonas, *Letter* 2.1 (PO 10.6:570).

76. Ammonas, *Letter* 2.1 (PO 10.6:570; Derwas J. Chitty, trans., with Sebastian Brock, *The Letters of Ammonas, Successor of St. Antony* [Oxford: SLG, 1979], 2; I offer and note several exceptions to Chitty's translation below).
77. Ammonas, *Letter* 8.1 (PO 10.6:586–87).
78. Ammonas, *Letter* 2.2 (PO 10.6: 572; trans. Chitty, *Letters of Ammonas*, 3, adjusted in the following way: Chitty translates the phrase ܥܕܡܐ ܕܢܫܪܐ as "so long as it dwells" in the person, meaning, the list contains the effects of the divine power's presence. I translate that phrase as "until [such time as] it dwells" in the person, meaning, the list is a prescription of the "divine labor" needed to attract the power. This creates a natural progression, from the labor required, to the promise following in the text that God will not wait to grant the power, implying "if these acts are followed," and the condition that "once you have received it ... you will find great boldness," clauses that do not make sense if the list of actions represents the presence of a power already inhabiting the monk.)
79. Ammonas, *Letter* 8 (PO 10.6:587).
80. Ammonas, *Letter* 3.2 (PO 10.6:574–75); cf. *Letter* 2.3 "And because your hearts are upirght, you are able to acquire for yourselves this divine power, so that you may spend all your time in freedom and joy, so that every work which is of God may be easy for you" (Chitty, *Letters of Ammonas*, 3).
81. Ammonas, *Letter* 3.4 (PO 10.6:577).
82. Ammonas, *Letter* 12.2 (PO 10.6:605), see also *Letter* 12.3, where Ammonas described how ascetics do not want to leave the quiet because they know that is where the divine power joined them.
83. Ammonas, *Letter* 12.4 (PO 10.6:606).
84. Ammonas, *Letter* 11.2 (PO 10.6:599). See also a little further on in *Letter* 11.2: "If we proceed by our own mind, God will not send his power."
85. Ammonas, *Letter* 3.2 (PO 10.6:574).
86. Ammonas, *Letter* 12.5 (PO 10.6:606–7); cf. *Letter* 10.1, where ascetics whose bodies are not "good" lose their divine power, or *Letter* 12.1, where such ascetics experience "various kinds of heaviness of the soul" (PO 10.6:603).
87. Ammonas remarked on the small numbers who received it in *Letter* 8.1, 12.5, and 13.2.
88. Ammonas, *Letter* 2.2 (PO 10.6:572; Chitty, *Letters of Ammonas*, 2)
89. Macarius of Egypt, *Letter* 1.8 (ed. Strothmann, ed., *Die syrische Überlieferung*, xix).
90. Macarius of Egypt, *Letter* 1.9 (Strothmann, *Die syrische Überlieferung*, xix).
91. Macarius of Egypt, *Letter* 1.10 (Strothmann, *Die syrische Überlieferung*, xx).
92. Macarius of Egypt, *Letter* 1.11 (Strothmann, *Die syrische Überlieferung*, xx).
93. Macarius of Egypt, Letter 1.15 (Strothmann, *Die syrische Überlieferung*, xxi); cf. Antony, *Letter* 1.43–44.
94. Macarius of Egypt, *Letter* 1.12 (Strothmann, *Die syrische Überlieferung*, xx), citing Ps 50.19.

95. Brakke, *Demons*, 52–56.
96. Evagrius, *Thoughts* 4, cf. *Thoughts* 28 (Sinkewicz, *Evagrius of Pontus*, 155, cf. 173).
97. For the tradition of responding to demons with snippets from Scripture, see Brakke, *Talking Back*, 7–14.
98. Evagrius, *Talking Back* Pride 3 (Brakke, *Talking Back*, 159; Syriac text [ed. Frankenberg, *Euagrius Ponticus*, 536], has “angel”).
99. Evagrius, *Talking Back* Pride 7 (Brakke, *Talking Back*, 160; Frankenberg, *Euagrius Ponticus*, 538 has “holy angels”).
100. Evagrius, *Talking Back* Sadness 9 and 10 (Brakke, *Talking Back*, 101; Frankenberg, *Euagrius Ponticus*, 504 has “angels”).
101. Evagrius, *Talking Back* Sadness 26, cf. Sadness 27, directed to “the soul that does not believe that the air is filled with holy angels that help us” (Brakke, *Talking Back*, 105, cf. 106; Frankenberg, *Euagrius Ponticus*, 506 has “holy angels” and ܥܕܪ as “help”).
102. Evagrius, *Talking Back* Fornication 14 (Brakke, *Talking Back*, 72; Frankenberg, *Euagrius Ponticus*, 486 has “angel”).
103. Angels, archangels, powers are all included among positive divine beings by Evagrius in *Foundations* 9 (Sinkewicz, *Evagrius of Pontus*, 9 and 10); cf. *Skemmata* 2.30.
104. Evagrius, *Scholia on Proverbs* 189 (Paul Géhin, ed. *Évagre le Pontique: Scholies aux Proverbes*, SC 340 [Paris: Éditions du Cerf, 1987], 282–84); cf. *On Prayer* 80–81 (PG 79:1184–85; Sinkewicz, *Evagrius of Pontus*, 201–202).
105. Evagrius, *Talking Back* Acedia 17 (Brakke, *Talking Back*, 137; Frankenberg, *Euagrius Ponticus*, 524).
106. Evagrius, *Talking Back* Fornication 42 (Brakke, *Talking Back*, 78; Frankenberg, *Euagrius Ponticus*, 490 has “holy angels” in Syriac).
107. For the longer story, see Sinkewicz, *Evagrius of Pontus*, preface and introduction.
108. Brakke, *Demons*, 145–46.
109. These two works have a complicated and interwoven manuscript history, *History of the Monks in Egypt* sometimes appearing as an appendix to the *Lausiac History* (A. J. Festugière, “Le problème littéraire de l’*Historia monachorum*,” *Hermes* 83 [1955]: 257–84).
110. Palladius, *Lausiac History* 28 (Cuthbert Butler, ed., *The Lausiac History of Palladius*, Texts and Studies, 2 vols. [Cambridge: Cambridge University Press, 1904], 2:83–84, whose notes suggest that there were a number of ways the guardian was described—“not with her,” “left her,” and “departed her” all are attested; trans. Robert T. Meyer, *Palladius: The Lausiac History*, ACW [London: Longmans, Green, 1965], 88).
111. Palladius, *Lausiac History* 47.9 (Butler, *Lausiac History*, 139). If we read “providence” as a shorthand for the angelic guide, other stories in the *Lausiac History* appear to confirm the tradition: see 22.1, for example.

112. AP systematic collection 5.23 (Jean-Claude Guy, ed., *Les apophtegmes des pères: Collection systématique: Chapitres I-IX*, SC 387 [Paris: Éditions du Cerf, 1993], 258–60), cf. N 169. In the alphabetical collection, Paul the Simple sees the demons that follow monks and the angels that stand alongside them.
113. AP anonymous collection N 34 (F. Nau, "Histoires des solitaires Égyptiens," *ROC* 12 [1907]: 64–66): ἀπεστάλη ἄγγελος κυρίου πρὸς βοήθειαν αὐτοῦ.
114. AP anonymous collection N 20, 74 (F. Nau, "Histoires des solitaires Égyptiens," *ROC* 12 [1907]: 56, 397).
115. AP anonymous collection N 592/45 (Lucien Regnault, ed. and trans., *Les sentences du pères du désert, série des anonymes* [Solesmes: Bellefontaine, 1981], 225–26). See also N 369 (ed. and trans. Regnault, *Les sentences*, 125): "It was said of an old man who had asked God for the ability to see demons, that it was revealed to him: 'you have no need of seeing them.' But the old man insisted, saying, 'Lord, you can protect me by your hand.' Then God opened his eyes and he saw the demons, like bees, encircling the man and grinding their teeth against him, and the angels of the Lord chased them." Cf. AP alphabetical collection Macarius the Great 33, where Macarius sees the combat taking place around other monks and notices the angels protecting their athletes.
116. AP systematic collection 7.1 (SC 387:336).
117. AP alphabetical collection Antony 7 (PG 65:77); cf. *First Greek Life of Pachomius* 108, in which Theodore is accompanied by two angels who coach him.
118. AP alphabetical collection Antony 26 (PG 65:84).
119. See, for example, Eusebius's *Demonstration of the Gospel* 4.6 and Basil of Caesarea, *Against Eunomius* 3.1, *Homily in Psalms* 33.6.

CHAPTER 4

1. Brakke, *Athanasius and the Politics of Asceticism*, 201–45.
2. For the entire list of ancient authors who refer to the *Life of Antony*, see G. J. M. Bartelink, ed., *Vie d'Antoine*, SC 400 (Paris: Éditions du Cerf, 1994), 68–70; for the list of ancient translations, 95–101.
3. John of Shmun, *Encomium on Antony* (ed. G. Garitte, "Panégyrique de Saint Antoine par Jean, évêque d'Hermopolis" *Orientalia Christiana periodica* 9 [1943]: 100–134, 330–65); interestingly enough, John cites Basil of Caesarea as having made much of Antony's example, though no citation of the *Life of Antony* has been identified among Basil's extant works.
4. Augustine, *Confessions* 8.
5. See Ambrose, *de Josepho* 1; Jerome *Letter* 52.4 *ad Nepotianum* and *Letter* 24.1 *ad Marcellam* (all cited in SC 400:127 n3).
6. Driver, *John Cassian*, 46.

7. A. M. C. Casiday explains how the *Life* and texts like it obscured diversity among portraits of Egyptian asceticism in *Tradition and Theology in St John Cassian*, OECS (Oxford: Oxford University Press, 2007), 119–60.
8. Patricia Cox Miller, *Biography in Late Antiquity: A Quest for the Holy Man* (Berkeley: University of California Press, 1983); Samuel Rubenson, "Antony and Pythagoras: A Reappraisal of the Appropriation of Classical Biography in Athanasius' *Vita Antonii*," in *Beyond Reception: Mutual Influences between Antique Religion, Judaism, and Early Christianity*, ed. David Brakke, Anders-Christian Jacobsen, and Jörg Ulrich, ECCA 1 (Frankfurt am Main: Peter Lang, 2006), 191–208.
9. Robert C. Gregg and Dennis E. Groh, *Early Arianism—A View of Salvation* (Philadelphia: Fortress Press, 1981), "Claims on the Life of St. Antony," 131–60.
10. *Life of Antony* prologue (SC 400:128).
11. See, for example, *Life of Antony* 2 (SC 400:132), where these locutions occur within a few lines of each other. Elsewhere, Athanasius used κυριακόν as an adjective, for things like the "dominical body" of Christ (see *Life of Antony* 90, for example) but never as a stand-alone word meaning a church. See Tetz, "Athanasius und die Vita Antonii," 22–25.
12. *Life of Antony* 7 (SC 400:150).
13. Tetz, "Athanasius und die Vita Antonii," 20–21, and see the rest of the article for several more examples.
14. See, for example, the first few lines of *Life of Antony* 28.
15. *Life of Antony* 20 (SC 400:188–90).
16. *Life of Antony* 20 (SC 400:190).
17. Clement, *Paedagogus* 3.1.1.2; see the discussion of the use of this phrase in the *Life of Antony* in Gregory A. Smith, "How Thin Is a Demon?" *JECS* 16 (2008):479–512, at 503, with n99.
18. See Antony, *Letters*, especially 5 and 6, as discussed by Rubenson, *Letters*, 64–71.
19. *Life of Antony* 45 (SC 400:256).
20. *Life of Antony* 89 (SC 400:364); for how Antony identifies angels as "holy ones," see the discussion of *Life of Antony* 43 later in this chapter.
21. *Life of Antony* 55 (SC 400:282); cf. later in 55 where daily confession keeps the monk from entertaining these "filthy thoughts" (SC 400:286). The repetion of the same distinct phrase (ῥυπαροὶ λογισμοί, in multiple cases) here and in 23 and 89 may be a clue toward a common written source underlying these passages.
22. *Life of Antony* 20 (SC 400:190).
23. *Life of Antony* prologue (SC400:126); elsewhere Athanasius or Antony the character praises "purpose" (*Life of Antony* 5, 12, 27).
24. *Life of Antony* 40 (SC 400:244): μὴ ἐκκακεῖν ἐν τῇ ἀσκήσει; cf. *Life of Antony* 16, 89. This directive survives in a later Greek collection of ascetic advice: Ps-Ephrem, *de recta vivendi ratione* 23 (Clavis Patrum Graecorum 4138.035).

25. *Life of Antony* 7; 16; 40.
26. *Life of Antony* 5 (SC 400:142).
27. *Life of Antony* 23 (SC 400:198).
28. *Life of Antony* 27 (SC 400:210).
29. *Life of Antony* 10 (SC 400:162–64). I have omitted the first phrase of section 10 for reasons that will become clear later in the chapter.
30. Brakke, *Demons and the Making of the Monk*, 31 (ray of light: "the sudden appearance of a ray of light sends the demons away and ends his pain") and 32–33 (the voice as God). In *Athanasius and the Politics of Asceticism*, Brakke leaves the identity of the agents less determined: "Athanasius' notion of the co-operation between divine grace and human effort stands behind the famous scene in chapter 10, in which the Lord provides 'assistance' to the struggling Antony by dispersing the demons with a 'ray of light.' 'Antony, I was here,' a voice tells the monk, who is relieved" (225).
31. Brian Brennan, "Athanasius' Vita Antonii: A Sociological Interpretation," *VC* 39 (1985): 209–27, at 212.
32. Tim Vivian, *The Life of Antony: The Greek Life of Antony and the Coptic Life of Antony, and an Encomium on Saint Antony by John of Shmûn, and a Letter to the Disciples of Antony by Serapion of Thmuis* (Kalamazoo, MI: Cistercian, 2003).
33. *Life of Antony* 10 (SC 400:162): Ὁ δὲ Κύριος οὐδὲ ἐν τούτῳ ἐπελάθετο τῆς ἀθλήσεως Ἀντωνίου, ἀλλ' εἰς ἀντίληψιν αὐτῷ γέγονεν.
34. While different scholars at different times have argued for the primacy of the current Coptic or Syriac versions, it is clear that neither precedes the extant Greek version; see the exchange between T. D. Barnes and Andrew Louth (Barnes, "Angel of Light or Mystic Initiate? The Problem of the *Life of Antony*," *JTS* 37 [1986]: 353–68; Louth, "St Athanasius and the Greek *Life of Antony*," *JTS* 39 [1988]: 504–9).
35. *Life of Antony* 9.11–10.4, Sahidic version (G. Garitte, ed., *S. Antonii vitae versio Sahidica*, CSCO 117 [Paris: Imprimerie National, 1949], 15–16): "They tried to do many things to him and they ground their teeth at him [Acts 7.54]. [10] He looked up and he saw the roof, as if it were opening, and he saw something like a ray of light coming down toward him. And immediately the demons ceased living, the pain of his body stopped in an instant, and the place where he was living was restored to its fashion. Antony sensed that the Lord saved him, and when he started breathing again, he sensed that he lightened his pain. He asked the one that appeared to him, 'where are you from? and why did you not appear to me at the first so that you could heal me?' A voice came to him, saying, 'I was in this place, but I remained to see your struggle. And since you perservered and were not conquered, I will be to you a helper in every time, and I will make you famous everywhere.' When he heard these things, he got up and he prayed."
36. There are two Syriac versions—a long and a short recension—but they are fundamentally in agreement about this scene. *Life of Antony* 9.11–10.4, Syriac

(René Draguet, ed., *La vie primitive de S. Antoine, conservée en syriaque*, CSCO 417, Scriptores syri 183 [Leuven: Secrétariat du CorpusSCO 1980], 26–27): "Now our Lord did not neglect to help his athlete, but appeared to him before his victory. The blessed one [Antony] lifted his eyes and he saw the roof uncovered and a ray of light descending from there toward him. And at that moment, the demons dispersed quickly and the pains of his body eased. Then blessed Antony perceived and recognized the help of our Lord. And when he went on a bit and he was saved from his tribulations and he had help from the comforting of the vision of our Lord, he raised his voice and said, 'I love your deeds, but where were you before these pains and tribulations came to me?' And then a voice came to him, 'I was here beside you, Antony, and I did not abandon you, but I waited to see your struggle. So now that you have been perfectly illumined and you were not grieved [by your torments], I will be for you a director and paraclete and I will make you a faithful servant and one famous in all the Earth'...and he got up, knelt, and prayed to God, who had visited him."

37. Compare this to the specificity of Evagrius of Antioch's Latin translation, which substitutes "Jesus" for "Lord," so that Antony asks, "Jesus, where were you?" (Pascal Henricus Elisabeth Bertrand, "Die Evagriusübersetzung der Vita Antonii: Rezeption—Überlieferung—Edition: Unter besonderer Berücksichtigung der Vitas Patrum-Tradition" [PhD diss., Utrecht University, 2006], 164).
38. To be clear, I do not think that Athanasius had access to Antony's letters but rather that he used texts that represented Antony in ways cohering with the letters.
39. *Life of Antony* 12 (SC 400:166).
40. *Life of Antony* 49 (SC 400:266).
41. *Life of Antony* 49 (SC 400:268).
42. *Life of Antony* 66, 89 (SC 400:308, 362).
43. Evagrius, *On Prayer* 95 (PG 79:1188; ed. Sinkewicz, *Evagrius of Pontus*, 203).
44. *Life of Antony* 40 (SC 400:242).
45. On Evagrius's extensive use of the *Life of Antony*, see Brakke, *Demons and the Making of the Monk*, 65.
46. Evagrius, *Talking Back* Vainglory 23 (ed. Frankenberg, *Euagrius Ponticus*, 534; trans. Brakke, *Talking Back*, 152).
47. *Life of Antony* 43 (SC 400:252; for my translation of ἅγιοι as "holy ones," thus "angels," rather than simply "saints," cf. *Life of Antony* 91 and 92, where context makes clear that "angels" is the meaning).
48. *Life of Antony* 27.
49. *Life of Antony* 35 (SC 400:230–32).
50. Tetz, "Athanasius und die Vita Antonii."
51. Smith, "How Thin Is a Demon?" 504.
52. Jean Daniélou, *Platonisme et théologie mystique: Doctrine spirituelle de Saint Grégoire de Nysse* (Paris: Éditions Montaigne, 1944).

53. Though see now a turning of the tide: B. Pottier, "Le Grégoire de Nysse de Jean Daniélou," *Nouvelle revue théologique* 128 (2006): 258–73.
54. See, for example, Sarah Coakley's rendering in *Re-thinking Gregory of Nyssa* (Oxford: Blackwell, 2003), esp. "Introduction—Gender, Trinitarian Analogies and the Pedagogy of *The Song*," 1–14.
55. *Life of Moses* 1.3 (ed. Musurillo, *De Vita Moysis*, 2).
56. *Life of Moses* 1.6 (ed. Musurillo, *De Vita Moysis*, 4).
57. *Life of Moses* 2.132 (ed. Musurillo, *De Vita Moysis*, 75).
58. *Life of Moses* 1.17 (ed. Musurillo, *De Vita Moysis*, 7).
59. *Life of Moses* 1.30 (ed. Musurillo, *De Vita Moysis*, 14).
60. *Life of Moses* 1.31 (ed. Musurillo, *De Vita Moysis*, 14).
61. *Life of Moses* 1.38 (ed. Musurillo, *De Vita Moysis*, 18).
62. *Life of Moses* 1.42 and 1.49 (ed. Musurillo, *De Vita Moysis*, 19 and 23).
63. *Life of Moses* 1.44 (ed. Musurillo, *De Vita Moysis*, 21).
64. *Life of Moses* 1.21 (ed. Musurillo, *De Vita Moysis*, 10).
65. *Life of Moses* 1.29 and 1.33 (ed. Musurillo, *De Vita Moysis*, 13 and 16).
66. Michel Barnes, *The Power of God: δύναμις in Gregory of Nyssa's Trinitarian Theology* (Washington, DC: Catholic University of America Press, 2001), 240, cf. 224 n14, in which Barnes places the *Life of Moses* later in Gregory's career because of its increased use of the term "divine power."
67. *Life of Moses* 1.3, 1.29 (ed. Musurillo, *De Vita Moysis*, 2 and 13–14).
68. *Life of Moses* 2.169 (ed. Musurillo, *De Vita Moysis*, 89).
69. Sinkewicz, *Evagrius of Pontus*, xxxiv, cf. *Kephalaia Gnostica* 2.4. See the larger discussion of Evagrius's program in Chapter 1.
70. *Gregory of Nyssa: The Life of Moses*, ed. and trans. Abraham J. Malherbe and Everett Ferguson (New York: Paulist Press, 1978), 97.
71. *Life of Moses* 2.154, 2.156 (ed. Musurillo, *De Vita Moysis*, 83–84).
72. *Life of Moses* 2.162 (ed. Musurillo, *De Vita Moysis*, 86.)
73. *Life of Moses* 2.44 (ed. Musurillo, *De Vita Moysis*, 45) διὰ προσοχῆς τε καὶ ἐπιμελείας. Cf. 2.55 (ed. Musurillo, *De Vita Moysis*, 49).
74. *Life of Moses* 2.89 (ed. Musurillo, *De Vita Moysis*, 60).
75. *Life of Moses* 2.44 (ed. Musurillo, *De Vita Moysis*, 45). Note the allusion to Theanor's speech from the dialogue in *de genio Socrates*, discussed in the first part of Chapter 3.
76. *Life of Moses* 2.43 (ed. Musurillo, *De Vita Moysis*, 45).
77. *Life of Moses* 2.45 (ed. Musurillo, *De Vita Moysis*, 46); cf. 2.118: Aaron is there described as "the brother who met with Moses as he was opposing the Egyptians as God had willed, whom the discourse has revealed is in the order of angels" (ed. Musurillo, *De Vita Moysis*, 70).
78. Brakke, *Demons and the Making of the Monk*, 11–12, 230, with notes.
79. Evagrius, *Talking Back* prologue (ed. Frankenberg, *Euagrius Ponticus*, 472; trans. Brakke, *Talking Back*, 49).

80. *Life of Moses* 2.209 (ed. Musurillo, *De Vita Moysis*, 106); cf. 2.51, which affirms that this angel is kin to the "intellectual and incorporeal part of the soul" but that it was also created first, before humanity.
81. *Life of Moses* 2.46 (ed. Musurillo, *De Vita Moysis*, 46).
82. *Life of Moses* 2.47 (ed. Musurillo, *De Vita Moysis*, 46).
83. Evagrius, *Talking Back* prologue (ed. Frankenberg, *Euagrius Ponticus*, 472; trans. Brakke, *Talking Back*, 49).
84. *Life of Moses* 2.36 (ed. Musurillo, *De Vita Moysis*, 43).
85. *Life of Moses* 2.54 (ed. Musurillo, *De Vita Moysis*, 48).
86. *Life of Moses* 2.310 (ed. Musurillo, *De Vita Moysis*, 139–40).
87. *Life of Moses* 2.14 (ed. Musurillo, *De Vita Moysis*, 37).
88. *Life of Moses* 2.42, 47 (ed. Musurillo, *De Vita Moysis*, 45, 46).
89. *Life of Moses* 2.117 (ed. Musurillo, *De Vita Moysis*, 69).
90. *Life of Moses* 2.56 (ed. Musurillo, *De Vita Moysis*, 49), cf. 59: Gregory reveals the opponent's intent, saying that "the demon that injures and corrupts human beings deeply desires that none look to heaven" (ed. Musurillo, *De Vita Moysis*, 50).
91. *Life of Moses* 2.117 (ed. Musurillo, *De Vita Moysis*, 69).
92. *Life of Moses* 2.120 (ed. Musurillo, *De Vita Moysis*, 70).
93. *Life of Moses* 2.122 (ed. Musurillo, *De Vita Moysis*, 71).
94. *Life of Moses* 2.298–99 (ed. Musurillo, *De Vita Moysis*, 136).
95. Kevin Corrigan, *Evagrius and Gregory: Mind, Soul and Body in the 4th Century* (Burlington, VT: Ashgate, 2009), discusses both writers at length without suggesting a direct link between the two.

CHAPTER 5

1. *History of the Monks in Egypt* prologue 5 (A.-J. Festugière, ed. and trans., *Historia Monachorum in Aegypto: Édition critique du texte grec*, SH 34 [Brussels: Société des Bollandistes, 1961], 7).
2. See my discussion of previous scholarship in "Ambivalence about the Angelic Life: The Promise and Perils of an Early Christian Discourse of Asceticism," *JECS* 16 (2008): 448–49, and n4.
3. Robin Lane Fox, *Pagans and Christians* (New York: Knopf, 1986).
4. Peter Brown, *The Body and Society: Men, Women, and Sexual Renunciation in Early Christianity* (New York: Columbia University Press, 1988), chapter 16, 323–38.
5. Robin Darling Young, "Cannibalism and Other Family Woes in Letter 55 of Evagrius of Pontus," in *The World of Early Egyptian Christianity: Language, Literature, and Social Context*, ed. James E. Goehring and Janet A. Timbie (Washington, DC: Catholic University of America Press, 2007), 130–39. The phrase that Young translates as "those being made holy in light" corresponds

in Syriac to the "saints in light" of Colossians 1.12. She sees this as a reference to "those becoming angelic—here surely the monastic community, typically self-described as living the *angelikos bios*" (137).

6. Guy G. Stroumsa, "The Scriptural Movement of Late Antiquity and Christian Monasticism," *JECS* 16 (2008): 75.
7. Dyan Elliott, "Tertullian, the Angelic Life, and the Bride of Christ," in *Gender and Christianity in Medieval Europe: New Perspectives*, ed. Lisa M. Bitel and Felice Lifshitz (Philadelphia: University of Pennsylvania Press, 2008), 16–33.
8. Some earlier Christian writers had used the language of being "equal to the angels" as a reference for virginity; see Elliott, "Tertullian, the Angelic Life, and the Bride of Christ." Others had used it for an advanced state of Christian living; Clement of Alexandria refers to Christians who are advanced in their development as "equal to angels" in *Paedagogus* 1.36.6 and *Stromata* 6.105.1 and 7.57.5. I thank Judith Kovacs for drawing these references to my attention. My interest here lies with the application of this discourse, associated with the phrases "equal to the angels" or "living the angelic life," to particular ascetic practices in the fourth and fifth centuries.
9. Elm, *"Virgins of God,"* viii, ix, 29–39. See Elm's discussion of the shift from several different species of female virginity toward monastic structures, facilitated by the rhetorical redefinition of models of piety by bishops and other Christian writers, in *Virgins*, 373–85. See also Sterk's review of the earliest developments in Christian asceticism and note the recent turn in scholarship toward finding diversity rather than unity in the origins of asceticism: *Renouncing the World*, 13–34.
10. For one reading of the genre of virginity sermons, see Thomas Camelot, "Les traités 'de virginitate' au IVe siècle," *Études carmélitaines* 31 (1952): 273–92.
11. *Peri Parthenias* (D. Amand de Mendieta and M. Ch. Moons, "Une curieuse homélie grecque inédite sur la virginité adressée au pères de famille," *Revue bénedictine* 63 [1953]: 18–69, 211–38); Gregory of Nyssa, *On Virginity* (M. Aubineau, ed., *Grégoire de Nysse: Traité de la virginité*, SC 119 [Paris: Éditions du Cerf, 1966]).
12. Compare Josephus *Jewish War* 2.165 as well as *Antiquities* 18.16, two passages where Josephus reports on the Sadducees's ideas about the mortality of the soul.
13. Elizabeth A. Clark, *Reading Renunciation: Asceticism and Scripture in Early Christianity* (Princeton, NJ: Princeton University Press, 1999), 199–200.
14. *On Virginity* 14.4 (SC 119:440–43). This passage, Aubineau notes, has an almost direct parallel in the *Sermo Asceticus* attributed to Basil of Caesarea (SC 119:443, n3). For a discussion of those sources that may have influenced Gregory, including Methodius and Basil of Ankyra, see Aubineau, *Grégoire de Nysse*, 97–142. Basil of Ankyra goes further by saying that virgins are "already angels on Earth" (*virg.* 37 [PG 30:744], cf. 51 [772]).
15. Gregory of Nyssa, *On Virginity* 4.8 (SC 119:328–31).

16. David Brakke, ed., *Pseudo-Athanasius: On Virginity*, CSCO 592 (Leuven: Peeters, 2002), x–xii.
17. Pseudo-Athanasius, *On Virginity* 42 (CSCO 592:17; trans. CSCO 593:16).
18. John Chrysostom, *Baptismal Homilies* 7.20 (Antoine Wegner, ed., *Huit catéchèses baptismales*, SC 50 [Paris: Éditions du Cerf, 1957], 238–39). In addition, see *Baptismal Homilies* 1.2.
19. *Against the Opponents of the Monastic Life* 3.4 (trans. David G. Hunter, *A Comparison between a King and a Monk/Against the Opponents of the Monastic Life: Two Treatises by John Chrysostom*, Studies in the Bible and Early Christianity 13 [Lewiston, NY: Edwin Mellen Press, 1989], 132). Cf. Sterk's mention of a similar viewpoint of monasticism, *Renouncing the World*, 22–23.
20. *Against the Opponents of the Monastic Life* 3.11 (trans. Hunter, *Two Treatises by John Chrysostom*, 146–47). Hunter notes that there is a very similar passage in John's *Homilies on Matthew* 72.3 (PG 58:671–73).
21. Elsewhere, John makes the case that poverty and sexual renunciation are angelic qualities; cf. *Homilies on Matthew* 90.3 and *Homilies on Genesis* 19.4, respectively.
22. *Homilies on Matthew* 8.5 (PG 57:87–88); this is also not the only place where John refers to monks as "angels" or living the "angelic life."
23. *On First Timothy* 14 (PG 62:575).
24. *Homilies on Matthew* 8.4–5 (249–50), quotation at 8.4 (249).
25. Georgia Frank, *The Memory of the Eyes: Pilgrims to Living Saints in Christian Late Antiquity*, TCH 30 (Berkeley: University of California Press, 2000), 2.
26. Theodoret of Cyrrhus, *Religious History* 26.11 (Pierre Canivet and Alice Leroy-Molinghen, ed. and trans., *Théodoret de Cyr: Histoire des moines de Syrie*, SC 234, 257 [Paris: Éditions du Cerf, 1977, 1979], at 257:182), cited by Frank, *Memory of the Eyes*, 2. For more evidence that the numbers of pilgrims bound for ascetic viewing were high, see Frank's list of references here, n4.
27. Patricia Cox Miller treats this style of depiction in *History of the Monks in Egypt* as well as other works in her well-known article, "Desert Asceticism and 'The Body from Nowhere'," *JECS* 2 (1994): 137–53.
28. *History of the Monks in Egypt* Abba Or 1 (SH 34:35).
29. *History of the Monks in Egypt* Abba Bes 1 (SH 34:40).
30. *History of the Monks in Egypt* Theon 1 (SH 34:44).
31. *History of the Monks in Egypt* Apollo 18–19 (SH 34:54).
32. This is also the case with other texts, like Palladius's *Lausiac History*, in which angels assist ascetics, especially in their pursuit of chastity. See *Lausiac History* 8, 29, and 38 for examples of angelic intervention.
33. Goehring, "The World Engaged,"39–52.
34. Bentley Layton, "Rules, Patterns, and the Exercise of Power in Shenoute's Monastery: The Problem of World Replacement and Identity Maintenance," *JECS* 15 (2007): 45–73.

35. AP anonymous collection N186 (ed. F. Nau, "Histoires des solitaires égyptiens," *ROC* 13 [1908]: 47–57, 266–83; 14 [1909] 357–79; 17 [1912]: 204–11, 294–301; 8 [1913]: 137–40; here cited at 13 [1908]: 272); cf. *Verba sen.* 5.5.34 (PL 73:882D).
36. AP anonymous collection N186. The sentiment is echoed in the expurgated version of Evagrius's *Kephalaia Gnostica* 4.74 (ed. Frankenberg, *Evagrius Ponticus*, 307: "whoever keeps the commandment of God and rejects the world will not be put out of the community of angels").
37. *Abraham Our Father* (*Canon* 3; Johannes Leipoldt, ed., *Sinuthii Archimandritae Vita et opera omnia*, vol. 4, CSCO 73 [Paris: Imprimerie Nationale, 1913], 32.13–18). Shenoute's other advice from this text, considered later in this chapter, suggests that he may have been casting himself as "God" to his ascetics' "angels" in this remark. Rebecca Krawiec discusses the situation that led to Shenoute's scolding of the women's community in *Shenoute and the Women of the White Monastery*, 38–40.
38. *Scholia on Luke* (Angelo Mai, ed., *Scriptorum veterum: nova collectio e Vaticanis codicibus*, vol. 9 [Rome: Typis vaticanis, 1837] 721–22; trans. A. M. Casiday, *Evagrius Ponticus*, The Early Church Fathers [London: Routledge, 2006], 157).
39. AP systematic collection 11.122 (SC 474:202).
40. AP systematic collection 5.52 (SC 387:306). See Brakke, *Demons and the Making of the Monk*, 148 for a longer discussion of this passage.
41. AP anonymous collection N199 (ed. Nau, *ROC* 13 [1908]: 278); cf. AP systematic collection 7.38 for parallel.
42. In AP anonymous collection N176 (ed. Nau, *ROC* [1908]: 266; see parallel at AP systematic collection 5.46), an old man gives in to the temptation of fornication and when he repents, he laments having brought sorrow to "the spirit of God, the angels, and the holy fathers."
43. Shenoute of Atripe, *Canon* 1 (Johannes Leipoldt, ed., *Sinuthii Archimandritae Vita et opera omnia*, vol. 3, CSCO 42 [Paris: Imprimerie Nationale, 1908], 199.20–21); cf. *Canon* 4, BZ 331 (available in Dwight Wayne Young, ed. and trans., *Coptic Manuscripts from the White Monastery: Works of Shenute* [Vienna: Hollinek, 1993], 96 #16, where Shenoute adjures monks "by God, and our Lord Jesus, and his holy angels.")
44. AP anonymous collection N359 (ed. Nau, *ROC* 18 [1913]:137).
45. Graham Gould, *The Desert Fathers on Monastic Community*, OECS (Oxford: Clarendon, 1993), 123, but see also the discussion that ranges over 123–32.
46. Gould, *Desert Fathers*, 129.
47. At least one saying in the *Apophthegmata* collections directly contradicts me, saying that to judge another is indeed worse than slander. See AP anonymous collection N417, cited by Gould, *Desert Fathers*, 123.
48. AP Isaias 10; I was directed to this reference by its mention and translation in Sinkewicz, *Evagrius of Pontus*, 18. For other references to the monastic injunction against gossip, see Sinkewicz, 18 n18, 19, and 21.

49. "Visiting and News: Gossip and Reputation-Management in the Desert," *JECS* 6 (1998): 501–21, at 503.
50. "Visiting and News," 503, emphasis in original.
51. AP Hyperechius 4 (PG 65:429; trans. Gould, *Desert Fathers*, 121).
52. AP Hyperechius 5 (PG 65:429; trans. Gould, *Desert Fathers*, 121).
53. Gould, *Desert Fathers*, 121. In AP Poemen 154, slander and fornication are spoken of in once piece, while in AP Matoes 8, Matoes discusses with another brother whether slander is worse than fornication. Matoes argues that it is not, with the brother holding the other view. For the idea that slander is worse than lying, see Basil of Caesarea, who reports that "he who makes a statement against someone in order to slander or disparage him is a detractor, even though the statement be true"; *Letter* 22.3.8, cited and translated by Sinkewicz, *Evagrius of Pontus*, 18, n118. Worse than lying about a murderer? AP Alonius 4 (cited in Gould, *Desert Fathers*, 125): "Suppose two men have committed murder before you, and one of them has fled to your cell. Then the magistrate comes to look for him, and asks you whether you have seen a murder. If you do not lie, you are handing the man over to death. You should leave him before God without censure, for God knows everything."
54. AP Agathon 5 (PG 65:109; trans. Gould, *Desert Fathers*, 65).
55. AP Theodore of Pherme 4 (PG 65:188; trans. Gould, *Desert Fathers*, 93).
56. Gleason, "Visiting and News," 504.
57. *Paralipomena* 7 (Armand Veilleux, trans., *Pachomian Koinonia, vol. 2: Pachomian Chronicles and Rules* [Kalamazoo, MI: Cistercian Publications, 1981], 28–29). Cf. AP anonymous collection N19, in which angels cannot smell a dead body, but can smell the soul that has sinned.
58. *Paralipomena* 7 (trans. Veilleux, *Pachomian Koinonia*, 2:29).
59. Theodore's appointment as head of the federation was a compromise solution to a dispute about the proper successor to Pachomius. Apparently, the *Letter of Ammon* is aware of the slight taint surrounding Theodore and in the text, Theodore's leadership is confirmed by angelic appearances: the letter recounts a story in which Pachomius claims that Theodore's appropriateness as successor was clear to him because when Theodore joined the community, an angel appeared to Pachomius to tell him that Theodore was "full of the Holy Spirit," citing Acts 7.55 (James E. Goehring, ed., *The Letter of Ammon and Pachomian Monasticism*, Patristische Texte und Studien 27 [New York: de Gruyter, 1986], text: 130, trans.: 163–64). In addition to this, while Pachomius is still alive, Theodore has a night vision in which he sees angels enacting a sort of Eucharist at the altar of the church, one in which Theodore himself is fed "an alien food" (ξένην τροφήν) that helps him see more such visions (Goehring, *Letter of Ammon*, text: 134, trans.: 166–67). As James Goehring has pointed out, the *Letter of Ammon*, like most of the extant Pachomian texts, should be dated to the time of Theodore and Horsiesius (ca. 346–400), and thus any story about Pachomius in texts like the *Letter of Ammon* must be read as representing this later time

period's interpretation of Pachomius. That is to say, these appearances have more to do with authenticating Theodore as a leader than they do with reporting Pachomius's experience. See Goehring, "New Frontiers in Pachomian Studies," in *Ascetics, Society, and the Desert*, 162–86, particularly 163–64.

60. To be fair, I should point out that in two other instances, the text indicates that Theodore receives word of heresy via the Holy Spirit (*Letter of Ammon* 22, 23 [Goehring, *Letter of Ammon*, text: 143–46, trans.: 172–74]).
61. *Letter of Ammon* 20 (Goehring, *Letter of Ammon*, text: 141, trans.: 171).
62. *Letter of Ammon* 26 (Goehring, *Letter of Ammon*, text: 148, trans.: 175–76).
63. For a detailed account of the controversy, see Elizabeth A Clark, *The Origenist Controversy: The Cultural Construction of an Early Christian Debate* (Princeton, NJ: Princeton University Press, 1992).
64. Evagrius, *On Prayer* 115 (PG 79:1192–93; ed. Sinkewicz, *Evagrius of Pontus*, 205–6). One might think this advice is a bit difficult to take, since the rewards of good behavior can include visions of angels. Consider the contrast Evagrius makes between the angry person and the patient person in *Eight Thoughts*. On the subject of anger, Evagrius finishes the section by summing up this way: "The irascible person sees disturbing nightmares, and an angry person imagines attacks of wild beasts. A patient person has visions of encounters with holy angels, and one free from resentment discourses on spiritual matters and receives in the night answers to mysteries" (Sinkewicz, *Evagrius of Pontus*, 81).
65. John Cassian, *Conferences* 10.2 is the other source for this encounter, where neither Aphou nor the angel are mentioned.
66. Tim Vivian, trans., *Four Desert Fathers: Pambo, Evagrius, Macarius of Egypt and Macarius of Alexandria* (Crestwood, NY: St. Vladimir's Seminary Press, 2004), 183; cf. Étienne Drioton, "La discussion d'un moine anthropomorphite audien avec le patriarche Théophile d'Alexandrie en l'année 399," *ROC* 10 (1915–17): 92–100, 113–28.
67. The text of the *Life of Aphou* marks this difference in the ways it chooses to depict the monk. When Aphou joins the celebration of Easter, he leaves behind the wild beasts he lives with (5). As he prepares to go to Alexandria, Aphou puts on a "raggedy garment" (7). His appearance is so meager that he is ignored for three days after he arrives and the bishop's servants are afraid to present him at court (7). As if these clues weren't enough, Aphou identifies himself as a "poor man."
68. Vivian, *Four Desert Fathers*, 187.
69. I reproduce Vivian's translation, but add "[for my part]" in order to point out the particularly telling nature of the construction here. By using a pronoun unnecessary to the Coptic, Aphou may be emphasizing that it is he, and no one else, that is confident. See the discussion of "personal independents" in Bentley Layton, *A Coptic Grammar with Chrestomathy and Glossary: Sahidic Dialect*, Porta Linguarum Orientalium 20 (Wiesbaden: Harrassowitz, 2000), 65 (§77).
70. See Clark, *Origenist Controversy*, 37–38.

71. AP Megethios 4 (PG 65:300).
72. See the litany of religious laments for the splendor of the past in Annie Dillard, *For the Time Being* (New York: Knopf, 1999), 60–62. For the way this functioned in early Christian ascetic circles, see Teresa M. Shaw, *The Burden of the Flesh: Fasting and Sexuality in Early Christianity* (Minneapolis, MN: Fortress, 1998), especially chapter 5, "Return to the Golden Age."
73. AP systematic collection 16.7 (SC 474:396).
74. AP anonymous collection N332 (ed. Nau, *ROC* 17 [1912]: 210).
75. AP anonymous collection N224 (ed. Nau, *ROC* 17 [1912]: 359); cf. AP systematic collection 10.138.
76. AP anonymous collection N310 (ed. Nau, *ROC* 17 [1912]: 206).
77. AP systematic collection 15.115 (SC 474:360).
78. AP anonymous collection N311 (ed. Nau, *ROC* 17 [1912]: 356).
79. Daniel Caner, *Wandering, Begging Monks: Spiritual Authority and the Promotion of Monasticism in Late Antiquity*, TCH 33 (Berkeley: University of California Press, 2002), 43, for example.
80. AP John the Dwarf 2 (PG 65:204–205); cf. AP Ethiopic collection 14.52, about Silvanos. See also Caner's discussion of "free from care" (*Wandering, Begging Monks*, 33 n. 68). This word—ἀμέριμνος—has a long history in the monastic movement; consider that it is the contemplation of Matt 6.34 ("Do not worry about tomorrow") that moves Antony to leave society (Athanasius, *Life of Antony* 3.1; SC 400:134).
81. See Bentley Layton's discussion of the formation of monastic expectations in "Rules, Patterns, and the Exercise of Power," esp. 58–65.
82. For an extended account of Shenoute's life, see Stephen Emmel, *Shenoute's Literary Corpus*, 2 vols., CSCO 599–600 (=Subsidia 111–112) (Leuven: Peeters, 2004), 1:6–14.
83. Shenoute *Canon* 1 (CSCO 42:199). ⲟⲩⲛ̅ϩⲉⲛⲙⲏⲏϣⲉ ϯⲉⲟⲟⲩ ⲛⲁⲛ ϩⲓⲃⲟⲗ ⲁⲛⲟⲛ ⲇⲉ ⲧⲛ̅ⲉⲓⲣⲉ ⲛϩⲉⲛϩⲃⲏⲩⲉ ⲉⲩⲙ̅ⲡϣⲁ ⲙ̅ⲡⲥⲱϣ ϩⲛ̅ϩⲉⲛⲡⲉⲑⲟⲟⲩ ⲉⲙⲛ̅ⲧⲟⲩⲏⲡⲉ.
84. This is an unpublished portion of a florilegium of Shenoutean texts; I thank Stephen Emmel for allowing me its use here. He has identified this particular fragment as a part of *So Listen*, from *Canon* 8 (XL297=FR-BN 130[4] f.149). ⲙⲏ ⲉⲩⲙⲟⲩⲧⲉ ⲁⲛ ⲉⲣⲟ ⲧⲥⲩⲛⲁⲅⲱⲅⲏ ⲉⲃⲟⲗ ϩⲓⲧⲛ̅ⲛⲉⲧϯⲉⲟⲟⲩ ⲛⲉ ϫⲉ ⲑⲓ̅ⲗ̅ⲏ̅ⲙ̅ ⲛ̅ⲧⲡⲉ ⲁⲩⲱ ⲛⲉⲧⲟⲩⲏϩ ⲛ̅[ϩ]ⲏⲧⲉ ϫⲉ ⲁⲅⲅⲉⲗⲟⲥ; ⲛ̅ⲧⲟ ⲛ̅ⲧⲟ ⲟⲛ ⲡⲉ ⲑⲓ̅ⲗ̅ⲏ̅ⲙ̅ ⲛ̅ⲧⲡⲉ ⲁⲩⲱ ϩⲉⲛⲁⲅⲅⲉⲗⲟⲥ ⲛⲉ ⲛⲉⲧⲣ̅ϩⲟⲧⲉ ϩⲏⲧϥ ⲙ̅ⲡⲛⲟⲩⲧⲉ ϩⲣⲁⲓ̈ ⲛ̅ϩⲏⲧⲉ ⲉⲧϩⲁⲣⲉϩ ⲉⲛⲉϥϣⲁϫⲉ....ⲉϣϫⲉ ⲛⲉⲧⲟⲩⲁⲁⲃ ⲉⲧⲛ̅ϩⲏⲧⲉ ⲉⲩⲉⲓⲛⲉ ⲛ̅ⲁⲅⲅⲉⲗⲟⲥ ⲏ ⲉⲩⲧⲛ̅ⲧⲱⲛ ⲉⲣⲟⲟⲩ ϩⲛ̅ⲛⲉⲩϩⲃⲏⲩⲉ ⲛ̅ⲇⲓⲕⲁⲓⲟⲥⲩⲛⲏ ⲉⲓ̈ⲉ ⲉⲩⲛⲁϣⲱⲡⲉ ⲟⲛ ⲙ̅ⲛ̅ⲛ̅ⲁⲅⲅⲉⲗⲟⲥ ϩⲛ̅ⲧⲙⲛ̅ⲧⲉⲣⲟ ⲙ̅ⲡⲛⲟⲩⲧⲉ ⲛ̅ⲑⲉ ⲉⲧⲉⲣⲉⲧⲉⲅⲣⲁⲫⲏ ϫⲱ ⲙ̅ⲙⲟⲥ: ⲉϣϫⲉ ⲛⲉⲧϫⲁϩⲙ̅ ⲇⲉ ⲟⲛ ⲏ ⲛⲉⲧⲛⲁϫⲁϩⲙⲟⲩ ϩⲣⲁⲓ̈ ⲛ̅ϩⲏⲧⲉ ⲛⲟⲩⲟⲉⲓϣ ⲛⲓⲙ. ⲉⲩⲉⲓⲛⲉ ⲏ ⲉⲩⲧⲛ̅ⲧⲱⲛ ϩⲛ̅ⲛⲉⲩϩⲃⲏⲩⲉ ⲛ̅ⲗⲟⲓⲙⲟⲥ ⲉⲛⲁⲅⲅⲉⲗⲟⲥ ⲛ̅ⲧⲁⲩⲣⲛⲟⲃⲉ ⲛ̅ⲁⲣⲭⲁⲓⲟⲥ ⲉⲓ̈ⲉ ⲉⲩⲛⲁϣⲱⲡⲉ ⲟⲛ ⲙⲛ̅ⲛⲉⲧⲙ̅ⲙⲁⲩ ϩⲣⲁⲓ̈ ϩⲛ̅ⲁⲙⲛⲧⲉ.

85. ϥⲙⲟⲕ̄ϩ ⲅⲁⲣ ⲁⲩⲱ ⲟⲩⲛ̄ϩⲉⲛⲕⲟⲟⲩⲉ ⲙⲟⲕ̄ϩ ⲛ̄ϩⲏⲧ ⲛⲙ̄ⲙⲁϥ ⲉⲧⲃⲉⲛⲉⲧⲉⲓⲣⲉ ⲛ̄ϩⲉⲛϩⲃⲏⲩⲉ ⲛ̄ⲇⲓⲁⲃⲟⲗⲟⲥ ϩⲣⲁï ⲛ̄ϩⲏⲧⲉ. ϥⲣ̄ϩⲟⲩⲟⲧⲏⲧ ⲟⲛ ⲛ̄ϩⲏⲧ ⲁⲩⲱ ⲟⲩⲛ̄ϩⲉⲛⲕⲟⲟⲩⲉ ⲧⲏⲧ ⲛ̄ϩⲏⲧ ⲛⲙ̄ⲙⲁϥ ⲉⲧⲃⲉⲛⲉⲧⲉⲓⲣⲉ ⲛ̄ϩⲉⲛϩⲃⲏⲩⲉ ⲛ̄ⲁⲅⲅⲉⲗⲟⲥ ϩⲣⲁï ⲛ̄ϩⲏⲧⲉ. This is a portion of *Canon* 6, XM 550, and perhaps a part of a work titled *Then Am I Not Obliged* (Emmel, *Shenoute's Literary Corpus*, 1:172–74); it is reproduced by Dwight W. Young, "Two Unplaced Fragments from a Copy of Shenute's *Sixth Canon*," *Göttinger Miszellen* 189 (2002): 99–110, at 107. Though the Coptic is written in third person, it is customary for Shenoute to refer to himself this way; for the ease of the English reader, I translate his references to himself in first person.

86. [ϩⲉ]ⲛⲇⲓⲁⲃⲟ[ⲗⲟ]ⲥ ϩⲱⲟⲩ [ⲛ]ⲉ ϫⲉⲙ̄ⲡⲟⲩϫⲱ̄ ⲉⲣⲟⲟⲩ ⲉⲩⲉⲓⲣⲉ ⲛ̄ϩⲉⲛϩⲃⲏⲩⲉ ⲛ̄ⲇⲓⲁⲃⲟⲗⲟⲥ. ⲛ̄ⲑⲉ ⲉⲧⲉϩⲉⲛⲁⲅⲅⲉⲗⲟⲥ ⲛⲉ ⲛⲉⲧⲉⲓⲣⲉ ⲟⲛ ⲛ̄ϩⲉⲛϩⲃⲏⲩⲉ ⲛ̄ⲁⲅⲅⲉⲗⲟⲥ ⲙ̄ⲡⲉⲩⲁϩⲉ ⲧⲏⲣϥ̄. (Young, "Two Unplaced Fragments," 107).

87. What remains of *Canon* 4 is, as much of Shenoute's work, a composite of many different manuscript pieces. For complete details about the *Canon* and its representation in the manuscripts, see Emmel's discussion in *Shenoute's Literary Corpus*, 1:155–63 and 2:573–75, along with the table on 2:719–26.

88. *Canon* 4 *Why, O Lord* (ed. Leipoldt, who called this portion of the text *De eis qui e monasterio discesserunt*, CSCO 42:116–51), cited at 148–49: the operative part of the citation reads in Coptic: ⲉⲛϩⲩⲡⲟⲙⲉⲓⲛⲉ ⲉⲛϩⲙⲟⲟⲥ ⲉⲛⲥⲟⲟⲩϩ ⲉϩⲟⲩⲛ ⲉⲛϫⲱ ⲛϩⲉⲛϣⲁϫⲉ ⲛ̄ⲧⲉⲓⲙⲓⲛⲉ ϫⲉ ⲉⲩⲧⲱⲛ ⲛⲉⲛϣⲃⲉⲉⲣ ⲉⲧϩⲓⲃⲟⲗ ⲉⲧⲛⲏⲩ ⲛⲁⲛ ⲉⲧⲙⲟⲩⲧⲉ ⲉⲣⲟⲛ ϫⲉ ⲁⲅⲅⲉⲗⲟⲥ; See also Shenoute's comment about being mocked by others ("Were they the people who were thought to dwell with angels?") in *Some Kinds of People Sift Dirt*, a part of *Discourses* 5 (É. Amélineau, *Oeuvres de Schenoudi: Texte copte et traduction française* [Paris: Leroux, 1907], #6).

89. Shenoute's litany serves another purpose, namely, to project Shenoute as a "suffering servant," one who must work constantly to overcome the difficulties created by those in his community who err. See Rebecca Krawiec's discussion of this trope in Shenoute's writing (*Shenoute and the Women of the White Monastery*, 69–71).

90. *Canon* 4 (BN 130[1]136; Young, *Coptic Manuscripts from the White Monastery*, 98).

91. AP systematic collection 11.12 (SC 474:142); see also Ammoes 2.

CHAPTER 6

1. Jerome, *On Famous Men* 129.
2. *On the Priesthood* 6.4 (*Sur le sacerdoce*, ed. Anne-Marie Malingrey, SC 272 [Paris: Éditions du Cerf, 1980], 316–18).
3. Paul Meyendorff, "Liturgy and Spirituality I. Eastern Liturgical Spirituality," in *Christian Spirituality: Origins to the Twelfth Century*, ed. Bernard McGinn and John Meyendorff, World Spirituality 16 (New York: Crossroad, 1985), 350–63, at 352.

4. Consider, for example, the place occupied by catechetical treatises in the collection of sources for the study of Christian liturgy cataloged in Paul F. Bradshaw's *The Search for the Origins of Christian Worship: Sources and Methods for the Study of Early Liturgy* (London: SPCK, 1992; reprint New York: Oxford University Press, 2002), particularly in the chapter, "Other Major Liturgical Sources," 98–117.
5. There is nothing more promising for the study of the late ancient Christian habitus, in its local incarnations, than these detailed documents.
6. See, for example, *2 Enoch* 8.
7. Clement, *Stromata* 5.11, citing from "Zephaniah the prophet," presumably the *Apocalypse of Zephanaiah*, of which fragments remain (Otto Stählin, ed., *Clemens Alexandrianus*, GCS, 2 vols. [Leipzig: Hinrichs, 1906], 2:377).
8. Is 6.1–3.
9. For an overview of the scholarship reconstructing the place of Isaiah's vision in Jewish and Christian liturgy, see Albert Gerhards, "Crossing Borders—The Kedusha and the Sanctus: A Case Study of the Convergence of Jewish and Christian Liturgy," in *Jewish and Christian Liturgy and Worship: New Insights into its History and Interaction*, ed. Albert Gerhards and Clemens Leonhard (Leiden: Brill, 2007), 27–40. For a more in-depth study, consult Gabriele Winkler, *Das Sanctus: über den Ursprung und die Anfänge des Sanctus und sein Fortwirken*, Orientalia Christiana Analecta 267 (Rome: Pontificio Istituto Orientale, 2002).
10. *Imagined Communities: Reflections on the Origin and Spread of Nationalism* (London: Verson, 1983, repr. 2006).
11. *Imagined Communities*, 6.
12. Carol Newsom, "'He has established for himself priests': Human and Angelic Priesthood in the Qumran Shabbat *Shirot*," in *Archaeology and History in the Dead Sea Scrolls: The New York University Conference in Memory of Yigael Yadin*, ed. Lawrence H. Schiffman (Sheffield: Sheffield Academic Press, 1990), 113–18.
13. Seth Schwartz, *Imperialism and Jewish Society: 200 B.C.E. to 640 C.E.* (Princeton, NJ: Princeton University Press, 2001), 259.
14. See Bradshaw, *Search for the Origins of Christian Worship*, 91–92, on how church orders, often taken to be snapshots of Christian practices in the first three centuries, are better understood as "living literature" that may not accurately represent the time periods it recounts.
15. The majority of manuscripts are missing the key verse of the story, John 5.4 ("an angel of the Lord went down at certain seasons into the pool, and stirred up the water; whoever stepped in first after the stirring of the water was made well from whatever disease that person had"). Though this line is not extant in P66, P75, or Sinaiticus, they all contain John 5.7, which refers to the water being stirred and assumes something had stirred the water.
16. Tertullian, *On Baptism* 5 (Ernest Evans, ed., *Tertullian's Homily on Baptism* [London: SPCK, 1964], 14).

17. For example, Clement of Alexandria quoted from a work that scholars have tied to the Valentinian Christian movement, and in it, angels in heaven were baptized in a ritual parallel to the ritual of human beings on earth to whom they belong. See Clement, *Excerpts from Theodotus* 22 (F. Sagnard, ed. *Extraits du Théodote*, SC 23 [Paris: Éditions du Cerf, 1948], 102). See also the descriptions of baptism in 76, 69–77, and 81–86. These latter two passages diverge from the ritual represented in 22, and for that reason, scholars have suggested these may be Clement's own words, or that the *Excerpts from Theodotus*, like the *Gospel of Philip*, may be an anthology. If the work was an anthology, it does not seem that Clement was aware of it.
18. Cyprian *Ad Fortunatem*, preface. A century later, Optatus of Milevus, writing against his rival Parmenian, argued that the Donatist church could not be authoritative, despite the fact that it represented the majority, because the Donatists did not have the gifts that Christ spoke of. Among the gifts Optatus listed was the "angel that agitated the water" of baptism. Optatus of Milevis, *Against Parmenian* 2.6.1–2 (Mireille Labrousse, ed., *Optat de Milève: Traité contre les Donatistes*, vol. 1, SC 412 [Paris: Éditions du Cerf, 1995], 256).
19. Cyril was not bishop during the Bordeaux pilgrim's likely trip, but seems to have been the bishop during Egeria's extensive stay in the early 380s. As for the subtle way that Cyril asserted his vision of Jerusalem through ritual training, see Dayna S. Kalleres, "Cultivating True Sight at the Center of the World: Cyril of Jerusalem and the Lenten Catechumenate," *CH* 74 (2005): 431–59.
20. See Edward Yarnold, *Cyril of Jerusalem* (New York: Routledge, 2000), 4–5.
21. Cyril of Jerusalem, *Catechesis* 1.1 (Wilhelm C. Reischl, ed., *S. Patris nostri Cyrilli Hierosolymorum archiepiscopi opera quae supersunt omnia*, 2 vols. [Munich: Keck, 1848, 1860], 1:28).
22. *Catechesis* 1.6, 3.1 (ed. Reischl, *Cyrilli opera*, 1:36, 64).
23. *Catechesis* 3.3 (ed. Reischl, *Cyrilli opera*, 1:66).
24. *Catechesis* 16.22 (ed. Reischl, *Cyrilli opera*, 2:232).
25. *Catechesis* 16.22 (ed. Reischl, *Cyrilli opera*, 2:232). Cyril's practice resonates with earlier rhetorical goading of the imagination for emotional response. See Ruth Webb, "Imagination and the Arousal of the Emotions in Greco-Roman Rhetoric," in *The Passions in Roman Thought and Literature*, ed. Susanna Morton Braund and Christopher Gill (Cambridge: Cambridge University Press, 1997), 112–27.
26. *Catechesis* 16.23 (ed. Reischl, *Cyrilli opera*, 2:234). See how Cyril asks listeners to envision the multiple levels of heaven in *Cat.* 6.3, using the same progression: city to province to Empire to world to heaven to more heavens (ed. Reischl, *Cyrilli opera*, 1:156–58).
27. *Catechesis* 15.24 (ed. Reischl, *Cyrilli opera*, 2:188).
28. *Catechesis* 15.24 (ed. Reischl, *Cyrilli opera*, 2:190). I would be remiss were I not to point the way this creates an angelic version of the Panopticon, a prison building that Michel Foucault used as the central metaphor of his critique of modern

bureaucracies in *Discipline and Punish: The Birth of the Prison* (New York: Random House, 1975).

29. Georgia Frank, "'Taste and See': The Eucharist and the Eyes of Faith in the Fourth Century," *CH* 70 (2001): 621.
30. Frank, "Taste and See," 621.
31. Alexis James Doval has argued that the *Mystagocial Catechesis* and Cyril's *Catechesis* are, despite earlier doubts, both authentically Cyril's work (*Cyril of Jerusalem, Mystagogue: The Authorship of the Mystagogical Catecheses*, NAPS Patristic Monographs 17 [Washington, DC: Catholic University of America Press, 2001]).
32. Cyril of Jerusalem, *Mystagogical Catechesis* 5.6 (Auguste Piédagnel, ed., and Pierre Paris, trans., *Cyrille de Jérusalem: Catéchèses Mystagogiques*, SC 126bis [Paris: Éditions du Cerf, 2004], 152–54).
33. The texts of Theodore's *Catechetical Homilies* survive in Syriac and are available in the *Commentary of Theodore of Mopsuestia on the Lord's Prayer and on the Sacraments of Baptism and the Eucharist*, ed. Alphonse Mingana, Woodbrooke Studies 6 (Cambridge: W. Heffer and Sons, 1933), here cited at 144 (text), 17 (trans., slightly altered). A facsimile of the manuscript from which Mingana worked is available in *Les homélies catéchétiques de Théodore de Mopsueste: Reproduction phototypique du MS. Mingana syr. 561*, ed. Raymond Tonneau and Robert Devreesse (Vatican City: Biblioteca apostolica vaticana, 1949). The appoximate date of these homilies is the judgment of Peter Bruns (cf. *Dictionary of Early Christian Literature*, ed. Siegmar Döpp and Wilhelm Geerlings, trans. Matthew O'Connell [New York: Crossroad, 2000], 563), but see also Paul Bradshaw's discussion of the date of the homilies—as well as the possibility that they were preached when Theodore was a bishop, not a presbyter—in *Search for the Origins*, 109.
34. *On Baptism* (Mingana, *Commentary*, 151–52 [text], 23–24 [trans.]). Theodore was alluding to Hebrews 12.22–23 in this passage.
35. *On Eucharist and the Liturgy* (Mingana, *Commentary*, 219 [text], 83 [trans.]).
36. *On Eucharist and the Liturgy* (Mingana, *Commentary*, 220 [text], 83 [trans.]).
37. *On Eucharist and the Liturgy* (Mingana, *Commentary*, 215, 220 [text], 79, 84[trans.]).
38. Frank, "Taste and See," 638.
39. Frank, "Taste and See," 638–40. Frank also reports this phrase of Theodore's ("Taste and See," 638, citing Theodore *On Eucharist and the Liturgy* [Mingana, *Commentary*, 86]); the Syriac text appears on 223, ܫܘܡܠܝܐ ܓܡܝܪܐ and is perhaps better translated as "complete reproduction" or "a total accomplishment," suggesting that Theodore has more in mind than a simple reference to the Passion; perhaps he considers the Eucharist a replication or reproduction of the Passion.
40. *On Eucharist and the Liturgy* (Mingana, *Commentary*, 222–23 [text], 85–86 [trans., slightly altered]).

41. Paul Meyendorff, "Liturgy and Spirituality," 358, emphasis mine.
42. This is not to say that I think Theodore found the Eucharist solely representative. For a previous debate about whether Theodore emphasized an empty symbol of the Eucharist or a real ritual, see Frederick G. McLeod's article, "The Christological Ramifications of Theodore of Mopsuestia's Understanding of Baptism and the Eucharist," *JECS* 10 (2002): 37–75, esp. 41–50, in which McLeod rehearses the positions of Wilhelm de Vries (symbolic) and Ignatio Oñatibia and Luise Abramowski (real).
43. *On the Priesthood* 3.4 (SC 272:142).
44. *On the Priesthood* 3.5 (SC 272:148).
45. *On the Priesthood* 6.4 (SC 272:316).
46. *Baptismal Instructions* 2.20 (SC 50:145).
47. *Baptismal Instructions* 3.8 (SC 50:155).
48. *Baptismal Instructions* 10.2 (A. Papadopoulos-Kerameus, ed., *Varia Graeca sacra* [St. Petersburg: Kirschbaum, 1909], 155).
49. On John's audiences, see Wendy Mayer, "Who Came to Hear John Chrysostom Preach? Recovering a Late Fourth-Century Preacher's Audience," *Ephemerides Theologicae Lovanienses* 76 (2000): 73–87.
50. *Homilies on Ephesians* 3.5 (PG 62:29).
51. *Homilies on Ephesians* 14.4 (PG 62:104).
52. *On the Ascension of our Lord Jesus Christ* (PG 50:443D).
53. "Controlling Contested Places: John Chrysostom's *Adversus Iudaeos* Homilies and the Spatial Politics of Religious Controversy," *JECS* 15 (2007): 483–516.
54. *Homily* 22 *On Baptism* (Alphonse Mingana, ed., *Narsai Homiliae et carmina*, 2 vols. [Mosul: Fratrum praedicatorum, 1905], 1:358). Since the publication of these homilies, the authenticity of *Homily* 17 has been brought into question. At least one interpreter does not think this sermon belongs to Narsai (Frederick G. McLeod, "The Soteriology of Narsai," [PhD diss, Pontificium Institutum Orientale, Rome, 1968], 38). Adam H. Becker has suggested that Narsai went beyond Thedore's depiction of liturgical events using "metaphor" to show ritual as an enactment of a heavenly service, a technique that drew upon Neoplatonic assumptions (*Fear of God and the Beginning of Wisdom: The School of Nisibis and the Development of Scholastic Culture in Late Antique Mesopotamia*, Divinations [Philadelphia: University of Pennsylvania Press, 2006], 124).
55. *Homily* 21 *On the Mysteries of the Church and On Baptism* (ed. Mingana, *Homiliae*, 1:351); see also a later portion of the same homily (ed. Mingana, *Homiliae*, 1:355).
56. At times, Narsai's dependence on these sources was quite heavy, as he reproduced patterns and even phrases from earlier writers. It is also possible, and suggested by Richard Connolly (*The Liturgical Homilies of Narsai*, Texts and Studies [Cambridge, 1916]), that Narsai had read and used Cyril of Jerusalem's *Catechetical Lectures*. The evidence for that possibility includes Narsai's assertions that angels watch and enjoy the repentance and baptism of new Christians (*Homily* 21 *On*

the Mysteries of the Church and On Baptism [ed. Mingana, *Homiliae*, 1:348–49]); the trope that these new Christians are athletes whose spiritual development takes place in an arena (*Homily* 22 *On Baptism* [ed. Mingana, *Homiliae*, 1:368]); that arenas, shows, and the circus are the devil's work (*Homily* 22 *On Baptism* [ed. Mingana, *Homiliae*, 1:361; cf. Cyril *Cat.* 19.6]); the dual nature of Christ as human being, fulfilling some roles, and God, fulfilling others (*Homily* 17 *An Exposition of the Mysteries* [ed. Mingana, *Homiliae*, 1:284–85]; cf. Cyril *Cat.* 4.9–11); and the generally fearful nature of the Eucharist itself (*Homily* 17 *An Exposition of the Mysteries* [ed. Mingana, *Homiliae*, 1:275–76]; and *Homily* 22 *On Baptism* [ed. Mingana, *Homiliae*, 1:363, 365]). As for his use of Theodore, see *Homily* 32 *On the Church and the Priesthood* (ed. Mingana, *Homiliae*, 2:146), in which Narsai suggests that rituals point to mysteries in time and a heavenly liturgy. On the continuing importance of the images of angels in the processional for Syrian Christians, see Sebastian Brock, "Gabriel of Qatar's Commentary on the Liturgy," *Hugoye* 6.2 (2003):197–248, in which he records an early seventh-century text that suggests, again, that priest and deacons represent angels (sections 44 and 62 of the text). For other instances in which Narsai was influenced, see Becker, *Fear of God and the Beginning of Wisdom*, particularly chapter 5, "The Reception of Theodore of Mopsuestia in the School of Nisibis," 113–25.

57. *Homily* 21 *On the Mysteries of the Church and On Baptism* (ed. Mingana, *Homiliae*, 1:342–43). Cf. *Homily* 17 *An Exposition of the Mysteries* (ed. Mingana, *Homiliae*, 1:273) in which Narsai exhorts the priest, "See, you have been exalted above cherubim and seraphim!"

58. *Homily* 32 *On the Church and On the Priesthood* (ed. Mingana, *Homiliae*, 2:151): cf. *Homily* 17 *An Exposition of the Mysteries* (ed. Mingana, *Homiliae*, 1:280): "It is offered on behalf of angels and human beings.... It is offered on behalf of sinners and the righteous.... It is offered for the departed and for the living," and Narsai summarized by saying that the Eucharist was offered on behalf of "all creatures." It is possible that Narsai's consistent comparison of priests with angels, and his insistence that angels are dependent on the sacrifice worked by priests, was merely for the building up of the priestly office; when Narsai recounted the actual list of pentitents for whom the Eucharist is offered, angels are not on the list. See the list of those "brought to mind" in the sacrifice in *Homily* 17 *An Exposition of the Mysteries* (ed. Mingana, *Homiliae*, 1:286–87).

59. *Homily* 17 *An Exposition of the Mysteries* (ed. Mingana, *Homiliae*, 1:276).

60. *Homily* 17 *An Exposition of the Mysteries* (ed. Mingana, *Homiliae*, 1:294).

61. *Homily* 17 *An Exposition of the Mysteries* (ed. Mingana, *Homiliae*, 1:298).

62. *Rule of the Master* 48.7 (Adalbert de Vogüé, ed., *La règle du maître*, SC 105–7 [Paris: Éditions du Cerf, 1964–65], 106:218–20). Indelicate though it may seem, this warning was not unique; objections to and advice about spitting in ritual settings abound in late ancient and early medieval Christian documents. See the examples collected in L. Gougaud's article, which is modestly titled, "Anciennes

règles de bienséance pour le choeur" (*Ephemerides Liturgicae* 41 n.s. 1 [1927]: 186–88), but is actually all about spitting, its products, and its perpetrators.

63. Jason Moralee, "The Stones of St. Theodore: Disfiguring the Pagan Past in Christian Gerasa," *JECS* 14 (2006): 194.

64. *Life of Jacob* (E. W. Brooks, ed., *Lives of the Eastern Saints*, PO 19 [Paris: Firmin-Didot, 1923], 265, cited by Sebastian Brock, in "Fire from Heaven: From Abel's Sacrifice to the Eucharist, a Theme in Syriac Christianity," in *Fire from Heaven: Studies in Syriac Theology and Liturgy* [Aldershot: Variorum: 2006], 229–43, at 229. Brock follows the trail of fire that attends ritual in Syriac contexts; here I am interested in the angels in attendance. See also the *Chronicle of Seert* 59 [PO 13:467], cited by Brock).

65. *Homily on the Archangel Gabriel*, attributed to Celestinus of Rome (William H. Worrell, ed., *The Coptic Manuscripts in the Freer Collection* [New York: Macmillan, 1923], 240–41). Worrell estimates that the homily, though not by Celestinus, dates to before 641 CE (126).

66. Giulio Jacopi, "Le miniature dei codici di Patmo," *Clara Rhodos* 6–7.3 (1932–33): figure 145, lower left.

67. *Homily on the Holy Sacraments* 5 (cited in Simon Weber, *Ausgewählte Schriften der Armenischen Kirchenväter*, 2 vols. [Munich: Kösel and Pustet, 1927], 2:226; Armenian available in *Tearn Hovhannu Mandakunwoy Hayots' Hayrapeti chark'* [Venice: Ghazar, 1860]).

68. Gregory the Great *Dialogues* 4.60.3 (Adalbert de Vogüé, ed., *Grégoire le Grand: Dialogues*, vol. 3, SC 265 [Paris: Éditions du Cerf, 1980], 202).

69. Indeed, there is an alternate thread running through the evidence I have presented in this chapter, namely that angels were increasingly imagined to be present at Christian rituals because Christians increasingly imagined Christ to be present at them, especially the Eucharist. That is certainly true—Christian literature does show a significant increase in the gravity Christians attest to the ritual, based on the sanctity of the presence of Christ—but I am interested in the effects such imaginative works had on the estimation of the person doing the ritual. The increasing gravity of the ritual speaks also to the increasing superiority of the priest.

CONCLUSION

1. In reference to the Eucharist, for example, the author lists the steps of the ritual, then, in his fuller description, appeals directly to ritual itself to reveal its secrets. "Lift up the symbolic garments of the enigmas which surround you. Show yourself clearly to our gaze. Fill the eyes of our mind with a unifying and unveiled light." *Ecclesiastical Hierarchy* 428 C (Günter Heil and Adolf Martin Ritter, ed., *Corpus Dionysiacum II: Pseudo-Dionysius Areopagita* [Berlin: de Gruyter, 1991], 82; trans. Colm Luibheid, *Pseudo-Dionysius: The Complete Works* [New York: Paulist Press, 1987], 212). Readers will see in the title of this chapter an allusion to Karl

Barth's statement in *Church Dogmatics: The Doctrine of Creation* on "The Limits of Angelology."

2. *Ecclesiastical Hierarchy* 429B (*Corpus Dionysiacum II*, 83; *The Complete Works*, 213).
3. The scholarly literature on the Dionysian corpus is enormous. There are many entry points, but particularly helpful are Andrew Louth's *Denys the Areopagite* (London: Continuum, 1987); the collected essays in *Denys l'Aréopagite et sa postérité en Orient et en Occident, Actes du Colloque International Paris, 21–24 septembre 1994*, ed. Ysabel de Andia, Collection des Études Augustiniennes, Série Antiquité 151 (Paris: Institut d'Études Augustiniennes, 1997); Paul Rorem and John C. Lamoreaux, *John of Scythopolis and the Dionysian Corpus: Annotating the Areopagite*, OECS (Oxford: Clarendon, 1998); or more recently, Charles M. Stang, *Apophasis and Pseudonymity in Dionysius the Areopagite: "No Longer I,"* OECS (Oxford: Oxford University Press, 2012).
4. Rorem and Lamoreaux, *John of Scythopolis*, 9–22.
5. For his allusions to Proclus, which eventually led nineteenth-century readers to abandon the conceit that these works were written by Paul's first-century convert, see Josef Stiglmayer, "Der Neuplatoniker Proclus als Vorlage des sogennante Dionysius Areopagita in der Lehre vom Übel," *Historisches Jahrbuch* 16 (1895): 253–73, 721–48; H. Koch, "Proclus als Quelle des Pseudo-Dionysius Areopagita in der Lehre vom Bösen," *Philologus* 54 (1895): 438–54; as well as Jan Opsomer and Carlos Steel, ed., *Proclus: On the Existence of Evils* (Ithaca, NY: Cornell University Press, 2003), 4–7.
6. Among the details that help readers assign the identity of Dionysius to the author are his suggesting that he has been in the presence of James and Peter (*Divine Names* 3.2), his discussion of Greeks being changed by a new revelation of the "wisdom of God" of which Paul spoke (*Letter* 7.2), and his naming himself "Dionysius" (*Letter* 7.3).
7. See the complaints of the sixth-century bishop of Constantinople Hypatius cited in Rorem and Lamoreaux, *John of Scythopolis*, 18.
8. Stang, *Apophasis and Pseudonymity*, 198; cf. Louth, *Denys the Areopagite* and Christian Schäfer, "The Anonymous Naming of Names: Pseudonymity and Philosophical Program in Dionysius the Areopagite," *American Catholic Philosophical Quarterly* 82:4 (2008): 561–80.
9. *Celestial Hierarchy* 145B (*Corpus Dionysiacum II*, 16; *The Complete Works*, 153). The concept of dissimilar similarities has inspired quite a bit of attention among post-structuralist thinkers and those seeking to understand them. A good entry point for the reception of Pseudo-Dionysius and his tools of language in contemporary philosophical and critical discourse is Mary-Jane Rubenstein's "Dionysius, Derrida, and the Critique of 'Ontotheology,'" *Modern Theology* 24 (2008): 725–41.
10. *Celestial Hierarchy* 164D (*Corpus Dionysiacum II*, 17; *The Complete Works*, 153).
11. *Celestial Hierarchy* 165B (*Corpus Dionysiacum II*, 18; *The Complete Works*, 154).

12. *Ecclesiastical Hierarchy* 373C (*Corpus Dionysiacum II*, 65–66; *The Complete Works*, 197).
13. *Evil Incarnate: Rumors of Demonic Conspiracy and Satanic Abuse in History* (Princeton, NJ: Princeton University Press, 2006), 21, 27.
14. *Celestial Hierarchy* 205C (*Corpus Dionysiacum II*, 27–28; *The Complete Works*, 162).
15. *Celestial Hierarchy* 257B (*Corpus Dionysiacum II*, 36; *The Complete Works*, 170).
16. Rorem, *Commentary*, 75.
17. See Rosemary A. Arthur, *Pseudo-Dionysius as Polemicist: The Development and Purpose of the Angelic Hierarchy in Sixth Century Syria* (Burlington, VT: Ashgate, 2008), especially "Christian and Non-Christian Sources," 1–41, as well as Daniel F. Stramara, Jr., "The Angelology of Cyril of Jerusalem as Source for Pseudo-Dionysius' Celestial Hierarchy," *Patristic and Byzantine Review* 27 (2009): 11–21.
18. Alexander Golitzin contextualizes the Dionysian works as an expression of a monastic community in *Et introibo ad altare dei: The Mystagogy of Dionysius the Areopagite* (Thessalonica: Patriarchikon Idruma Paterikōn Meletōn, 1994).
19. Brakke, "Scriptural Practices in Early Christianity."
20. Several examples: Friedrich Andres, "Die Engel- und Dämonenlehre des Klemens von Alexandria," *Römische Quartalschrift für christliche Altertumskunde und Kirchengeschichte* 34 (1926): 13–37, 129–40, 307–29; Winfrid Cramer, *Die Engelvorstellung bei Ephräm dem Syrer*, Orientalia Christiana Analecta 173 (Rome, 1965); J. Rousse, "Les anges et leur ministère selon Saint Grégoire de Nazianze," *Mélanges de science religieuse* 22 (1965): 133–52; Bernhard Lohse, "Zu Augustins Engellehre," *Zeitschrift für Kirchengeschichte* 70 (1959): 278–91.
21. Andres, *Die Engellehre der griechischen Apologeten des zweiten Jahrhunderts und ihr Verhältnis zur griechisch-römischen Dämonologie* (Paderborn: Schönigh, 1914).
22. C. D. G. Müller, *Die Engellehre der koptischen Kirche* (Wiesbaden: Harrassowitz, 1959).
23. The fact that I am the first to do this, despite the investigation of the diversity of cultural forms now grouped under the rubric of "late ancient Christianity," or even "late ancient Christianities," further points to the rhetorical force of the hierarchy.

Bibliography

PRIMARY SOURCES

Ammonas. *Letters.* Greek: *Ammonas, successeur de Saint Antoine: Textes grecs et syriaques.* Edited by F. Nau. PO 11.4. Paris: Firmin-Didot, 1915. Syriac: *Ammonii eremitae epistolae.* Edited by M. Kmoskó. PO 10.6. Paris: Firmin-Didot, 1915. Derwas J. Chitty, translator, with Sebastian Brock, *The Letters of Ammonas, Successor of St. Antony* (Oxford: SLG, 1979).

Antony. *Letters. The Letters of St. Antony: Monasticism and the Making of a Saint.* Minneapolis: Fortress Press, 1990.

Apophthegmata Patrum, anonymous collection. "Histoires des solitaires Égyptiens," *ROC* 12 (1907): 43–69, 171–89, 393–443; 13 (1908): 47–57, 266–83; 14 (1909): 357–79; 17 (1912): 204–11, 294–301; 18 (1913): 137–40. Additional sayings in Lucien Regnault, editor and translator, *Les sentences du pères du désert, série des anonymes.* Solesmes: Bellefontaine, 1981.

Apophthegmata Patrum, systematic collection. *Les apophtegmes des pères: Collection systématique.* Edited by Jean-Claude Guy. SC 387 and 474. Paris: Éditions du Cerf, 1993 and 2003.

Apuleius. *On the God of Socrates. Apulée: Opuscules philosophiques et fragments.* Edited by Jean Beaujeu. Paris: Belles lettres, 2002. Translated by Thomas Taylor. *Apuleius' Golden Ass, or, The Metamorphoses, and Other Philosophical Writings.* Somerset: Prometheus Trust, 1997. First published 1822.

Arius. *Thalia.* Surviving in Athanasius. *De synodis.* Edited by H. G. Opitz. *Athanasius Werke* II/1. Berlin: de Gruyter, 1939. *A New Eusebius: Documents Illustrating the History of the Church to AD 337.* Edited by J. Stevenson; rev. ed., W. H. C. Frend. London: SPCK, 1987; repr. in Ehrman and Jacobs, *Christianity in Late Antiquity*, 158–59.

Athanasius. *Life of Antony. Vie d'Antoine.* Edited by G. J. M. Bartelink. SC 400. Paris: Éditions du Cerf, 1994. Sahidic version: *S. Antonii vitae versio Sahidica.* Edited by G. Garitte. CSCO 117. Paris: Imprimerie National, 1949. Syriac version: *La vie primitive de S. Antoine, conservée en syriaque.* Edited by René Draguet. CSCO 417. Scriptores syri 183. Leuven: Secrétariat du CorpusSCO 1980. Latin translation by Evagrius of Antioch: Pascal Henricus Elisabeth Bertrand, "Die

Evagriusübersetzung der Vita Antonii: Rezeption—Überlieferung—Edition: Unter besonderer Berücksichtigung der Vitas Patrum-Tradition" (PhD diss., Utrecht University, 2000).

———. *Orations against the Arians. The Orations of St. Athanasius against the Arians according to the Benedictine Text.* Edited by William Bright. Oxford: Clarendon, 1873.

Athanasius [pseud.]. *On Virginity. Pseudo-Athanasius On Virginity.* Edited by David Brakke. CSCO 592. Leuven: Peeters, 2002.

Augustine. *City of God. Sancti Aurelii Augustini De civitate Dei.* Edited by Bernhard Dombart and Alphons Kalb. CCL 47–48. Turnhout: Brepols, 1955. Translated by Henry Bettenson. *St Augustine: Concerning the City of God against the Pagans.* London: Penguin Classics, 2003.

———. *Enchiridion. Sancti Aurelii Augustini Opera.* Edited by E. Evans. CCL 46. Turnhout: Brepols, 1969.

———. *New Sermons. Discorsi Nuovi XXXV/2: Supplemento II (Dolbeau 21–31); Étaix 4–5.* Edited by François Dolbeau. Rome: Città Nuova Editrice, 2002.

———. *On the Trinity. Sancti Aurelii Augustini de trinitate libri XV.* Edited by W. J. Mountain. CCL 50. Turnhout: Brepols, 1968. Translated by Edmund Hill. *The Trinity.* The Works of Saint Augustine: A Translation for the 21st Century. Brooklyn: New City Press, 1990.

———. *To Orosius. Contra adversarium legis et prophetarum: Commonitorium Orosii et sancti Aurelii Augustini contra Priscillianistas et Origenistas.* Edited by K. D. Daur. CCL 49. Turnhout: Brepols, 1985.

Basil of Caearea. *Against Eunomius. Basile de Césarée Contra Eunome, suivi de Eunome Apologie.* Edited by Bernard Sesboüé. SC 299 and 305. Paris: Éditions du Cerf, 1982, 1983.

Celestinus of Rome [pseud.]. *Homily on the Archangel Gabriel. The Coptic Manuscripts in the Freer Collection.* Edited by William H. Worrell. New York: Macmillan, 1923.

Clement of Alexandria. *Stromata. Clemens Alexandrianus.* Edited by Otto Stählin. 2 vols. GCS. Leipzig: Hinrichs, 1906.

———. *Excerpts from Theodotus. Extraits du Théodote.* Edited by F. Sagnard. SC 23. Paris: Éditions du Cerf, 1948.

Cyril of Jerusalem. *Catechesis. S. Patris nostri Cyrilli Hierosolymorum archiepiscopi opera quae supersunt omnia.* Edited by Wilhelm C. Reichsl. 2 vols. Munich: Keck, 1848, 1860.

———. *Mystagogical Catechesis. Cyrille de Jérusalem: Catéchèses Mystagogiques.* Edited by Auguste Piédagnel and translated by Pierre Paris. SC 126bis. Paris: Éditions du Cerf, 2004.

Damasus. *Letter to Paulinus.* PL 13:364.

Dionysius [pseud.]. *Celestial Hierarchy. Corpus Dionysiacum II: Pseudo-Dionysius Areopagita.* Edited by Günter Heil and Adolf Martin Ritter. Berlin: de Gruyter,

1991. Translated by Colm Luibheid. *Pseudo-Dionysius: The Complete Works*. New York: Paulist Press, 1987.

———. *Ecclesiastical Hierarchy. Corpus Dionysiacum II: Pseudo-Dionysius Areopagita*. Edited by Günter Heil and Adolf Martin Ritter. Berlin: de Gruyter, 1991. Translated by Colm Luibheid. *Pseudo-Dionysius: The Complete Works*. New York: Paulist Press, 1987.

Evagrius. *Letters. Euagrius Ponticus*. Edited by W. Frankenberg. Abhandlungen der königlichen Gesellschaft der Wissenschaften zu Göttingen, Philologisch-historische Klasse, Neue Folge 13.2, 564–611. Berlin: Weidmannsche Buchhandlung, 1912.

———. *Kephalaia Gnostica. Les six centuries des "Kephalaia Gnostica" d'Évagre le Pontique*. Edited by Antoine Guillaumont. PO 28. Paris, 1958; repr. Turnhout: Brepols, 2003.

———. *On Prayer*. PG 79:1165–1200. Translated by Robert E. Sinkewicz. *Evagrius of Pontus: The Greek Ascetic Corpus*. OECS. Oxford: Oxford University Press, 2003.

———. *On Thoughts. Sur les pensées*. Edited by Paul Géhin, Claire Guillaumont, and Antoine Guillaumont. SC 438. Paris: Éditions du Cerf, 1998. Translated by Robert E. Sinkewicz. *Evagrius of Pontus: The Greek Ascetic Corpus*. OECS. Oxford: Oxford University Press, 2003.

———. *Praktikos. Traité pratique ou Le moine*. Edited by Antoine Guillaumont and Claire Guillaumont. SC 171. Paris: Éditions du Cerf, 1971. Translated by Robert E. Sinkewicz. *Evagrius of Pontus: The Greek Ascetic Corpus*. OECS. Oxford: Oxford University Press, 2003.

———. *Scholia on Luke. Scriptorum veterum: nova collectio e Vaticanis codicibus*. Edited by Angelo Mai. Volume 9. Rome: Typis vaticanis, 1837. Excerpts translated by A. M. Casiday. *Evagrius Ponticus*, The Early Church Fathers, 153–161. London: Routledge, 2006.

———. *Talking Back. Euagrius Ponticus*. Edited by W. Frankenberg. Abhandlungen der königlichen Gesellschaft der Wissenschaften zu Göttingen, Philologisch-historische Klasse, Neue Folge 13.2, 472–544. Berlin: Weidmannsche Buchhandlung, 1912. Translated by David Brakke. *Evagrius of Pontus Talking Back: A Monastic Handbook for Combating Demons*. Cistercian Studies 229. Collegeville, MN: Liturgical Press, 2009.

Gregory the Great. *Dialogues*. Edited by Adalbert de Vogüé. *Grégoire le Grand: Dialogues*, Volume 3. SC 265. Paris: Éditions du Cerf, 1980.

Gregory of Nazianzus. *Oration 28. Discours 27–31 (Discours théologiques)*. Edited by Paul Gallay. SC 250. Paris: Éditions du Cerf, 1978.

———. *Prayer Texts*. "Demons and Divine Illumination: A Consideration of Eight Prayers by Gregory of Nazianzus." Edited by Dayna Kalleres. *VC* 61 (2007): 157–88.

Gregory of Nyssa. *Against Eunomius. Contra Eunomium Libri, pars altera: Liber III (vulgo III–XII), Refutatio confessionis Eunomii (vulgo Lib. II)*. Edited by Werner Jaeger. Leiden: Brill, 1960.

———. *Life of Moses. Gregorii Nysseni De vita Moysis.* Edited by Herbert Musurillo. Leiden: Brill, 1964.

———. *On Virginity. Grégoire de Nysse: Traité de la virginité.* Edited by M. Aubineau. SC 119. Paris: Éditions du Cerf, 1966.

———. *Letters. Grégoire de Nysse: Lettres.* Edited by Pierre Maraval. SC 363. Paris: Éditions du Cerf, 1990.

Gregory Thaumaturgus. *Panegyric on Origen. Grégoire le Thaumaturge: Remerciement à Origène.* Edited by Henri Crouzel. SC 148. Paris: Éditions du Cerf, 1969.

History of the Monks in Egypt. Historia Monachorum in Aegypto: Édition critique du texte grec. Edited by A.-J. Festugière. SH 34. Brussels: Société des Bollandistes, 1961.

Jerome. *Letter to Algasia. Sancti Eusebii Hieronymi epistulae.* Edited by Isidor Hilberg. CSEL 56. Vienna: Verlag der Österreichischen Akademie der Wissenschaften, 1996.

John Cassian. *Institutes. Institutions cénobitiques.* Edited by Jean-Claude Guy. SC 109. Paris: Éditions du Cerf, 1965.

John Chrysostom. *Against the Opponents of the Monastic Life.* PG 47:387–92. Translated by David G. Hunter. *A Comparison between a King and a Monk/Against the Opponents of the Monastic Life: Two Treatises by John Chrysostom.* Studies in the Bible and Early Christianity 13. Lewiston, NY: Edwin Mellen Press, 1989.

———. *Baptismal Homilies. Huit catéchèses baptismales.* Edited by Antoine Wegner. SC 50 Paris: Éditions du Cerf, 1957. Other homilies are edited by A. Papadopoulos-Kerameus in *Varia Graeca sacra.* St. Petersburg: Kirschbaum, 1909.

———. *Homilies on Ephesians.* PG 62:9–176.

———. *Homilies on Genesis.* PG 53:21–385; 54:385–580.

———. *Homilies on Matthew.* PG 57:13–472; 58:471–794.

———. *On the Ascension.* PG 50:441–52.

———. *On First Timothy.* PG 62:501–600.

———. *On the Priesthood. Sur le sacerdoce.* Edited by Anne-Marie Malingrey. SC 272. Paris: Éditions du Cerf, 1980.

John Mandakuni. *Homily on the Holy Sacraments.* Cited in Simon Weber, *Ausgewählte Schriften der Armenischen Kirchenväter.* 2 vols. Munich: Kösel and Pustet, 1927. Armenian available in *Tearn Hovhannu Mandakunwoy Hayots' Hayrapeti chark'.* Venice: Ghazar, 1860.

John of Shmun. *Encomium on Antony.* "Panégyrique de Saint Antoine par Jean, évêque d'Hermopolis." Edited by G. Garitte. *Orientalia Christiana Periodica* 9 (1943): 100–134, 330–65.

Justin. *Dialogue with Trypho. Iustini Martyris Dialogus cum Tryphone.* Edited by Miroslav Marcovich. Patristische Texte und Studien 47. Berlin: de Gruyter, 1997.

Lactantius. *Divine Institutes. Lactance: Institutions divines livre I.* Edited by Pierre Monat. SC 326. Paris: Éditions du Cerf, 1984.

Letter of Ammon, The. The Letter of Ammon and Pachomian Monasticism. Edited and translated by James E. Goehring. Patristische Texte und Studien 27. New York: de Gruyter, 1986.

Life of Aphou, The. "La discussion d'un moine anthropomorphite audien avec le patriarche Théophile d'Alexandrie en l'année 399." Edited by Étienne Drioton. *ROC* 10 (1915–17): 92–100, 113–28. Translated by Tim Vivian. *Four Desert Fathers: Pambo, Evagrius, Macarius of Egypt and Macarius of Alexandria.* Crestwood, NY: St. Vladimir's Seminary Press, 2004.

Life of Jacob, The. Lives of the Eastern Saints. Edited by E. W. Brooks. PO 19. Paris: Firmin-Didot, 1923. Excerpts translated in "Fire from Heaven: From Abel's Sacrifice to the Eucharist, a Theme in Syriac Christianity." In *Fire from Heaven: Studies in Syriac Theology and Liturgy*, 229–43. Aldershot: Variorum: 2006.

Macarius of Egypt. *Letter. Die syrische Überlieferung der Schriften des Makarios, Teil 2: Übersetzung*, xvi–xxii. Edited by Werner Strothmann. Göttinger Orientforschungen, Reihe Syriaca 2. Wiesbaden: Harrassowitz, 1981.

Narsai. *Homilies. Narsai Homiliae et carmina.* Edited by Alphonse Mingana. 2 vols. Mosul: Fratrum praedicatorum, 1905. Translated by Richard Connolly. *The Liturgical Homilies of Narsai.* Texts and Studies. Cambridge: Cambridge University Press, 1916.

Optatus of Milevis. *Against Parmenian. Optat de Milève: Traité contre les Donatistes.* Edited by Mireille Labrousse. SC 412. Paris: Éditions du Cerf, 1995.

Orac. Apoll. Cited in J. Fontenrose, *Didyma: Apollo's Oracle, Cult, and Companions.* Berkeley: University of California Press, 1988.

Origen. *Commentary on Matthew. Origenes Werke: Origenes Matthäuserklärung.* Edited by Erich Klostermann. GCS 40.1. Leipzig: Hinrichs, 1935.

———. *Homilies on Luke. Die Homilien zu Lukas in der Übersetzung des Hieronymus und die griechischen Reste der Homilien und des Lukas-Kommentars.* Origenes Werke 9. Edited by Max Rauer. GCS 49. Berlin: Akademie-Verlag. 1959.

———. *Against Celsus. Origène: Contre Celse, Tome I.* Edited by Marcel Borret. SC 132. Paris: Éditions du Cerf, 1967.

———. *Homilies on Jeremiah. Origène: Homélies sur Jérémie, vol. 1.* Edited by Pierre Nautin and Pierre Husson. SC 232. Paris: Éditions du Cerf, 1976.

Palladius. *Lausiac History. The Lausiac History of Palladius.* Edited by Cuthbert Butler. Texts and Studies. 2 vols. Cambridge: Cambridge University Press, 1904. Translated by Robert T. Meyer. *Palladius: The Lausiac History.* ACW. London: Longmans, Green, 1965.

Paralipomena. Pachomian Koinonia. Vol. 2. *Pachomian Chronicles and Rules.* Translated by Armand Veilleux. Kalamazoo, MI: Cistercian Publications, 1981.

Peri Parthenias. D. Amand de Mendieta and M. Ch. Moons. "Une curieuse homélie grecque inédite sur la virginité adressée au pères de famille." *Revue bénedictine* 63 (1953): 18–69, 211–38.

Philokalia. Sur les Écritures: Philocalie, 1–20. Edited by Marguerite Harl. SC 302. Paris: Éditions du Cerf, 1983. *Philocalie 21–27: Sur le libre arbitre.* Edited by Éric Junod. SC 226. Paris: Éditions du Cerf, 1976.

Plato. *Republic. The Republic: Books VI–X.* Edited and translated by Paul Shorey. LCL. Cambridge, MA: Harvard University Press, 1935.

———. *Apology. The Trial and Execution of Socrates: Sources and Controversies.* Edited by Thomas C. Brickhouse and Nicholas D. Smith. New York: Oxford University Press, 2002.

Plutarch. *On the God of Socrates. Plutarch's Moralia in Fifteen Volumes: Volume 7.* Edited and translated by Phillip H. DeLacy and Benedict Einarson. LCL. Cambridge, MA: Harvard University Press, 1927.

Pseudo-Dionysius. *See* Dionysius [pseud.].

Regula Magistri. La règle du maître. Edited by Adalbert de Vogüé, SC 105–7. Paris: Éditions du Cerf, 1964–65.

Shenoute. *Canon* 1. Edited by Johannes Leipoldt. *Sinuthii Archimandritae Vita et opera omnia.* Volume 3. CSCO 42. Paris: Imprimerie Nationale, 1908.

———. *Abraham Our Father* (*Canon* 3). Edited by Johannes Leipoldt. *Sinuthii Archimandritae Vita et opera omnia.* Volume 4. CSCO 73. Paris: Imprimerie Nationale, 1913.

———. *Canon* 4. *Coptic Manuscripts from the White Monastery: Works of Shenute.* Edited and translated by Dwight Wayne Young. Vienna: Hollinek, 1993.

———. *Canon* 6. Dwight W. Young. "Two Unplaced Fragments from a Copy of Shenute's *Sixth Canon.*" *Göttinger Miszellen* 189 (2002): 99–110.

———. *Some Kinds of People Sift Dirt* (*Discourses* 5). É. Amélineau. *Oeuvres de Schenoudi: Texte copte et traduction française.* Paris: Leroux, 1907.

Tertullian. *On Baptism. Tertullian's Homily on Baptism.* Edited by Ernest Evans. London: SPCK, 1964.

Theodore of Mopsuestia. *Catechetical Homilies. Commentary of Theodore of Mopsuestia on the Lord's Prayer and on the Sacraments of Baptism and the Eucharist.* Edited by Alphonse Mingana. Woodbrooke Studies 6. Cambridge: W. Heffer and Sons, 1933. Facsimile of manuscript: *Les homélies catéchétiques de Théodore de Mopsueste: Reproduction phototypique du MS. Mingana syr. 561.* Edited by Raymond Tonneau and Robert Devreesse. Vatican City: Biblioteca apostolica vaticana, 1949.

Theodoret of Cyrrhus. *Religious History or History of the Monks in Syria. Théodoret de Cyr: Histoire des moines de Syrie,* Edited by Pierre Canivet and Alice Leroy-Molinghen. SC 234 and 257. Paris: Éditions du Cerf, 1977, 1979.

SECONDARY SOURCES

Anderson, Benedict. *Imagined Communities: Reflections on the Origin and Spread of Nationalism.* London: Verson, 1983. Reprint, 2006.

Andres, Friedrich. *Die Engellehre der griechischen Apologeten des zweiten Jahrhunderts und ihr Verhältnis zur griechisch-römischen Dämonologie*. Paderborn: Schönigh, 1914.

———. "Die Engel- und Dämonenlehre des Klemens von Alexandria." *Römische Quartalschrift für christliche Altertumskunde und Kirchengeschichte* 34 (1926): 13–37, 129–40, 307–29.

Arthur, Rosemary A. *Pseudo-Dionysius as Polemicist: The Development and Purpose of the Angelic Hierarchy in Sixth Century Syria*. Burlington, VT: Ashgate, 2008.

Ayres, Lewis. *Nicaea and Its Legacy: An Approach to Fourth-Century Trinitarian Theology*. Oxford: Oxford University Press, 2006.

———. *Augustine and the Trinity*. New York: Cambridge University Press, 2010.

Barnes, Michel. *The Power of God: δύναμις in Gregory of Nyssa's Trinitarian Theology*. Washington, DC: Catholic University of America Press, 2001.

Barnes, T. D. "Angel of Light or Mystic Initiate? The Problem of the *Life of Antony*." *JTS* 37 (1986): 353–68.

———. *Athanasius and Constantius: Theology and Politics in the Constantinian Empire*. Cambridge, MA: Harvard University Press, 2001.

Barth, Karl. *Church Dogmatics, Volume 3.3: The Doctrine of Creation*. London: T & T Clark, 1960.

Becker, Adam H. *Fear of God and the Beginning of Wisdom: The School of Nisibis and the Development of Scholastic Culture in Late Antique Mesopotamia*. Divinations. Philadelphia: University of Pennsylvania Press, 2006.

BeDuhn, Jason David. *Augustine's Manichaean Dilemma, 1: Conversion and Apostasy, 373–388 C.E.* Divinations. Philadelphia: University of Pennsylvania Press, 2010.

Bergjan, Silke-Petra. "Qualifying 'Angel' in Justin's Logos Christology." *Studia Patristica* 50 (2003): 353–57.

Boyarin, Daniel. *Border Lines: The Partition of Judaeo-Christianity*. Divinations. Philadelphia: University of Pennsylvania, 2004.

Bradshaw, Paul F. *The Search for the Origins of Christian Worship: Sources and Methods for the Study of Early Liturgy*. London: SPCK, 1992. Reprint, New York: Oxford University Press, 2002.

Brakke, David. "Canon Formation and Social Conflict in Fourth-Century Egypt: Athanasius of Alexandria's Thirty-Ninth *Festal Letter*." *HTR* 87 (1994): 395–419.

———. *Athanasius and the Politics of Asceticism*. OECS. Oxford: Oxford University Press, 1995.

———. "The Making of Monastic Demonology: Three Ascetic Teachers on Withdrawal and Resistance." *CH* 70 (2001): 19–48.

———. *Demons and the Making of the Monk: Spiritual Combat in Early Christianity*. Cambridge, MA: Harvard University Press, 2006.

———. "A New Fragment of Athanasius's Thirty-Ninth Festal Letter: Heresy, Apocrypha, and the Canon." *HTR* 103 (2010): 47–66.

———. "Scriptural Practices in Early Christianity: Towards a New History of the New Testament Canon." In *Invention, Rewriting, Usurpation: Discursive Fights over Religious Traditions in Antiquity*, edited by Jörg Ulrich, Anders-Christian Jacobsen, and David Brakke, 263–50. ECCA 11. Frankfurt am Main: Lang, 2012.

Brennan, Brian. "Athanasius' Vita Antonii: A Sociological Interpretation." *VC* 39 (1985): 209–27.

Brock, Sebastian. "Gabriel of Qatar's Commentary on the Liturgy." *Hugoye* 6.2 (2003): 197–248.

———. "Fire from Heaven: From Abel's Sacrifice to the Eucharist, a Theme in Syriac Christianity." In *Fire from Heaven: Studies in Syriac Theology and Liturgy*, 229–43. Aldershot: Variorum: 2006.

Brown, Peter. *Augustine of Hippo: A Biography*. Berkeley: University of California Press, 1967 (1969).

———. *The Body and Society: Men, Women, and Sexual Renunciation in Early Christianity*. New York: Columbia University Press, 1988.

———. *Power and Persuasion in Late Antiquity: Towards a Christian Empire*. Madison: University of Wisconsin Press, 1992.

Bunge, Gabriel. "Évagre le Pontique et les deux Macaire." *Irénikon* 56 (1983): 215–27, 323–60.

Camelot, Thomas. "Les traités 'de virginitate' au IVe siècle." *Études carmélitaines* 31 (1952): 273–92.

von Campenhausen, Hans. *Kirchliches Amt und geistliche Vollmacht in den ersten drei Jahrhunderten*. Beiträge zur historischen Theologie 14. Tübingen: Mohr Siebeck, 1953.

Caner, Daniel. *Wandering, Begging Monks: Spiritual Authority and the Promotion of Monasticism in Late Antiquity*. TCH 33. Berkeley: University of California Press, 2002.

Casiday, A. M. C. *Tradition and Theology in St John Cassian*. OECS. Oxford: Oxford University Press, 2007.

Chin, Catherine M. *Grammar and Christianity in the Late Roman World*. Divinations. Philadelphia: University of Pennsylvania Press, 2008.

———. "Who Is the Ascetic Exegete? Angels, Enchantments, and Transformative Food in Origen's *Homilies on Joshua*." In *Asceticism and Exegesis in Early Christianity*, edited by Hans-Ulrich Weidemann. Göttingen: Vandenhoeck and Ruprecht, 2013.

Clark, Elizabeth A. *The Origenist Controversy: The Cultural Construction of an Early Christian Debate*. Princeton, NJ: Princeton University Press, 1992.

———. *Reading Renunciation: Asceticism and Scripture in Early Christianity*. Princeton, NJ: Princeton University Press, 1999.

———. *History, Theory, Text: Historians and the Linguistic Turn*. Cambridge, MA: Harvard University Press, 2004.

Coakley, Sarah, editor. *Re-thinking Gregory of Nyssa*. Oxford: Blackwell, 2003.

Conybeare, Catherine. *The Irrational Augustine*. OECS. Oxford: Oxford University Press, 2006.

Corrigan, Kevin. *Evagrius and Gregory: Mind, Soul and Body in the 4th Century*. Burlington, VT: Ashgate, 2009.

Cramer, Winfrid. *Die Engelvorstellung bei Ephräm dem Syrer*. Orientalia Christiana Analecta 173. Rome: Pont. institutum Orientalium studiorum, 1965.

Daniélou, Jean. *Platonisme et théologie mystique: Doctrine spirituelle de Saint Grégoire de Nysse*. Paris: Éditions Montaigne, 1944.

———. *The Angels and Their Mission according to the Fathers of the Church*. Translated by David Heimann.Westminster, MD: Christian Classics, 1976. Originally published as *Les anges et leur mission d'après les Pères de l'Église*. Chevetogne: Éditions de Chevetogne, 1953.

de Andia, Ysabel, editor. *Denys l'Aréopagite et sa postérité en Orient et en Occident, Actes du Colloque International Paris, 21–24 septembre 1994*. Collection des Études Augustiniennes, Série Antiquité 151. Paris: Institut d'Études Augustiniennes, 1997.

DelCogliano, Mark. *Basil of Caesarea's Anti-Eunomian Theory of Names: Christian Theology and Late-Antique Philosophy in the Fourth Century Trinitarian Controversy*. Supplements to VC 103. Leiden: Brill, 2010.

Demetracopoulos, John A. "Glossogony or Epistemology? The Stoic Character of Basil of Caesarea's and Eunomius' Epistemological Notion of *epinoia* and its Misinterpretation by Gregory of Nyssa." In *Gregory of Nyssa: Contra Eunomium II*, edited by Lenka Karfíková, Scot Douglass, and Johannes Zachhuber, 387–98. Leiden: Brill, 2007.

Digeser, Elizabeth DePalma. *Making of a Christian Empire: Lactantius and Rome*. Ithaca, NY: Cornell University Press, 1999.

———. "Origen on the *Limes*: Rhetoric and the Polarization of Identity in the Late Third Century." In *The Rhetoric of Power in Late Antiquity: Religion and Politics in Byzantium, Europe and the Early Islamic World*, edited by Robert M. Frakes, Elizabeth DePalma Digeser, and Justin Stephens, 197–218. London: I. B. Tauris, 2010.

Dillard, Annie. *For the Time Being*. New York: Knopf, 1999.

Dombrowski, D. A. "Asceticism as Athletic Training in Plotinus." *Aufstieg und Niedergang der römischen Welt* 2.36.1 (1987): 701–12.

Döpp, Siegmar, and Wilhelm Geerlings, editors. *Dictionary of Early Christian Literature*. Translated by Matthew O'Connell. New York: Crossroad, 2000.

Doval, Alexis James. *Cyril of Jerusalem, Mystagogue: The Authorship of the Mystagogical Catecheses*. NAPS Patristic Monographs 17. Washington, DC: Catholic University of America Press, 2001.

Draguet, René. "Une lettre de Sérapion de Thmuis aux disciples d'Antoine (A.D. 356) en version syriaque et arménienne." *Mus* 64 (1951): 1–25.

Drake, H. A. *Constantine and the Bishops: The Politics of Intolerance*. Baltimore, MD: Johns Hopkins University Press, 2000.

Driver, Steven D. *John Cassian and the Reading of Egyptian Monastic Culture*. New York: Routledge, 2002.

Elliott, Dyan. "Tertullian, the Angelic Life, and the Bride of Christ." In *Gender and Christianity in Medieval Europe: New Perspectives*, edited by Lisa M. Bitel and Felice Lifshitz, 16–33. Philadelphia: University of Pennsylvania Press, 2008.

Elm, Susanna. *"Virgins of God": The Making of Asceticism in Late Antiquity*. Oxford: Clarendon Press, 1994.

———. "A Programmatic Life: Gregory of Nazianzus' *Orations* 42 and 43 and the Constantinopolitan Elites." *Arethusa* 33 (2000): 411–27.

Emmel, Stephen. *Shenoute's Literary Corpus*. 2 vols. CSCO 599–600 (= Subsidia, vols. 111–112). Leuven: Peeters, 2004.

Ernest, James D. *The Bible in Athanasius of Alexandria*. Leiden: Brill, 2004.

Festugière, A. J. "Le problème littéraire de l'*Historia monachorum*." *Hermes* 83 (1955): 257–84.

Foucault, Michel. *Discipline and Punish: The Birth of the Prison*. New York: Random House, 1975.

Fox, Robin Lane. *Pagans and Christians*. New York: Knopf, 1986.

Frank, Georgia. *The Memory of the Eyes: Pilgrims to Living Saints in Christian Late Antiquity*. TCH 30. Berkeley: University of California Press, 2000.

———. "'Taste and See': The Eucharist and the Eyes of Faith in the Fourth Century." *CH* 70 (2001): 619–43.

Frankfurter, David. *Evil Incarnate: Rumors of Demonic Conspiracy and Satanic Abuse in History*. Princeton, NJ: Princeton University Press, 2006.

Gaddis, Michael. *There Is No Crime for Those Who Have Christ: Religious Violence in the Christian Roman Empire*. TCH 39. Berkeley: University of California Press, 2005.

Garrett, Susan R. *No Ordinary Angel: Celestial Spirits and Christian Claims about Jesus*. New Haven, CT: Yale University Press, 2008.

Gerhards, Albert. "Crossing Borders—The Kedusha and the Sanctus: A Case Study of the Convergence of Jewish and Christian Liturgy." In *Jewish and Christian Liturgy and Worship: New Insights into Its History and Interaction*, edited by Albert Gerhards and Clemens Leonhard, 27–40. Leiden: Brill, 2007.

Giulea, Dragoş-Andrei. "The Watchers' Whispers: Athenagoras's Legatio 25,1–3 and the *Book of the Watchers*." *VC* 61 (2007): 258–81.

Gleason, Maud. "Visiting and News: Gossip and Reputation-Management in the Desert." *JECS* 6 (1998): 501–21.

Goehring, James E. "New Frontiers in Pachomian Studies." In *Ascetics, Society, and the Desert: Studies in Early Egyptian Monasticism*, 162–86. Harrisburg, PA: Trinity Press International, 1999.

———. "The World Engaged: The Social and Economic World of Early Egyptian Monasticism." In *Ascetics, Society, and the Desert: Studies in Early Egyptian Monasticism*, 39–52. Harrisburg, PA: Trinity Press International, 1999.

Golitzin, Alexander. *Et introibo ad altare dei: The Mystagogy of Dionysius the Areopagite*. Thessalonica: Patriarchikon Idruma Paterikōn Meletōn, 1994.

Gougaud, L. "Anciennes règles de bienséance pour le choeur." *Ephemerides Liturgicae* 41 n.s. 1 (1927): 186–88.

Gould, Graham. *The Desert Fathers on Monastic Community*. OECS. Oxford: Clarendon, 1993.

Gregg, Robert C., and Dennis E. Groh. *Early Arianism—A View of Salvation*. Philadelphia: Fortress Press, 1981.

Guillaumont, Antoine, and Claire Guillaumont. "Evagrius Ponticus: Persönlichkeit, Leben, Wirkung." *Reallexicon für Antike und Christentum* 6 (1966): 1088–107.

Hadot, Pierre. *Philosophy as a Way of Life*. Translated by Michael Chase. Oxford: Blackwell, 1995.

Harmless, William. *Desert Christians: An Introduction to the Literature of Early Monasticism*. New York: Oxford University Press, 2004.

———. "Patristics Bibliography #7: Augustine & the Latin West." http://moses.creighton.edu/harmless/bibliographies_for_theology/Patristics_6.htm, last modified August 20, 2012.

Heidtmann, Dieter. *Die Engel: Grenzgestalten Gottes: über Notwendigkeit und Möglichkeit der christlichen Rede von den Engeln*. Neukirchen-Vluyn: Neukirchener Verlag, 1999.

Humfress, Caroline. *Orthodoxy and the Courts in Late Antiquity*. Oxford: Oxford University Press, 2007.

Jacobs, Andrew S. "Dialogical Differences: (De-)Judaizing Jesus' Circumcision." *JECS* 15 (2007): 291–335.

Jacopi, Giulio. "Le miniature dei codici di Patmo." *Clara Rhodos* 6–7.3 (1932–33): 573–705.

Jenott, Lance, and Elaine Pagels. "Antony's Letters and Nag Hammadi Codex I: Sources of Religious Conflict in Fourth-Century Egypt." *JECS* 18 (2010): 557–89.

Jensen, Robin M., and J. Patout Burns, Jr. *The Practice of Christianity in Roman Africa*. Grand Rapids, MI: Eerdmans, 2013.

Kalleres, Dayna. "Cultivating True Sight at the Center of the World: Cyril of Jerusalem and the Lenten Catechumenate." *CH* 74 (2005): 431–59.

———. "Demons and Divine Illumination: A Consideration of Eight Prayers by Gregory of Nazianzus." *VC* 61 (2007): 157–88.

Kalvesmaki, Joel, editor. "Guide to Evagrius Ponticus." evagriusponticus.net

Keck, David. *Angels and Angelology in the Middle Ages*. New York: Oxford University Press, 1998.

Klejna, Franz. "Antonius und Ammonas: Eine Untersuchung über Herkunft und Eigenart der ältesten Mönchsbriefe." *Zeitschrift für katholische Theologie* 62 (1938): 309–48.

Koch, H. "Proclus als Quelle des Pseudo-Dionysius Areopagita in der Lehre vom Bösen." *Philologus* 54 (1895): 438–54.

Konstantinovsky, Julia S. *Evagrius Ponticus: The Making of a Gnostic*. Burlington, VT: Ashgate, 2009.

Krawiec, Rebecca. *Shenoute and the Women of the White Monastery: Egyptian Monasticism in Late Antiquity*. New York: Oxford University Press, 2002.

Layton, Bentley. *A Coptic Grammar with Chrestomathy and Glossary: Sahidic Dialect*. Porta Linguarum Orientalium 20. Wiesbaden: Harrassowitz, 2000.

———. "Rules, Patterns, and the Exercise of Power in Shenoute's Monastery: The Problem of World Replacement and Identity Maintenance." *JECS* 15 (2007): 45–73.

Layton, Richard A. *Didymus the Blind and His Circle in Late-Antique Alexandria: Virtue and Narrative in Biblical Scholarship*. Urbana: University of Illinois Press, 2004.

Lienhard, Joseph T. "On 'Discernment of Spirits' in the Early Church." *JTS* 41 (1980): 505–29.

Lim, Richard. *Public Disputation, Power, and Social Order in Late Antiquity*. TCH 23. Berkeley: University of California Press, 1995.

Lohse, Bernhard. "Zu Augustins Engellehre." *Zeitschrift für Kirchengeschichte* 70 (1959): 278–91.

Long, A. A. "How Does Socrates' Divine Sign Communicate with Him?" In *A Companion to Socrates*, edited by Sara Ahbel-Rappe and Rachana Kamtekar, 68–73. West Sussex: Wiley-Blackwell, 2009.

Louth, Andrew. *Denys the Areopagite*. London: Continuum, 1987.

———. "The Use of the Term ἴδιος in Alexandrian Theology from Alexander to Cyril." *Studia Patristica* 19 (1987): 198–202.

———. "St Athanasius and the Greek *Life of Antony*." *JTS* 39 (1988): 504–509.

Malherbe, Abraham J., and Everett Ferguson, editors and translators. *Gregory of Nyssa: The Life of Moses*. New York: Paulist Press, 1978.

Markus, R. A. *Saeculum: History and Society in the Theology of St. Augustine*. New York: Cambridge University Press, 1970. Reissued with a new introduction, 2007.

Martin, Dale B. *Inventing Superstition: From the Hippocratics to the Christians*. Cambridge, MA: Harvard University Press, 2004.

———. "When Did Angels Become Demons?" *Journal of Biblical Literature* 129 (2010): 657–77.

Mayer, Wendy. "Who Came to Hear John Chrysostom Preach? Recovering a Late Fourth-Century Preacher's Audience." *Ephemerides Theologicae Lovanienses* 76 (2000): 73–87.

McLeod, Frederick G. "The Soteriology of Narsai." PhD diss., Pontificium Institutum Orientale, Rome, 1968.

———. "The Christological Ramifications of Theodore of Mopsuestia's Understanding of Baptism and the Eucharist." *JECS* 10 (2002): 37–75.

Meyendorff, Paul. "Liturgy and Spirituality I. Eastern Liturgical Spirituality." In *Christian Spirituality: Origins to the Twelfth Century*, edited by Bernard McGinn and John Meyendorff., 350–63. World Spirituality 16. New York: Crossroad, 1985.

Miller, Patricia Cox. *Biography in Late Antiquity: A Quest for the Holy Man*. Berkeley: University of California Press, 1983.

———. "Desert Asceticism and 'The Body from Nowhere'." *JECS* 2 (1994): 137–53.

———. *The Corporeal Imagination: Signifying the Holy in Late Ancient Christianity*. Divinations. Philadelphia: University of Pennsylvania Press, 2009.

Moralee, Jason. "The Stones of St. Theodore: Disfiguring the Pagan Past in Christian Gerasa." *JECS* 14 (2006): 185–215.

Muehlberger, Ellen. "Ambivalence about the Angelic Life: The Promise and Perils of an Early Christian Discourse of Asceticism." *JECS* 16 (2008): 447–78.

Müller, C. D. G. *Die Engellehre der koptischen Kirche*. Wiesbaden: Harrassowitz, 1959.

Newsom, Carol. "'He has established for himself priests': Human and Angelic Priesthood in the Qumran Shabbat *Shirot*." In *Archaeology and History in the Dead Sea Scrolls: The New York University Conference in Memory of Yigael Yadin*, edited by Lawrence H. Schiffman, 113–18. Sheffield: Sheffield Academic Press, 1990.

O'Daly, Gerard J. P. *Augustine's City of God: A Reader's Guide*. Oxford: Clarendon, 1999.

O'Donnell, James J. *Augustine: A New Biography*. New York: Ecco/HarperCollins, 2005.

Opsomer, Jan, and Carlos Steel, editors. *Proclus: On the Existence of Evils*. Ithaca, NY: Cornell University Press, 2003.

Parvis, Sara. *Marcellus of Ancyra and the Lost Years of the Arian Controversy 325–45*. OECS. Oxford: Oxford University Press, 2006.

Peers, Glenn. *Subtle Bodies: Representing Angels in Byzantium*. TCH 32. Berkeley: University of California Press, 2001.

Peterson, Erik. *The Angels and the Liturgy*. Translated by Ronald Walls. New York: Herder and Herder, 1964. Originally published as *Das Buch von den Engeln: Stellung und Bedeutung der heiligen Engel im Kultus*. Leipzig: Hegner, 1935.

Pottier, B. "Le Grégoire de Nysse de Jean Daniélou." *Nouvelle revue théologique* 128 (2006): 258–73.

Radde-Gallwitz, Andrew. *Basil of Caesarea, Gregory of Nyssa, and the Transformation of Divine Simplicity*. OECS. Oxford: Oxford University Press, 2009.

Rapp, Claudia. *Holy Bishops in Late Antiquity: The Nature of Christian Leadership in an Age of Transition*. TCH 37. Berkeley: University of California Press, 2005.

Reed, Annette Yoshiko. "The Trickery of the Fallen Angels and the Demonic Mimesis of the Divine: Aetiology, Demonology, and Polemics in the Writings of Justin Martyr." *JECS* 12 (2004): 141–71.

Rorem, Paul, and John C. Lamoreaux. *John of Scythopolis and the Dionysian Corpus: Annotating the Areopagite*. OECS. Oxford: Clarendon, 1998.

Rousse, J. "Les anges et leur ministère selon Saint Grégoire de Nazianze." *Mélanges de science religieuse* 22 (1965): 133–52.

Rousseau, Philip. *Basil of Caesarea*. TCH 20. Berkeley: University of California Press, 1994.

———. *Ascetics, Authority, and the Church in the Age of Jerome and Cassian*. 2nd ed. Notre Dame, IN: University of Notre Dame Press, 2010.

Rubenson, Samuel. *The Letters of St. Antony: Monasticism and the Making of a Saint*. Minneapolis, MN: Fortress Press, 1990.

———. "Evagrios Pontikos und die Theologie der Wüste." In *Logos: Festschrift für Luise Abramowski zum 8. Juli 1993*, Zeitschrift für die neutestamentliche Wissenschaft und die Kunde der älteren Kirche 67, edited by Hanns Christof Brennecke, Ernst Ludwig Grasmück, and Christoph Markschies, 384–401. Berlin: de Gruyter, 1993.

———. "Wisdom, Paraenesis and the Roots of Monasticism." In *Early Christian Paraenesis in Context*, edited by James Starr and Troels Engberg-Pedersen, 521–78. Berlin: De Gruyter, 2004.

———. "Antony and Pythagoras: A Reappraisal of the Appropriation of Classical Biography in Athanasius' *Vita Antonii*." In *Beyond Reception: Mutual Influences between Antique Religion, Judaism, and Early Christianity*, edited by David Brakke, Anders-Christian Jacobsen, and Jörg Ulrich, 191–208. ECCA 1. Frankfurt am Main: Peter Lang, 2006.

Rubenstein, Mary-Jane. "Dionysius, Derrida, and the Critique of 'Ontotheology.'" *Modern Theology* 24 (2008): 725–41.

Schäfer, Christian. "The Anonymous Naming of Names: Pseudonymity and Philosophical Program in Dionysius the Areopagite." *American Catholic Philosophical Quarterly* 82:4 (2008): 561–80.

Schroeder, Caroline T. *Monastic Bodies: Discipline and Salvation in Shenoute of Atripe*. Divinations. Philadelphia: University of Pennsylvania Press, 2007.

Schwartz, Seth. *Imperialism and Jewish Society: 200 B.C.E. to 640 C.E.* Princeton, NJ: Princeton University Press, 2001.

Shaw, Teresa M. *The Burden of the Flesh: Fasting and Sexuality in Early Christianity*. Minneapolis, MN: Fortress, 1998.

Shepardson, Christine. "Controlling Contested Places: John Chrysostom's *Adversus Iudaeos* Homilies and the Spatial Politics of Religious Controversy." *JECS* 15 (2007): 483–516.

Sinkewicz, Robert E. *Evagrius of Pontus: The Greek Ascetic Corpus*. OECS. Oxford: Oxford University Press, 2003.

Smith, Gregory A. "How Thin Is a Demon?" *JECS* 16 (2008): 479–512.

Smith, Jonathan Z. *Drudgery Divine: On the Comparison of Early Christianities and the Religions of Late Antiquity*. Chicago: University of Chicago Press, 1990.

Stang, Charles M. "Dionysius, Paul and the Significance of the Pseudonym." *Modern Theology* 24 (2008): 541–55.

———. *Apophasis and Pseudonymity in Dionysius the Areopagite: "No Longer I."* OECS. Oxford: Oxford University Press, 2012.

Stead, G. C. "Athanasius' Earliest Written Work." *JTS* 39 (1988): 76–91.

Stefaniw, Blossom. *Mind, Text, and Commentary: Noetic Exegesis in Origen of Alexandria, Didymus the Blind, and Evagrius Ponticus.* ECCA 6. Frankfurt am Main: Lang, 2010.

Sterk, Andrea. *Renouncing the World Yet Leading the Church: The Monk-Bishop in Late Antiquity.* Cambridge, MA: Harvard University Press, 2004.

Stiglmayer, Josef. "Der Neuplatoniker Proclus als Vorlage des sogennante Dionysius Areopagita in der Lehre vom Übel." *Historisches Jahrbuch* 16 (1895): 253–73, 721–48.

Storin, Bradley. "In a Silent Way: Asceticism and Literature in the Rehabilitation of Gregory of Nazianzus." *JECS* 19 (2011): 225–57.

Stramara, Daniel F. "The Angelology of Cyril of Jerusalem as Source for Pseudo-Dionysius' Celestial Hierarchy." *Patristic and Byzantine Review* 27 (2009): 11–21.

Stroumsa, Guy G. "The Scriptural Movement of Late Antiquity and Christian Monasticism." *JECS* 16 (2008): 61–77.

Stump, Eleonore and Norman Kretzmann. *The Cambridge Companion to Augustine.* New York: Cambridge University Press, 2001.

Tetz, Martin. "Athanasius und die Vita Antonii: Literarische und theologische Relationen." *Zeitschrift für die Neutestamentliche Wissenschaft und die Kunde der älteren Kirche* 73 (1982): 1–30.

Thompson, Robert W., editor. *Contra Gentes and De Incarnatione.* Oxford Early Christian Texts. Oxford: Oxford University Press, 1971.

Vaggione, Richard Paul. *Eunomius: The Extant Works.* Oxford Early Christian Texts. Oxford: Clarendon, 1987.

———. *Eunomius of Cyzicus and the Nicene Revolution.* OECS. Oxford: Oxford University Press, 2001.

Van Dam, Raymond. *Families and Friends in Late Roman Cappadocia.* Philadelphia: University of Pennsylvania Press, 2002.

———. *Kingdom of Snow: Roman Rule and Greek Culture in Cappadocia.* Philadelphia: University of Pennsylvania Press, 2002.

———. *Becoming Christian: The Conversion of Roman Cappadocia.* Philadelphia: University of Pennsylvania Press, 2003.

van Nuffelen, Peter. "Episcopal Succession in Constantinople (381–450 C.E.): The Local Dynamics of Power." *JECS* 18 (2010): 425–51.

Vivian, Tim. *The Life of Antony: The Greek Life of Antony and the Coptic Life of Antony, and an Encomium on Saint Antony by John of Shmun, and a Letter to the Disciples of Antony by Serapion of Thmuis.* Kalamazoo, MI: Cistercian, 2003.

Watts, Edward J. *City and School in Late Antique Athens and Alexandria.* TCH 41. Berkeley: University of California Press, 2006.

Webb, Ruth. "Imagination and the Arousal of the Emotions in Greco-Roman Rhetoric." In *The Passions in Roman Thought and Literature*, edited by Susanna Morton Braund and Christopher Gill, 112–27. Cambridge: Cambridge University Press, 1997.

Williams, Rowan. *Arius: Heresy and Tradition*. London: Darton, Longman, and Todd, 1987.

Wills, Garry. *Saint Augustine: A Life*. New York: Viking, 1999.

Winkler, Gabriele. *Das Sanctus: über den Ursprung und die Anfänge des Sanctus und sein Fortwirken*. Orientalia Christiana Analecta 267. Rome: Pontificio Istituto Orientale, 2002.

Wipszycka, Ewa. "Les clercs dans les communautés monastiques d'Égypte." *Journal of Juristic Papyrology* 26 (1996): 135–66.

Yarnold, Edward. *Cyril of Jerusalem*. New York: Routledge, 2000.

Young, Robin Darling. "Cannibalism and Other Family Woes in Letter 55 of Evagrius of Pontus." In *The World of Early Egyptian Christianity: Language, Literature, and Social Context*, edited by James E. Goehring and Janet A. Timbie, 130–39. Washington, DC: Catholic University of America Press, 2007.

Index